FEVER SWAMP

FEVER SWAMP

A Journey through the Strange
Neverland of the 2016 Presidential Race

RICHARD NORTH PATTERSON

Quercus

New York • London

Quercus

New York • London

ISBN 978–1-68144165–8

Library of Congress Control Number: 2016956580

Distributed in the United States and Canada by
Hachette Book Group
1290 Avenue of the Americas
New York, NY 10104

Manufactured in the United States

10 9 8 7 6 5 4 3 2 1

www.quercus.com

For the next generation,
Shannon, Brooke, Katherine,
Adam and Chase

And the next,
Finley, Soren, and Miles

Contents

Foreword

Sometime near the end of the 2016 US presidential campaign—
I think it was at the end of the third debate—I publicly suggested that if the Founding Fathers in Philadelphia had found
themselves watching the proceedings, they might well have
said, "You know what? Let's call the whole thing off." A race
that often seemed soaked in bile, that raised accusations of
sexual, political, financial, and governmental misconduct,
left even the most optimistic campaign watchers wondering
if something had gone seriously wrong with the body politic,
the mechanisms of American self-government, or both.

Given the dyspeptic mood that had engulfed so many
citizens by campaign's end, there is one obvious question
a book like this raises: Why in God's name would anyone
want to revisit this train wreck of a campaign?

Well, it turns out there are compelling answers to this
question.

First, just as real train wrecks require a thorough, detailed
investigation, so does the metaphorical wreck of a campaign.
How did one of our great political parties, offering a platoon's
worth of experienced, credentialed candidates, wind up with
the most manifestly unfit nominee in the 165-year history
of our current two-party system? How did our mass media,
so conditioned to self-congratulatory back-patting about its
"speak truth to power" role, open its airwaves to (literally)
a few billon dollars worth of free publicity before finally
deploying its resources to shine a light on the temperament,

character, biography, and veracity of one Donald Trump? Why did the other major party clear the field for the "obvious" nominee and why was there such discontent with that choice that a back-bench, seventy-four-year-old, self-proclaimed socialist US senator from Vermont managed to come within a relative hairbreadth of upending Hillary Clinton?

These are questions that go to the heart of what has happened to our politics, and their consequentiality alone demands our attention. But in this case, the overriding reason for journeying back into the recent past is the nature of your guide.

I first discovered Richard North Patterson—if that's the right word for my relatively late encounter with a writer whose books have sold well into the millions—by picking up one of his books at the airport before a transcontinental flight. It was *Protect and Defend*, and it was set in the world of big-time politics. My defenses immediately went up. As someone who spent his life working in and then covering politics, I had developed an abiding suspicion of "political" novels; most, I had concluded, were written by people whose grasp of politics was roughly equivalent to my skill at microsurgery.

So I was surprised—and then delighted—to discover that Patterson had a grasp of politics and government that would have done any journalist proud. His characters, and the story itself, reflected a rich understanding of both issues and process. I went out and picked up an armful of Patterson's other novels, which reflected that same sure-handed grasp of our system.

I later learned why. Patterson, who was trained as a lawyer, researched his novels intensely. He read, he interviewed, he immersed himself in the issues he was covering so that— unlike so many other writers—he was actually describing a plausible account of what might happen.

So when he decided to write about the 2016 campaign, he brought with him two critical tools: first, he knew the terrain; second, because of his analytical and novelistic skills, he was able to go deeper into questions of policy and character than 99 percent of working journalists. In this journey, Patterson makes no pretense of impartiality. He is an ardent liberal, and none of the Republican candidates he scrutinizes escape some withering assessments. But it's critical to understand that he has deep respect for many in the Republican Party, ranging from the first President Bush to John McCain. And that's what gives his account such moral force. It is *because* he has seen the Republican Party nominate good, decent, credentialed candidates (if burdened by what he would see as bad ideas) that Patterson can recount, with mounting disbelief and shock, the surrender of the party to a mountebank. This respect for the GOP gives him the authority to examine Trump not just from a political perspective, but from the perspective of character—specifically, a character hobbled by serious disorders.

Patterson also had the advantage of working in what for him was a new medium: digital publishing. He came late to the world of computers, smartphones, PDAs, and the like. He is a writer who prefers the pen, a reader who prefers the feel of dead trees. But in writing for The Huffington Post, Patterson was freed from the limits of space. A newspaper or magazine might have told him: "eight hundred words, tops." In the digital universe, Patterson was able to offer far more detailed arguments about what he was seeing—what the journalistic community now calls "deep dives." As you read through this account of what happened, you will find yourself encountering an observation or an argument that makes his account that much richer.

Finally, Patterson has folded into this book something all too rarely seen in such works: a reassessment of his original reporting. Throughout these essays are marginal notes that point to what he got right—and, more impressively—what he got wrong, and why. (He was, for example, convinced that the Republican Party would at some point defend itself against a hostile takeover; to his—and my—astonishment, the institutional wing of the party proved itself a paper tiger, paralyzed by the constituencies it had encouraged to embrace the scorched-earth approach to politics Trump embodied.)

All this may not make for reassuring reading; that's all to the good. It's not just political operatives or journalists who need to learn the painful lessons of the 2016 election. It's all of us—as citizens—who need to grasp what happened, and why.

You'll find no better resource than the book you're holding in your hands.

—Jeff Greenfield, November 2016

JEFF GREENFIELD is an award-winning television journalist and author focusing on politics, media, and culture. In the course of his career, he served as a senior political correspondent for CBS, a senior analyst for CNN, and a political and media analyst for ABC News.

He has also authored or co-authored 13 books and written for *Time Magazine*, *The New York Times*, *The Los Angeles Times*, *National Lampoon*, *Harper's Magazine*, and *Slate*, among other publications.

Introduction

In August 2016, on a beautiful summer day, instead of going out I found myself watching Donald Trump on television, his hue a bright tangerine, promising to cut my taxes "bigly."

How bigly, I wondered, my bemusement at his syntactical flexibility overcome by astonishment: at an age where one is conscious that each wasted hour moves you one hour closer to death, I was deliberately expending precious oxygen on the poverty of language and thought emanating from a narcissist. Then I remembered that I was suffering so that others would not—specifically, by bearing witness to what was, by far, the most bizarre and unpredictable presidential campaign in the memory of anyone under the age of, say, two hundred.

Worse, no one had asked me to—I was a volunteer. I wasn't even a journalist; I was a novelist. So why was a guy who made up stuff for a living writing about a campaign you couldn't make up? And why in the world was I doing this to myself?

The real answer was: How could I not?

In my view, this was the most consequential election of my lifetime—for multiple reasons. The country was gripped by a great contagion: insecurity, confusion, fear. The leading candidates, both controversial, offered radically different visions and solutions. And one of them was so unusual no one quite knew what to make of him—or why so many people were willing to gamble on someone so untested and unbound.

Over the years, as an incident of my career as a novelist, I had written numerous opinion pieces on political issues. To my great pleasure, The Huffington Post offered me the chance to write a column every week and, if I liked, more often. So I set out to write as well as I could about American politics through the election of 2016, trying to capture every aspect of this fascinating, troubling, and fateful campaign saga—including what it said about who we have become and where we are going.

No small project. But I realized that I came to it armed with some helpful, if unorthodox, qualifications.

One was sheer enthusiasm. This fresh ambition, I recalled, had also been my first ambition as a writer. Under the pressure of career and family, I set the idea aside. But now, given a second chance, I realized how much I wanted to do this, and do it well. And, forty-plus years later, I had a bit more game.

For one thing, seventeen years as a lawyer—I understood the ins and outs of law, including Supreme Court opinions on such salient subjects as abortion and voting rights. Pretty useful given that these issues were integral to the campaign, and that the future of the Supreme Court was hanging in the balance.

Even more useful was that, out of professional necessity, I had immersed myself in the world of politics. As a novelist, I had written several political novels that depended on grasping that world and the sensibility of those who lived there— presidents, legislators, staffers, reporters, pundits, strategists, and consultants. To get things right I had interviewed— quite literally—hundreds of them.

Along the way, I had come to know figures like George H. W. Bush, Ted Kennedy, and John McCain. On one memorable day Bob Dole gave me a master class on how to defeat a Supreme Court nominee, and Bill Clinton, then president, had countered with a learned tutorial on how to save one. While everything they told me enriched my understanding, nothing we discussed was for attribution. So I had a perspective on their lives and thoughts sometimes foreclosed to journalists.

So, too, with the other habitués of politics in every segment of the business. If I had a question or an opinion to test out, there were people I could call—then and now. Over time, I couldn't help but develop my own theories about politics.

Two examples became particularly germane to 2016. One was the perception, which for years I'd thrust on any Republican pro who would listen, that the party was made up of factions—the donor class, Chamber of Commerce types, Tea Party dead-enders, frustrated evangelicals, and the restive whites who increasingly comprise the party's voting base—whose interests were irreconcilable. In particular, I insisted that the party's ideology was tailored to its donor class, not its legions of discontented white folks.

So I started this project expecting the crack-up that, nonetheless, came with astonishing speed. By the end of 2015, with beginner's luck, I was guessing in print that Donald Trump or Ted Cruz would be the GOP nominee, and that no white knight would rescue the party establishment.

Nor did the rise of Bernie Sanders seem all that mysterious. 2008 had made it clear that Hillary Clinton was vulnerable and there was an underserved constituency on the Democratic left awaiting a candidate in 2016. The question was whether Sanders could go all the way despite his weakness with the minorities who had helped propel Barack Obama. I thought not—a judgment that prevented me from overreading a truly impressive showing by Sanders and his millions of contributors and admirers.

But perhaps most helpful in this strange and unsettling year was three decades spent as a novelist. Essential to this was the study of character—including motivation and psychology and how they played out under the pressure of events. If anything, the crucible of high-stakes politics magnifies the importance of who the candidates are as people. In my youth, Richard Nixon exemplified this for us all. But never was a focus on character more essential than during the campaign of 2016.

It was jammed with interesting characters to write about—the candidates themselves. And some of them seemed quite peculiar. From the outset, it was apparent that Ben Carson's logic train was more than a bit unusual, and that Ted Cruz, to put it gently, was inadequately socialized even by the standards of politics. But they paled by comparison. For Donald Trump was someone special—a man driven by an inner landscape that transcended the normal analytic boxes of issues, strategy, or demographic appeal.

Reporters operating within the standard rules could report dubious statements by a candidate as they occurred. They could note individual incidents that suggested a lack of empathy, or obliviousness about what the presidency actually required. They could record moments of self-involvement, or unreasoning defensiveness, or irresponsible rhetoric. But what does it mean when all these characteristics—and more—repeatedly converge in a single human being?

And so those writing about the campaign were presented with uncomfortable but pivotal questions. With respect to Donald Trump, did the traditions of journalistic restraint and objectivity risk normalizing the abnormal? Were the usual methods of political reportage, focused on reporting and analyzing events as they occur, sufficient to this highly unusual candidate or to the volatile environment in which he arose?

As a non-journalist who was writing opinion pieces, I was freer than most to frame my own answer. As you will see, beginning in the spring of 2016, I did.

This did not provoke universal approval. Friends schooled in the admirable constraints of traditional journalism questioned, understandably, whether it was responsible to venture a psychological diagnosis of a candidate. But Trump's own behavior made some sort of journalistic reckoning unavoidable.

By late summer, prominent mainstays of conventional commentary were questioning his psychological stability. And in September major print and broadcast outlets began labeling his misstatements for what they were. For 2016 was the year in which the standard verities no longer seemed to suffice.

One can, and should, view this with some unease. I surely do. For Trump presented the media with a terrible choice. Its reportage of Trump became fodder for his charge that the election was rigged against him. One of his many dubious gifts to us is sowing yet more distrust of the media and, within journalism itself, the question of how its role has changed.

But this was only one issue among many that I was compelled to write about. Never in my lifetime, not even in 1968, had so many Americans been so insecure, alienated, and confused—and so bitterly opposed to so many of their fellow citizens. The campaign became a potent additive to this volatile mix of uncertainty and fear: of displacement, violence, terrorism, and "the other"—Muslims, Mexicans, minorities, and, yes, even Russian hackers. Few dared to imagine what would happen next—including whether the chief protagonist of this drama would crack up before our eyes, and what would become of us if he became our president.

As I wrote, a metaphor occurred to me. With Trump as the principal agent of contagion, this campaign was becoming a fever swamp where lies blossomed, anger thrived, conspiracy theories mushroomed, and reason went to die. Like all of us, the principal figures of the campaign would have to navigate the swamp.

These included Bernie Sanders, Joe Biden, Marco Rubio, Ted Cruz, Paul Ryan, Ben Carson, Carly Fiorina, and Mike Pence. Even more notable were Barack and

Michelle Obama and, especially, Hillary Clinton. I wrote about them all, some extensively, for how they negotiated the swamp said much about who they were and what choices lay before us.

For Clinton, this was a harrowing journey through emails, an FBI investigation, a bitter primary season, suspicions about her ethics, renewed scrutiny of her marriage, a daunting level of voter mistrust, and twenty-five years of attacks from all sides. Only in a year featuring Donald Trump would Clinton not be the central character. For whether and how she surmounted these difficulties said much about her resilience, discipline, and stamina—and whether enough Americans would come to trust her enough to select her over Trump.

For the candidates, and all of us who watched, this gauntlet provided more surprises then anyone could imagine. Still, until close to the end I was convinced that Trump would lose—and said so.

And then, eleven days before the election, a final shock—an ambiguous letter to Congress from FBI director James Comey about newly discovered emails, about whose contents he knew nothing, which nonetheless might bear on the FBI's investigation of Clinton's email practices. This single act set off a media avalanche, transforming the dynamic of the race, tarnishing the FBI's reputation, and giving Trump a startling last-minute path to victory.

We were living in truly dangerous times, and I was writing about them. So I tried to do that with as much insight, clarity, style, and, when appropriate, humor as I could muster. And, above all, I resolved to tell the truth as I saw it.

This book contains my pieces precisely as I wrote them, week by week, with a few edits to avoid repeating points made in prior pieces. Where it is helpful to add additional detail or insight, or note subsequent events, I have done so through annotations. Taken together, these articles comprise a comprehensive narrative of the campaign.

All in all, it was a remarkable journey, and I'm glad that I decided to take it. So I'm grateful to all the readers who accompanied me, and whose comments chastened, illuminated, or simply helped me keep on going. And I'm especially grateful to you, for reading this now.

PART I

*Plutocrats, Birthers, Climate Deniers,
a Reality Star, a Socialist from Vermont,
a Scrum of Candidates Killing Each Other,
and an Entire Political Party Gone Mad*

SOMETIME DURING THE SUMMER OF 2015 I HAD A TRULY alarming perception: the Republican presidential debates resembled the bar scene from *Star Wars*.

The characters were feral and scruffy. Menace hung in the air. Nothing anyone said made sense. It was like a transmission from an alternative galaxy. Mexicans were pouring over our borders; Muslims were celebrating 9/11; Obamacare was like slavery; the Chinese were occupying Syria. And an audience full of people who looked something like us—only a lot more Caucasian—were cheering wildly.

One of the characters was orange and kept insulting everyone else. The only black man spoke largely in haiku; the only woman seemed mean as a snake. The young guy kept sweating and repeating himself. And the guy who looked like Joseph McCarthy sounded like a televangelist. Like the inmates of an insane asylum, all kept insisting they would be our next president.

Scary.

Worse, this was not a movie, and Donald Trump was not a sideshow but an increasingly serious candidate for the Republican nomination. Was he a meteor, or a death star, or the GOP's great white hope? The question was not premature—though no votes would be cast until February, the great winnowing had already begun.

A putative front runner, Scott Walker, vanished beneath the weight of his own weightlessness. Weighed down by establishment support, Jeb Bush languished in the doldrums. As Trump rose to the top, oddities like Ben Carson and Carly Fiorina nipped at his heels. Marco Rubio kept repeating the same origin speech, like a man whose perpetual Groundhog Day was the Fourth of July. Ever watchful, the predatory Ted Cruz lurked in Trump's nativist slipstream.

In the footlights swarmed rich donors unleashed by *Citizens United,* disconcerted by Trump and trying to pick winners in a political auction with public policy on the block. As always, they knew what they wanted—more. But for once they were confused about who could best give it to them.

Offstage, terrorists murdered innocents at home and abroad. Millions of Americans feared losing their place, and the party establishment was losing its grip. And the GOP was afflicted by distemper so severe that the once powerful elephant threatened to become a multiheaded beast.

In the chaos, Trump's competitors jockeyed for second place, betting that Trump would implode all by himself. This had a considerable fascination of its own—the characters were interesting, their maneuvers complicated, and the fissures they exposed acute. As they stalked one another, their chosen enemies, tricks, and tactics kept on shifting. In the chaos, Trump remained untouched—even when, in debate after debate, he insulted his rivals in the most coarse and personal terms.

Indeed, some of his competitors demeaned themselves by flattering him, hoping to inherit his support. Instead his lead in the polls burgeoned ever more, propelled by billions in free media, as the addled GOP establishment took refuge in delusional passivity. It was hard to pick what was most astonishing: that a man so ignorant and vulgar was the Republican front-runner; or that the vaunted GOP establishment was so completely feckless.

So what did this portend—not just for the party, but the country?

And what of the Democrats? In any other year, their drama would have been front and center—and for good reason. Was it truly possible that a septuagenarian loner would spur a mass movement so powerful that it would topple their presumptive nominee? Could Hillary Clinton—by sheer grit and persistence—overcome years of attacks, a generational divide, and her own mistakes? And would the party's flawed but beloved vice president try one last time to seize the prize?

Whatever the answers, the election of 2016 was poised to become the most surprising, strange, dramatic, and consequential election in living memory—a journey through a fever swamp we had never visited before.

And the story was only beginning.

The Faux Humility of Dr. Ben Carson

SEPTEMBER 18, 2015

In the fevered political moment captured so well by the second Republican presidential debate, Dr. Ben Carson has improbably emerged as the leading challenger to the improbable Donald Trump. Recently asked to distinguish himself from his rival, Dr. Carson humbly singled out his faith-based humility. One must assume that he equates humility with the disarming persona he once again displayed in debate on Wednesday evening—his soft-spoken manner seemingly detached from the conflict around him, his most memorable response a pleasing tribute to his hardworking mother.

But that muted volume shrouds pronouncements that, in both their strangeness and self-certainty, are stunning even by Trumpian standards. For little in Dr. Carson's campaign thus far suggests the slightest awareness of the feeble qualifications, rhetorical excess, and monumental self-regard he brings to his pursuit of the presidency.

His rise began at the 2013 National Prayer Breakfast. He began by noting: "My role model is Jesus," a statement that might have given pause to a man less humble. With President Obama two seats away, he then proceeded to critique

Even more remarkable is that this never changed. Thus Carson's debate appearances—a portrait in incomprehension.

Obama's health care plan and offer up his own. Even some evangelicals felt that he had hijacked a religious event with unseemly arrogance.

But Carson knew better. He then went on television to criticize the president's own remarks, saying that they made him "feel that perhaps we're being betrayed, perhaps we don't have a leader who feels the same thing as most of us do," adding that "we will have another opportunity, coming up in 2016, looking at all the senators and congressmen who rabidly support this man."

With this, movement conservatives began urging him to seek the presidency. And, much like his role model, Dr. Carson was prepared to sacrifice himself for the higher good.

His subsequent self-evaluations suggest why. "I'm ready for leadership on the world stage," he has assured us, "not just sitting around waiting to see what other people do." When asked about his lack of knowledge of that stage, he countered that "the most important thing is having a great brain"—his own, it would seem. After all, as he remarked in closing out the first debate, "I'm the only one [onstage] to separate Siamese twins." That last statement, at least, is beyond peradventure.

And it was one of many moments where his statements provoked bewilderment and bemusement, as in his dubious claim to have nearly killed someone as a teenager.

On one level, this serene self-assurance is not wholly surprising. For a superb surgeon, which Dr. Carson surely was, self-confidence is a prerequisite. But it is an unsettling leap for a brain surgeon to suggest that staving off global disaster is not, well, brain surgery. And it is outright unnerving when this lofty self-concept is fused with the certainty on which fundamentalism so often rests—as recently illustrated by the Kentucky county clerk who rejected same-sex marriage applicants "on God's authority."

Even in less dangerous times than these, one hopes for a president who, before making momentous decisions, consults not just God, but advisers with deep intelligence and experience—especially when that president is so inexperienced himself. But Carson's tidy solution to the protean dangers posed by ISIS—that he would "order the military to destroy the group"—did not, to put it gently, seem to reflect a meaningful consultation with military experts, let alone a comprehension of the poisonous complexities of the Middle East. In this matter, as in others, divine inspiration should be infused with worldly wisdom.

But there is disturbingly little sign of that in Dr. Carson. Think what one will about Obamacare, it is surely not "the worst thing that has happened in the United States since slavery." However quiet Dr. Carson's voice, he sounds more than a bit like Trump—not to mention un-Christian—when he suggests that President Obama is "sitting there saying, 'These Americans are so stupid they'll believe anything I say.'"

It is passing strange for a man of science to disdain the scientific community by repudiating the theory of evolution, and labeling any discussion of man-made climate change "irrelevant." And when his intellectual isolation propels the workings of his mind to interplanetary levels—asserting that Americans "live in a Gestapo age," then paradoxically proposing a "covert division" of civil servants to spy on their fellow workers—one can only question the operating manual for this particular "great brain."

Among all of the habitués of the fever swamp, including Trump, Carson's statements and behavior were often the least predictable and most bizarre.

This continued throughout the debates. Even in the odd ménage of GOP contenders, Carson seemed to be debating in his own space bubble.

Like Trump, Dr. Carson appeals to those for whom loathing of government suffices as policy; unlike Trump, he channels this rage through a mien of self-effacement that has religious resonance, deepening his appeal to evangelicals and others uncomfortable with bombast. But our long campaigns are as grueling as a marathon, as telling as a microscope—even now, the residue of this last debate may be of a candidate only tenuously connected to the larger discussion. In the end, even many of Dr. Carson's would-be admirers may conclude that they have seen this man before—perhaps in an airport bar or on a park bench. He has a gentle demeanor, a kindly aura, a soft and pleasing voice. And then we come closer and realize that he is speaking in tongues.

The Shallow Salesmanship of Carly Fiorina

SEPTEMBER 20, 2015

In the wake of Wednesday's debate, Carly Fiorina has become the latest Republican meteor of the moment, trailing only Donald Trump in the most recent polling. Asked why by Chris Wallace, Fiorina argued that voters respond to her once they "know what I've done and, more importantly, what I will do"—citing her business skills as a negotiator. In both her self-assured delivery and its substance, this answer illuminates the paradox in Fiorina's claim to world leadership.

For Ms. Fiorina is of a very different stamp than her "outsider" peer group: Trump and Ben Carson. However unlikely it is that their skills preordain a successful presidency, Trump has made himself a billionaire, while Carson had a remarkable career as a surgeon. The irony of Fiorina's rise is that far from reflecting success as a business executive, it stems from the presentational skills of a superior politician: polished delivery, rigorous message discipline, and the ability to assimilate facts, neatly packaged to please the party's right-wing base.

Thus the program she offers America includes shutting down the government to defund Planned Parenthood and disowning the nuclear agreement with Iran. In this, the past is prologue. For, as at Hewlett-Packard, her persona is that of a world-class salesperson whose gifts obscure glaring questions about her judgment and abilities.

Beyond aggressively marketing herself as the female anti-Hillary, hardly a credential in itself, her candidacy rests solely on a tenure as CEO, which ended in her firing. By comparison to other business leaders who have run for president or pondered doing so—Wendell Willkie, Lee Iacocca, Ross Perot, and even Herman Cain—Fiorina's record at Hewlett-Packard is less uplifting saga than dead weight, suggesting that she lacks the capacities essential in a successful president.

The problem is not that she fired a lot of people—CEOs will do that, sometimes unavoidably. Rather, the prevailing narrative in the tech sector and beyond is that her tenure was marked by bad decisions, poor interpersonal relations, and a leadership style that placed self-promotion above the nitty-gritty of making HP work.

To be fair, it is widely acknowledged that Fiorina arrived at a troubled company on the cusp of an industry-wide downturn. But it is also true that she left HP more troubled yet. Silicon Valley insiders describe a leader who was often manipulative, devious, and self-absorbed, focused on building a cult of personality blinding even in an era of celebrity CEOs.

Privately, they often say much worse. I heard "sheer evil" more than once.

The manifestations of such *folies de grandeur* abounded, from rock star entrances at annual meetings, to approving the hanging of her portrait at headquarters, to travel for personal appearances, even as HP descended into crisis. Equally significant, her frequently imperious manner and penchant for over-centralizing authority alienated colleagues, causing some of the more gifted to leave. This "cult of Carly," said Roy Verley, HP's former director of corporate communications, obscured that "[s]he didn't know what she was doing, and couldn't deliver in the process."

That judgment goes to the heart of Fiorina's credentials, most prominently the centerpiece of her tenure, HP's merger with Compaq. To be sure, she has her defenders, including those who argue that HP would have stalled regardless of who was CEO. But her insistence on negotiating a merger to jump-start the company's growth precipitated what is widely viewed as a disaster. Despite her subsequent claim to have doubled the company's size, its profits as a percentage of revenues fell sharply, its stock price plummeted far more than that of HP's competitors, and the failure to smoothly merge the companies became a millstone, miring HP in the doldrums. In 2005, the HP board delivered its verdict on her skills as a negotiator and CEO—it fired her.

It is telling that, in over a decade, Fiorina has never found another job as a corporate CEO.

Within HP, her departure was greeted by an outburst of celebrations. The stock price rose dramatically. She became a staple of "worst CEO" lists. A Wall Street analyst delivered the common conclusion: "[N]obody liked Carly's leadership all that much. The Street had lost all faith in her, and the market's hope is that anyone will be better."

However harsh this sentiment may be, the record that engendered it is hardly an affirmative credential for her current and much more grand ambition. And it lends a tinny ring to Fiorina's claim that she should be president because "I understand how the economy actually works."

But once again, she is selling herself superbly, tapping in to the magical thinking of those who believe that only an outsider can cure all the ills they attribute to traditional political leaders. But it is even more magical to imagine that, as president of the United States in uniquely complex and dangerous times, Fiorina will be transformed, succeeding where she failed as a mere corporate CEO. In assessing her performance in that job, her former colleague Roy Verley may have delivered the most devastating judgment of all: Fiorina, he says, is a "born politician."

Though not a successful one. Her last gasp was an ignominious week as Ted Cruz's putative running mate—spent a heartbeat away, as one humorist put it, from never becoming president.

Marco Rubio's Empty Suit

SEPTEMBER 23, 2015

Some GOP professionals are suggesting that the quest for an antidote to the dreaded Trump and Carson may land on Marco Rubio. Given that his chief assets are an affecting life story and superior performance skills, this seems an odd choice. For Rubio personifies the Republican complaint against Barack Obama, reflected in the fun house mirror of primary politics: the starter senator whose capacities for world leadership are unproven. Indeed, Rubio is the ultimate "pop-up" candidate, whose sole aim on entering the Senate was to leapfrog his inexperience in order to run for president.

But there is little of substance to commend promoting Rubio to president in the political blink of an eye. His policy positions seem to involve positioning himself with the party's right-wing base.

Though forcefully delivered, his foreign policy prescriptions are no more novel than Dick Cheney's: disavow the opening to Cuba and the Iran nuclear deal, pledge allegiance to Benjamin Netanyahu, consider intervening militarily in Syria and Iraq, and bulk up the military to project American power. His anodyne budget proposals include that chestnut of political fantasies, the balanced budget amendment. The current Rubio is so pro-life that he grants no exception to

This persisted throughout the campaign. Rubio was a candidate without identity, with little to offer but hysterical denunciations of Barack Obama. Eventually, he was reduced to puerile jibes about Trump's body parts, another candidate maddened by the fever.

victims of rape or incest. His switch from believer to climate change denier was augured when he coined the dodge "I'm not a scientist"—which, given that he is also not a general, an economist, or an educator, if taken literally would seem to limit his role as president to pardoning turkeys and lighting Christmas trees.

The most egregious example of Rubio's evanescence on principles may be his head-spinning about-faces on immigration. Running for the Senate in 2010 he disdained a path to citizenship for illegal immigrants. But by 2013, he became instrumental in a bipartisan group of senators whose comprehensive immigration reform bill included just such a path, underscoring his zeal with impassioned speeches inside and outside the Senate.

To his apparent surprise, the Republican base erupted in anger. When his legislation passed the Senate, Rubio did not appear with his colleagues at the press conference that followed. And four months later he publicly opposed his own bill's passage in the House. These dizzying changes seem particularly soulless in a man who asserts that his parents' immigrant experience is at the core of his political soul.

Equally problematic, Rubio is the poster child for the post-*Citizens United* systemic distortion that surfaced in 2012: candidates disproportionally financed by wealthy patrons (e.g., Newt Gingrich/Sheldon Adelson; Rick Santorum/Foster Friess). But Rubio's ties to Florida billionaire Norman Braman suggest more than a short-term rental. Once Rubio became a Florida legislator, Braman funded his campaigns, financed his legislative agenda, and subsidized his personal finances, employing Rubio as a lawyer and his wife as a philanthropic adviser. While Speaker of the Florida House, Rubio helped steer $85 million in state funds to Braman's favorite causes. And now Braman is expected to spend at least $10 million to help Rubio become president.

As the weeks wore on, his image as a candidate of the future—a youthful Latino American—became ever more threadbare. His slogan seemed to be: "I'm great political horseflesh."

But Rubio is also a leading contender for the largess of Sheldon Adelson, the right-wing ideologue who spent

$100 million in the presidential campaign of 2012. In addition to courting Adelson at a half-dozen private meetings last summer, during which he laid out his foreign policy vision, Rubio cosponsored the casino mogul's top legislative priority: a bill to outlaw Internet gambling. Lest Braman's and Adelson's interests seem merely parochial, both men vehemently oppose the Iran nuclear deal and criticize the proposed two-state solution between Israel and the Palestinians. For whatever reason, Rubio now espouses both positions, vowing to hamstring implementation of the Iran nuclear pact by rear-guard legislative tactics.

The presidency is serious business—too serious, one would hope, to entrust to inexperienced candidates with malleable ideas and wealthy patrons whose desires are far from malleable. In more serious times, Rubio would be running for reelection to the Senate or, perhaps, for governor of Florida, hoping to benefit his state while preparing himself for national leadership. The current primary field contains at least two such candidates, Jeb Bush and John Kasich—both successful Republican governors who tested their ideas in the crucible of diverse and important states with major problems. In 2016, they are the adults in the room. By comparison, Rubio is a political adolescent, still dressed in short pants, dependent on a scholarship funded by powerful benefactors.

After repeatedly denigrating the Senate and stating that he would never run for reelection, Rubio did precisely that—trampling the hopes of an old friend of his who was already running in the process.

Ted Cruz

The Lone Stranger

SEPTEMBER 28, 2015

Armchair psychoanalysis of political figures can be a dubious and even disreputable business. But one presidential candidate presents the following symptoms: feral aggression, reflexive demagoguery, self-absorption, paranoia, grandiosity, disdain for social norms, and an inability to cooperate with others. When such a person habitually imagines himself as Winston Churchill, the effect is truly destabilizing. So let us add to the *DSM* a newly discovered malady: Ted Cruz Syndrome.

These qualities were a major component of Cruz's failure. They were simply too obvious to ignore.

For the historic figure Cruz most evokes is not Churchill, but a nascent Joseph McCarthy. It is not his fault that he resembles the young McCarthy (though he does), but that his words and actions bring the vulpine loner from Wisconsin to eerie recall. Like McCarthy, Cruz is capable of a casual cruelty that is startlingly gratuitous. Hard upon the death of Beau Biden, Cruz chortled to an audience, "Joe Biden. You know what the nice thing is? . . . [J]ust walk up to someone and say, 'Vice President Joe Biden,' and just close your mouth. They will crack up laughing."

Shortly after Jimmy Carter revealed his grim cancer diagnosis with admirable grace, Cruz ridiculed Barack Obama and Carter as having identical failed presidencies, as if merely attacking Obama was not pleasure enough.

Sometimes, it seems, all one has to do is cross the senator's radar screen, no matter how tragic the circumstances. For with Cruz, like McCarthy, merely calling his endless array of self-selected opponents wrong does not suffice to slake his psychic need to demean and disparage.

The targets of these rhetorical drive-by shootings are often his fellow Republicans. During Chuck Hagel's confirmation hearings, Cruz implied that Hagel had received money from North Korea. In the skirmishing over the Export-Import Bank, Cruz accused his own Majority Leader of telling a "flat-out lie." And when John Boehner resigned under fire from hard-right House members whose ire Cruz relentlessly stoked, without citing any source the senator danced on the Speaker's political grave, suggesting that Boehner had "cut a deal with Nancy Pelosi to fund the Obama administration for the rest of the year—and then presumably to land a cushy K Street job."

As for his policy pronouncements, they seem contrived to feed the gnawing victimization felt by those most alienated from society. His claims that there is a "war on faith in America today," and that those "who are persecuting [Kentucky county clerk] Kim Davis believe that Christians should not serve in public office," suggest an ignorance of law and history too profound to be credible in a graduate of Princeton and Harvard Law. Just as dubious is that Cruz believes his comparison of scientists concerned about climate change to the flat-Earthers who rejected scientific truth. Asked to measure Cruz against his understanding of McCarthy, a prominent Republican professional with four decades of experience makes this troubling distinction: calling Cruz "the most calculating man I've seen in this business," he posits that the newer version is much more "calculating and Machiavellian" than his predecessor in recklessness.

Unsurprisingly, beneath such venom and demagoguery lurks a man who dramatizes himself as beset by venal

Republican colleagues bent on punishing him for his lonely
and courageous efforts to save America from the abyss.
"Sometimes," Cruz writes, "people ask me, 'When you have
a room full of Republican senators yelling at you to back
down and compromise your principles, why don't you just
give in?' I just remember all those men and women who
pleaded with me, 'Don't become one of them.'" It never
occurs to Cruz that his colleagues' uniform contempt stems
from a deeper reason—that he has made the Senate a soundstage for his own psychodrama, good only for garnering
money and attention while he pursues his larger ambition
with relentless monomania.

One curiosity is why Cruz seems to revel in his oppositional persona. On one hand, Cruz is relentlessly tactical; the question is if his need to attack springs from something deeper.

As his colleagues suffer, so do we. In 2013, he infuriated his fellow Republicans by prompting a government
shutdown without the slightest hope of achieving his
stated purpose—defunding Obamacare. He preceded his
twenty-one-hour filibuster by quoting Churchill that "we
will fight on the beaches," then went on to compare his
GOP peers to "Neville Chamberlain, who told the British people, 'Accept the Nazis.'" When his efforts ended in
political disaster, he blamed his fellow Republicans in order
to inflame the right-wing base, dishonestly ignoring that a
presidential veto made his alleged goals impossible. Now,
still blithely dismissing the separation of powers, he again
proposes to force another government shutdown—drawing
a rare public letter from Senator Kelly Ayotte asking him
why this effort will be any less disastrous for the party or
the country.

Cruz hears no voices but his own, and it has ever been
thus. A college classmate has been quoted as saying, "It was
my distinct impression that Ted had nothing to learn from
anyone else. . . . Four years of college education altered nothing." His rise to prominence on the national stage personifies the degree to which our politics is gripped by a political
distemper, drowning our capacity to seize the future in a

Not quite. But Trump prevailed in part because many establishment Republicans—especially Cruz's senatorial colleagues—loathed Cruz even more. At least until, too late, they grasped the essence of Donald Trump.

tsunami of nihilism and fury. For our own sake as well as their party's, his colleagues need to seal off his path to power, inflicting on Cruz the public ostracism that befell McCarthy and sent him skulking to the political margins with Joseph Welch's famed admonition still ringing in his ears.

The Biden Dilemma

OCTOBER 1, 2015

Ever more, Democrats worried about the Clinton campaign hope that Joe Biden will jump into the race with all his capacious humanity. In this politically breathless moment, they will be spending the next few days waiting for Joe.

It is easy enough to see why. At whatever distance, Joe Biden is an easy man to like. Those who have worked with him closely describe the Biden that voters see—a politician who loves people, as warm and generous as one could ask. It is no mean feat in his Darwinian milieu that almost everyone seems to like Biden. For Democrats, the sight of him in a crowd conjures a warmth the vice president clearly returns.

And he is never better than in times of sorrow or adversity. His remembrance of Ted Kennedy at the senator's memorial service was a marvel of empathy—not least when he addressed each family member with a memory preceded by "your uncle" or "your dad." His grief over the loss of his son Beau is affecting beyond words, even more so when he struggles to find them. It is surely an asset for voters to see a candidate as someone they could turn to in the toughest of moments. And President Obama has done so—time and again, Biden has worked with his former colleagues to advance the president's agenda, becoming in the process a truly consequential vice president.

Like Bill Clinton, Biden savors every aspect of politics—except, unlike Clinton, raising money. To him the

This was a stunning moment for all of us in attendance. In a gifted roster of memorialists, Biden evoked tears.

art of persuasion is a joyous pursuit, fueled by a commitment to the average American with whom he still identifies. For Biden, engagement with the maelstrom of politics and its inhabitants is as natural as breathing.

But running for president does not engender fondness in one's opponents. It seems no accident that a spate of recent articles has exhumed the roughest moments in Biden's political past. Feminists with long memories challenge his performance in chairing the Clarence Thomas hearings, asserting that he allowed Thomas and his allies to savage Anita Hill without calling witnesses who could have corroborated her account of sexual harassment. Those who question his judgment as a candidate reach back to the 1988 campaign, when Biden appropriated details from the life of a British politician as his own.

Progressives point to Biden's votes in favor of the Iraq war resolution and a bankruptcy law that favored Delaware-based credit card companies. Other critics resurrect his advice to Obama not to go after Osama bin Laden. Should Biden run, these zombie issues will arise anew.

To be unscripted and unpredictable is in Biden's DNA. Most often this is engaging and fun to watch. But his powers of speech seem overprogrammed for output, creating the perpetual risk of a cringe-making *lapsus linguae*. Though the vice presidency has muted this, historically he has sometimes seemed defensive about his intellect, creating twitchy moments of public insecurity. And the high-stakes debates that lie ahead conjure Biden's 2012 face-off with Paul Ryan, when Biden squandered his clear edge on substance through an overcaffeinated show of smirks, chuckles, and grins, punctuated with eye rolling and shakes of the head.

As a reporter who has followed him remarked to me, at times Biden can seem "a click off."

But the central question is this: What, at its core, is the rationale for choosing Biden over Hillary Clinton? Their bases of support largely overlap, as do their stands on issues—unlike Bernie Sanders, Biden cannot claim to be fighting Clinton for the soul of the Democratic Party.

The real differences are stylistic, and the implicit message of a Biden run would be that Clinton is too damaged to win. This is as hard to articulate as it is to assert with any confidence Biden's long-run superiority as a candidate. Indeed, Kevin McCarthy's dunderheaded admission that the Benghazi committee is a political witch hunt may help stiffen Clinton's support. And among those Democrats who fear that nominating Sanders would be electoral disaster lurks the fear that Biden could widen the self-proclaimed socialist's path to daylight.

> McCarthy bragged that the hearings had dragged down her poll numbers by showing that she was "untrustable." This tongue-tied blunder helped derail his bid to become Speaker of the House.

In the end, Biden's decision comes down, as it so often does with him, to the human element. He is a seventy-two-year-old man who has overcome great hardship to achieve a truly estimable career at the apex of American politics. Though it may be hard to gaze into the chasm of retirement, for Biden grace and honor are no small things. He surely questions the siren song of poll numbers buoyed by sympathy for his loss, also knowing that the tyranny of state filing deadlines will force a decision far too soon.

In some recess of his mind he must recoil at the thought of a failed campaign and, far worse, at being remembered as a spoiler who weakened the Democrats' chances. And those who watch and wait are left to wonder if a Biden candidacy would be a kindness to his party, or to the man himself.

> One possible result would have been to fracture the party's center-left, delivering a nomination to Bernie Sanders. Thus Biden's legacy would have been a hitherto unimaginable Trump–Sanders race.

The Paradox of Bernie Sanders

OCTOBER 5, 2015

The surge of money and enthusiasm propelling Bernie Sanders has long since trampled conventional wisdom. The question now is where that takes us.

Through a progressive lens, the systemic inequities Sanders eviscerates are a blistering rebuke to politics as usual. The soul-shriveling gap between the fortunate and the rest in the essentials of a decent life—education, economic opportunity, health care. A system of campaign finance that is elegant bribery. Ordinary people losing their homes as Wall Street malefactors go unpunished. The cynical equation of "class warfare" with increased taxes on the very rich. To many who feel this social corrosion most acutely, Hillary Clinton personifies a party adrift from its liberal moorings. They long for a truth-teller free of Super PACs and pollsters, primed to at last take the gloves off.

Now comes Senator Sanders—not only with attitude, but an agenda. Single-payer health care. Free tuition at public colleges. Affordable day care. Billions more for Social Security. Higher taxes on the wealthy to cover an estimated $4 trillion price tag. And, necessarily, the most dramatic expansion of government in three generations.

Universal free tuition was at the heart of Sanders's appeal to the young. Understandable. But many wondered whether it made social or fiscal sense for American taxpayers to send rich kids to college.

But as of now these proposals are political ships in a bottle, faced with inescapable threshold questions. Can Sanders win the presidency? If so, can he enact any part of his vision? And what is the balance between primary voting as an act of self-expression and a cold-eyed look at a candidate's prospects in a general election? Resolving this cage match between head and heart is vexing work. For the Sanders phenomenon presents the impassioned but thoughtful progressive with a painful electoral paradox: When might the most heartfelt vote for a better society preserve the ills one seeks to banish? And here we start with Sanders himself.

For Democrats of a certain age, Sanders evokes a familiar figure from the '60s: the committed ideologue transfixed by a vision of tectonic change and driven by total fidelity to principle. Such people would rather lose an election than trim their sails to the winds of the electorate. And Sanders did lose—six elections in a row before, with admirable persistence, becoming the first socialist mayor of Burlington, Vermont.

Beyond achieving some concrete civic good, Sanders launched his modest burg into the arena of foreign policy, writing letters of reproof to Ronald Reagan and Margaret Thatcher and imploring the UK, China, and the Soviet Union to embrace military disarmament. He climaxed these efforts by visiting Daniel Ortega in Nicaragua, writing Reagan on his return proposing to help resolve America's conflict with the Sandinistas. The results beg stating.

Which raises questions for the present day. While Sanders has been giving the same basic speech—keyed to income inequality—for decades, the turn of history's wheel has given him a megaphone of impressive power. His career in Congress is noteworthy for his votes against the Iraq war and the Patriot Act, and progressives dearly wish that more Democrats could say that. But his legislative accomplishments are slight. And none of the 250 Democrats in Congress support him, nor any governor—including Vermont's.

This is not simply because of policy differences—some Democrats overlap Sanders on key issues—but because in a business where personal relations count, Sanders is viewed as a brusque and inflexible loner. The indubitably progressive Barney Frank summarized the common view of the senator's ability to move the body politic: "He went for the ideal, but he was not part of the legislative process. He chose to be an outsider." Asked to imagine a Sanders presidency, an avowedly liberal insider expresses the worries of many who know him, ruefully concluding that "Bernie would be among the least effective presidents ever."

One hope among progressives aware of his flaws is that a President Sanders could channel his current grassroots support into a tidal wave that would overwhelm congressional opposition. But President Obama tried just that. What he learned is that campaigns are different than governance. A Senate closely divided between red states and blue states, and a House with a vast majority of members insulated from defeat by gerrymandering, are immune to a tsunami of emails.

In these fractious times, enacting any part of the Sanders agenda calls for more than principled consistency—it requires a Ted Kennedy or, at least, someone skilled at working with Congress as they find it. Sanders's most recent bills—promoting free college and universal health care—drew zero Democratic cosponsors. These bills are the canary in the mine shaft of reality. For, given the electoral base of Congress, there is no scenario—none—that delivers us a legislature that embraces Bernie Sanders.

But from the progressive point of view there is one way Congress could change for the worse: a decisive presidential defeat. As Gene McCarthy and George McGovern learned—the latter disastrously for his party—white liberals by themselves are not nearly enough to compete. While Sanders's appeal to progressives is turbocharged by the class divide, McGovern had enraptured crowds, deep grassroots

One underreported story is the intense dislike for Sanders among many of his colleagues, often captured in epithets. One senator suggested to me that the only reason Sanders was not the most disliked senator was the existence of Ted Cruz. Ditto journalists, one of whom told me: "You can't imagine what a relief it is to experience Bernie at a distance."

And Sanders surely knew it. Hence the call for a "political revolution" that, to all but his most fervent followers, was obviously fantastical in light of gerrymandering, polarization, and a widespread aversion to government.

support, and the galvanizing issue of our tragedy in Vietnam. He carried Massachusetts.

Fervent crowds of the committed do not of themselves augur a mass revolution in voting patterns that will transform the electoral map. Perhaps, as some insist, this year it's different—so different as to transcend the unpleasant truths of a long campaign. But it is inconceivable that Sanders will moderate his stance to propitiate the majority of voters to his right, or that the GOP won't trumpet all that many voters will need to know: that Sanders is a self-proclaimed socialist who became a Democrat solely to run for president. So progressives must decide whether to risk this election on the willingness of Americans of varying political stripes to choose him.

Given political polarization and the nature of Donald Trump, in a general election Sanders would have done far better than George McGovern. It is possible, if barely, to imagine President Bernie Sanders.

"Yes," one can imagine some responding, "when to our eyes Hillary Clinton and the GOP dine at the same table." But the most casual glance at issues reveal stark differences between Clinton and the Republican field on economics, education, the environment, and gun control—one area where she is markedly stronger than Sanders. Here, again, history provides us with lessons. No true progressive can look at the current Supreme Court, which has turned back affirmative action and voting rights while gutting campaign finance reform, and say that President Gore would have made no difference.

This lesson dogged Jill Stein, limiting her prospects of garnering Sanders voters.

That election mattered. So does this one.

Trump's Character Is His Fate

OCTOBER 8, 2015

The Greek philosopher Heraclitus famously wrote, "A man's character is his fate." This truth neatly captures Donald Trump's rise—and inevitable fall—as a presidential contender.

Already there are hints of his collapse beneath the weight of his quest. Trump's performance in the second debate resembled the slow leak of a balloon, overinflated by an indulgent media that viewed him as ratings helium. Though he now promises that his candidacy will have a "second act," Trump has within him but one act—his own. Thus polls suggest that he has reached his ceiling, and it is hard to imagine him drawing mass support from the adherents of his rivals.

For the Trump campaign—if such a happening can be called that—does not reward more serious scrutiny. His persona is not that of a seasoned political leader, but an entertainer, a combustible mix of P. T. Barnum updated by Kim Kardashian. His seeming supernova exemplifies how social media and reality TV have debased our sense of who to admire, and for what. His puerile jibes—at Bush's energy, Fiorina's looks, and Rubio's sweat glands—suggest the tiresome braying of a witless frat boy. And his reflex to demean

anyone who displeases him—especially women—combines
the pollution of our civic dialogue with our appetite for seeing others humiliated as entertainment.

Trump offers no real program—he offers himself. While
many politicians may be narcissists, Trump alone treats narcissism as a contest he must win. To him, his dominance of
the airwaves must have seemed absurdly easy, confirming
his rightful place at the center of public attention. After all,
as he recently remarked, were he not in the race "there'd be
a major collapse of television ratings."

To put it mildly, this suggests an underappreciation of
the seriousness of his current enterprise. The goal of becoming the most powerful man in a dangerous world has not
moved him to undertake the difficult task of truly understanding that world. In Trump's inner world, the world will
come to him.

> This disinterest in learning became glaring, including in debate with Clinton.

So in place of substance, he channels the primal scream
of those so gripped by media-fueled outrage that contempt for government and those who lead it is program
enough. His ignorance of governance is a klieg-lit embarrassment; his pronouncements on policy self-preening
blather. His immigration plan is incoherent, unachievable,
inhumane, budget-busting, and borderline racist. His for-

> Forget "borderline."

eign policy, when he deigns to have one, consists of chest
thumping. His economic program is a muddled mélange
of populism, protectionism, and tax proposals that don't
add up. As a political thinker, he is Herman Cain on
steroids.

> If that. Throughout the campaign he was contradictory and incoherent on policy or issues.

In this intellectual Sahara, a credulous media has greeted
any sprout of sanity—his renunciation of the Iraq war,
repealing tax breaks for hedge fund managers—as a sign of
growth. And the twenty-four-hour cacophony of Trump as
a political colossus by commentators with their jaws agape
obscures the fact that, as a candidate, he has not been with us
for four years, but merely four months, with thirteen months
to go until November 2016.

> This is a key point. One big mistake I made was underrating the degree to which the media would enable him throughout the primary season.

His GOP rivals never exploited this weakness. Clinton did.

This was my biggest error: believing that the GOP establishment would put up more resistance than, say, the French Army in 1940. Fearful of alienating Trump's supporters, the other candidates trashed their nearest rivals, imagining that The Donald would self-destruct. Instead, they killed one another off.

Another serious mistake was underrating the degree to which Trump was channeling his followers' deep resentment and alienation, cementing their unwavering loyalty. In the hermetically sealed world of the GOP primaries, this was enough. Not until after the primary season did his offenses begin to matter—though not to his millions of true believers.

He will never get that far, for whatever months remain to him will come to feel like a merciless persecution. The flip side of his self-involvement is that he is a thin-skinned bully, and such people do not endure attacks with grace. Forty years of self-celebration have scattered nuggets of video that his detractors will convert to bullets. They will be fired at his heart by the Republican establishment and donor classes, their own hearts filled with a particularly ruthless loathing—not simply because they fear that Trump would lose a general election, but because his intimation of tariffs and tax hikes is, to them, an economic sacrilege that threatens their own place in the firmament.

As the primary field continues to narrow, one or two well-financed opponents will—as Romney did to his rivals in 2012—carpet-bomb Trump with viciously crafted negative ads from state to state, a drumbeat of humiliation that will make Megyn Kelly's recitation of sexism look like a Caribbean cruise. Conservative media will peel back his curtain of red meat and expose that, as a conservative, Trump is a phony; his all-too-ripe personal life will begin repelling evangelicals. Slowly, inevitably, Trump will crack, flooding the maws of an avid media with a cascade of whining, petty feuds and overblown grievances, mindlessly feeding the hunger for a new story line in which Trump consumes himself.

His audience will be watching, and not kindly—some out of sheer fascination with his self-destruction, more because most Americans are, at bottom, sensible. They want an optimistic leader who imbues them with hope, not a self-obsessed whiner whose endless psychodrama is, in the end, exhausting. Not only will they not want Donald Trump in the White House; they won't want him in their living rooms. And one by one they will switch the channel until Trump is left alone on a soundstage, and the lens into which he stares becomes an empty mirror.

Debating Hillary Clinton

OCTOBER 14, 2015

Beneath the din, the essence of Tuesday's debate can be distilled with relative ease. If consistent ideology is the sine qua non, one can stop at Bernie Sanders. But those concerned with the yawning political chasm between naming problems and solving them must employ a wider lens. Which brings us to Hillary Clinton, whose crisp and substantive performance served, at last, to resurrect her better self.

By now one can recite her problems on autopilot. For restive Democrats, she embodies the party's tilt toward the financial classes. Critics decry her speaking fees or see her ties to Wall Street as a mortgage on her political soul. Too often her campaign can feel like a series of tactical feints bereft of an uplifting vision—at times a thought bubble seems to appear above her head, filled with focus groups, poll numbers, and the conflicting voices of too many advisers. While smart at strategy, her recent shifts on TPP, the Keystone Pipeline, and Obamacare's Cadillac Tax reinforce this image of a calculating politician, driven less by principle than by a rival whose principles never change. The ironic upshot is an all-too-familiar figure who seems all too elusive.

Her portrait has been further blurred by fuzzy campaign optics. Years of fending off attacks have bred an instinctive

The dynamic established in this debate never changed, because Hillary Clinton never cracked. Her discipline and command of the issues proved to be an underrated asset.

caution that can smother spontaneity. Her long history in public life overshadows that her quest is potentially historic, while serial reintroductions of each new persona have served only to obscure the person. A kaleidoscope of shifting accounts has made the email issue feel eternal, each thread tying Clinton down like Gulliver among the Lilliputians, hostage to the trope that she is entitled and disingenuous. All this has threatened to gel into a dispiriting ennui.

Driven largely by the email story, this problem persisted throughout her campaign, becoming a magnet for voter distrust.

But such a litany disserves the effort to truly assess this complex woman. For she is neither the feminist icon of her fiercest devotees nor the stock villain of the GOP's demented melodrama.

One starts by dismissing the zealots for whom she has become a human Rorschach test. Whatever toxins emanate from House Republican Trey Gowdy's oh-so-selective committee, she did not abandon the victims of Benghazi. However ill-judged her use of a private server, the emails themselves amount to little. No credible evidence suggests that she subcontracted policy decisions to the Clinton Foundation. Only those gripped by the psychic need to hate Hillary Clinton need linger in this fever swamp. The rest of us, at least, can note her hardihood in slogging through it.

Other qualities prepare her for this race. The marathon of 2008 produced an able and durable campaigner. Her skills as a debater—potentially critical in a close election—were again evident last night, likely foreclosing a Biden candidacy. Her proposals on key issues like financial regulation, tax policy, and college debt relief are detailed and considered. She remains strong among Democrats writ large. And as a manner of electoral math, she can block the GOP from making headway where they need it most—white women.

As for her claim to higher office, it rests on capacities that few dispute. Strong-minded adversaries like John McCain and Lindsey Graham respect her intellect and grasp of policy. Colleagues describe a woman who works hard, assimilates complex information, and tests conventional wisdom, her high expectations leavened by good humor. Whatever her limitations in large settings, in smaller groups she is engaging, cogent, and persuasive. Despite glaring misjudgments—e.g., Iraq—she has amassed deep knowledge of foreign and domestic policy. By consensus she is prepared to fill the presidency.

The harder question is what core beliefs would inform this President Clinton. True, many challenges facing a president require acumen instead of ideology—as ever, competence matters. But what a president cares most about day to day matters just as much. Three decades of public engagement prove Clinton to be solidly left of center, sometimes markedly so. But it is colder comfort to assume that her judgments will reflect the political interests—and interest groups—associated with any Democratic president.

So a clear-eyed Democrat must measure Clinton and Sanders against a complex calculus. What candidate has the best chance to win, and to what end. How much does preventing a Republican president matter in itself. When does expedience on one issue promote success on another, and the refusal to compromise morph into comprehensive failure. Who has the skill and temperament to wrest results from a fractious Congress in such divisive times, pushing forward the party's stated agenda. And who can best confront the disparate challenges thrust at an American president.

For some the hope of seismic change will outweigh its probability, binding them to Bernie Sanders's impassioned crusade. But others who look past November 2016 to envision the difference between victory and defeat may conclude that, in the end, Hillary Clinton's dogged quest is the safest place to be.

This aura of competence became Clinton's version of "trust"—voters could trust her to be up to the job.

Plutocrats and Their Pets

OCTOBER 20, 2015

Wikipedia defines plutocracy as a society "controlled by the small minority of its wealthiest members." In 2010, the Supreme Court set out to help us join the list.

By common consensus, this is the worst Supreme Court decision since *Dred Scott v. Sanford*. And it is one of only a handful of decisions—*Roe v. Wade* being another—that became a persistent political issue.

The case, of course, is *Citizens United*. After an unseemly series of maneuvers by Chief Justice John Roberts expanded the case far beyond the issues presented, a five-to-four majority of Republican appointees held that unlimited expenditures to elect political candidates are "speech protected" from regulation by the First Amendment. Stating bluntly in dissent that "the Court changed the case so it could change the law," Justice Stevens warned: "A democracy cannot function effectively when [voters] believe laws are being bought and sold."

The post–*Citizens United* conduits for such barter, super PACs, funnel millions from the ultra-wealthy to support their human vessels—a counterweight, one supposes, to the parlous effects of letting ordinary people vote. The ads spawned by this money now flood our airwaves: a prominent Democratic consultant estimates that his party's nominee must raise at least $1.5 billion to compete with the tidal wave unleashed by the Supreme Court. This spiraling financial arms race drives candidates away from voters in order to grovel before demanding would-be patrons in big-dollar "money primaries." And there is much groveling to be done. The 2012 campaign produced over $1 billion in soft money. A drastic increase is coming in 2016: already a mere 156 families have put $176 million on the electoral table.

As anyone—surely Chief Justice Roberts—could foresee, this constitutionally cosseted class is overwhelmingly white and to the right. With honorable exceptions, such people are characterized by vaulting self-esteem and tend to perceive the national interest by looking in the mirror. And while support from rich donors does not in itself ensure victory, at the least it badly skews the discussion of policy and issues within the campaign as a whole.

It hardly matters if these donors' desires precede, or match with, the candidates' positions—though often the symmetry is so striking as to suggest an answer. This unwholesome symbiosis between plutocrats and their pets is epitomized by two of the most well fed, Ted Cruz and Marco Rubio.

Take Cruz. As of July, pro-Cruz super PACs had raised $38 million. Fifteen million dollars came from Dan and Farris Wilks, Texan brothers who made billions through fracking. No surprise that they oppose regulation of pretty much anything that relates to oil and gas. Far odder is their leadership of a tiny and socially conservative cult that believes every word of the Bible as originally written is literally true. In a nifty double pander to his patrons, Cruz calls fracking a "providential blessing." And Cruz's program for the rest of us is manna for any fundamentalist fracker: barring the EPA from regulating greenhouse gases; adamant denial of climate science; disdain for reproductive rights; and—in direct response to the Court's approval of same-sex marriage—subjecting justices to electoral review.

Then there is the combined $21 million from Robert Mercer, a hedge fund kingpin whose enterprise is under IRS investigation, and Toby Neugebauer, a Texas financier who decamped for Puerto Rico after it erased the capital gains

Here Bernie Sanders deserves considerable credit. His campaign was the one bright spot in a dismal and corrupting landscape.

Mercer later became a key Trump supporter, instrumental in the shake-up that installed the extreme right-wing founder of *Breitbart News*, Stephen Bannon, as the head of Trump's campaign.

tax. Cruz's tax program? Abolish the IRS, enact a flat tax, and roll back the capital gains rate. Whatever his proposals might do to the country, no doubt President Cruz would strive to bring balm to this afflicted duo, liberating Mercer from the IRS while facilitating Neugebauer's repatriation.

Even so, for the experience and zest he brings to the role of rich man's hireling, Marco Rubio stands out. Here one starts with Norman Braman, who has pledged $10 million to help bring us President Rubio. Since Rubio entered Florida's legislature, Braman has funded his campaigns and subsidized his personal finances, employing Rubio and his wife and underwriting Rubio's stint as a college instructor. As a legislator, Rubio steered $85 million to Braman's favorite causes. And as a candidate for president, Rubio echoes Braman's adamant support for Benjamin Netanyahu, no matter what the issue.

Along with ambition, the pursuit of soft money from billionaires is the one unifying explanation for Rubio's shape shifting on multiple issues.

But even more adamant is the billionaire Rubio is courting most assiduously—casino magnate Sheldon Adelson, by many multiples the biggest donor of soft money in 2012. Though Adelson has other requirements—notably a bill to ban Internet gambling now sponsored by Rubio—it is Israel that best illuminates Rubio's political permeability.

For Adelson is committed to investing a staggering amount in the candidate who best demonstrates absolute fealty to his hard-line views. And they are not merely extreme—they run counter to the most basic tenets of American policy with respect to Israel. An unbroken line of presidents—all staunchly committed to Israel's security—have supported the establishment of a demilitarized Palestinian state on the West Bank, home to several million Palestinians. This is no small matter. A half century of Israeli occupation has fed a festering anger that, now as before, threatens to explode in a cascade of violence that could destabilize an already dangerous region. American and Israeli national security experts believe that indefinite occupation will end in tragedy for all concerned: the collapse of the Palestinian Authority; a third intifada; the bloody intervention of more Israeli troops; and a radicalized populace bereft of hope and dotted with extremists.

But this is precisely what Adelson wants America to support: an Israeli annexation of the West Bank and the subjugation of its people. As for the nuclear deal with Iran, Adelson would have the next president rip it up. His alternative? A preemptive American nuclear strike on the Iranian people.

This would be so much park-bench babbling but for Adelson's resolve to spend tens of millions to elect his chosen candidate. And so Republican aspirants flock to Las Vegas in the hope that winning the "Adelson primary" will make them our next president. But Rubio goes the extra thousand miles. As *New York* magazine quoted an Adelson intimate, every two weeks "Rubio calls and says 'Hey, did you see this speech? What do you think I should do about this issue?' It's impressive. Rubio is persistent." And now Rubio has backed away from the two-state solution and pledged to hamstring the multinational nuclear pact with Iran.

This is not just Rubio's problem. Cynically, the GOP has made unreasoning support of Benjamin Netanyahu a political wedge issue, distorting American foreign policy in the process.

Rubio's panders abound. But what marks this callow candidate—and the shame of *Citizens United*—is his willingness to delegate his views on vital foreign policy issues to an ignorant and imperious donor. For once Donald Trump is trenchant: "Adelson is looking to give his money to Rubio because he feels he can mold him into his perfect little puppet." He has every reason to hope. For Marco Rubio and Sheldon Adelson, money buys so much more than speech.

Despite Rubio's efforts, Adelson remained neutral between Rubio and his wife's ardent courtier, Ted Cruz.

The GOP's Faith-Based Climate

NOVEMBER 2, 2015

Webster's defines *faith* as a "belief that does not rest on logical proof or material evidence." Traditionally, this connotes theology. But the Republicans now offer us faith-based politics—that intellectual lotus land where dogma, blissfully unmoored from fact, suffocates reality. One stellar example, climate change, captures the party's intricate pas de deux between ignorance and venality.

By now, denying global warming should be no more respectable than it was, thirty years ago, to assert that those hacking coughs emitting from terminal cancer patients could be ameliorated by smoking. The scientific consensus is no less compelling: a recent survey of scientific papers on the subject showed that 97 percent affirmed man-made climate change.

Little wonder. Nine of the ten hottest years on record have occurred since 2001; the tenth was three years earlier. Reaching further back, the concentration of carbon dioxide in the atmosphere has risen 40 percent since the dawn of the Industrial Revolution. The evidence accumulates—droughts, melting ice caps, cod dying off New England, rising sea levels menacing the Florida coast. Worldwide, 2015 will be the hottest year ever. And for those sentimentalists who care about the world we leave behind, by century's end the Persian Gulf will be close to uninhabitable. Given all that, most Republican voters are inclined to believe in climate change.

But not for those Republicans we would call the party's thought leaders was there any thought involved. Their cartoonish face is Senator James Inhofe, a man whose words and deeds cry out for H. L. Mencken. Global warming, Inhofe assures us, is the "greatest hoax ever perpetrated on the American people." Deriding climate science as a "secular religion," he gives us the real thing: "[A] lot of alarmists forget God is still up there." The actual problem? It's "the arrogance of people who think that we [can] change what He is doing to the climate."

To preserve our faith in the Almighty, Inhofe and his confrere, Representative Lamar Smith of Texas, seek to prevent us from biting the apple of knowledge—Inhofe by hostile inquisitions into federal climate research; Smith by cutting $300 million from NASA's budget in order to defund it. Inhofe's sense of the scientific method refutes the need for such extravagance, as exemplified by the priceless moment he rebutted global warming by throwing a snowball onto the Senate floor.

Only cynics would note that the oil and gas industry is his leading funder; a more charitable assessment of the senator's intellect and grasp of science gives one ample reason to credit his sincerity. So let us leave him in that so very sunny world where, as he tells it, "increases in global temperature may well have a beneficial effect on how we live our lives."

But one must cast a more wintry eye on his senatorial colleagues, all but five of whom opposed a resolution stating that "human activity significantly contributes to climate change." Of particular interest are two senators now widely touted as presidential finalists: Marco Rubio and Ted Cruz.

On the subject of climate change Rubio is, as ever, finely attuned to the political moment. While a Florida legislator, he believed that action on climate change—including "emissions

Including Donald Trump, who echoed James Inhofe in his fervent embrace of scientific ignorance. Trump has pledged to reverse Obama's efforts to reduce carbon emissions while peddling extravagant nonsense about reviving the coal industry. To a depressing degree, his most fervent supporters have swallowed his biggest lies—furthering the damage he is doing to our politics.

caps and energy diversification"—could make Florida "the Silicon Valley of [the energy] industry." Such was his fervor that he voted in favor of regulating greenhouse gases.

But that, truly, was then. Five years later, Rubio coined the "I'm not a scientist" dodge to avoid opining on the subject altogether. Now, as a candidate, he is a full-fledged climate change denier, armed with a three-pronged attack: first, "I do not believe that human activities are causing these dramatic changes;" second, it is "absurd" that laws could change our weather; and third, instead these laws "will destroy our economy." One is left to imagine Rubio staring at his backyard in perplexity as it sinks beneath the Atlantic.

But for those inclined to see Rubio as a perfectly lubricated weathervane, Ted Cruz is made of sterner stuff. With his usual ferocity, he denounces climate science as a front for "power-greedy politicians" who want to control the energy industry. As for the scientists themselves, these "global warming alarmists are the equivalent of the flat-Earthers." And Cruz? He is, well, the modern Galileo in his intellectual bravery: "It used to be it was accepted scientific wisdom that the Earth was flat, and this heretic named Galileo was branded a denier."

Here we pause for some corrective science. First, Galileo had nothing to do with refuting flat Earth theory. Second, his actual belief—that the Earth revolves around the sun—was supported by scientists but opposed by the Catholic Church as heresy. No surprise, then, is Cruz's stunningly counterfactual insistence that "satellite data demonstrate for the last seventeen years there has been zero warming."

It is cold comfort that Rubio and Cruz are nowhere near that clueless, because their reality is so much worse. They signed a pledge to "oppose any legislation relating to climate change that includes a net increase in government revenues" for the simplest of reasons: the Koch brothers wrote it. Which returns us to the brave new world of *Citizens United*.

The Kochs' many billions are rooted in the fossil fuel industry; after *Citizens United*, the only limit on the brothers' political spending is their estimate of how much it takes to purchase their own US president. And they are vehement climate deniers. In recent years, they have poured an estimated $79 million into front groups that oppose climate legislation. Now the Koch funding network has pledged nearly $900 million to elect their candidates in 2016—more than double the amount spent by the Republican National Committee in 2012.

In sheer seductive power, this pending windfall dwarfs the $15 million Cruz's Super PAC received from two billionaire frackers, the Wilks brothers, in appreciation of his proposal to ban federal regulation of greenhouse gases. So it is also unsurprising that Rubio, Cruz, and other candidates flock like lemmings to conferences held by the Kochs' donor network, or that Rubio would "love to earn their support" because, after all, "we are clearly aligned on issues." No doubt that is why he is deemed the favorite to receive the Koch brothers' ultra-lucrative anointment—Marco Rubio will never, ever be out of alignment.

Indeed Rubio has already hit pay dirt—three days ago, New York venture capitalist Paul Singer, the epicenter of a huge soft-money network, pledged the senator his support. As it happens, Singer also helps fund a foundation that castigates climate science as "utopian alarmism." At whatever cost to the planet, Rubio and Cruz will keep on fighting to outdo each other in assuring Republican voters that climate science is a luxury and a fraud, the better to propitiate their wealthy patrons.

In a more innocent time, Daniel Patrick Moynihan adjured, "You're entitled to your own opinion, but not your own facts." No more. In post–*Citizens United* America, billionaires can not only buy their own facts, but their own environment.

Fun Questions for the Next GOP Debate

DECEMBER 1, 2015

Throughout the primary season, the Republican debates seemed to take place in an alternative GOP universe. In debate, Sanders and Clinton argued about recognizable issues: trade, money in politics, regulation of Wall Street, income inequality, and the cost of higher education. But the Republicans seemed to be competing with each other in describing how badly Obama had ruined America. As much as anything, this captured the closed intellectual system in which the Republican base lived, and which helped to make Trump's rise possible.

Trump never retracted his false claim that crowds of Muslims in New Jersey had celebrated wildly after 9/11.

Let's get real. For four GOP debates now, watching journalists solicit crazy answers to serious questions—mostly serious, anyhow—has become as surreal as taking acid. In between, all we can do is listen to the most amazing stuff and talk back to our television. So wouldn't the next debate be much more fun if we took the candidates' positions to their logical conclusion? Before it's too late, don't you want to find out how nuts some of these people really are?

I sure do. So here are my suggested questions for a truly enlightening evening:

Mr. Trump, you have called for surveillance of mosques and requiring Muslims to register. Do you intend to identify Muslims by pigmentation, or by the wild look in their eyes? If so, how do you tell them apart from Mexicans? Looking forward, do you see Japanese internment camps as a definitive model for solving both problems? In conceiving such camps, will you wall off the Mexican section, and will you allow the Muslims to celebrate their favorite holidays, like Ramadan and 9/11?

Dr. Carson, you have compared Obamacare to slavery. In your mind, was slavery more like being stuck in the emergency room or paying high deductibles? Have you ever interviewed a slave? If so, did you inquire about their health care? And do you think the movie *12 Years a Slave* was wildly exaggerated?

Ms. Fiorina, you scored points by sticking it to Donald Trump when he ridiculed your appearance. Did you get this idea from your 2010 Senate race, when you ridiculed Barbara Boxer's hairstyle? In your view, is same-sex ridicule okay? Is it conceivable that California's voters rejected you because they didn't like you? Or, like you, did they see the presidency of the most powerful nation on earth as a more appropriate entry-level job for a woman with your mastery of factually dubious talking points?

Senator Rubio, you bravely advocate special operations against ISIS in which "we strike them, we capture or kill their leaders, we videotape the operations" because "I want the world to see how these ISIS leaders cry like babies" and "begin to sing like canaries . . ." Have you run your cinematic ambitions past the generals charged with filming this operation, then getting American soldiers and their captives out of hostile territory alive? How do you know that these erstwhile jihadists will begin acting like stoolies in a '30s gangster movie? Has it occurred to you that, as a military strategist, you may resemble George Patton less than George Armstrong Custer? Have you imagined the Battle of Little Big Horn reenacted by jihadists with videocams who think scalping is for sissies? As president, how will you react if murderous fanatics begin starring captured American soldiers in special movies of their own?

Senator Cruz, in claiming Galileo as a model for your vigorous denial of climate change, you confused his opponents with flat-earth advocates. Do you, in fact, believe that the earth is round? Does your remark reflect a genuine lack of basic scientific knowledge? Or are you striving to make your enthusiasts forget that you graduated from Princeton and Harvard?

Senator Rubio, you have advocated the "sunlight" of disclosing a candidate's donors, while a "dark-money" group

What brought down Carson was that he sounded increasingly like a space alien, even in the interplanetary precincts of the GOP. Though he was never going to be president, the mere idea had seriocomic filmic possibilities.

As always, Trump was inexcusable. Still, I must admit that, for me, Fiorina's overall demeanor evoked the scary Nurse Ratched in *One Flew over the Cuckoo's Nest*.

One of Rubio's fatal flaws was his transcendent callowness. He seemed even younger than he looked—which is younger than he is.

channels millions from undisclosed sources to pay for pro-Rubio commercials. Were you "shocked" to discover this, like the cop in *Casablanca*? Are there, in fact, two Marco Rubios? Or, like Sybil in the movie, do you have multiple personalities dedicated to each of your biggest soft-money donors?

Governor Christie, you favor refusing asylum to Syrian orphans. Might you, instead, vet people of small stature to screen out murderous jihadist midgets? Are traumatized six-year-old Syrians uniquely skilled and vicious? If radicalized children are such a threat, what would you do about Muslim preschools?

After Trump co-opted him, it was Christie who looked traumatized whenever standing next to The Donald.

Ms. Fiorina, you have said that among your first acts as president would be to "call my friend Bibi Netanyahu." How many times have you actually met your friend Bibi, and how elastic is your definition of friendship? Do you, in fact, have friends? Or is Bibi more like the imaginary friend kids make up when they're five years old?

Mr. Trump, your solution to ISIS is to "take away all their oil." Did you get this idea from watching retired army officers on *Meet the Press*? Can you be more precise about logistics? Or is the only problem how many oil tankers to send after your rhetoric reduces hardened jihadist killers to supplicants desperate to please you? If so, would you make them pay for the tankers?

Senator Cruz, your strong professions of evangelical faith seem to affect your stated view of science. Do you still believe that fracking is not just an oil extraction technique, but a "providential blessing"? If so, did God give us global warming to put date palms in our backyards? On the subject of evolution, do you believe that *The Flintstones* was a cartoon or a documentary?

Dr. Carson, you have referred to prospective Syrian refugees as "rabid dogs." Given your fondness for Nazi references, are you by any chance familiar with how the Nazis characterized Jews? Do you still think that an armed Jewish populace could have taken out the entire SS and Gestapo, and that the shooting victims in Oregon should have tried harder? Back to Syria, are the Chinese still there?

Senator Rubio, by the estimate of a conservative tax research group, your tax cut for the wealthy would virtually double the deficit every year, adding about $4 trillion to the national debt over the next decade. How do you relate this problem to your experience with credit cards? Is there an undisclosed foreign entity—like, say, the Chinese—who would be willing to balance your budget by funneling $4 trillion through your dark-money group?

Ms. Fiorina, you claim to be qualified to be president because you "actually know how the economy works." When did you acquire this knowledge? Was it after you got kicked out of Hewlett-Packard? Given that no one has offered you another CEO job, did you learn how the economy works by reading? If so, was your principal source of information *Atlas Shrugged*?

Mr. Trump, a recent Pew Research survey shows that more Mexicans are leaving the US than staying. How do you explain this? Do you have a formula for making sure that the millions of "rapists and murderers" are leaving, and the handful of "good people" are staying? Will Mexicans in both categories have to register?

Governor Bush, let's talk. Do you ever wonder what you're doing in the company of these pretenders? Would one of the "cool things I could be doing" include hanging out with a smarter group of people? For that matter, do you ever feel like you wandered into an insane asylum and can't get out?

If so, I sure do understand. You're awfully stoic about it all, but that's how it looks from here.

Clearly so, as evidenced by Bush's refusal to endorse Trump after he left the race.

The GOP's Tax Warfare

DECEMBER 8, 2015

The discovery was startling—since the millennium, middle-class and blue-collar whites are dying at sharply increased rates. The reasons are equally stunning. The primary causes are self-inflicted: drugs, alcohol, suicide. The victims are the least educated; the triggers are poor health and financial distress. Yet the mortality rate for blacks and Latinos is declining; so, too, for comparable groups in other economically advanced countries. In short, a segment of once secure Americans is suffering an epidemic of shattered dreams. This, it seems clear, is death by class.

One must include this burgeoning social tragedy as a factor spurring struggling white Americans to rally behind Trump.

How ironic, then, is the current Orwellian twist on the term "class warfare." In Marxian parlance, this connotes the struggle for economic and political power between capitalists and workers. But for the GOP it means only this: opposing tax cuts for the rich. Thus the conservative echo chamber bewailed Obama's plan to let Bush-era tax cuts expire—but only for the top earners—as "full-throated class warfare," nothing less than "a pitchfork and torches attack on Republicans and America's rich."

But before imagining our first black president as America's Robespierre, a brief look at the embattled class trembling behind the barricades.

To say the least, it is hard to fathom their self-pity. In 2013, the top 1 percent received 20 percent of the national income and held an equal percentage of our wealth—double their share thirty years ago. And a principal driver of their ever-cascading riches is our tax code, markedly more favorable to the privileged few than in other developed countries.

For, far from being victims, they are the beneficiaries of an enormous tax windfall—over the last fifty years, our top income tax rate has fallen by 48 percent. As their assets swell, those of the poor and middle class decline, a trend accelerated by the Great Recession. Labor unions—a primary target of class warfare from the right—have weakened. Debt has increased; bankruptcies have quintupled. In macroeconomic terms, shifts in income to the wealthy slow consumption and retard growth—even as more political power flows to those who have the most and, all too often, care the least about those below them.

As to the phenomenon of rising deaths among the middle class, the late historian Tony Judt described the causal links: "There has been a collapse in intergenerational mobility: in contrast to their parents and grandparents, children born . . . in the US have very little expectation of improving [their] condition. . . . The poor stay poor. Economic disadvantage for the overwhelming majority translates into ill health, minimal educational opportunity, and—increasingly—the familiar symptoms of depression: alcoholism, obesity, gambling, and minor criminality."

So what does the GOP offer us? More tax cuts for the rich.

This would make sense only if the cuts served some larger social benefit. But they don't. So the GOP dresses them up as the Tax Fairy, cloaked in a hoary myth that history has long since proven false: that tax cuts magically pay for themselves or, at least, offset much of their cost by stimulating economic growth.

With apologies to my readers, the truth resides in numbers.

The first great tax cutter, Ronald Reagan, slashed the upper income tax rate by 42 percent; the deficit exploded by $1.4 trillion. Fans of economic reality noticed. When the second President Bush proposed cutting the top rate by 4.5 percent, 450 economists—including ten Nobel Prize winners—sent a letter protesting that "these tax cuts will weaken the long-term budget outlook . . . will reduce the capacity of the government to finance Social Security and Medicare benefits as well as investments in schools, health, infrastructure, and basic research . . . [and] generate further inequities in after-tax income."

All true. In the end, these cuts increased the deficit by another $5 trillion. The cause was a reprise from the Reagan years, and worth remembering now: large tax cuts combined with increased military spending.

By contrast, Bill Clinton raised the upper income tax rate by 11.6 percent, achieving a budget surplus of $236 billion by the end of his term. Barack Obama's more modest achievement is to hike the top rate by 8.5 percent, while the percentage of the deficit to gross domestic product (GDP) fell from 10 percent to 3 percent. Add to this the small matter of creating jobs: under Clinton, the economy added more than 20 million new jobs—the highest total for the last five presidents.

The concurrent myth that tax cuts spur economic growth is demolished by a five-decade comparison. In the '60s, the highest marginal rate was a whopping 91 percent; the average annual growth in GDP was 4.5 percent. In the '70s, the upper rate declined to 70 percent—so did GDP growth, to 3.2 percent. It remained at 3.2 percent in the '80s, when Reagan drastically lowered rates, and in the '90s, when Clinton raised them. When George W. Bush lowered the rates again, average GDP growth declined to 1.5 percent, only to rise again, in the wake of Obama's tax hikes, to a little over 2 percent.

The American economy is a complex thing, driven by myriad factors in any given time span. But one thing is

clear: the Republican fairytale notwithstanding, there is
no correlation between tax cuts and economic growth.
In 2012, the non-partisan Congressional Budget Office
(CBO) said just that; so has a study by Martin Feldstein,
Reagan's principal economic adviser. The coup de grace
comes from another Republican, Keith Hall, the current
head of the CBO. Hall was brought in by the GOP to
calculate projected budgets through a process known as
"dynamic scoring," a highly speculative method favored
by tax-cut advocates, in that it incorporates the presumed
growth effects of prospective tax cuts. But Hall is an honest man: "[T]he evidence is that tax cuts do not pay for
themselves. And our models show that."

> The persistence of the GOP's "zombie economics" owes less to logic than to the power of its donor class.

But here is the most persuasive proof of all: the near-
infinite self-interest of most elected officials. If the GOP's
tax cut voodoo actually worked, Democrats would be trampling all over Republicans in a frenzied race to enact it. They
aren't.

Not so the GOP. Remarkably, its current candidates are
doubling down on tax cuts for the wealthy. Here, as often,
Marco Rubio and Ted Cruz are salutary examples.

To an almost comical extreme, Rubio's plan scatters
golden eggs meant solely for the rich—the total elimina-
tion of taxes on capital gains, estates, dividends, and interest
income. As for the income tax, he cuts the highest rate by
4.6 percent. In all, Rubio's gifts to the top 1 percent would
hand them 11 percent more income.

Down the ladder, Rubio increases taxes on much of the
middle class, but provides some relief at the lower rungs
through child tax credits. But the overall effect is ruinous, particularly to the vulnerable. The Tax Policy Center
estimates that Rubio would nearly double the deficit over
the next ten years—an average of $414 billion annually
above the current $474 billion. And the least affluent would
pay the price. Rubio has pledged to boost military spending, and expenditures required by entitlement programs

can't be slashed. To cover his deficit requires massive borrowing—which retards economic growth—or spending cuts. All that is left to cut are infrastructure projects that create jobs or programs for the poor and disadvantaged.

But Ted Cruz is no lightweight. On top of his own exclusive enticements for the rich is a flat income tax of 10 percent. This would increase the income of the top 1 percent by about 20 percent; for the next level by about 17 percent. The ostensible benefit to everyone else plummets to from 1 to 4 percent.

But even this is a Trojan horse. For within the Cruz plan is a 16 percent value-added tax on corporations that, like sales taxes, would be passed on to consumers in the form of higher prices—a far more crushing burden on low-income families than the income tax itself. Another regressive feature is that, like Rubio, Cruz balloons the deficit—$3.7 trillion over the next decade—with the same attendant damage.

At this point, it was hard to find Trump's economic program. But eventually he proposed tax rates that would add a staggering $4 trillion to the deficit.

Just for fun, let's imagine what would happen if these candidates actually proposed to raise the rate on the top 1 percent. An increase of 7 percent in the overall tax rate, experts say, would generate about $157 billion in revenue—more than enough to pay for Rubio's child tax credit without any serious impact on economic growth. And even without raising taxes for the upper tier, keeping their rates as they are would lessen the impact on the deficit of tax relief for the middle class and poor.

So why do Republicans insist on cutting taxes for the ultra-rich while shrouding their impact in mendacious nonsense? Because that's what their ultra-richest donors want. Rubio's billionaire soft-money man, Paul Singer, is a fierce proponent of tax cuts for the wealthy. Cruz's leading patron, tax-phobic billionaire Robert Mercer, clocks in at $20 million; his business is being investigated for $6 billion in alleged tax evasion by an IRS Cruz proposes to abolish. And his next largest soft-money nest egg, $15 million, comes from the Wilks brothers, two billionaires who support the Koch brothers' anti-tax crusade.

Here we get to the biggest plutocratic prize awaiting the winner of the GOP's tax cut derby: the $900 million pledged by the Kochs to elect the president of their choice. And the brothers are deadly serious about cutting their own taxes—through abolishing the estate tax, drastically cutting capital gains and corporate taxes, and, above all, completely eliminating progressive income tax rates. After all, as their anti-tax front group grouses, a graduated tax rate "removes individuals in the lower brackets from the reality of the cost" of anti-poverty programs. For modest earners, apparently, bankruptcy and suicide is not reality enough.

As to who will receive the Kochs' $900 million in prize money, the betting favorite is Marco Rubio—when it comes to the brothers, cravenness counts. But the real victor won't be their chosen candidate. No one knows this better than the Kochs' fellow billionaire Warren Buffett: "There's class warfare, all right, but it's my class, the rich class, that's making war, and we're winning."

No kidding.

Trump is a believer in self-help. If you credit his claim to be worth $10 billion, his proposed abolition of the estate tax would have been a $4 billion gift to his heirs.

After Trump became the GOP front-runner for president, the Koch's focused their largesse on trying to help Republicans keep control of the Senate.

True enough. Trump eventually adopted the GOP's discredited tax cut dogma so beloved by its donors.

Ted Cruz's Holiday Spirit

DECEMBER 22, 2015

This holiday season has offered far too little respite from humanity's dark side—the hatred and fanaticism that gave us Paris, San Bernardino, Colorado Springs. How consoling, then, is Ted Cruz, who offers us the power of prayer and the balm of faith.

More massacres followed, including in Brussels and Orlando. In the primaries, this wound up helping Trump, whose vapid posturing was taken for "strength."

For Thanksgiving, Cruz called on the Almighty "to render our National government a blessing to all the people" and "promote the practice of true religion and virtue." His Christmas card quoted the Bible: "I have trusted in your loving kindness. My heart will rejoice in your salvation." Not content with mere random prayer, his website proposed to bind us in a "National Prayer Team." "Heidi and I," Cruz assured us, "are grateful for the prayers of people all over this great nation."

Lest we need guidance in placing our lips to God's ears, the website directs that our efforts be "dedicated to a focused season of prayer on behalf of the nation, presidential candidate Ted Cruz, his family and staff, and the campaign"—presumably including its pollsters and fundraisers. "Members," we are told, "will receive weekly emails containing prayer requests and short devotionals."

Promptly, "Prayer Warriors for Ted Cruz" assured us on Facebook that "God is empowering #TedCruz in such a mighty way." Wafted by this wave of prayer, Cruz is currently brightening our holidays with a twelve-city "Take Off with Ted Cruz Country Christmas Tour" through the southern primary states—the spiritual uplift of which, serendipitously for the senator, has him pressing Donald Trump for first place in this morning's latest national poll.

So let us examine the senator's holiday rhetoric, the better to grasp what he is asking us to pray for.

He predicts that "2016 will be a religious liberty election." But liberty for whom? Not gays or lesbians, evidently, for whom Cruz has prescribed conversion therapy to cure them of their "choice."

The freedom Cruz has in mind is for people like Kentucky county clerk Kim Davis, who denied gay couples marriage licenses. After all, Cruz memorably explained, gays are behind the "jihad"—such an evocative choice of words—"being waged [against] people of faith who respect the biblical teaching that marriage is the union of one man and one woman." So deep is Cruz's respect that he pledges his best efforts to repeal same-sex marriage. "For the sake of this cause," he adds without apparent irony, "we need to bring people together."

Cruz's God, it seems, is also a gun enthusiast. Shortly after the slaughter in San Bernardino, he starred at a gun-rights rally put on by a group whose self-described mission is to "glorify God in all we do." Cruz himself reacted to the massacre by proclaiming: "You don't get rid of the bad guys by getting rid of our guns" but "by using our guns."

In Cruz's world, we may have to. Hours after the massacre, Cruz voted against a Senate measure to bar people on the FBI terrorist watch list from purchasing guns—including the assault weapons used to murder fourteen people. For those puzzled by the senator's seemingly circular reasoning,

At this point I thought Cruz might stop Trump in the South. But the defection of evangelicals to Trump gave us a revealing new slant on their motivations.

it is, perhaps, salient that the NRA vehemently opposed the measure.

Cruz's reaction to the Planned Parenthood killings in Colorado Springs was truly original. The shooter's cry of "no more body parts" caused some to wonder if the heated rhetoric against Planned Parenthood—fervently stoked by Cruz himself—had resonated in the mind of a deranged killer who, like so many other deranged killers, too easily acquired weapons. Not Cruz. Instead, he found a way to conflate two favorite themes: the murderer, he speculated, was a "transgendered leftist activist."

Trump's disregard for truth has, regrettably, overshadowed Cruz's gifts in this area.

With respect to the tragedy in Paris perpetrated by ISIS, Cruz swiftly cut to the heart of the problem: that President Obama is "willing to use military force [only] if it benefits radical Islamic terrorists"—presumably including, though he chose not to mention this, those on the FBI's terrorist watch list whose right to acquire weapons of mass murder he voted to protect. But President Cruz will have the answer: "We will carpet-bomb them into oblivion. I don't know whether sand can glow in the dark, but we're going to find out."

Less aglow was the former commandant of the Army War College—"carpet-bomb," he remarked, "is just one of those phrases that people with no military experience throw around." Which perhaps explains Cruz's bewildering claim that during the first Gulf War "we carpet-bombed them into oblivion" when, as one would expect in the age of smart weaponry, no "carpet-bombing" ever occurred.

Were your holidays lightened a bit by the Paris Climate Agreement? Not Cruz's. He seized the moment to chair hearings denouncing climate change as a hoax perpetrated by liberals who "want massive government control over every aspect of our lives." Among the GOP candidates, Cruz is by far the most vehement in his rejection of climate science: remarkably, the senator purports to believe—in utter defiance of the scientific community—that according to satellite data "there has been no significant global warming for the past eighteen years."

One suspects that Cruz knows very well that his climate denial is nowhere close to intellectually respectable. Thus his diversionary suggestion that Obama's efforts to battle climate change are just another manifestation of weakness in a president who "apparently thinks having an SUV in your driveway is more dangerous than a bunch of terrorists trying to blow up the world"—including, one supposes, those folks on the terrorist watch list. For those attempting to follow this rhetorical bait and switch, it is worthy to note that in only one segment of Americans does a majority reject the overwhelming scientific consensus that man-made climate change is all too real: conservative Republican primary voters, including those clustered in Iowa.

A particularly dispiriting lump of holiday coal was Donald Trump's nativism—espousing a massive deportation of Mexicans while proposing to "register" Muslims in America and bar Muslims abroad from traveling here. Artfully aping Trump, Cruz proclaimed himself a "big fan of Donald Trump's," commending Trump for "focusing on the need to secure our borders" and echoing his hard line on immigration, and his "Christmas Tour" features an echo of George Wallace's segregationist pledge, promising to oppose legal status "today, tomorrow, forever." While modestly demurring to Trump's worst rhetoric with respect to Muslims, Cruz abandoned his erstwhile devotion to "religious liberty"—opposing a Senate resolution against imposing a religious test for entry into the United States.

Perhaps, by now, you've lost the thread of Cruz's Thanksgiving call to "promote the practice of true religion and virtue." Unwittingly recorded at a private fund-raiser, Cruz helped clear things up: stating that Trump and Ben Carson will never become president, he confided that "my approach has been to bear hug both of them, and smother

them with love . . . [until] the lion's share of their supporters come to me."

This, for once, is a window into the depths of Cruz's
soul, long apparent to the political cognoscenti. As a key
Republican insider of four decades says flatly, Cruz is relentlessly "Machiavellian—the most calculating man I've seen
in this business."

His current calculation was on sharp display in the most
recent Republican debate: eliminate Marco Rubio by tar-
ring him with conservatives as a supporter of "amnesty
and citizenship," and keep in good stead with Trump so
as to inherit his nativist vote. Indeed, his Christmas stump
speech includes a fresh appeal to the lowest common political denominator: "I think the new politically correct term is
no longer illegal aliens; it's undocumented Democrats"—to
which he adds the implication that Rubio talks more favorably about legalization when speaking Spanish on Spanish-
language television.

The simple truth about Cruz, says Eliana Johnson of the
National Review, is that "the man who boasts of his ideological purity is perhaps the most obviously tactical candidate." His path to the nomination runs through Iowa and the
Deep South—through evangelicals, gun fanatics, nativists,
climate deniers, and social conservatives—and every position he takes is laser focused on winning them over. And it's
working—Cruz has surged past Trump in Iowa and into second place in the latest national polls, and the growing consensus within the Clinton campaign is that Cruz will be the GOP
nominee. Cruz, not Trump, is becoming the man to watch.

And he bears watching. His holiday rhetoric is not that
of a God-smacked extremist prone to verbal excess, but a
cold-eyed cynic, a top-tier graduate of Princeton and Harvard who condescends to his target audience for his own
narrow ends. For the construct that defines him is not a
hard right-wing belief system, but something far more
frightening: the barren psyche of a demagogue.

Nothing captures Cruz's hypocrisy—and misguided strategy—better than his cynical embrace of Trump. Cruz thought he would inherit Trump's followers once The Donald imploded. Instead Trump and his followers swallowed Cruz whole.

Wrong. A big part of the reason is that Cruz didn't try to take Trump down until it was too late.

Classically defined, a demagogue is "a political leader who appeals to the emotions, fears, prejudice, and ignorance of the lower socioeconomic classes in order to gain power." Thus, as with Cruz, for the sake of stirring excitement, demagogues "oppose deliberation" and "accuse moderate and thoughtful opponents of weakness."

Bad enough. But consider the psychology of someone for whom personal advancement obliterates truth or fairness, and who sees others as chess pieces instead of human beings. A week before Christmas, Congress passed a rare bipartisan compromise by wide margins: a spending bill that prevented a potentially ruinous government shutdown—which, had it happened, would have been politically ruinous to Republicans. Protected from the consequences of such a disaster by the Republican leadership, Cruz used conservative talk radio to throw them under the bus: "This is Mitch McConnell and Paul Ryan passing the Democratic agenda, funding Obamacare, funding amnesty, expanding low-skilled immigration. . . . It's an absolute betrayal."

This is Cruz—a loner who routinely uses his Republican colleagues as foils for personal attacks, whose private conversation is little different than his self-aggrandizing stump speeches, and who is widely proclaimed as "the most hated man in the Senate." In self-exculpation for this universal loathing, Cruz mocks Rubio for being adequately socialized—"he's a wonderful communicator, he's a charming individual, he's very well-liked in Washington"—and argues: "If you want someone to grab a beer with, I may not be that guy. But if you want someone to drive you home . . . I will get you home."

To a person, Cruz's colleagues would rather have a beer at home. How else to react to a nakedly ambitious man whose behavior and persona suggest the following characteristics: "manipulative," "cunning," and "callous," with a "grandiose sense of self," "a penchant for pathological lying," and a

Again, one must not forget that, as a demagogue, Cruz is competitive with Trump.

It will be interesting to see whether Cruz mounts a primary challenge against Trump in 2020. Certainly, he will still be waiting for Trump to implode.

"marked lack of empathy for others." Which, as it happens, are among the hallmarks of a sociopath.

It says something about Republican politics that the leading contestants in 2016 were such alarming characters. The difference between Trump and Cruz is that the latter is sufficiently sane that one can locate his behaviors on the map of political calculation. By comparison, much of Trump's behavior during the campaign seemed less strategic than symptomatic of a mind prone to solipsism and impulsiveness.

Small wonder, then, that of the fifteen candidates followed by the *Washington Post*'s fact checker, Cruz trailed only Trump and Carson in the percentage of statements rated as "false or mostly false." It is sobering to realize that if Ted Cruz assures us that something is a fact, there's a two-thirds chance he's lying.

"Any president," Cruz informs us, "who doesn't begin every day on his knees isn't fit to be commander in chief of this nation." In truth, pious frauds are not fit to be president, demagogues even less so—whether on their knees or on the stump, seeding America with ignorance and hate for their own narcissistic ends.

Let us pray.

The GOP Establishment's Not So Happy New Year

JANUARY 5, 2016

For the established Republican order, the vista presented by this new year is filled with bewilderment and foreboding. For the last twenty-eight years of presidential primaries, the consultants, donors, and loyalists who constituted the party's so-called mainstream have taken it for granted that, in the end, the "most electable conservative" would once again ward off insurrection by the Visigoths of the GOP's outer reaches. This serene state of self-assurance has come to an abrupt and unseemly end.

The only surprise is that they seem so surprised. Over that span of time the meaning of *conservative* has moved ever rightward in the gravitational pull of evangelicals, gun-rights absolutists, economically and socially threatened whites, and, most recently, indignant Tea Party adherents who, collectively, have come to dominate the primary electorate. In the House, the Visigoths have already breached the wall, unhorsing John Boehner and hemming in Paul Ryan; in the Senate, the leadership avoided a similar fate only through the contentious stratagem of fighting off the Tea Party in primaries.

Yet despite the fevered passions of those on whom they have come to depend, the establishment's ever more dubious premise was that, at least in presidential primaries, its base would continue to settle on the candidate most congenial to the party's grandees. But how unruly those passions might be had already become apparent in 2012, when Mitt Romney was dragged into the malarial marshland of the right, merely to ward off the unlikely trio of Newt Gingrich, Herman Cain, and Rick Santorum. Instead of giving the establishment a president, this ordeal contributed to Romney's defeat by compelling him to take highly conservative stands unattractive to the electorate as a whole.

Fearful of a recurrence, for 2016 the party cut down on debates and condensed the primary schedule, hoping to spare the next "electable conservative" such a protracted and damaging gauntlet. As public opinion expert Peter Hart points out, and as the GOP professionals well appreciate, the party's image among the electorate as a whole is negative, not least because of the hard-line stance on social issues—such as same-sex marriage and reproductive rights—embraced by the party's base. Thus a post-election autopsy by the Republican National Committee emphasized the party's urgent need to expand its demographic appeal in presidential elections, notably to Latinos and women, whose disaffection was another ingredient in its primary-driven defeat.

Too little, and way too late. Four more years of frustration with the political classes has left the base seething with negative feelings of anger and distrust, the visceral instinct that the only way to stop America's perceived downward spiral is by cleaning house. Far from wanting to expand its appeal to minorities, many of these voters resent them. And so the GOP's electoral Frankenstein has at last escaped the lab, running amok in the form of the two-headed monster Donald Cruz as its creators shrink back in astonishment and horror.

Summoned by the monster's virulent roar, nativism and rigid social conservatism dominate the Republican landscape. Suddenly nothing works as party strategists intended—there is no consensus establishment choice, and the monster has rudely shouldered aside more acceptable prospects in a headlong lurch toward the primary season, leaving Dr. Frankenstein to pray that its two heads start devouring each other. In short, the formerly smug and powerful are reduced to depending on luck.

To kill the monster, they will need a lot of it. The rise of Ted Cruz was predictable enough—he is simply a more ruthless and calculating version of the right-wing candidates who came before him. Completely contemptuous of the establishment and anyone else who stands in his way, and fueled by a recent surge in campaign contributions, Cruz is a demagogue to watch.

But the true agent of disaster is the uncontrollable Donald Trump, not simply because he has harnessed the equally predictable outrage of a primary electorate inflamed by toxic GOP rhetoric, but because his amorphous appeal has stunted the growth of the presumptive mainstream candidates. In an age inundated with social media, he is the candidate of trash talk, each noxious phrase made to go viral.

This is where Trump bested Cruz—instead of embracing the programs of the donor classes, he became the middle finger of restive blue-collar whites.

Alienated by years of hostile attacks on government and its elected leaders of any stripe, the GOP base is ready-made for Trump's siren song of resentment—nativist, self-congratulatory, and utterly free of content save for the anti-immigrant venom that propelled his rise. After all, 2015 was the year in which Trump tied a presumably grateful Pope Francis for second place as Americans' most admired man.

It still seems probable that Trump will self-destruct—or that the remorseless Cruz will cast aside his Halloween mask of amity and destroy him. And come the various election days, Trump's support may be softer than it now appears: focus groups conducted last fall by Peter Hart indicate misgivings about his temperament and judgment, even among

Wrong again—because Cruz bet that Trump would self-destruct without his help. Trump's most strenuous efforts at self-immolation did not occur until after he won the nomination.

Republicans inclined to favor him. But there is no assurance that his decline will match the accelerated rhythms of the primary season, clearing the path for a challenger to swiftly emerge from the mainstream pool.

A look at the calendar explains why. After Iowa and New Hampshire, between February 20 and March 5 Republican contests occur in eighteen states that are overwhelmingly southern, otherwise conservative, or open to Trump's insurrectionist appeal. Altogether, these first twenty states will select roughly 990 delegates out of 2,472, out of which only half—1,237—are needed to clinch the nomination. In this volatile season, prognostication is dicey—in the wake of Paris and San Bernardino, Cruz rose as quickly as Ben Carson fell. But it is very hard to see a natural path through these early states for the mainstream contenders—Jeb Bush, Marco Rubio, Chris Christie, or John Kasich.

This was always the problem: in the angry precincts of the GOP, no one else had a path to victory.

Which means that New Hampshire is not merely critical but potentially fateful. Often the state has been the bulwark that saved mainstream candidates from the vicissitudes of the Iowa caucuses, which this year are poised to give Cruz a rousing liftoff. But while New Hampshire's more moderate profile makes Cruz unlikely to win there, Iowa should give him a bit of a bump, and going forward he is positioned to be the chief beneficiary of a Carson tailspin.

In early February, Cruz won Iowa handily, surprising Trump and fortifying his candidacy.

More ominously, as of now Trump has a significant lead in the polls of New Hampshire primary voters, and his lack of political definition gives him a broader ideological reach, especially in a year roiled by concerns about national security. The establishment's fondest wish is for a precipitous Trump collapse in New Hampshire, leaving the field wide open. At this point there is little sign that such a game changer can happen so quickly. This leaves the establishment desperately hoping that one of the four mainstream candidates can emerge as a strong consensus alternative.

This is always possible in a primary process where momentum shifts as swiftly as perceptions, transforming voter preferences and abruptly dooming candidacies. A poor showing in New Hampshire could kill off two or more contenders—including at least one of the two most plausible long-term hopes, Rubio or Bush.

In tacit acknowledgment of this, the Bush campaign has canceled television advertising to invest in beefing up their organization in Iowa and New Hampshire. Seeking to rally conservatives, Rubio has called for a constitutional convention to enact a balanced budget amendment and impose term limits on Congress and the Supreme Court—hoping, obviously, that voters are not aware that this is a political impossibility. In the next five weeks all this maneuvering may yield a survivor. By finishing lower than expected, Rubio could collapse; conversely, by exceeding his dramatically lowered expectations, Bush could reverse his decline. And a dismal finish in a state where they have staked their hopes would finish Christie and Kasich.

Still, it is equally possible that the four contenders will split what now appears to be about 40 percent of the expected primary vote, yielding no obvious savior. Recently, both Chris Christie and Jeb Bush have been going after Rubio, even as Trump, Bush, and Rubio go after Christie. These attacks will intensify even as negative ads proliferate, increasing the chance of mutual damage and fragmentation. Further, as Hart notes, in a year where national security matters, none of the contestants has credentials that would elevate him above the others. And whatever happens in New Hampshire, every one of them has significant problems going forward.

Take Marco Rubio. Insiders are murmuring that beneath the surface of his oft-repeated and uplifting biographical speech there is, well, nothing much and no one at home. This is not a helpful reading of a one-term senator with little accomplishment, a spotty voting record, suspiciously mutable positions, a leisurely campaign schedule, an acolyte's eagerness to please wealthy political benefactors, and

For the Republican base, it turned out, ignorant bellicosity was as intoxicating to hear as it was for Trump to spout. That proved to be enough to buoy a mindless draft-evader who asserted that "I know more than the generals." Even George Armstrong Custer was whirling in his grave.

To say the least. Down the road, Gail Collins would call Rubio "an annoying twit."

a demeanor that verges on the callow. Most damning, his flip-flop on immigration has tarred him with opportunism without pacifying the anti-immigrant base.

So whatever Rubio's gifts, it is far from clear that he can strike sparks with primary voters in an angry and ideological year. And the downside of soaking up soft money is that it seems to have distracted Rubio's campaign from sufficiently organizing in key primary states. Among the early primaries, it is hard to pick one for Rubio to win, including his home state of Florida, where another switch—this time favoring bondholders who are among his donors—threatens to alienate 1 million or so Puerto Ricans.

Despite wide expectations that Sheldon Adelson and his millions would come to Rubio's aid, this has yet to happen, perhaps because Adelson's wife, Miriam, is reportedly drawn to Ted Cruz. And the relentless Cruz has zeroed in on Rubio as his principal competitor, working overtime to trash him with the base. Even should he be viable after New Hampshire, Rubio could be a dead man walking well before he reaches Florida.

Which turned out to be true. After Trump decimated him in Florida, Rubio dropped out, and then, reversing himself, ran for reelection to the Senate.

By taking on Trump while the others vacillate, Jeb Bush has newly shown his mettle, and his more effective stump appearances have engendered needed enthusiasm. More than his competitors, he retains a national fund-raising and political network that could be reenergized, including in the South, and access to seasoned political talent that could upgrade his campaign. But as suggested by Bush's challenge of Trump to a one-on-one debate, he risks getting bogged down with a master of personal insult, while alienating voters he will need down the road.

In fact, what Hart told me in the fall was that Bush would "never happen." After New Hampshire, the truth of this prediction was clear.

Another difficulty, Peter Hart suggests, is that too many of these voters already feel that Bush is not their guy. His daunting task is to defy the zeitgeist in a year when the Republican base treats experience as a curse, persuading them that the qualifications of a successful conservative governor matter in choosing a president.

But both Rubio and Bush are better positioned than their mainstream rivals. Chris Christie is a first-rate political talent and often fun to watch. His ready-made town hall style gives him a shot to do well in New Hampshire, dealing a serious blow to the other mainstreamers. His focus on the state and his endorsement by its largest newspaper have made him the latest target of Trump's attacks. But even if he makes a good showing, where next?

Christie is dragging from New Jersey not just baggage, but boxcars full of it—the bridge scandal, faltering state finances, plunging approval ratings. In the South he has no discernible stronghold, or even a single state that holds out clear promise. And his claim that a stint as US Attorney gives him superior antiterrorism credentials is more rhetorical than real. All of which increases the danger that his Jersey Boy act will wear very thin very fast.

John Kasich has broad experience in Congress and as a governor, and his "ordinary guy" appeal to common sense makes him a viable New Hampshire–type candidate. But something—perhaps a tendency toward bumptiousness or a failure to shine in debates—has kept him stuck in single digits. And common sense is not what the party's angry base wants to hear. It's hard to see what delivers Kasich from the southern primaries with a discernible pulse.

Kasich lasted longer than some thought. Rumor has it that pressure from Reince Priebus forced him from the race. By early May, Priebus had become a "Vichy Republican," intent on giving Trump a glide path to the nomination.

And yet the establishment needs one of these men—and only one—to dispatch the others and survive past March 5 as a truly plausible alternative to Trump or Cruz. After that the promised land beckons—Michigan, Ohio, Illinois, Wisconsin, New York, Connecticut, Delaware, Maryland, Pennsylvania, Rhode Island, and, ultimately, California. Assuming that it's not already too late, these states offer a genuine, if belated, chance to change the dynamic of the race.

In the end, Trump virtually swept the South.

This prospect would be helped immensely if Trump and Cruz were to cancel each other out through the early primaries. But if Cruz skips New Hampshire and takes his campaign straight to South Carolina, he could precipitate a string of southern victories that deals Trump—and the establishment's hopes—a serious blow. And if by March 5 either man—most likely Cruz—takes out the other while amassing a significant delegate lead, the establishment's dilemma becomes very dire indeed.

Cruz went to New Hampshire—in retrospect, a mistake.

At that point, even with more promising primaries ahead, every scenario is problematic for the GOP's erstwhile powers that be. Trump may be both uncontrollable and unelectable. While the establishment might more readily choke down the odious Cruz, he too would have grave problems in a general election, and those Republicans fastidious enough to look past lower taxes to fitness for office might find themselves gagging. But what delivers them a nominee more to their liking?

Before March, perhaps, alarmed and ultra-wealthy donors will have put money behind advertising in an effort to bring down the two interlopers, most likely through an independent group that prevents their chosen candidate from being labeled as an establishment tool. But can big money, in itself, peel off voters from the tribunes of outrage in such a contrarian year?

They did. But too late, with too little money, without supporting a specific alternative.

And what of the mainstream alternative, should one of the four emerge? Will huge amounts of advertising suffice to overcome the momentum of Cruz or, perhaps, Trump? With what message does this white knight prevail? How does he distinguish himself as more inclusive and broadly appealing, and yet attract the support of the GOP's ever so restive base? How does he beat back Trump or Cruz without alienating their supporters?

And then there is the Hail Mary of desperate scenarios—resuscitating Romney, or conjuring a fresher face in Ryan. While labeling this a 100–1 long shot, Hart can imagine an uprising of GOP senators and congressmen unwilling to follow Cruz or Trump off the electoral cliff. In that event, Hart believes that Ryan, not Romney, would be broadly acceptable to conservatives.

But either man would face the same difficulties as a mainstreamer propped up by establishment money—worse, perhaps, in that the intervention of either could excite a counter reaction. Neither, even if successful, would be guaranteed to hold the party together. And what of the increased risk that one of the thwarted candidates, like Trump, would mount a third-party challenge lethal to the GOP's chances?

This kept the Republican establishment frozen in place.

Perhaps, indeed, the dominoes will fall in an improbable sequence of good fortune that once more bails out the establishment, or its remnants. But as of now the primary season ahead looks like more than a nightmare—it may foreordain the final tolling of a death knell that, for far too long, they stubbornly refused to hear.

Dog Whistles and Hypocrisy

The GOP's Selective Birthers

JANUARY 12, 2016

Let's get this straight. We spent the first several years of Barack Obama's presidency obsessing about whether he was born in Kenya. Why? Because a large segment of the GOP electorate—spurred on by Donald Trump—splenetically asserted that Obama's supposed foreign birth barred him from the White House. Merely to quell the rising political fever, Obama was forced to release a long-form birth certificate from Hawaii.

With me so far? Okay. Now Trump is raising the birther issue again, but this time the target is Ted Cruz. Ever selfless, Trump disclaims any worry that Cruz is polling ahead of him in Iowa. His sole concern is for his beloved, if recently adopted, Republican Party:

> Republicans are going to have to ask themselves the question: "Do we want a candidate who could be tied up in court for two years?" That'd be a big problem . . . for Republicans because he'd be running and the courts may take a long time to make a decision. You don't want to be running and have this kind of thing over your head.

Reliably Pavlovian when it comes to Trump, the media took his bait and ran with it. If foreign birth is disqualifying, this time Trump has his opponent dead to rights: beyond dispute, Ted Cruz was born in Canada. The senator's only defense—that his mother was an American citizen—also applies to Obama. So if the constitutional requirement that the president be a "natural born citizen" mandates birth in the United States, Cruz can never be president.

So why isn't the Cruz campaign sweating bullets and leaking oil? Where are all those constitutional purists in the Republican base who believe falsely about Obama what is true about Cruz? Whatever, pray tell, could the distinction be?

Oh no. It couldn't possibly involve . . .

Actually, it's worth stringing this out a little. So let's reprise the toils imposed by the birthers—and some elements of the elected GOP—on America's forty-fourth president.

The issue of whether Obama's alleged birth in Kenya disqualified him to be president surfaced during the 2008 campaign. It was not in dispute that his mother, like Cruz's, was an American citizen. Though there is no definitive Supreme Court ruling on the issue, the great weight of scholarly opinion was that, regardless of birthplace, his mother's citizenship made Obama a "natural born citizen" eligible to be president. This also applied to Obama's opponent John McCain, born in Panama to an American military family. Still, to put this issue to rest, before the election Obama released his official Hawaiian birth certificate.

It didn't help. A fresh round of accusations labeled the Hawaiian birth certificate a forgery. An actual forgery surfaced—a fake Kenyan birth certificate. Pondering a run in 2012, Donald Trump continued using his media megaphone to question Obama's eligibility for office. The birther movement went viral through the Internet, talk radio, and other channels of the conservative media, infesting Republican meetings and town halls.

To say the least, not all Republican officeholders distinguished themselves in response. Senator Richard Shelby said, "I haven't seen a birth certificate. You have to be born in America to be president"—a disqualifier he has not seen fit to repeat about Ted Cruz. In some way or another, birtherism was stoked by such luminaries as Senator Roy Blunt, Sarah Palin, Newt Gingrich, Mike Huckabee, Michele Bachmann, and numerous other Republican congressmen and candidates, some of whom implied that the president had a sensibility and viewpoint—indeed, loyalties—derived not from America, but Africa.

Proof that racism within the GOP did not originate with Trump, and will not follow him out the door.

Lest we forget the undertone of denigration that was birtherism's companion, the remarks of Gingrich and Huckabee were particularly gamy and insinuating—and, when deployed against our own president, strikingly xenophobic. Gingrich stated that Obama's sensibility could only be grasped by those who "understand Kenyan, anti-colonial behavior." Falsely claiming that the president had been raised in Kenya, Huckabee asserted that Obama "probably grew up hearing that the British were a bunch of imperialists who persecuted his grandfather." Their barely concealed implication was that America's president was, in fact, "the other"—a stranger to America and its values.

To be sure, other Republicans behaved with decency. Some were punished for it by birther-inflamed GOP voters. Confronted by birthers at a town hall in Delaware, Representative Mike Castle firmly rejected their claims—he was roundly booed and lost a Senate primary to a Tea Party candidate who dabbled in witchcraft. Fearful of such consequences, other GOP officeholders simply avoided public meetings.

Others ducked the issue by disclaiming knowledge of Obama's birthplace. Still others couched their evasions as respect for the electorate, as did John Boehner in asserting

his disinclination to tell voters what to think—a curious
objection from a man who attained high office by doing just
that. All in all, much of the official GOP allowed the issue to
keep boiling among the base, profiting from the unreasoning
antipathy to Obama it engendered.

The impact on the electorate was measurable, and distributed in telling ways. An opinion poll carried out for the
Daily Kos in 2009 found that 28 percent of Republicans
believed that Obama was not born in the United States,
and that an additional 30 percent were not sure. Notably,
support for birtherism was concentrated among whites and
was particularly strong in the South.

But the virus persisted nationwide. In 2011, a Gallup
poll reported that 23 percent of self-identified Republicans
thought that Obama was "probably born in another country," as opposed to 14 percent of Independents and 5 percent of Democrats. The 2011 release of Obama's long-form
birth certificate did little to extinguish this pervasive falsehood. In September 2015 a CNN/ORC poll showed that
20 percent of Americans continue to believe that Obama is
foreign-born.

Within the
Republican
base, all of these
delusions persist.

Again, it is well to recall the singular vituperation
directed at the president that has accompanied birtherism—
including a shout of "liar" from a Republican congressman
during his State of the Union Address. It is hard to perceive
such invective as wholly coincidental, a mere by-product
of partisan disagreement. For the inescapable essence of
birtherism is that Obama is not simply wrong on the issues
but an illegitimate president, a stranger who, by virtue
of his origins, is uniquely undeserving of the decent respect
otherwise due his office.

Now let us contemplate the current treatment of that
would-be president and child of Canada, Ted Cruz.

For once, one of Donald Trump's witch's shafts seems to
be missing its mark. In the week since Trump first hurled
it—a lifetime in this viral age—there is little sign that the

question of birthplace, which so bedeviled Barack Obama, is
seriously tarnishing the foreign-born Cruz with Republican
primary voters. In 2016, it seems, the contagion of birtherism is confined to the media, spurred on not by the GOP
base, but by Cruz's competitors and their allies—whose
obvious self-interest is augmented by a uniform loathing of
the Texas senator.

Seemingly frustrated at the initial paucity of grassroots
response, Trump has escalated his attacks, aware that taking down Cruz in Iowa could gravely damage his chances.
On Sunday's *Meet the Press*, Trump direly predicted: "If Ted
is the nominee, he will be sued by the Democrats." "Ted is
very glib," he complained in Iowa, "and he goes out and says
'well, I'm a natural born citizen,' but the point is you're not."
Professing bewilderment that he is trailing Cruz in most
Iowa polls, Trump said of his rival, "You can't have that
problem and go be the nominee."

But, apparently, Cruz can. Brushing off Trump's claims,
he ascribed them to the political "silly season." His campaign for the presidency rolls on; his stock as Trump's leading Republican challenger is holding steady. Untroubled by
birthers, Cruz finished a six-day run of Iowa town halls,
buoyed by the very Republican base that so despises Obama.
What Trump's political inner ear fails to pick up is the sound
of silence, the absence of the dog whistle that once animated
birthers. Instead, what he may be hearing is the sound of
Cruz's footsteps.

As noted, Cruz
won Iowa
handily—Canadian
or no.

For among the birthers, indifference reigns. This time
the issue is not visceral, as it was with Obama, bestirring the
deep emotions that gave us years of birtherism. Conservative
talk radio host Hugh Hewitt dismisses the question of Cruz's
eligibility as a nonissue for the Republican base. Cruz's principal Iowa backer, fiercely anti-immigrant representative Steve
King, neatly exemplifies their curious selectivity. With respect
to the president, King embraced the birther movement and
questioned Obama's birth certificate. As for Cruz, King insists

that his scholarly research proves that there is "no doubt" Cruz is a "natural born citizen" eligible to be president. Foreign birth, it seems, is less foreign in Canada than Kenya.

One reason for such disparity is surely garden-variety hypocrisy. Barack Obama is a progressive Democrat. Ted Cruz is a hard-right conservative with an enthusiastic following, no doubt including many erstwhile birthers who now find constitutional consistency ideologically inconvenient. But there is another distinction, peculiar to Obama, that Republicans need to own: the distinction that helped spread the infection of birtherism among the GOP base, the reason that almost half of Republican primary voters persist in believing that Barack Obama is another version of their "other"—a Muslim.

President Obama is black. Senator Cruz is not.

Cruz, of course, survived Trump's birther attack with nary a scratch. Proving the birtherism directed at Obama was not an issue, but a symptom.

PART II

Primaries, Guns, the Court,
Bernie vs. Hillary, the Rise of Trump,
and the Collapse of the GOP Establishment

ON FEBRUARY 1, 2016, THE IOWA CAUCUS BEGAN A FREN-
zied gauntlet of primary after primary, boosting Ted Cruz
and Bernie Sanders. By early May, Cruz was out and Sanders was effectively dead in the water, though his corpse kept
dog-paddling furiously. In three volatile months, much happened, and not just the brutal winnowing of candidates.

Antonin Scalia suddenly died, pouring gasoline on one
of our most incendiary issues: which party would win the
chance to transform the Court for a generation in areas
such as voting rights, reproductive choice, and gun control.
To preserve its chances, the GOP stalled the nomination
of Merrick Garland. Among the candidates, hopes were
dashed, reputations tarnished, and careers destroyed. The
Republican establishment collapsed. Terrorists and mad-
men slaughtered innocents with weapons of war. A fretful
populace feared for America's future—in part because they
feared one another.

In this heated moment, I set out to analyze what was
happening in the fever swamp—and why.

It quickly became apparent that the normal tools of
analysis simply would not do, for none of them explained
Donald Trump.

No matter how disturbing, nothing he said or did diminished his support within the GOP primary electorate—instead
it grew in numbers and intensity. But why?

A partial reason was the party's indifference to the
economic anxieties of its voting base—struggling whites.
Another was that Trump ripped the scab off the base's racial
anxieties, evoking a primal roar of anger against Mexicans,
Muslims, and minorities. Still another was his hallucinatory vision of American renewal—restoring traditional

manufacturing; repealing the realities of the global economy; walling off Mexico; and crushing ISIS with one blow of his iron fist.

But beneath this lurked a craving for authority, embodied by a man who delighted in the role of modern-day strongman. A man who promised his frightened and credulous followers that only his greatness could make America great again. Millions of our fellow citizens saw Donald Trump as their last chance, a human Powerball ticket.

The Rise of the Unfit
Trump, Cruz, and Rubio

FEBRUARY 9, 2016

This year it's different.

Breathlessly, Republicans await the outcome of today's New Hampshire primary. In times past, New Hampshire was, variously, a check on Iowa, a force for moderation, a safe haven for front-runners, a boon to long shots, and badlands for the presumably anointed. In this unconventional year, it will likely alter the trajectory of the presumptive leaders—not least because of Marco Rubio's Saturday night train wreck—as well as of those in the second tier, muddling the contest for "mainstream" candidate while winnowing the brace of also-rans.

But that death knell we are hearing is not just the mercy killing of walking footnotes like Carly Fiorina. It is for the GOP establishment and, more profoundly, for the very idea of what a president should be.

The ruin of the established order—big donors, lobbyists, and professionals—has been a long time coming. For decades the establishment has resembled the once proud family who keeps selling off pieces of their estate so they can keep the house. In exchange for lower taxes and laissez-faire, the establishment subcontracted its electoral fortunes to an overlapping—and increasingly hostile—compendium of evangelicals, gun-rights advocates, Tea Party fanatics, and

Cruz's victory in Iowa eight days before had made him the leading challenger to Trump.

Apparently unable to frame a responsive answer to a debate moderator's questions, Rubio four times repeated—virtually word for word—an inane attack on President Obama. This confirmed the widespread view that Rubio was a shallow poseur programmed to recite prepackaged talking points, an astonishing act of self-immolation underscored by an instantaneous and withering takedown by Chris Christie. In the history of political debates, one struggles to recall a more devastating flameout.

less-educated whites who feel that their security, and their country, are being snatched from their grasp. Now it is no longer enough to surround the mansion—they want to burn it down.

The incongruous agent of their resentment has been the self-proclaimed billionaire Donald Trump, followed by self-styled bomb-thrower Ted Cruz. But in great measure what empowers them is the establishment's surrender to nihilistic rhetoric directed at Washington, DC. A throng of voters willing to shut down the government is unlikely to nurture tender feelings for the grandees of the GOP. Trump has simply focused their free-floating hostility on a larger group of scapegoats—Mexicans, Muslims, rich Republican donors and financiers, and, Lord help us, Megyn Kelly.

In doing so, he has become an unlikely symbol for socially vulnerable whites who feel threatened by forces they can't control. Too late, the GOP establishment has found out what "class warfare" really means, and they are on the wrong end.

Financiers and party professionals feel free to perceive the economic and political upside of resolving the immigration mess. Not so with blue-collar workers fearful that immigrants—legal or not—will take away their jobs or swell the ranks of welfare recipients who sponge off their hard-earned tax money. For them, the GOP establishment has become another instrument of the Great Sell-Out, the smug proponents of free trade agreements that savage American workers.

In due course, the man became a shill for Trump on talk shows and spearheaded a pro-Trump super PAC, proving, for those who are so inclined, that one can never be too cynical about the political classes.

Like so many elites who discover that they are widely loathed, the establishment has responded with dithering and wishful thinking. The result is a vacuum that has consumed the very idea of leadership.

A widely respected GOP professional attempted to raise money for a Stop Trump campaign and found no takers. Even before Iowa, elements of the established order began gingerly propitiating their antagonists—choosing between Trump and the widely hated Cruz. Bob Dole mused aloud that at least Trump has "the right personality and he's kind of a deal maker"; Mary Matalin hosted a fund-raiser for Cruz. And then Iowa reshuffled the deck a bit, with Cruz banishing the panicky myth that Trump was invincible, while Marco Rubio surfaced in third place.

Abruptly, some in the party's elite began clutching Rubio like a human lifeline, praying that he emerges from the scrum of New Hampshire as the alternative to Trump and Cruz. Beyond ratifying the impotence of the establishment, their desperation confirms the demise within the GOP of something far more important—the very idea of what qualifies a person to assume the most complex and demanding office in a dangerous world.

In saner times, there was a general understanding of those elements that might commend a candidate. Sound judgment. A reasonable command of the issues. At least some relevant experience. A grasp of what the job demands that transcends canned speeches and talking points. A balanced temperament. A certain capacity for dignity and grace. At least a few real achievements, not least in the realm of politics.

One of the most telling features of the GOP race was that experience counted for nothing—let alone sane policy positions. This confirmed the restiveness and alienation of the Republican base.

Add to this the ability to inspire, but also to appreciate the political environment. And something less tangible but no less critical—some combination of intellectual integrity and emotional health that keeps self-regard from spinning into sociopathy turbocharged by power: lying without shame, governing without some genuine regard for the governed, a narcissism so deep that it obliterates all else.

In the recent history of the GOP, there were harbingers that these standards were eroding—that, among a portion of the electorate, all that mattered was anger and disdain for government. One can cite Pat Robertson, Pat Buchanan, and, even more ludicrous, Herman Cain and Michele Bachmann. But the party's eventual nominees reached the threshold of presidential plausibility—George H. W. Bush, Bob Dole, George W. Bush, John McCain, Mitt Romney.

This year is very different indeed. Of the three most likely Republican nominees, none is remotely qualified to be president. Indeed, their unfitness is so patent as to inspire fear.

The challenge with Donald Trump is where to start. Even Ted Cruz pretends that his campaign is about other people. Trump doesn't even get that he's supposed to fake it. His candidacy is, indeed, all about him, his default expression one of aggrieved displeasure at not being "treated fairly," his mouth the pursed "*O*" of a beached flounder sucking oxygen.

Imagine year upon year of crudity, petulance, self-preening, and puerile bluster. Imagine Americans' sickening realization that they are trapped in a dysfunctional relationship with a boorish narcissist who has no idea how to protect their interests and whose only interest is himself. Imagine the face of America in the world as the face of Donald Trump.

That's for openers. Trump understands nothing that a president needs to understand. His nationalistic promise to "make America great again" is hucksterism devoid of substance. He has no idea of governance. He has no coherent policy for anything—the economy, foreign policy, ISIS, or trade. His "solution" to immigration is fantastical and racist.

He measures his candidacy by Nielsen ratings. He exudes sexism. He demeans anyone who displeases him—opponents, reporters, women, a wide assortment of ethnic groups, even the disabled—the hallmark of a thin-skinned bully wholly focused on himself. Forget Megyn Kelly. Imagine Trump's conduct at a press conference—let alone a summit conference.

But then imagine a president who is flat-out ignorant of the world. You can't make "great deals" if you don't know what the deal is about, let alone negotiate with counterparts you've made no effort to understand. Even an intellectual pygmy like Scott Walker tried to memorize a world globe. Trump can't be bothered. The ego that empowers such obliviousness is a dangerous thing—even more dangerous

After the conventions, the larger electorate began imagining all these things. Like hanging, a general election tends to concentrate the national mind.

A modest word, it later emerged, for a proudly predatory serial groper for whom consent was irrelevant. Each new account of his conduct raised nauseating images of a panting, orange-haired, emotionally barren sexual aggressor.

when dealing with adversaries in treacherous times. One cringes to imagine the fallout when ISIS or Putin decline to treat Donald fairly.

Thus it says a lot about Ted Cruz that his colleagues would prefer to jump into the abyss with Trump. Indeed, one of the striking features of the GOP debates is his fellow senators' visceral loathing for their peer.

If Trump is Huey Long without a program, Cruz is Elmer Gantry without the charm—oleaginous, transcendently phony, relentlessly manipulative, and intellectually dishonest to the point of demagoguery. His triumph in Iowa was buoyed by dirty tricks—including lies on caucus night about Ben Carson's fictitious "withdrawal," which Cruz then tried to cover up by repeating more blatant and deliberate lies blaming CNN for his campaign's "mistake." He is the dank prince of darkness, playing on the resentments of evangelicals and others who feel marginalized—without offering them, or anyone else, an uplifting vision of the future.

Even on the campaign trail, he seems to exist in emotional isolation, viewing voters less as people than as interchangeable pawns. One-on-one, he responds to voters' heartfelt expressions of concern about their lives not by answering in kind, but by reciting right-wing boilerplate from his stump speeches. There is something deeply disturbing in his disassociation, a lack of empathy that suggests an inner void.

In his self-scripted political psychodrama, Cruz casts himself as a lonely ideological purist surrounded by spineless sellouts. Routinely, he castigates the "Washington, DC, cartel," portraying the GOP establishment and its leaders as self-serving liars, the better to galvanize the embittered voters of the right. But this is a matter of convenience, not principle—far from being a true believer, Cruz sought establishment support for years, and his villainization of them now is a cold-eyed tactic. His only permanent loyalty is to his own ambition.

In the end, this obvious disassociation from voters helped to drag Cruz down. Trump never cared about them either, but he was better at channeling their anxieties and outrage.

Perhaps the most frightening thing about Cruz's act is that it is so transparently that—an act. His stump speeches are performances, scripted down to the last breathy pause, and delivered with the histrionic stage whisper of a grade B evangelist entranced with his own performance. All this cloaked in a cloying religiosity, often capped with an invocation to "awaken the body of Christ to pull this country back from the abyss."

But as is often true of genuine hypocrites, this patina of piety covers the meanness beneath. He savors insults and revels in his own slurs, no matter how gratuitous. Hence his mockery of the last GOP nominee: "I'm pretty certain Mitt Romney actually French-kissed Barack Obama." Truly Christian; sublimely presidential. Quintessentially Ted Cruz.

And so it comes to this—the last, best hope of the establishment is Marco Rubio.

Here one struggles to capture the depths of his shallowness, a task akin to grasping at vapor. For it is grim testament to Trump and Cruz that they can frighten grown-ups into proposing Rubio as presidential hardwood.

In debate and on the stump, Rubio increasingly tries to compete with Trump and Cruz through hyperbolic excess directed at Obama. With a slightly unhinged zeal, he claims that Obama is so "completely overwhelmed" that he has "deliberately weakened America." Like his indictment of the president as an enemy of the Constitution and the free enterprise system, this over-the-top rhetoric is shamelessly stolen from the hysterical alternate reality of talk radio. "When America needed a bold plan of action from our commander in chief," Rubio proclaims, "we instead got a lecture on love, tolerance, and gun control designed to please the talking heads at MSNBC."

At times, the comical ferocity of Rubio's attacks on Obama evoked a Chihuahua yipping through a screen door.

But the effect Rubio achieves is not that of a prospective commander in chief, but that of a callow aspirant who is over-caffeinated, shrill, and willing to say anything—a man wholly lacking in balance or intellectual ballast. One thinks not of a leader, but of an overambitious sales guy looking for a promotion he doesn't deserve—say, perhaps, to district manager.

That marks a deeper problem. Supporters excuse the swiftness of Rubio's attempted rise by comparing him to Barack Obama. But unlike Obama, in Rubio there is little sign of a deep intellect or even keen intelligence—as opposed to just a certain gift for reciting a memorized sales pitch. Thus Rubio is the most cosseted of candidates, his campaign designed to protect him from exposure.

His speeches are canned, recited from a script; he "debates" by repeating whole chunks from memory. That was what made Rubio's breakdown in Saturday's New Hampshire debate so disastrous: he at last displayed for a national audience what has been obvious up close. It was dreadful to watch; worse to think of him in the Oval Office.

But this is Marco Rubio, the pretender who would be president. He meets reporters guarded by a press aide who selects those permitted to ask the androidal candidate a question. Observing this unearthly phenomenon, one reporter was reminded of "a computer algorithm designed to cover talking points." As political insults go, Christie's characterization of Rubio as "the boy in the bubble" is particularly apt. One wonders if he knows or cares that he appears to have so little pride or substance—or, in truth, whether he has the capacity to be any better than this.

His blatant abandonment of immigration reforms seems to capture his political essence. To appease the right, Rubio opposes abortion in the case of rape or incest, then hints at a softer line. Once a proponent of green energy, he flipped and coined the great dodge of climate deniers—"I'm not a scientist, man." Formerly not given to public pieties, when asked in debate whether he was the "Republican savior," he intoned, "There is only one Savior and it's not me. It's Jesus Christ, who came down to Earth and died for our sins." Including, one assumes, a reflexive political malleability driven by unwarranted ambition.

One was left to wonder whether helplessly chattering the same phrases over and over was a symptom of too many months in the fever swamp. In any case, this indelible moment proved to be Rubio's undoing as a credible candidate. After New Hampshire, he lost primary after primary, and donors fell away. He had become a political nowhere man, trudging inexorably toward failure.

The deeper shame of his attack on Obama for speaking to American Muslims at a mosque is that, coming from Rubio, it was no surprise.

Here, at least, Rubio was a leader, providing a template for Republicans who wish to dodge the question of climate change.

Indeed, it seems quite clear that Rubio's only reason for becoming a senator was to run for president—not on the basis of any real accomplishment, but by repeatedly reciting an uplifting biographical speech that has little or no bearing on his policy positions. Beneath that is a spotty voting record and an unseemly eagerness to appease wealthy donors, often to fund super PACs whose activities verge on the illegal.

So what, one might ask, is Rubio all about? What are the political passions that drive him? When has he ever done anything courageous, or even hard? And where, in all this, can one locate a president?

Yet, come November, it appears likely that one of our two major parties will ask Americans to imagine a President Trump or Cruz or Rubio. One can but hope that, in its collective good sense, the electorate will experience a massive failure of imagination.

Hillary, Bernie, and the Future of the Court

FEBRUARY 16, 2016

The death of Antonin Scalia highlights the Democrats' day of reckoning.

Pretty soon, Democratic primary voters will settle on Bernie Sanders or Hillary Clinton. The fallout could be toxic. Many partisans of both candidates harbor dire images of the other. Hillary is a slippery sellout. Bernie is an impractical loser. Hillary is several people. Bernie is just one—a cranky loner. And so on.

I'm not here to argue with anyone. Feelings run high—I get that. I got it in 1968, when many supporters of Eugene McCarthy and Robert Kennedy abandoned Hubert Humphrey, whom they saw as a weaselly supporter of the war in Vietnam. And then we all got Richard Nixon—and six wrenching years of perspective punctuated by carpet-bombing and needless deaths abruptly ending in Watergate.

During that time, by the way, Nixon also gave us William Rehnquist and transformed the Supreme Court.

To be sure, there are real and important differences between Sanders and Clinton. But no matter which Democrat wins the nomination, if she or he loses in November, then much that is dear to their supporters will take a beating—environmental protection, pay equity, gun control, voting rights, women's rights, combating money in politics, and, yes, whatever chance exists to curb the excesses of Wall Street. And there is one forum where virtually all of these issues are certain to play out, for good or ill: the Supreme Court.

With Scalia's passing, the Court is now in equipoise—four justices appointed by Republicans, four by Democrats. Hanging in the balance is the legal future of core issues like affirmative action, union rights, reproductive freedom, and environmental protection. Even if Barack Obama sends a nominee to the Senate, Mitch McConnell has pledged to block a vote. Thus the course of the court—and, in many ways, the fate of progressive values—depends on this election.

Here the past is truly prologue to the crucible of 2016. The 5–4 conservative majority that preceded Scalia's death included two justices appointed by George W. Bush—John Roberts and Samuel Alito. The result was a relentless right-wing judicial activism through which the court undertook to transform our society. So let's consider two controversial decisions by the Roberts Court that go to the heart of what kind of country we are, what kind of decisions we could expect if a Republican president chooses Scalia's successor, and—critically—how the Republicans will ensure that this new justice is a judicial clone of Antonin Scalia.

First, the Lilly Ledbetter case. Most of us know at least something about it, though perhaps less about what is most telling: the convoluted reasoning through which Republican justices got where they wanted to go.

The case involved an allegation of sex discrimination. Unknown to Ledbetter, her employer, Goodyear, determined to pay her less than its male employees for performing the same job. As a result, Ledbetter received paychecks that were significantly smaller than those of her male counterparts.

The single smartest thing Trump did during the primary season was to release a list of right-wing prospective appointees. This helped cement the support of many conservatives, including those who otherwise despised him, and helped win over wavering Republicans in the fall.

When at length she found this out, Ledbetter sued Good-year under federal anti-discrimination statutes. Despite the fact that Goodyear had concealed its original discriminatory decision, the Supreme Court ruled, in essence, that Ledbetter had discovered that decision too late to file suit within the statute of limitations. On these technical grounds, she was barred from the Court.

To reach this ruling, a 5–4 majority of justices—all Republicans, including Scalia—employed some truly Orwellian logic. The statute of limitations began running, they reasoned, at the time of Goodyear's secret decision. The unequal paychecks—though received because of this decision—did not themselves reflect an intention to discriminate on the basis of sex, because Goodyear had already decided to pay Ledbetter less. In the majority's view, the smaller paychecks given Ledbetter as a result just sort of happened on their own.

Think about that. Stripped of legal niceties, the Republican majority rewarded an employer for successfully concealing from its female employee its deliberate decision to discriminate against her, allowing it to underpay her with impunity. Justice Ruth Bader Ginsburg's piercing dissent pointed out that Goodyear had knowingly carried its discrimination forward every time it issued Ledbetter a smaller check. Obviously true—and to the Republican majority, irrelevant. Quite deliberately, they shaped the law to protect a corporate perpetrator of discrimination against its victim—one of many decisions slanted toward the interests of corporations.

There is an important coda. Outraged by the Ledbetter case, Democratic majorities in the House and Senate passed legislation to change the law, which Barack Obama signed on taking office—albeit too late for Lilly Ledbetter. Without Obama, the *Ledbetter* decision would stand as a bar to other women who suffered pay discrimination.

Which brings us to another 5–4 decision by the same Republican justices: *Citizens United*.

Had there been a Republican majority in Congress, the Ledbetter decision would remain in force.

We all know the essence of this decision—that corporations, and subsequently super PACs, have the First Amendment right to influence elections by flooding our campaigns with millions of dollars in special interest money, often through repetitive—not to mention mendacious—political advertising. The court's ruling ignores the obvious, that these millions do not just buy access to the politicians who benefit, but outcomes, changing the lives of citizens who lack the megaphone of money. And, in the process, the majority exploded the pretense of "judicial modesty" beneath which they concealed their right-wing political agenda.

No matter what pieties they invoked to cloak this as a victory for free speech, there is simply no doubt that this decision—as was surely obvious to the majority—helped the Republican Party and the wealthy donors who fund it. Clinton, and especially Sanders, have made quite a point of that. But what is less known about *Citizens United* is the degree to which the five Republican justices contorted the usual Supreme Court procedures to transform the political landscape.

For those fortunate enough to have skipped law school, a brief explanation. It is a basic tenet of Supreme Court jurisprudence that the court will only decide the issues presented by the case before it—and nothing more. Indeed, this principle is central to the judicial restraint the Roberts Court purported to embrace. Unless, it turned out, the majority could advance the political interests of the Republican Party and the forces it represents.

The *Citizens United* case originally presented the Court with a narrow and technical legal question under the campaign finance laws. It posed no threat to those laws, raised no constitutional issues, and gave no hint whatsoever of recasting billions of dollars in soft money as speech. Indeed, the distinguished conservative lawyer who argued the case—Ted Olson—stuck strictly to the narrow issue at hand.

But five Republican justices had other ideas. After Anthony Kennedy prepared a draft opinion gratuitously and dramatically expanding the scope of the Court's prospective ruling, Chief Justice Roberts scheduled the case for reargument. Following Kennedy's lead, Roberts widened the issues before the Court way beyond what the litigants themselves had argued. From there on, the Court's highly unusual departure from normal practice foreordained the obvious: five Republican justices—Kennedy, Roberts, Scalia, Thomas, and Alito—had hijacked the case in order to shape the financing of American political campaigns to their liking.

At the time, this judicial hijacking was widely noted by commentators like Jeffrey Toobin. The resulting damage to the Court's reputation may be one reason why Roberts chose not to comprehensively gut Obamacare. It is one thing for justices to function as political partisans; another, perhaps, when this becomes too obvious.

In dissent, an appalled Justice John Paul Stevens said precisely that: "Five Justices were unhappy with the limited nature of the case before us, so they changed the case to give themselves an opportunity to change the law." As to the ruling itself, Stevens called it "a rejection of the common sense of the American people, who have . . . fought against the distinctive corrupting potential of corporate electioneering since the days of Theodore Roosevelt."

Notably, Justice Stevens is himself a Republican. But he is a different kind of Republican—a distinguished lawyer who qualified for the Court by being just that. The new litmus test for Republican presidents is not quality, but ideology—whether a nominee is certain to use his or her position to advance a right-wing legal and political agenda. Thus the screening process for Republican judges has been profoundly changed—a seismic shift in which Justice Scalia himself was instrumental.

To be sure, federal judges were always appointed by the party in power, and often the criteria—particularly for the lesser federal courts—included political involvement as well as, or even above, achievement in the profession. But Republican presidents now draw their judicial appointments from a different pool of candidates—lawyers recruited, indoctrinated, and screened in order to turn judicial decision-making into right-wing politics by other means. The goal is to make sure that no Republicans like John Paul Stevens ever grace the Court again.

The principal agent of this slow-motion legal coup is the Federalist Society, an organization founded in the 1980s, for whom Justice Scalia was perhaps the most visible proponent. It has but one mission: to seed the government and federal courts with lawyers whose fidelity to hard-right conservative ideology is predictable and fixed. And it's succeeding.

The society currently has chapters in more than two hundred law schools and claims as members 10,000 law students and 60,000 lawyers. Among its many loyalists on the bench were three justices in the five-person majority for *Ledbetter* and *Citizens United*—Scalia, Thomas, and Alito, all members of the Federalist Society—and a fourth, Chief Justice Roberts, who was a member of the Society's Washington, DC, steering committee. Thus these two cases—and many other Supreme Court decisions that reflect modern conservative ideology—are progeny of the Federalist Society.

As a result, the Roberts court has graven into law a stunning agenda of right-wing activism that impacts every aspect of our society. It has narrowed voting rights and barred affirmative action. It has empowered corporations and weakened unions and workers' rights. It has gutted campaign finance laws, eroded environmental regulation, and chipped away at Obamacare. The notable decisions that contravene the agenda of the Federalist Society—like the same-sex marriage opinion—usually have occurred only because the four Federalist-affiliated justices could not bring along the Republican non-affiliate, Anthony Kennedy.

This dramatic shift in judicial appointees is further spelled out by an exhaustive empirical study of federal appellate judges published in 2009 by two political scientists, Nancy Scherer of Wellesley and Banks Miller of Ohio State. Their aim was to determine whether the Federalist Society does, indeed, have the far-reaching influence on judicial decision-making that is its reason for being.

The results were conclusive and deeply disturbing for anyone who cares about judicial independence. The short of the study's detailed findings is that judges who are members of the Federalist Society are twice as likely to cast votes that reflect conservative ideology as Republican nonmembers, let alone judges appointed by Democrats. The study further notes that Republican presidents now rely on the Society and its members to identify and screen judicial nominees.

Thus future Republican appointees—ever more reliably and, indeed, inevitably—will decide cases not on the basis of unbiased and dispassionate legal reasoning, but to advance the political and ideological preferences they were selected to uphold. To assert that this is merely a matter of "judicial philosophy" is to obfuscate the systematic and deliberate effort to transform the federal courts, packing them with political activists whose rulings are foreordained. Spurred by the Federalist Society, the Republican Party has not simply changed the law, but the very role and nature of the judiciary itself.

And so with Antonin Scalia's death, the Supreme Court is at a final crossroads. As are Democrats who may feel tempted to walk away from their party's nominee, whether it be Bernie Sanders or Hillary Clinton.

A Republican president empowered to choose Scalia's successor will leave nothing to chance—no more than when the next vacancy arises, and the next. Without exception, every new Republican justice will be an agent of the extreme conservatism advanced by the Federalist Society. Unless a Democratic president takes office in 2017, the Republicans will mold the Supreme Court for yet another generation, completing the transformation of our highest court into an agent of right-wing politics by other means. And, with that, the Court will change the essence of our society, and how we define justice, in ways too deep to ever be undone.

A great deal of damage has already been done. Routinely, presidential candidates promise to appoint justices who undo unpopular decisions, whether *Roe v. Wade* or *Citizens United*. It is equally routine in politically charged cases for the media to report whether a Republican or Democratic president appointed the judges in question. As a result, the credibility of our justice system has seriously eroded.

Which brings us back, yet again, to the past as prologue: the election that gave us the Roberts Court, *Ledbetter*, *Citizens United*, and a host of other decisions that advanced right-wing ideology at whatever cost—an election decided by another 5–4 Republican majority in a case called *Bush v. Gore*.

In 2016, disappointed Democrats should not do this to themselves, let alone to the country.

The GOP's Super Doomsday

MARCH 1, 2016

By this time tomorrow, the slumped figures of the walking dead may well clutter the Republican landscape. If so, the cause of death will look a lot like assisted suicide.

The GOP's Kevorkian is, of course, Donald Trump. This is not because he is a political colossus. Far from it—Trump is the luckiest candidate alive, not least because his opponents, and the party, have worked overtime to create him.

He could not have done this on his own. Time and again, he has played the bumptious idiot—trashing women, ridiculing a disabled reporter, whining about mistreatment, making misstatement after misstatement, and, in South Carolina, turning in the worst debate performance in memory. He has excoriated John McCain and George W. Bush and, God help us, rebuked the Pope. He lives from insult to insult, each more juvenile than the last.

As a candidate, he grows worse by the day. Over the weekend, he initially refused to disavow support from the vile racist David Duke and the KKK, claiming ignorance of what they stand for. He retweeted a quote from Benito Mussolini. He suggested disqualifying the Latino judge presiding over a suit against his bogus "Trump University"—apparently for being of Mexican descent. Instead of claiming the higher

ground of a front-runner, he brayed fresh venom at his reel-
ing opposition, lowering the depths of a campaign that is
ever more degrading to his party and his country.

In eight months since entering the race, he has learned
nothing. His platform, such as it is, packages the ludicrous
with the politically blasphemous, scorning both reality and GOP orthodoxy. His promise to "make America
great again" shreds the inclusiveness that is the essence of
our greatness. His proposals to ban all Muslims, wall off
Mexico, and deport 11 million illegal immigrants combine the unconstitutional and unachievable with appeals
to racial and religious animosity. His willful ignorance
of governance and policy is the frightening foretaste of a
floundering presidency dangerously lacking in direction or
even dignity—a reality driven home in Thursday's debate.
By now he should have been political roadkill, a long-dead
skunk in the GOP's rearview mirror.

Instead, he is the party's all too likely nominee. So how
did this happen?

Start with the petri dish of resentment that is the Republican Party. For years, the party establishment has propiti-
ated evangelicals, Tea Party enthusiasts, and other fearful
and angry white folks by tolerating a toxic brew of empty
promises and rhetorical nihilism that filled the GOP base
with mindless rage. Enter Donald Trump.

By accident or instinct, he discovered that the party had
served him up the perfect audience: modestly educated, low-
information voters who feel betrayed by the government and
social and financial elites. For such voters, Trump's castiga-
tion of Muslims, immigrants, and free trade is an intoxicating political cocktail. Beyond that, his post-modern
sans-culottes don't much care what else he says; they just
want their nativist would-be strongman to demolish the
established order.

Thus, to their astonishment, Republicans have watched
Trump build a cult of personality that transcends ideology

or experience. His fatuous bluster against his chosen foes fills his legions with a visceral pleasure. Such is their hatred of the establishment that they hear any critique of Trump as another condescending message from the despised elites. They follow Trump's abusive tweets with abusive tweets of their own, often filled with libelous virulence. They are impervious to reason, indifferent to policy, immune to fact. They don't want to think; they want to feel.

Crucial to this phenomenon was the GOP's failure to perceive that the broadcast media was enabling Trump to build an uncritical mass following, making him ever harder to take down. Here, again, Trump was lucky and also shrewd: shamelessly avid for ratings, cable news gave him priceless months of free media, a seemingly endless infomercial for his siren song of self. With the honorable exception of Fox News, his debate interrogators largely extended his free ride, even as morning chat shows built him into a political phenomenon. It became all too clear that Trump would ride this adulatory wave unimpeded unless Republicans launched a forceful counternarrative.

But they remained passive—no doubt, at least in part, because they feared alienating Trump's followers in the base, an ever-swelling cadre filled with the unreasoning rage the party had stoked for years. Months ago, two respected GOP professionals solicited the party's big-money donors help to take to the airwaves against Trump and were turned down cold. Instead, the GOP elite chose to play ostrich, hoping to stick their collective head up some lucky day to discover Trump's corpse without their fingerprints on it. So fond were they of this delusion that they clung to it as his poll numbers rose and the time for action dwindled by the week.

This was a grave mistake. For just as Trump was made for TV, he was built to facilitate his own destruction, amplified by the very media that helped create him. Here, Megyn Kelly should have been a role model, as Trump's oh-so-telling decision to flee the second Fox debate confirmed.

By this time, I had begun to appreciate a persistent phenomenon: among Trump's most fervent followers, no statement, however grotesque, could shake their support. The many analysts who had previously forecast Trump's demise in the primaries—including me in early October 2015—failed to foresee this. Even the revelation in October 2016 that Trump had allegedly assaulted numerous women—and was videotaped bragging about such practices—didn't seem to alienate his base.

This process blossomed after Trump clinched the nomination, weakening him as a general election candidate.

Quite obviously, he is a candidate prone to crack under pressure—a classic overdog who becomes verbally incontinent when attacked, combining ignorant and narcissistic rants with whiny complaints that invite exhaustion and disgust. A skilled and resolute opponent could have dismantled him before he got too big to fail.

Yet until Thursday's debate, the also-rans instead focused on killing one another off—hopeful that Trump would blow himself up unassisted, fearful that his gift for the unrestrained counterthrust would make them figures of fun. But the conventional wisdom that Trump would crash and burn assumed resolute opponents armed with pointed attacks and negative advertising, pounding away until self-involvement and self-pity brought him down. It seemed borderline inconceivable that, presented with the juicy feast that is Donald Trump, the GOP's carnivores would become vegetarians.

In the fall, Clinton did just that, showing a perfect grasp of the warped and vulnerable psyche beneath Trump's protective coating of insults and self-adoration.

If not vegans. Instead of throttling Trump in the cradle, his rivals imagined emerging from the overcrowded field as the party's surviving white knight, some lingering past their sell-by date. Mired in wishful thinking, they left Trump untouched for far too long. As of the South Carolina primary, of the many millions spent on advertising by his opponents, only 4 percent of ads targeted Trump. Now he is dominant—their money has been spent, and their attacks have come too late.

At this point almost all the primaries lay ahead. But the disarray of Trump's opponents, and of the party itself, had become apparent. In essence, they were allowing a wholly unqualified candidate to complete a hostile takeover.

What could have been was apparent on Thursday. When his opponents came after him at last, he looked like a blowhard with a dubious past whose only riposte is name-calling. All that survived was the vaulting ego that drives him to seek an office for which he is unfit.

This savaging should have started in the third debate, not the tenth—relentless attacks on Trump's knowledge and character, supplemented by mass advertising directed at a single theme: this man should not be president. Last fall, this could have worked. But now his base of support has solidified as it grows, his purchase on the nomination ever more assured. In their belated aggression, Trump's opponents conjured the party's most horrific nightmare—what Hillary Clinton and the Democrats will do to him in the fall.

A related mistake within the party was to misread Trump's appeal in the age of entertainment—the assumption that Trump and his trappings were too exotic for the Republican base. But exotic feeds fantasy. What exhausted worker wouldn't want to escape on his or her own private jet? Who, pray tell, was the audience for *Fifty Shades of Grey*? So why suppose that ordinary Republicans would find Melania, Ivanka, and the two preppy but gun-toting boys unthinkable in the White House?

The GOP elites may not watch reality TV, but millions do, including *The Apprentice*. And, for older folks, the Trump mélange may evoke nostalgia for the cast of *Dynasty* or *Dallas*, with an updated J. R. Ewing promising to bring American jobs back by steamrolling the Chinese.

Which brings us to a final demographic irony. It was widely assumed that Trump's aromatic personal life would alienate evangelical voters. But Trump has stumbled on a larger truth—a great many rank-and-file evangelicals are less godly than prey to the resentments shared by the other white folks who dominate the GOP.

In retrospect, this should not be a surprise. The evangelical Jesus has always been a distinctly right-wing savior—a gun-loving, ferociously nativist tax cutter for whom English is the first and only language. Now the truth is out—in threatening times, salvation may mean less than temporal fears and resentments, as Ted Cruz is learning fast.

Like many others, Cruz assumed that the evangelicals would be his rock of ages. The Super Tuesday primaries in the South exposed that as a myth.

The struggle of Trump's chief "outsider" rival highlights the ultimate ingredient of his good fortune—the weaknesses of his opponents. "This guy is sick," Trump says of Cruz. "There's something wrong with this guy."

More and more voters are inclined to agree. Cruz is the Halloween candidate, trying to frighten Republicans into voting for him. Where Trump conjures a new dawn of national greatness, for Cruz it is always midnight in America. It is not exactly heartwarming for a presidential candidate to say, as did Cruz in South Carolina, "I wake up scared every day."

In his telling, he is America's last chance of pulling back from the abyss. He is the polar opposite of the synthetically positive Marco Rubio—a human depressant with a dark and gloomy message. His claim to be a "consistent conservative" does not seem to include any concern for actual people. Hence the priceless moment in Thursday's debate when, confronted with Trump's insistence that he would not "let people die in the street," Cruz seemed to suggest that a consistent conservative would kick the corpses to the curb.

As noted, Cruz's most persistent failure was his inability to impersonate an actual human being. This casts more than a little shade on his prospects of ever becoming president.

And so his relentlessly dystopian campaign seems to have hit the wall. His hope of taking down Trump rested on expanding his base of Tea Party adherents and the deeply religious. Instead, Trump is swiping his evangelicals. As with the other also-rans, Cruz waited too long to go after Trump, flattering the solipsistic billionaire while transparently hoping he would implode.

To the contrary, Cruz is powering his own implosion. His campaign manager is a noted smear monger, and dirty tricks and mendacious ads have accentuated his charmlessness. The Nixonian fingerprints accumulate—the phony announcement of Ben Carson's withdrawal; a photoshopped picture of Rubio with Obama; a garbled videotape that wrongly portrayed Rubio as trashing the Bible; robocalls and radio ads that, even by the standards of South Carolina, were rankly deceptive.

Each new episode of sleaze summons fresh unctiousness from Cruz: "The Bible talks about if someone treats you unkindly, repay them with kindness. It has been the standard I've tried to follow." This must startle the fellow Republicans Cruz has attacked for his own political gain—in Washington, it can be fairly said of Cruz that even his friends don't like him.

Now this loathing is seeping into the electorate, spreading a sense of dishonesty and demagoguery that, as ever, suggests a contemporary Joe McCarthy. Every time that Cruz plays the victim of unfair and diversionary attacks, it becomes easier to imagine blood dripping from his fangs. Thus his freshly minted insinuation that Trump has committed tax fraud is caught in the undertow of Cruz's perceived mendacity. Cruz has created his own character issue and, it would seem, his own ceiling.

But Trump's good fortune abounds. Witness the ongoing fecklessness of the party elite. Belatedly stirring from their catatonic trance, they now resemble a forlorn tourist lost in a bad neighborhood during a rainstorm, vainly shouting at the last taxi as its taillights vanish into the night.

The more timorous are publicly making peace with the idea of Trump; the far less timorous Chris Christie has revenged a barrage of negative advertising in New Hampshire, kneecapping Marco Rubio by endorsing the bilious billionaire. Others have lapsed into hushed whispers, fearful of alienating a vengeful Trump. Still others are clutching at Rubio as their last hope, conjuring scenarios of rescue while, with comical frenzy, spurring a parade of meaningless endorsements that they somehow imagine will turn the tide in Rubio's favor.

It's hard to capture the haplessness of this. Don't they know that Bob Dole, however worthy, is from another time? What does it mean that the Koch brothers, ever in search of a puppet, have lent their chief political operative to the ever amenable Rubio? But oh, the establishment says, just wait until Mitt Romney gives his blessing to our boy Marco.

Seriously? If there is any message they should have grasped by now, it's that hordes of Republicans can't forget Mittens fast enough. His recent attack on Trump over, of all things, his failure to release tax returns provokes wonder at Romney's inability to look into the fun house mirror of his own flawed political persona. Whatever delusions the

Months later it emerged that Trump—if not guilty of tax fraud—had likely paid little or no income tax for a couple of decades. But it is dubious that this would have hurt him among the government-phobic legions of the GOP—in fact, it might have polished his image as their surrogate shark.

To his sorrow, Christie learned that Trump's capacity for gratitude is, shall we say, limited. His fateful decision to back Trump made him the poster child for public humiliation. By August he was reportedly fetching Big Macs for The Donald and privately expressing his disenchantment to the media.

establishment conjures, many in the base would rather buy a reverse mortgage from the late Fred Thompson than hear another word from Willard Romney.

But Trump's real stroke of luck is that the elites' last hope is a political mollusk. Marco Rubio is a concept, not a president. The concept is youth and diversity, packaged with a Horatio Alger story that passes the torch to the "children of the Reagan revolution." The reality is a rich man's pet—a drive-by senator with no achievements, mutable policy positions, and a reliance on comically excessive denunciations of Barack Obama.

When pressed, Rubio says little different than Ted Cruz, save when imitating Donald Trump on immigration and surveillance of American Muslims—the latest instance of which is his promise to begin deporting Dreamers on his first day in office. The remnant is Mitt Romney warmed over, save with a line of credit from soft-money donors instead of his own millions.

So where are the compelling attributes that would propel a last-minute surge? Campaigning with Rubio and African-American senator Tim Scott, Governor Nikki Haley compared this youthful and diverse triumvirate to a Benetton ad. But she came closer than intended to encapsulating Rubio's campaign—a glossy surface with little beneath, a reflection of Rubio himself.

Rubio has never displayed political courage of any kind—unless you count his desperate rearguard action in Thursday's debate where, losing in the polls and under pressure from donors, he took a truckload of opposition research and dumped it in Trump's lap. Give Rubio this—he didn't flinch, and at times he made Trump look like the buffoon he has always been. But by saving his onslaught for a single eleventh-hour attack, Rubio helped reduce the debate to a schoolyard brawl that was neither presidential nor even adult.

Too much, too late. And, as ever, Rubio's dependence on hysterical right-wing talking points was on full display, as when he pandered to the Sheldon Adelsons of the world by labeling Palestinians en masse as suicide bombers, making Trump sound almost statesmanlike. There was a brief, queasy moment where an awful thought presented itself: Would this lightweight be an even worse president than Donald Trump? Truly terrible to contemplate, and a measure of what the GOP establishment has come to.

As if to underscore this, since the debate Rubio has debuted a new political self, calling Trump an ignorant "con man" (fair enough) while hurling insults worthy of the master himself—including a suggestion of incontinence. In striving to derail Trump, Rubio has become Trump or, more accurately, the Apprentice. As Trump responds that Rubio is "a choker," his followers howl in glee. And so Rubio is taking the establishment on a demeaning and mind-numbing race to the bottom that shows little promise of stemming the Trump tsunami.

Like Cruz, Rubio became damaged goods as a presidential aspirant. His year was 2016, when he was a bright and shiny new object.

In embracing Rubio, the GOP elite are pressing the only survivor with the stuff to be president, John Kasich, to step aside. But as long as there is life in his candidacy, why should he? In Thursday's debate it was Kasich, not Rubio, who combined a presidential temperament with deep knowledge of the issues. He is an accomplished legislator and capable governor; Rubio is neither. In his heart, Kasich has to view the idea of Rubio as president with near contempt.

But again Trump benefits. By presenting himself as a conciliator, Kasich is running against the grain of the Republican electorate while taking a chunk out of Rubio. Over the weekend, Kasich called for civility yet again, labeling the GOP campaign "disgraceful"; the morning shows, riveted by their sudden discovery that Trump is truly loathsome, covered the GOP's tripartite food fight while paying Kasich little mind. In the upside-down world of 2016, attitude trumps experience.

That the GOP establishment—donors, professionals, and officeholders—did not back Kasich confirmed its bankruptcy.

Finally, even this year's primary schedule favors Trump. And, once again, the GOP elite did this to themselves.

After the corrosive primary fight of 2012, the party professionals front-loaded and condensed the primary calendar for 2016, hoping to squelch insurgents and quickly anoint an establishment candidate. But their tactic has backfired—empowering the surprise front-runner, Donald Trump, while narrowing the window for other candidates to rally or for voters to entertain second thoughts. By March 16, nearly 60 percent of all GOP delegates will have been chosen, cementing Trump's chokehold on the nomination.

The nature of the states holding primaries by mid-March also serves Trump's candidacy. The first four primary states were too demographically varied to produce a single challenger. Now the still-fractured field gives Trump a daunting advantage in today's primaries and beyond.

Most of today's contests take place in southern states where Trump is doing well. In polling for the thirteen primaries or caucuses, Trump appears to lead in all but Cruz's

As it happened, Trump swept pretty much everything but Texas.

home state of Texas. Sunday's endorsement by Senator Jeff Sessions of Alabama, an epicenter of anti-immigrant and anti-Muslim feeling, further fortified Trump in the more feverish precincts of the South. All he needs is for Rubio and Cruz to keep on splitting votes, with a likely assist from Kasich in less conservative states such as Massachusetts, Vermont, and Virginia. And a Trump win in Texas would wipe

Cruz won, allowing him to hang in by a thread.

Cruz off the board.

Texas aside, if Trump comes out of Super Tuesday with accelerated momentum, he could pick up three more states on March 5, and Michigan and Mississippi on March 8—places where Kasich hopes to do well. By then, Cruz and Rubio will be gasping for oxygen, if not expired altogether. And March 15 gives Trump the chance to knock off Kasich and Rubio in their home states, Ohio and Florida,

Kasich survived. Rubio did not.

while picking up Illinois and Missouri. Game over—if it isn't already.

By comparison, his rivals' path to the nomination is a tight-rope. In today's primaries, both Rubio and Cruz will be trying to limit Trump's haul of delegates by targeting specific areas: Cruz, the Bible Belt; Rubio, more mainstream states and suburban areas populated by affluent voters. Their hope is that the complicated proportional allocation rules for delegates in early primaries limits the impact of statewide pluralities for Trump. Yet if both succeed in surviving, they perpetuate the multi-candidate field that has given Trump plurality wins.

But even if Trump destroys Cruz's chances in today's contests, he may also deal Rubio a mortal wound. And if he does not, the pool of voters available to Rubio going forward is less than promising. There is no monolithic non-Trump vote; indeed, Trump is as likely to inherit as many Cruz voters as is Rubio, if not more. All in all, it is far from clear that there is a sufficient pool of voters for Rubio to salvage any hope. And Kasich will be vying for the very same votes.

Amid these tough scenarios, the most imaginable is that Rubio will get past March 15 with enough victories to reach delegate-rich winner-take-all states like New Jersey, Pennsylvania, and California. But query where Rubio's victories come from except, perhaps, Florida—where as of now he is trailing Trump. To ask the question is to confirm how close Trump is to completing his hostile takeover.

And so, tomorrow morning, the party may well wake up like a man with a hangover, a sour taste in his mouth, trying to remember how he got this way and wishing he were dead. And then a terrible image will slowly materialize from the night before—the gargoyle face of the GOP's new leader, Donald Trump.

With Rubio out, Cruz was left trying to beat Trump in mid-Atlantic and northeastern states, where his hard-line evangelical pitch never had a prayer.

The GOP's Morning After

MARCH 8, 2016

Repugnant beyond redemption.

Whatever its dire implications, for a time the GOP presidential race had the terrible fascination of a multicar collision. No more. Now we can see the casualties close-up—reason, dignity, honesty, and hope. And, not least, a once great political party reduced to the intellectual and moral level of a mindless fraternity house.

In belatedly attacking the repulsive Donald Trump, the party establishment and also-rans have stripped bare his appalling candidacy without giving voters a plausible alternative. The residue evokes that abysmal frat house the morning after a drunken party—stubbed cigarette butts leaving burn holes in the coffee table; a carpet stained with red wine spills; an acrid smell whose origins are nauseating to consider. A sodden lout is sprawled on the couch, snoring with his mouth agape; a pale young woman in the bathroom applies lipstick with trembling hands, dimly recalling the shame she wishes to forget. All one can do is rush outside, desperate for a gulp of air.

Faced with such debris, it seems almost trivial to analyze the political fallout. But it can be gamed out easily enough.

However damaged, Trump stands atop a scrum of rivals diminished in stature and prospects. Rubio has shrunk to his

One struggled for fresh metaphors to capture the GOP's debacle. By the time I wrote this, the race was effectively over. Only the commentariat kept it alive, struggling to feed the perpetual news cycle.

actual size, retreating to Florida as though it were Elba. Cruz has introduced America to the sanctimonious and treacherous tactician his colleagues loathe, shedding the evangelicals he so badly needs. With admirable persistence, Kasich is calling for uplift in a political landscape polluted by insults and lies, a thick smog of anger choking his intended audience.

The primary calendar remains Trump's friend. Over the weekend he added a brace of delegates by winning in Louisiana and Kentucky—albeit by lesser margins than expected, reflecting a slippage in late deciders. Continuing a pattern, Cruz took two closed caucuses in Maine and Kansas, but has yet to win a primary outside his home state. Rubio's decline accelerated despite the asterisk of Puerto Rico; Kasich achieved next to nothing.

Though very late polling suggests that Kasich is on the rise in Michigan, by tomorrow morning, in all likelihood, Michigan and Mississippi will have padded Trump's delegate count. Alone among the contenders, he has scored victories in all regions; his demographic reaches from blue-collar voters to evangelicals and so-called moderates. His sole ideology, anger and frustration, is the new opium of the GOP masses.

Trump won both, further deflating Cruz and Kasich.

This despite another wretched debate swathed in Trump's trademark squalor. His favorite organ, he advised us, is the equivalent of those "ninety-seven-story buildings" he boasts of erecting. Otherwise, it was the same now-stale act—insults, boasting, misstatements of fact, and empty promises of greatness personified by "Trump" alone. Enduring four years of this from our president would resemble being relentlessly pounded over the head with a bag of sand until one succumbs to stultitude.

But what Republican can now stop him? That Marco Rubio is the establishment hope captures his hopelessness—and theirs. True, he appeals to affluent Republicans with private-club manners for whom Mitt Romney was their kind. But he can't hijack the evangelicals or persuasively channel Trump's angry populist appeal. Worse, the reality of Rubio has been exposed—a candidate without a core, too callow and shallow to persuasively fill the office he seeks.

Ted Cruz? It is hard to imagine him cleaning up in delegate-rich states like California and New York, whose populace is not drawn to a hard-line conservatism wherein the smarmily pious Cruz summons a political Rapture. And John Kasich still appears better suited to another year, in a party that has voided its toxins.

Perhaps 2020, should President Trump flounder. But that contest promises to be a knife fight between contending Republican factions.

At this point in the calendar, it seems clear that none of them can stack up enough delegates to win outright. So now the establishment strategy is to deny Trump a majority of delegates by keeping all three rivals in the race from now until the convention. The idea is that Rubio takes Florida; Kasich Ohio; and Cruz a few conservative bastions, after which they collectively win enough states to block Trump's path.

This, at best, is deeply problematic. As a matter of arithmetic, it is certainly possible to deny Trump the roughly 54 percent of delegates he would need to win from here on out. But Rubio, Cruz, and Kasich are like the occupants of a life raft, allies by necessity, yet eyeing one another with self-interest and suspicion. Sooner or later, cannibalism will

Which it did. ensue.

Indeed, Ted Cruz is already poised to take the first bite—by investing more resources in Florida, he hopes to take votes from Rubio, effectively delivering the state to Trump. This will hardly be the last instance where, by accident or design, one of the also-rans snacks on another—Cruz in particular still seems bent on driving his rivals from the race. This go-it-alone strategy involves a very high-risk gamble: that in a two-man race Cruz can force the potentially volatile Trump to implode, having first helped him compile a daunting delegate lead.

Yet the establishment's stop-Trump strategy requires all three also-rans to live—especially, and ironically, Cruz, second only to Trump in filling the GOP establishment with fear and loathing. A special problem is that Rubio, fading badly, is another key component. The scenario for deadlock requires him—or Kasich—to ward off The Donald in mainstream states with large urban populations, venues where, no matter what he may imagine, Cruz is unlikely to thrive in a one-on-one race against Trump. But to survive, Rubio must win Florida—if he does not, it is hard to conceive what would sustain him in the miserable weeks to come.   In the end, nothing.

All this illustrates the problem with assuming that each of Trump's rivals can appropriate pieces of the electoral map. That construct is like a tower of building blocks assembled by a two-year-old: snatch away the blocks marked "Ohio" or "Florida" and the whole thing topples. Unless Kasich and Rubio beat him in their home states a week from today, Trump will seize a prohibitive delegate lead in a matchup with Cruz. Even a victory in one of those states would give him a commanding margin in a race where Cruz and whoever else survives are still dividing votes.

But let us suppose, however improbably, that the ill-matched trio makes it ashore in Cleveland and then manages to stop a wounded Trump on the first ballot. What is to keep one of them from then cutting a deal with Trump? And, if not, what awaits them? A fractured party; a mass of alienated Trump supporters; a potential third party that splits the GOP vote. In this environment, it seems unlikely that any of them can hold the GOP together.

So who is the savior? Mitt Romney? The base would spit him out. Paul Ryan? If Ryan remains sane, he will flee this invitation as though it were ebola. Presiding over the insane   He did. asylum that is the Republican House is sacrifice enough.

The absolute last gasp of poison gas is the idea of a third party should Trump prevail. Let me venture a fearless prediction—no elected official with any interest in his or her future will throw themselves on this funeral pyre. (Bill Kris-   No one did. tol, chronic promoter of fools like Dan Quayle and Sarah

Palin, has offered up Dick Cheney. I can't shake the idea of his campaign theme song: "Where have you gone, Richard Bruce Cheney? Our nation turns its lonely eyes to you.") Whatever comes of this idea will be pitiful indeed.

So now we have dispensed with the all-too-grim horserace. The larger question is when, if ever, the established GOP will take responsibility for the rise of Donald Trump.

Last week, several *New York Times* reporters exchanged anecdotes about when they first thought the threat of Trump was real. The median date fell in the latter part of 2015. So where was the Republican establishment all this time?

The answer is simple: living out the Faustian bargain through which they had long since swapped their political souls for dwindling pieces of Republican turf. Last week, a few GOP professionals surfaced with the truth. Having failed in his effort to raise money from GOP donors to fight Trump from the start, consultant Alex Castellanos wrote: "If our self-indulgent Republican Party establishment had really wanted to prevent a takeover of the GOP, they should not have gorged on political power while they failed to do anything to prevent the decline of the country. Our leaders could have led. They could have done more than say 'no' to Democrats while offering no alternative."

Castellanos resolved his own dilemma by becoming a fervent Trump supporter.

Veteran strategist Scott Reed remarked: "I'm amazed that people are acting surprised. Trump has been building for months, and the voters are speaking." And media mastermind Mike Murphy stated the obvious—that Trump "would set the party back decades."

Yet the sustained obliviousness of the GOP elite was truly impressive. The pompous panjandrums of the *Wall Street Journal* now wax indignant that Donald Trump has jumped the traces of bellicosity, free trade, and privatizing Social Security. Here is the small detail they've missed: the GOP has been offering the embattled middle and working classes tax cuts for the wealthy, wars they don't want, and trade policies that leave them fearful for their jobs. In thrall to a political orthodoxy dear to the donor classes, the Republican establishment has lost touch with the base, believing that rhetorical red meat was enough to satiate the great unwashed.

Now comes Trump, promising health care "to take care of everybody"; vowing to protect entitlement programs; and blaming Republican free-market policies for the plight of working people. Belatedly, the Republican elite is discovering the truth—when it comes to ideological purity, most voters care much more about the reality of their own lives. And a whole lot of them think that the GOP establishment has sold them down the river of free trade, lining its own pockets in the bargain.

I had long since made this point in various pieces—it was glaringly obvious. Yet many establishment Republicans kept insisting that Trumpism is a one-time phenomenon with a sell-by date of November 2016. Good luck with that.

This divide between the establishment and Trump supporters is a scalding rebuke to the politics of plutocracy. Which makes risible the establishment's warnings that Trump is playing these folks for fools. Who do they think wrote that playbook?

But looking in the mirror overtaxes their gifts for introspection. Hence—having awakened like Rip Van Winkle the day after Super Tuesday—their tardy and often hypocritical efforts to excommunicate Donald Trump.

Mitt Romney gave the speech of his lifetime, a comprehensive and searing excoriation of Trump's intellectual and personal unfitness. No minced words—it was perhaps Romney's finest political hour, and one of the few good ones in this pitiful GOP campaign.

In 2012, I often wondered if Romney believed what he was saying—his public persona had a synthetic quality. But in denouncing Trump he seemed almost happy, like a man freed at last from the shackles of contrivance. He plainly meant every word.

Romney reminded evangelicals about Trump's values, such as they are. He informed struggling Americans of the many ways that Trump has exploited their fellow workers. He awakened those worried about national security to Trump's stupefying ignorance of geopolitics and military affairs. He advised those enamored with Trump's business career that it is pocked with fraud and failure. He even extracted a little payback for John McCain, his erstwhile rival, noting that when McCain was a prisoner of war in Vietnam, the draft-avoidant Trump was racking up sexual scores so as to regale the world with his manliness.

Romney's speech was comprehensive and telling—and had no discernible effect.

But the GOP should have said all this six months ago, in a swelling chorus—Trump's odious qualities were ever in plain sight. His putrid response to Romney was embarrassingly typical of all that has come before—recycled insults and boasts, delivered in semicoherent sentence fragments. There was nothing that involved anything but himself—not a policy, not a thought. Just another chapter in the annals of his repulsiveness—in 2012, Trump informed us, Romney "was begging for my endorsement. I could've said, 'Mitt, drop to your knees.'"

This should have been a defining moment, confirming all that Romney said. But at this late date the message was blunted and, for some, incendiary. The truth of Romney's jeremiad was eclipsed by speculation that he is angling to become the party's savior. And, quite predictably, Trump supporters were infuriated by what they saw as another condescending message from the face of the elite.

Yet suddenly the establishment was transfixed by its own righteous indignation. A cadre of billionaires, at last perceiving that they are losing their grip on power, coalesced to spend millions on air time for scathing attack ads trashing Trump. Eleventh-hour denunciations rained down on Trump from all quarters of the GOP establishment—business interests, foreign policy mavens, elected officials. The two Whitmans—Meg and Christine Todd—respectively called Trump "a dishonest demagogue" and accused him of "hate-mongering and racism."

Truly, did they just discover this? Given the tone the GOP has struck on immigrants and Muslims, including American citizens, did they really think all this is unique to Donald Trump? What about Ted Cruz and Marco Rubio? Or, for that matter, the Republicans in 2012?

But the questions abound. Where were all these worthies when Ted Cruz and a cabal of Tea Party fanatics were shutting down the government? When birthers were inflaming the Republican electorate with race-based denunciations of Obama? Or when all three hundred elected Republicans in the House and Senate voted against the Iran deal, taking a grave foreign policy issue down the same low road of cynical partisan politics.

Where were these tribunes of truth when the GOP became a fact-free zone—immune to climate science, claiming that massive tax cuts could help balance the budget, rewriting history to blame partisan rancor solely on Barack Obama? Where were they when the kids of the less fortunate were being squandered in the neoconservatives' tragic misadventure in Iraq? Where were they when the anxious middle class was sliding into insecurity and despair?

And where were they eight months ago, when this man they so deplore was using racist dog whistles to run away in the polls—and with their party?

They were tending to their own parochial interests beneath a self-serving cone of silence while ignoring that Ted Cruz and Marco Rubio were shamelessly echoing Trump's rhetoric about Mexicans and Muslims. One must say it—the glee with which they seized on Trump's stupidity regarding David Duke as a fig leaf for theatrical outrage is a classic of pretext and hypocrisy. What courage indeed it takes to denounce the Ku Klux Klan.

In truth, Trump is not an accident thrust by fate on an undeserving party. He is a mirror of what the GOP has become. He is, quite simply, a particularly embarrassing manifestation of the party's aversion to fact, appeals to fear, immunity to reason, and nihilistic denunciations of government as the source of all our problems. The GOP has offered America no concrete solutions—instead, it has stoked political distemper for its own self-serving ends, repackaged in absurd and cynical dumbshows like the seventy or so votes to defund Obamacare. It has abdicated any claim to serious governance, let alone to be the steward of our collective future.

It should not be this way. Americans deserve real arguments and real choices grounded in the real world, not a Democratic president elected by default. Should the Republican party someday right its course and reenter the realm of reason, the country will be better off.

Let us hope. Until then, the GOP is the party that degraded itself and so gave us Donald Trump—not the other way around.

The GOP's Strongman Syndrome

MARCH 15, 2016

Has it struck you by now that Donald Trump is, in the deepest of ways, not right?

I don't mean on the issues, though that's true enough. I'm suggesting something far more troubling—a personality disorder that feeds, and is empowered by, a profound disturbance among Americans at large. 2016 is the year that megalomania became a movement.

The symptoms of personal instability and societal destabilization abound—not least the violence erupting from the mass anger Trump inspires—and the implications are grave indeed. The moral importance of this subject transcends, but emanates from, the state of the Republican race. So please hold the deeper thought while we pause to contemplate Trump's continuing rise, and thus the stakes in today's primaries and beyond.

Last Tuesday's victories in Mississippi, Michigan, and Hawaii have buttressed Trump's lead. While Ted Cruz's second-place showing drew notice, his strategy rested in large measure on doing much better in the South, where Trump stole his evangelicals and ate his lunch. Kasich took some votes from Rubio in Michigan and Mississippi; Rubio now stares into his political grave.

This is where I started raising the question of Trump's mental fitness for office. For the next three-plus months, it was a pretty lonely place to be—and then not so much.

The debate that followed proved only that the candidates could speak in muted tones. Trump gave us his version of statesmanship—he insulted no one save, of course, every Muslim on the planet, calmly advocated torture, and linked sucker punching a black protester to righteous anger about trade deals. No one really went after him, and nothing said changed much of anything. So what happened the next morning was at least worth noting: Ben Carson endorsed Trump—this despite the fact that Trump had once compared him to a child molester—giving Trump a further boost while confirming Carson's political and personal disorientation. One wished once again that Carson was still de-linking conjoined twins.

<blockquote>Carson's devotion to Trump, often curiously expressed, was one of the small wonders of 2016—even had not Trump once called him a psychopath.</blockquote>

So here we are on the cusp of five primaries—Ohio, Florida, Illinois, North Carolina, and Missouri—fateful to the fortunes of the contestants and, perhaps, our own.

The linchpins of fate are Kasich and Rubio, contesting their home states of Ohio and Florida. Should both lose to Trump, he would hold a commanding delegate lead over Cruz, whose hard-right positions underscore his noxious persona. Add an inescapable momentum, and Trump is the all but certain nominee.

In a last-ditch effort to prevent this, Republican donors are hitting Trump with at least $10 million worth of attack ads in Florida alone, with another few million in Ohio and Illinois. But Cruz is undercutting this strategy by going after Rubio with attack ads of his own. Wednesday morning, we will have likely seen the last of Marco Rubio.

<blockquote>Which is what happened. On Wednesday Rubio bowed out, while emphatically disclaiming any interest in seeking reelection to the Senate.</blockquote>

But even should Rubio vanish, if Kasich takes Ohio it will preserve the prospect, however difficult, of stopping Trump short of a delegate majority going into a contested convention. The immediate question is which way the donor classes will jump—toward Trump, Cruz, or Kasich.

<blockquote>Here the establishment failed once again.</blockquote>

Though Kasich is the least likely choice, he is the only honorable one. While hewing to Republican orthodoxy, he also calls for compromise, civility, and making government work. Instead of fomenting hyper-partisan hysteria, Kasich would campaign in the world as it exists, competing for voters in the middle. He might actually win, and in a way that would allow him to govern.

If the Republican donor classes were visionary or even smart, they would embrace Kasich like a long-lost son, hoping to somehow rally Republican voters and elected officials and repair the damage to the body politic that resulted from enabling Trump and Cruz. For the party does not simply need to be saved from Donald Trump—it needs to be saved from itself, and for the greater good of the country. But plutocrats obsessed with cutting their own taxes are dubious agents of salvation.

A major reason why the party is so lost.

Far from it. Should Trump take Ohio and Florida—or, alternatively, win Florida and do well in North Carolina, Missouri, and Illinois—much of the party establishment will claw at his bandwagon with the same craven self-interest that allowed Trump to rise. For those who have countenanced the bankrupt GOP agenda of the last several years, fighting for a high chair at Trump's table may feel like nothing new.

One can imagine their eyes growing big at the thought of their erstwhile bête noire as the instrument of their deliverance. A tempting vision may appear at the end of their very dark tunnel: that the fevers sweeping the land will place Trump in the White House, putting the party, and themselves, back in business. Leaving the rest of us, as ever, to live with the consequences.

In fact, many establishmentarians jumped on the Trump bandwagon—yet another example of the party's intellectual, ideological, and moral decline.

Which returns us to the most essential and disturbing question of all: whether Trump's megalomania matches our societal moment, and what that means for America's future.

Megalomania is defined as a "psychopathological condition characterized by fantasies of power, relevance, and omnipotence, and by inflated self-esteem." Among its hallmarks are extreme grandiosity, indifference to truth, and an inability to accept criticism or to see other people except as

Trump is where
the definitions
of megalomania,
narcissism,
and sociopathy
overlap. Symptoms
abound—the
challenge is
picking the most
appropriate label.

agents of one's own needs, fueling the reflex to devalue and disparage all those who fail to please.

Sound familiar? Then consider that, when linked to power, these attributes are "likely to lead to miscalculation as a byproduct of the subject's conceit."

Lest this seem far-fetched, consider the startling degree to which Trump is unable to separate self-celebration from his pursuit of the world's most powerful office.

In speech after speech, his principal subject is Donald Trump. He brags about his penile size. He touts his skyscrapers. He trumpets his golf game. A post-election press conference becomes an infomercial for Trump water, Trump wine, and (bogus) Trump steaks. All meaning evaporates in self-referential babble.

Granted, some of this has the buffoonish character of a comic opera satrap, parading his imaginary grandeur before a crowd of peasants in which he sees only himself. But imagine George W. Bush using a press conference to exhibit his paintings; or Barack Obama showing videos of his golf swing in the East Room. One can't, and for the simplest of reasons—a marginally normal president can separate the trivia of his life from the gravity of his office.

As much as anything,
this characteristic
defines Trump's
malady.

Not Trump. And when it comes to issues, any trace of comedy evanesces. His ignorance of policy—foreign or domestic—is as comprehensive as it is stunning. He knows nothing and, even worse, cares to learn nothing. In the cul-de-sac of his mind, his own greatness is enough.

So deep is Trump's romance of self that his solution to every problem is, quite simply, "Trump." Insulated by the impermeable solipsism of his inner landscape, he issues prescriptions with the preposterous insouciance of a three-year-old emperor. ISIS? He will simply take their oil. Mexico? He will make them pay for his wall. Homeland security? He will bar all Muslims from abroad and spy on those at home. China? He will bully them with tariffs until they send back all our jobs. Terrorists? He will waterboard their leaders and execute their families. He is, after all, Trump.

So why didn't Bush or Obama think of all this? Simple again, Trump tells us—they're "incompetent." Mired in fantasies of his own omnipotence, he never considers the possibility that they're sane.

Equally damning is his mercurial relationship with anyone but himself. His only prism for assessing others is whether they "treat me fairly." Those who criticize or oppose him are assaulted with insults. Those perceived to favor him—like that noted character witness, Vladimir Putin—develop qualities of leadership worthy of his notice. Because other people are not real to him as separate human beings, he shifts them from one category to another depending on whether they feed, or offend, his all-encompassing sense of self. Imagine, then, a political and geopolitical world where America's course is defined by "Trump."

> This is how Trump organizes his world and the people in it, making him chum for Vladimir Putin.

Funny, no. Dangerous for sure. Trump rarely speaks without reducing our reserves of empathy or understanding. Faced with an America that is an extension of Trump's psychodrama, the world will stop laughing soon enough.

Yet millions of Americans have cast him as our one-man-fits-all solution to all that besets us. So it is imperative to ask whether our social and economic flux is explanation enough.

To be sure, the anxieties besetting the middle and working classes are corrosive. Far too many have been battered by recession, ruined by the home mortgage crisis, displaced by globalization, and bypassed by the information economy. The GOP has offered them nothing but empty political theatrics and strident denunciations of Washington, deepening their belief that the financial elites have appropriated our politics for their own selfish ends.

As their sense of displacement and impotence swells, so does their fury—including at a growing social and racial diversity personified, for many, by Barack Obama. This is a breeding ground for magical thinking, scapegoating minorities, and false solutions promised by self-serving demagogues. In short, it is made for men like Donald Trump.

But Trump's rise as our tangerine would-be Caudillo is abetted by another factor—a growing strain of authoritarianism among the Republican electorate. Thus Trump's megalomaniacal prescriptions fuse neatly with a widespread craving for stern and simple answers.

This helps explain the seemingly unbreakable bond between Trump and many of his followers.

The GOP has long been seen as the "daddy party"—hierarchical, proscriptive, and committed to order. But lately social science has fleshed out this perception.

A doctoral student at UMass Amherst, Matthew MacWilliams, asked a survey group of Republicans which traits were most important in child rearing: independence or respect for elders; curiosity or good manners; self-reliance or obedience; being considerate or being well behaved. His purpose was to identify those inclined to favor hierarchy and direction from the top, characterized by psychologists as "authoritarians."

The results were striking. Half the Republicans who chose the second—or authoritarian—answer to each question supported Donald Trump. Recent articles by George Lakoff and Amanda Taub amplify these findings. The short is that Trump's persona meets a deep need for authority that is particularly strong among evangelicals, as well as the less religious who feel economically and socially threatened. And, unsurprisingly, authoritarianism tends to thrive among white Republicans of limited education.

These folks respond to promises of direct action to impose clear and simple solutions. This is precisely what Trump does—and, given his pathology, all he can do. And his disdain for "political correctness" in stereotyping minorities gives anxious authoritarians the empowering sense that their enemies will be repelled and their security restored—a need reinforced by the widespread fear of terrorism. Amanda Taub puts it this way:

Here, Trump's ignorance and magical prescriptions for instant success meld with the authoritarian mindset.

Trump's specific policies are not the thing that most sets him apart. . . . Rather, it's his rhetoric and style. The way he reduces everything to black-and-white extremes of strong versus weak, greatest versus worst. His simple, direct promises that he can solve problems that other politicians are too weak to manage.

And, perhaps most importantly, his willingness to flout all the conventions of civilized discourse when it comes to the minority groups that authoritarians find so threatening.

Inevitably, this must metastasize into a mass degradation of character and spirit. Hence the fruits of Trump's sulfurous penchant for using protesters as props, sinking to a level unseen in America since George Wallace in 1968.

From the safety of his podium, no doubt comforted by the memory of his multiple draft deferments, Trump throws verbal matches on gasoline: "I'd like to punch you in the face"; "Knock the crap out of him, will you? I promise to pay your legal fees"; "Get a job"; "Go home to your mother." Again and again, he evokes the supposedly good old days where such people were treated with a rough efficiency that would put them in their place.

To be sure, many of Trump's supporters feel uneasy about this; granted, as well, that the protesters are using Trump rallies as a megaphone to reach a larger audience. But Trump and his message have created a uniquely volatile environment that seethes with anger and racial animus. Reporters, too, are verbally abused, often by name; recently, a journalist was roughed up, allegedly by Trump's campaign manager. Lately the confrontations with protesters have turned violent—as when an old white man sucker punched a black kid who he said "wasn't acting like an American," proudly adding that "next time, we may have to kill him." When questioned about this, Trump's evasive evocation of the righteous anger of his followers confirmed him not merely as a demagogue, but as a moral cipher.

A dangerous one. For it is increasingly clear that, as a political leader, he has little sense of responsibility to

During the primary season, incitements to violence increasingly became a component of his campaign, even as he lashed out at a growing list of scapegoats.

anything or anyone beyond his needs of the moment. Over the weekend, he exploited his decision to cancel a rally in Chicago to further stoke the distemper of his crowds, attacking protesters in ever more vehement terms; suggesting that he might pay the legal fees for the racist sucker puncher; falsely claiming that protesters had been sent by Bernie Sanders; and threatening to "retaliate" by instructing his followers to disrupt Sanders rallies. Far from tamping down the potential for violence, he now escalates the risk to feed his hunger for votes and, even more disturbing, for the dominance and attention he cannot live without.

Yet this man is the probable Republican nominee for president of the United States.

In one sense, Trump is uniquely disturbing, if only because his character disorder is so obvious. But megalomania did not make The Donald great—our politics did.

For far too long, our political system has been foundering in the morass of polarization, rhetorical dishonesty, narrow partisanship by both parties, and cynical exploitation of our deepest problems. This intractable dysfunction was cemented by a Republican Party that appropriated the fear and anger of the most vulnerable to serve the most privileged, offered empty gestures and phony solutions that betrayed its contempt for those they purported to serve, and wallowed in an extremism that blamed Washington, DC, for every problem—until the only apparent "solution" was to shut down the government and blow the place up.

The inevitable result was a profound alienation and distrust among the GOP electorate, the craving for a strongman who will put things right. Trump's megalomania simply fills the need his party has created.

So we can take no comfort in believing that Trump is singular. Ted Cruz is right behind him. And the next demagogue, and the next, unless and until the GOP decides that the only solution to our problems is to confront them, challenging Democrats to an honest debate about how best to relieve the anxiety of our people and achieve the common good. Which means that the electorate—Republicans of conscience most of all—must shun this heartless joke of a party until it does or, failing that, meets the extinction it deserves.

Regrettably, Republicans of conscience were overcome by the forces of resentment unleashed by Trump—the primary process kills off what passes for moderates within the GOP.

An Open Letter to My Republican Friends

MARCH 22, 2016

Dear Cherished Friends,

The Republican Party has become intellectually and morally bankrupt, a mockery of its traditions—corrosive to our society, our civility, and our capacity to govern. This is not a temporary condition; it is woven into the fabric of the party. Unless and until it reverses course, you should take your votes and money and walk away.

This piece began as an effort to explain the party to friends who, like the habitually religious, cling to the faith long after events should have exposed its fraudulence.

I never thought I would presume to say this. I respect that your allegiance is rooted in considered beliefs and years of loyalty that, at the beginning of my political journey, I shared. I certainly don't think I have all the answers, and I enjoy exploring our differences. You inform me, correct me, and, most generously, tolerate me. You care, as do I, about the world we are leaving the next generations.

Our friendship far transcends our political beliefs. We share each other's celebrations, enjoy each other's successes. I value your advice. You've helped me through hard times, and some of you have helped my kids as well. You are loyal friends, generous members of the community, and deeply committed parents and grandparents. My world, and the larger world, would be a grayer place without you.

Knowing you as I do, I know that you are troubled by the direction of your party. Little wonder—you are mainstream Republicans whose mainstream has run dry. But I also accept that, for you, the Democrats may not be the answer—that you see them as feckless devotees of identity politics and too much government, don't trust Hillary Clinton, and believe that Bernie Sanders would drive us off the fiscal cliff. I'm not writing to quarrel with these beliefs. Nor do I suggest that unchallenged dominance by the Democrats would serve the country well.

But to compare the two parties at this time in our history is to indulge in false equivalency. For rationalizing the GOP's pathology by responding with a partisan tit-for-tat is not adequate to the circumstances. The sins you perceive in Democrats are the usual ones—misguided policies, ill-chosen means for dubious ends, and the normal complement of rhetorical dishonesty and political squalor. However mistaken you may find Clinton and Sanders on the issues, their debate is addressed to the world as it exists and therefore open to a sensible critique. The squalor to which the GOP has sunk, an alternate reality rooted in anger and mendacity, transcends mere differences in policy, threatening the country with profound, perhaps irreparable, damage.

This is not simply about Donald Trump. For Trump is not the result of forces that will come and go, but of a deterioration within the Republican Party that has been accelerating for years. The GOP has become a political mutation, stirred from dysfunction, demagoguery, myopia, and myth, nurtured in that fever swamp where lies and hysteria kill off reason. Nothing better will arise until you help drive a stake through its heart.

One of our ongoing disagreements has been about the nature of the party, and where you fit within it. With respect to GOP extremism in areas like climate denial, gun violence, or reproductive rights, you often say, "but I'm not like that." But the party is. You may be moderate in your views; the party is not. Even candidates with temperate instincts must go along to survive, or meet the fate of Jon Huntsman, mocked for publicly accepting climate change and evolution.

One can argue that Huntsman might well have done better in 2012 than Mitt Romney to win the nomination; Romney ran too far to the right. But in the hothouse of the GOP primaries, Huntsman never had a chance. This encapsulates the party's problem in presidential elections.

Long since, the GOP killed its moderates and trashed everything they stood for. It has replaced respected figures like William Cohen, Richard Lugar, and John Danforth with rigid ideologues like Ted Cruz and Mike Lee, and social illiterates like James Inhofe, Jeff Sessions, and Richard Shelby. On issue after issue, they have embraced an orthodoxy rooted in extremism and divorced from fact. These dynamics forced Mitt Romney to win the nomination by running so far right that he could never get back. And what was the lesson learned among the party base? That Romney was not nearly extreme enough.

In short, the Republican Party no longer belongs to you, or you in it. The year 2016 has proven the point.

I saw this coming not because I'm uniquely prescient, but because I began writing reality-based political novels twenty years ago. I hung around with party pros, consultants, lobbyists, donors, pollsters, officeholders, and political partisans, some of whom became my friends. Bit by bit, I saw the party sell out its agenda for short-term gains with disastrous long-term consequences. Eventually the GOP's train wreck became inevitable—no longer a matter of if, but when.

How did this happen? Start with the relationship between the party establishment and its base. Your family, and mine, occupy a privileged slice of American society. Not so for most members of the GOP electorate. They are folks that few of us know very well: evangelicals; modestly educated whites threatened by economic dislocation; and people whose distrust of government partakes of paranoia.

Economically, they are not natural allies of the party of business or its wealthy donors, who tend to focus on tax cuts and free-market principles irrelevant to the base. So in exchange for pursuing its economic agenda, the party offered evangelicals a faith-based vision of America: barring abortion, banning same-sex marriage, and giving government preferences to fundamentalist religious institutions. Why should business people care, the reasoning went, when we can rally these voters with promises that, however illusory, cost us nothing?

But as "promise keepers," the party failed its fundamentalist flock. Abortion remains legal; same-sex marriage became a right; the Constitution prevents government from enshrining religious preferences as law. So there was nothing to stop evangelicals from noticing that their own lives were often harder and less secure.

Ditto other members of the middle and working classes. The real causes of their woes are globalization, the Great Recession, the housing crisis, and an information society that marginalizes blue-collar jobs. But the GOP never addressed these complex forces with any kind of candor—let alone proposed solutions like job retraining and educational access for their kids.

> Throw in automation and globalization. Trump's promises notwithstanding, these jobs are never coming back. If anything, the end product of his demagoguery will be yet more public cynicism and despair.

Barren of ideas for helping its base voters, it resorted to blame shifting and scapegoating—of government, Obama, illegal immigrants, and Muslims and other minorities. Instead of looking forward, the party indulged a primal nostalgia for simpler times, an imaginary white folks' paradise that can never be resurrected.

Some of this was shameful. The GOP countenanced a race-based birtherism directed at our first black president, giving Donald Trump a political foothold. It nurtured xenophobia that targeted all Muslims at home and abroad. It pretended that illegal immigrants were poisoning our economy. It aped the mindless masters of talk radio and trafficked in conspiracy theories. It embraced Tea Party dead-enders who claimed that shutting down the government, at whatever cost, was the only answer.

In Congress, the party resolved to deny Obama reelection by grinding the legislative process to a halt, then blaming him for gridlock as if its tactics played no role. Political polarization polluted foreign policy—as when all three hundred Republicans in Congress turned the Iran deal into a political wedge issue, shunning the careful consideration it deserved in favor of shrill and simpleminded denunciations. In the world of the GOP, our many and complex problems had but one misbegotten cause: that Barack Obama was president.

So-called mainstream Republicans competed to fan the flames of outrage, poisoning political discourse. Typical was the establishment's darling, Marco Rubio, who claimed that Obama was not simply wrong, but trying to destroy America as we know it. Republican politics became not faith-based, but hate-based.

For the Republican base, nothing changed.

Except, of course, their rising anger, stoked by yet more empty and diversionary anti-Washington rhetoric that only deepened their sense of impotence. Focused on the donor class, party leaders charged the Democrats with "class warfare" against the less than embattled rich, while still failing to acknowledge through substantive policies the very real struggles of its rank and file. The election in 2014 of yet more Republican senators and congressmen made no difference in the lives of the people who supported them.

Not unreasonably, the base came to believe that our governmental and financial institutions—including the Republican Party—were controlled by an elite that was indifferent to their plight. And so demagogues like Donald Trump and Ted Cruz became the agents of their frustration and despair. Like the sorcerer's apprentice, the party lost control.

Among the casualties was the agenda most dear to the Republican establishment. Its insensitivity to the base has eroded support for free trade. Despite its claims of fiscal probity, the GOP continued its meretricious complaints about deficit spending—for which, as ever, it blamed the Democrats' self-serving rhetoric about protecting Social Security and Medicare—while proposing tax cuts for the wealthy that would explode the national debt. And consider this: How do tax cuts at the top benefit the struggling middle and working classes? And wouldn't slashing or privatizing Social Security further threaten their fragile place in our society?

But set aside the party's disingenuousness with respect to the economic and fiscal concerns that, in many cases, have gained it your allegiance. In other important areas the party has abandoned serious thought. Instead, the alternate reality of the GOP has created a closed intellectual system immune to fact or reason, imposing a mindless political fundamentalism on its candidates that no reflective person, least of all you, can any longer support.

Here is the fact-free theology one supports every time one votes for a Republican candidate for president, senator, or representative:

Climate denial. In the anti-science world of the GOP, man-made global warming is a hoax—just ask Ted Cruz or Donald Trump. This is one of many areas where the party perpetuates ignorance among its base, separating them from the populace at large. In a recent Gallup poll asking if human activity was a factor in climate change, 85 percent of Democrats and 68 percent of independents answered yes. Republicans? Only 38 percent. Faced with overwhelming scientific consensus, the party will not even consider how to combat this existential menace.

This, of course, is amplified by avatars of anger like Rush Limbaugh, Sean Hannity, and their cousins in talk radio and the alt-right.

Denial of evolution and general scientific knowledge. I know you can't believe this, but a Pew Research poll showed that more than 50 percent of Republican voters don't accept the theory of evolution. When the core of the party thinks that *The Flintstones* was a documentary—and none of its presidential candidates dare say otherwise—the broader implications for policies rooted in scientific inquiry are disturbing. Hence people like Trump who profit by suggesting that vaccination engenders autism.

Gun violence. The GOP slavishly follows the NRA line. It has opposed any effort to curb gun violence, hiding behind paranoid nonsense about disarming all Americans. Its only answer to our unique and devastating mass slaughter is that more Americans should carry guns—quite literally, that the black churchgoers in Charleston mowed down by a madman should have brought weapons to their place of worship.

Racism. Given that all of you deplore it, I can feel you bridling. But the troubling signs proliferate. Voter suppression laws aimed at minorities in states where no evidence of fraud exists. Scapegoating American Muslims—many of whom have more experience defending our country than any of us—as potential terrorists. Targeting illegal immigrants whose presence owes as much to American business interests as to their own desperation.

Want more? Ignoring the glaring evidence of unequal law enforcement against blacks that, in some cases, includes unjustified police shootings. Upholding a death penalty that disproportionately targets minorities and the poor—not a few of whom turn out to be innocent.

With the summer came a new spate of officer-involved shootings that Trump tried to exploit.

And still more? Gutting programs that seek to recognize the impact of race and class, often because they are deemed "unfair" to far more advantaged whites. Tolerating a relentless disparagement of our president that reeks of racism—imagine, if you will, the outcry if a black congressman had shouted "liar" at George W. Bush during a State of the Union Address. The party that claims to be "race blind" has become blind to its own tacit bigotry.

Curbing reproductive rights. Protected by *Roe v. Wade* and our own privilege, it is easy for us to ignore what the GOP is doing beyond our field of vision—our daughters, after all, have access to safe and legal abortion and any form of birth control they need. But this is not so in America at large, where Republican legislatures and the Congress are working overtime to limit access to abortion and reproductive care, often at great cost to women and their families.

The GOP's senseless war on Planned Parenthood is only part of it. How many of us know that, due to draconian laws sponsored by Republicans, 90 percent of American counties have no legal abortion provider? How many of us have stopped to consider that no healthy family needs GOP-sponsored parental consent laws, which in authoritarian, abusive, and incestuous families can lead to the murder of a daughter?

All this is central to the rigid orthodoxy that Republican presidents and legislators will be forced to follow, now and in the future. Mitt Romney did; Marco Rubio has; Paul Ryan will. No matter how personally attractive, no candidate will change this party until forces outside the party make dramatic change imperative.

This will be a real problem for traditional Republicans, in part because of the populist strain introduced by Trump.

I appreciate that this conclusion is depressing. No doubt many of you will object to some aspect of my indictment. Fair enough. But I doubt that you are much inclined to dispute most of its particulars—if only because you've acknowledged them yourselves.

And there are still more issues to consider. Why hasn't the GOP made creative efforts to confront the problems of struggling middle-class and working people—many of whom have now turned to Donald Trump—seeking solutions that are consistent with its philosophy? Are we squandering the talents of our young people by saddling them with prohibitive student debt, cheating our society in the bargain? Are we stifling struggling families by not trying to retrain their breadwinners?

For that matter, what sense does this phony war on Obamacare make when the GOP offered no alternatives—even to deal with preexisting conditions or the ruinous effects of catastrophic illness? When did the GOP stop caring—I mean really caring, not offering bromides about liberating the engines of free enterprise—about the everyday life of citizens who are falling behind?

One can debate the best policies and solutions for all this—and we should. But the GOP has utterly abdicated its responsibility to participate in reasoned governance, and so gave us Donald Trump.

Trump's policies, such as they may be, are a disastrous expression of bottled-up resentment among the base, a blind lashing out at all they feel besets them. Again and again, he offers phony and dangerous prescriptions that betray his complete ignorance of the most basic rudiments of governance, economics, domestic policy, and national security. He caters to racial antagonism, spreading it within the party and the country as a whole. As a man, he is an intellectually vacant and self-obsessed misogynist lacking the most rudimentary qualifications to be president. He is not simply a disgrace to the party, but a product of all that disgraces it.

I can't imagine you will ever choose to support him. That this is the only choice your party has given you makes it imperative to leave the GOP.

I'm not urging you to become Democrats. I'm not even trying to win an argument. I simply want our political arguments to make sense in the world of reality, the better to move our country forward with the goodwill and considered judgment required by these challenging times.

So what I profoundly hope is that, collectively, you will abandon the Republican Party until it becomes worthy of the country we love in common. Because, in the end, a big chunk of our common future may depend on you.

With abiding friendship,
Ric

Spurred by Trump, this began to happen. The exodus included movement conservatives, commentators, foreign policy and national security experts, religious leaders, officeholders, and party officials who refused to support Donald Trump. More abandoned him in October, when he was exposed as a self-professed sexual predator. But none of this mattered to Trump's legions.

Partners in Death
The GOP and the NRA

MARCH 29, 2016

The tragic toll of war stupefies and stuns. In the 240 years since the Revolutionary War, we have sacrificed nearly 1.4 million Americans to war. In itself, this number is hard to grasp.

But harder yet is to reckon the human cost—of husbands, wives, fathers, mothers, sons, daughters; of perished potential; of achievements and kindnesses that will never be; of families forever shattered. However justified some wars may be, war sobers us, diminishes us, cheats us. We struggle to find some national purpose to console us, some nobility of spirit to uplift us. We mourn the tragedies of Vietnam, Afghanistan, and Iraq, the wars of our last half century.

In less than that same half century, from the murders of Martin Luther King Jr. and Robert Kennedy until now, guns have claimed over 1.5 million Americans—100,000 more deaths than in all the wars of our history.

Here there is no nobility, no consolation, no parades or speeches or monuments or national days of remembrance. Nothing but the indelible stain of mindless butchery and private sorrow.

Every year, year after year, we lose over 30,000 more of us to homicides, suicides, and preventable accidents. Every day, we average more than one mass shooting—four or more people dead or wounded. Perhaps a name attaches to that day: Charleston, San Bernardino, Sandy Hook; perhaps we see a memorial service on our screen. Beneath such days are buried the deaths of eighty-eight more people that day, and every other.

And the carnage moves inexorably forward. In the first two months of 2016, we have had twenty-eight mass shootings. In two weeks' time, we have added the names of Kalamazoo and Hesston, Kansas, to this litany of shame. And yet nothing changes.

Why? It is not that America has more crime—our crime rates are comparable to other advanced countries. Instead we are stalked by something uniquely American: death by gunshot—four times more per million than the next highest country, Switzerland; twenty more times than Australia. America is the first world's slaughterhouse.

Most Americans deplore that. A solid majority believes the epidemic of deaths by gunshot is a serious problem; that mass shootings are something that can be stopped; and that our gun laws should be aimed at stemming these tragedies. Indeed, more than 90 percent of Americans support background checks for all gun purchases. So why hasn't Congress taken steps to protect our safety?

Because Republicans refuse.

Amid the comprehensive moral and intellectual collapse of the GOP, nothing captures its utter bankruptcy more than the issue of gun violence. Lest this seem too stark, we must consider its stunning record of rhetorical and legislative obedience to the NRA.

Start with the party's most recent presidential candidates. At the height of the campaign season, the massacres in Kalamazoo and Kansas provoked no comment. To a person, they oppose any legislation or government measures whatsoever to prevent gun violence. Instead, their answer is more guns in the hands of more Americans, no matter how dangerous an individual may be. As for gun safety legislation,

Throughout the campaign, the slaughter continued apace.

they consistently—and falsely—characterize it as an effort to confiscate guns from law-abiding citizens.

Three of the principal contenders suffice to capture this cowardice and cynicism: "You don't stop the bad guys by taking away our guns," Ted Cruz says. "You stop the bad guys by using our guns, and a free and armed American citizenry is how we keep ourselves safe." The recently departed "mainstream" choice, Marco Rubio, asserts that "gun laws fail everywhere they're tried."

Attempting to outdo his rivals, the probable nominee Donald Trump claims that "we already have tremendous regulations. Now, if you look at my opponents, they're very weak on the Second Amendment. I'm very, very strong." Again and again, Trump suggests that the only solution to gun violence is for Americans to carry weapons wherever they go.

At one point during the campaign, the NRA was running more ads supporting Trump than his own campaign was.

And they mean it. For example, as senators both Cruz and Rubio voted against expanded background checks to keep dangerous people from acquiring guns. Both opposed banning high-capacity magazines of over ten bullets. And on and on, for there is not a single measure to reduce the toll of death that they support.

This opposition is not grounded in reason. Instead, the GOP hides behind a shopworn litany of excuses that do not withstand scrutiny.

First, there are the myths perpetuated by the gun lobby about self-defense. No question that law-abiding citizens have the perfect right to buy a gun for self-defense or any other lawful purpose. Advocates for gun safety laws don't debate this. To the contrary, they believe that, to the extent possible, the law should protect all of us—whether we choose to own guns or not—by keeping dangerous people from acquiring weapons.

There is certainly a need for such protections. Gun ownership alone won't keep us safe—to the contrary, the assertion that guns used for self-defense keep us safer is counterfactual. A 2012 study by the Violence Policy Center showed that for every justifiable homicide there were thirty-two criminal gun deaths. The study concluded that: "The reality of self-defense gun use bears no resemblance to the exaggerated claims of the gun lobby and gun industry." With respect to women and domestic violence, a study by researchers at Boston University confirms a grim reality: in states where gun ownership is higher, more women are killed by people they know.

As for the claim that gun safety legislation will do no good, it is bogus, a logical fallacy. The goal of such legislation is not the impossible—to stop every possible death—but to make it more difficult for dangerous people to kill with a gun.

And it works. Incremental measures to stop deaths from smoking and drunk driving have drastically reduced both. Obviously, they did so without banning driving or even smoking. So, too, the effort to keep guns out of the hands of criminals and others with a propensity for violence—as the shooter in Hesston, Kansas, freshly served with a domestic violence restraining order, so tragically exemplifies.

Which brings us to the greatest falsehood of all—that gun safety legislation means denying law-abiding Americans the right to own a weapon, whether for self-defense or any other lawful purpose. Not only would such legislation be unconstitutional, but nothing the Republicans so adamantly oppose remotely resembles the straw man of confiscation they so conveniently invoke.

Yet again and again, the NRA and GOP deploy a preposterous perversion of the "slippery slope" argument—that any legislation to prevent criminals or terrorists from buying guns is a step toward barring gun ownership by all Americans. Bereft of rational arguments and terrified of fact, they traffic in demagoguery and paranoia. The NRA's propaganda marks the absolute bottom of American political discourse—rooted in fear, fomented by hysteria, dependent on lies, and, in some cases, fueled by fantasies of blowing away "the other."

As for the assertion that the 5–4 Supreme Court decision finding a constitutional right to bear arms means that guns cannot be regulated to protect law-abiding citizens, it is nonsense. No constitutional right—including free speech—is absolute. As to guns, the Supreme Court made clear that nothing in its opinion barred reasonable regulation to protect the public safety, such as background checks to screen out gun purchases by criminals, spousal abusers, and the adjudicated mentally ill. The Second Amendment protects the rights of law-abiding Americans to buy a gun, not the rights of violent felons to endanger the law-abiding.

When all else fails, the NRA and its Republican handmaidens traffic in a particularly distasteful brand of diversion. A lot of homicides are gang related, they argue, so why should we care? Besides, they say, many gun deaths are suicides, not homicides—ignoring that the prevalence of guns means that a person in despair has a quick and easy way of placing themselves beyond second thoughts or the help of others. Particularly odious is the suggestion that a mass murderer like the demented young man in Sandy Hook would simply have found another weapon to wipe out so many kids and teachers so quickly. With what—a knife or slingshot?

And, finally, this: given the NRA's success in promoting gun ownership and opposing gun safety legislation, why aren't we dramatically safer? Why so many mass murders? Why so many more killings than in any other first-world country? Is the only answer that more Americans should carry weapons? Do the Republicans in Congress really believe—for one tragic example—the only protection for the black churchgoers murdered in Charleston would be bringing guns to their place of worship? Do they ever ask themselves whether our society is truly that helpless?

In truth, it doesn't matter what Republican officceholders know or believe in their hearts. They are the NRA's legislative arm—without them, the NRA could not have succeeded in making America the first world's most dangerous place. Because, quite simply, they are the craven servants of the gun lobby—their services bought and paid for at whatever cost in human lives.

They don't come cheap. Since 2010, the NRA and its allies have spent more than $46 million in soft money alone to influence federal elections. In the last election cycle, the NRA spent $18.6 million on candidates. Throw in lobbying, and the NRA spent $32.5 million in 2015. Virtually every dollar spent on candidates went to Republicans. Along with that comes a small cadre of voters obsessed with guns who respond to whatever scare tactic the NRA comes up with.

Money is one explanation. Another is that all but a handful of GOP primaries occur in gerrymandered districts that reward extreme positions and candidates—including with respect to guns.

What have the Republicans given the NRA in return? Anything it wants.

Take background checks. The current law exists to prevent felons, fugitives, domestic abusers, and the adjudicated mentally ill from purchasing weapons. This is no small matter: in 2013, for example, 61 percent of women killed with guns were killed by intimate partners; in 57 percent of mass shootings, one of the victims was the shooter's partner or family member. Since taking effect in 1994, the law has blocked more than 2.4 million gun sales to dangerous people.

Patently, this has nothing to do with taking guns from law-abiding citizens—it exists to protect them. But the law needs to be strengthened. Due to a gaping loophole that exempts gun shows and the Internet, roughly 40 percent of gun sales occur without a background check. That's millions of guns every year—imagine what Republicans would say if the TSA failed to check 40 percent of airline passengers. And even the existing system is hampered by a process of record keeping that is badly underfunded.

But Republicans have blocked absolutely all legislative efforts to strengthen the system, extend background checks, and close loopholes. Conspicuously, that includes Senators

Rubio and Cruz. Just who are they protecting? No one but dangerous people who can't pass a background check. Their rationale—that they are protecting gun rights from an oppressive government—is shamefully dishonest, the fig leaf of a political lapdog.

And shamefully typical. Days after the terrorist attack in San Bernardino killed fourteen people, the House and Senate considered a bill to ban the sale of guns and explosives to people on the FBI's terrorist watch list. After the NRA opposed the measure, the legislation was voted down by all 241 Republicans in the House, and 53 of 54 Republican senators—including Ted Cruz and Marco Rubio.

At the time, President Obama asked, "What could possibly be the argument for allowing a terrorist suspect to buy a semi-automatic weapon?" Rubio's answer? He was worried about "people that basically just have the same name as everybody else, who don't belong on the no-fly list." Incredibly, Rubio claims to be more concerned about bureaucratic error than allowing terrorists to buy weapons of mass murder.

The GOP's duplicity and hypocrisy is exposed by another favorite excuse—that the problem is not guns but mentally ill people with guns. "The country," Rubio says, "should examine mental illness."

By this logic, the GOP would want to extend background checks on the mentally ill by closing the gun show loophole—which, of course, it opposes. But there is more. As part of a relatively modest gun safety measure, in 2013 Obama proposed to increase funding for mental health programs designed to identify and help people who are potentially dangerous. At the behest of the NRA, Republicans in the Senate killed it. Note here an ironic coda—two weeks ago, an Idaho pastor who appeared with Ted Cruz was gravely wounded by a shooter with a history of mental illness. But there is no incident, however personal, that causes Republican politicians to reflect on their obedience to the gun lobby.

Indeed, another important part of the Republican cover-up is to help the NRA suppress research into the cost and causes of gun violence. This is critical to deceiving the American public—to the gun lobby, facts are more deadly than bullets.

Thus for twenty years Republicans in Congress have banned the Centers for Disease Control and Prevention from conducting basic research into gun violence and its impact on public health. No other research topic is subject to a ban—which Republicans in Congress extended yet again in December 2015. The reason is simple: the NRA fears the research will refute its propaganda against gun safety laws and expose its bogus claims that measures like concealed carry laws save lives.

Little wonder—a recent research project showed that, since 2007, 763 people were killed by shooters with concealed carry licenses, including 29 mass killings that took 139 lives; the murder of 17 police officers; and, ironically, 223 suicides. Only after he left Congress did the NRA's point man, Republican congressman Jay Dickey, admit that "I wish we had started the proper research and kept it going all this time. I have regrets." Adds Dickey, "If we had somehow gotten the research going, we could have somehow found a solution to the gun violence . . ." If the Republicans still in Congress feel any regret, they keep it to themselves.

Indeed, at the insistence of the NRA, the GOP has enacted more, and more deadly, suppressions of potentially life-saving information regarding guns. A 2003 Republican-sponsored measure prohibits the ATF from releasing information to cities and states that would allow them to trace crime guns. This effectively prevents law enforcement agencies from examining patterns of gun trafficking to criminals or identifying crooked gun dealers linked to large numbers of gun crimes.

Another GOP-backed provision frees dealers from submitting inventories to the ATF, allowing crooked dealers to supply guns to criminals and then claim they were "stolen." Yet another provision requires the FBI to destroy within twenty-four hours all records of approved purchasers gained from background checks. This makes it very hard to retrieve guns issued to dangerous people by mistake—like Dylann Roof, the Charleston shooter—or from purchasers later shown to be criminals, mentally ill, or spousal abusers.

A major cause of gun death is assault weapons. In 2004, Republicans in Congress voted to allow the federal assault weapons ban to expire. As the *New York Times* comments, "As a result, gun manufacturers have been allowed to sell all manner of war weaponry to civilians. Including the super destructive .50-caliber sniper rifle. . . . Why any civilian would need this weapon, designed to pierce concrete bunkers and armored personnel carriers, is a question that should be put to the gun makers who profit from them in the politicians who shamelessly do their bidding."

The Republicans' only coherent answer is to cite the difficulty in defining an "assault weapon"—without, of course, entering into any effort to address the problem. Beyond that, they are reduced to insisting that Americans have the right to purchase any gun they want, up to and including military-style weapons designed for mass killing. But such guns are hardly necessary or even suitable for self-defense; as for hunting, their use on a deer would yield not a trophy, but ground venison.

In truth, all that such weapons are good for is killing a lot of people quickly at close range. Which is why they were used by the shooters in the massacres at San Bernardino; Fort Hood; Sandy Hook Elementary School; Aurora, Colorado; Umpqua Community College in Oregon; and on and on. Offered a chance to rethink this after Sandy Hook, Republicans in Congress blocked an effort to renew the ban.

As a result, gun companies are aggressively marketing military-style weapons to boost their profits. As the *Times* reports, their advertising says it all: "'As Close as You Can

Get Without Enlisting,' reads one tagline under a photo of a poised shooter aiming the civilian version of a military rifle. An ad for a semi-automatic shotgun promises security whether in 'Iraq, Afghanistan, Your Living-room.' An ad for an armor-piercing handgun shows an embattled infantryman above the line: 'Built for Them . . . Built for You.'"

They will face no consequences for manufacturing unreasonably dangerous guns and selling them in ways that only enhance the dangers. Why? Because in 2004 a Republican majority in Congress passed one of the NRA's top legislative priorities: a bill granting gun manufacturers and dealers—no matter how crooked—broad immunity from lawsuits in state or federal court.

They were joined by Bernie Sanders, no doubt driven by a politicians usual desire to please the more militant gun owners of Vermont. This became an issue in the Democratic primaries.

Similarly, Republicans in Congress have blocked the Consumer Product Safety Administration from requiring that guns have even basic safety features. Cars and food and aspirin and kids' toys must be made safer—only guns are sacrosanct.

But there is seemingly no end to the NRA's appetite, or the GOP's servility. Recently, stymied by the Republicans in Congress, President Obama took modest administrative steps to try to strengthen background checks, expand access to mental health treatment, and improve gun safety technology. At once Ted Cruz rushed forward to claim that the president was proposing "taking away our guns."

But Marco Rubio equally captured the spineless servility of the GOP to the NRA's dystopian demagoguery. President Obama, he claimed, "has waged war on the Constitution. He is obsessed with gun control." He charged that Obama's measures were "meant to further erode the Second Amendment." But, of course, the ever-vigilant Rubio promised to protect us: "I believe that every single American has a constitutional—and therefore God-given—right to defend themselves and their families. . . . On my first day in office, behind a desk, don't worry, those orders are gone."

For sheer fear-mongering and dishonesty, that is hard
to beat. One wonders whether Rubio ever asks himself who
will pay the price in blood for this kind of "leadership." But
if you want to define the word *servility* with pellucid clarity,
you will not require a dictionary. Far better to contemplate
Mitch McConnell.

After President Obama nominated Merrick Garland to
the Supreme Court, McConnell was asked if, as Majority
Leader, he would permit a vote on Garland in the event that
a Democrat won the presidency in November. McConnell
flatly said that he would not. Here is his reason: "I can't
imagine that a Republican majority in the United States
Senate would want to confirm, in a lame duck session, a
nominee opposed by the National Rifle Association."

Truly, ineffably, servile.

The annals of American politics are rife with self-serving
hypocrisy. But the Republicans' cowardly and contemptible
servitude to the NRA stands alone in its cravenness and in
its costs: the death and maiming of so many thousands of
Americans, year after year, shattering families and inflicting
the stain of violence on our country. And the GOP's only
answer is to promise us more.

It is long past time for Americans to call them on it.

Though Trump tried hard. Increasingly, he embraced the NRA's most extreme positions on pretty much everything.

The problem here is salience. Most voters, including Democrats, care about many things and do not prioritize gun control. For many gun fanatics, gun rights are paramount.

The Reckoning of 2016

The Supreme Court and Reproductive Rights

APRIL 5, 2016

By then it was apparent that Clinton would win the nomination. In candor, one of my concerns was reminding disaffected Sanders supporters that this would be a binary choice, and that the stakes included the direction of the court for a generation—or more. Republicans devoted to judicial conservatism understood this very well.

Whether you support Bernie or Hillary, how many of you want Republicans to abolish freedom of reproductive choice?

I thought so. But here's the kicker—in much of the country, the GOP already has.

For millions of American women, freedom of choice is writ on water. And if you abandon your party's nominee, whoever that may be, millions more may suffer.

By musing aloud about punishing women once the GOP completes its relentless drive to stamp out abortion rights, Donald Trump has reminded us yet again of the stakes in this election. On the issue of choice, as with so much else, our national reckoning is now at hand and cannot be wished away.

Put simply, the president who selects Antonin Scalia's successor will determine the future of reproductive rights. That is not hyperbole—it is already graven on the American landscape.

Start with access to a safe and legal abortion. For the less privileged women in most American states, this right is close to extinction.

Across the country abortion clinics are closing at a record pace. A little over seven hundred remain—forty-three years after *Roe v. Wade*, 90 percent of American counties have no clinics at all. In a large swath of red states, 400,000 women of reproductive age live more than 150 miles from the nearest clinic. Five states—Mississippi, Missouri, North Dakota, South Dakota, and Wyoming—have just one.

So how did this happen?

A principal cause is GOP-sponsored state laws that shut down clinics by imposing unnecessary and onerous requirements. Some mandate prohibitively expensive renovations so that clinics resemble hospitals for no good reason—broader hallways, for example. Others demand that doctors performing abortions have admitting privileges at a nearby hospital—difficult at best, and impossible in areas where the hospital refuses.

If these laws are upheld by the Supreme Court, the impact will not simply be to cement them, but to encourage the GOP to expand their reach into yet more states. And the obliteration of choice will proceed apace.

The transparently bogus rationale for such laws is the tender concern of Republican legislators for women's health. Yet abortion is one of the safest of all medical procedures, with a complication rate below 1/10 of 1 percent. By comparison, a routine colonoscopy is riskier. Oddly enough, there is no crusade within the GOP to stem the nightmare of colonoscopy.

The real agenda, of course, is finding a palatable rationale for gutting *Roe v. Wade*. After the passage of one such law, the lieutenant governor of Texas tweeted a map of all the clinics that would have to close, capped with an exultant message: "We fought to pass S.B. 5 thru the Senate last night, & this is why!"

The social myopia of privileged Republicans is captured by this issue. It simply doesn't affect anyone they know.

Less exultant were the poor or rural women denied access to a safe abortion. In the name of women's health, Republicans give these women three choices: bear unwanted children, travel sometimes prohibitive distances, or run the risk of an illegal abortion. One does not have to be a keen observer to fear for women when Republicans start protecting them.

One very keen observer—a distinguished Republican federal judge—has sliced through the hypocrisy.

Judge Richard Posner is a renowned conservative legal scholar. As a judge on the United States Court of Appeals, he was faced with a similar law from Wisconsin, requiring doctors at abortion clinics to obtain admitting privileges at hospitals within a thirty-mile radius—and to do so in three days. In an opinion striking down the law, Posner shredded the pretense that the Republican legislature was protecting women's health:

Posner is that increasingly rare breed—a conservative judge with a fully formed judicial philosophy who, nonetheless, eschews political partisanship.

"Wisconsin," Posner writes, "appears to be indifferent to complications of any other outpatient procedures, even when they are far more likely to produce complications than abortions are." The alleged health concerns, he finds, are in fact "nonexistent." In contrast the impediments to abortion are very real: "[M]ore than 50% of Wisconsin women seeking abortions have incomes below the federal poverty line. . . . For them a round trip to Chicago . . . may be prohibitively expensive. The state of Wisconsin is not offering to pick up the tab, or any part of it."

He then cuts to the quick. "A great many Americans are passionately opposed to abortion—as they are entitled to be. . . . Some of them proceed indirectly, seeking to discourage abortion by making it more difficult for women to obtain. They may do this in the name of protecting the health of women who have abortions, yet . . . the specific measures they support may do little or nothing for health but rather strew impediments to abortion."

Finally, Posner eviscerates the cynical pretense behind requiring admitting privileges—the usual method used to shut down clinics. This requirement, he writes, "cannot be taken seriously as a measure to improve women's health because the transfer agreements that abortion clinics make with hospitals, plus the ability to summon an ambulance by phone call, assure the access of such women to a nearby hospital in the event of a medical emergency."

As a particularly egregious example of this legislative masquerade, Posner cites the Texas law praised by its lieutenant governor for its effectiveness in shutting down clinics. Which brings us back to the judicial stakes in this election—the constitutionality of that very law is now before the United States Supreme Court.

The law reduced the number of clinics in Texas from forty to ten, all clustered in four metropolitan areas. No clinics are located west or south of San Antonio, an area larger than California. Yet despite—or perhaps because of—the fact that it places abortion out of reach for women in most of Texas, a conservative panel of federal appeals judges upheld the law. After all, the court said, women in West Texas could always travel to New Mexico.

But the context for this law makes its impact even worse. Other Texas laws require most women to get a sonogram at least twenty-four hours prior to an abortion, from the same doctor, and require all abortions past sixteen weeks to be done in surgical centers—the nearest of which is in San Antonio. Ironically, the inevitable overcrowding of those clinics that remain has caused delays that, in some cases, mean that women seeking an abortion pass the sixteen-week deadline—a nasty Republican catch-22.

The legal test for such laws is clear: whether they impose an "undue burden" on a woman's right to an abortion under *Roe v. Wade*. Obviously, they do—as the Texas law exemplifies, their impact is not simply "undue," but draconian.

Yet at the hearing before the Supreme Court, the justices appeared to be divided 4–4, with the four Republican justices—Roberts, Alito, Thomas, and Kennedy—in favor of upholding the law. Such a tie will leave Texas's anti-choice scheme in place. And had Scalia lived, there is no doubt that the Court's ruling would have protected such laws in every state that has passed them—including the Wisconsin law struck down by Judge Posner. As matters stand, freedom of choice for millions of American women hangs in the balance, awaiting the selection of the Court's ninth justice.

On June 27, 2016, with Justice Kennedy casting the deciding vote, by a 5–3 majority the Supreme Court invalidated the Texas law. To many observers, including me, Kennedy's vote came as somewhat of a surprise.

Instead, all similar laws were effectively invalidated.

There could be no better illustration of how critical it is that a Democrat appoint Scalia's successor. Yet this same term provides another example—a case that threatens to limit access to contraception under the Affordable Care Act (ACA).

Under a prior ruling of the Roberts Court, an employer can claim a religious exemption to the ACA's mandate to provide contraception as part of an employee's health insurance plan. To opt out, all the employer need do is notify the Department of Health and Human Services that it will not subsidize a plan that offers contraception. At that point, the government can require the insurer to offer contraception using funds not derived from the employer who objects.

One would think this would satisfy employers who object to contraception. Not so. Seven religiously affiliated employers brought suit challenging this compromise, claiming that being required to opt out of providing contraception in itself violates their religious freedom. Or, more starkly, that their concept of religious freedom entitles them to block the government and their insurance company from providing contraception to their employees.

On June 16, 2016, apparently deadlocked, the Court returned the case to the lower court with instructions to find a compromise. In this case, Scalia would, indeed, have been the deciding conservative vote.

Remarkably, the Supreme Court hearing made it clear that the same four Republican justices agree. Their sole concern was Orwellian: that by requiring the employers to opt out of providing contraception, the ACA was making them complicit in the provision of contraception by others.

This narrowness of view was truly striking. Instead of focusing on a woman's right to contraception, both Chief Justice Roberts and Justice Kennedy accused the government of "hijacking" the objectors' insurance plans. In the name of "religious freedom," the four justices would empower the objectors to impose their religious beliefs on others—a dangerously elastic concept with implications well beyond the present case.

Again, Scalia would have been the fifth. And, again, the resolution of this issue may well depend on who appoints his successor—though a subsequent order suggests that the Court is searching for an alternative to let itself, and the religious objectors, off the hook of a tie vote that would effectively uphold the opt-out. Whatever the case, it is clear that a Republican president can not only narrow a woman's access to abortion, but also to contraception, simply by restoring the Court's conservative majority.

Together, the two cases illustrated how precarious Roe itself has become, and how much depended on the outcome in November.

But the long-term impact could be even more severe. For both Donald Trump and Ted Cruz, repealing *Roe* is an explicit litmus test for appointing the next justice. Indeed, Trump's recent *lapsus linguae* about punishing women obscures the fact that Cruz is even worse. Piously, Cruz responded that, far from prosecuting women, he would "affirm their dignity and the incredible gift they have to bring life into the world." Care for a translation? Here it is: Ted Cruz wants to impose this "gift" on the adolescent victims of rape or incest.

As if all this were not enough, the election of a Republican president would diminish reproductive rights more broadly yet, threatening women's health in the bargain. In the most obvious example, Republicans in Congress and state legislatures are attempting to hamstring Planned Parenthood by cutting off public funds to organizations that provide abortions—even though abortion is a small portion of its services, which include contraception, sex education, and treatment for sexually transmitted diseases.

Without Planned Parenthood, these essential services could become scarce to unavailable. The proponents' list of supposed alternatives available to women smacks of dark comedy. For example, Florida helpfully specified elementary and middle schools, dental practices, and, believe it or not, an eye doctor as potential providers of women's health services—leaving one to wonder whether Republican legislators require not only sex education, but anatomical instruction.

One struggles to locate any benefit to women. But that, of course, is not the point. The real point is this: the Republican Party is carrying out a fundamentalist religious agenda in which it is the father who knows best.

In this area, as in the voting rights cases, the GOP's pretenses are becoming increasingly threadbare. They are not protecting women's health, any more than they are heading off a wave of in-person voter fraud.

Thus the election of a Republican president in 2016 would erode reproductive rights and threaten *Roe* itself. The next president could appoint up to four new justices, transforming the law for generations to come. So it is time for us to ask again those fundamental questions that informed the battle for choice from its beginnings:

Should concern for fetal life cause us to order women to have children because their birth control has failed—the predicate for the majority of abortions?

Should religious opposition to contraception strip women of protection from unwanted pregnancies?

Should we force families to have more children when they can't support the ones they have?

Should the law require women traumatized by rape or incest to become mothers against their will?

Should we compel pregnant women in desperate circumstances to seek illegal abortions that endanger their life and health?

Should pregnant teenagers forfeit their future to an accidental pregnancy, thus becoming, as they often do, depressed and undereducated mothers with minimal parenting skills?

Should we consider a woman's life or health a fair exchange for imposing compulsory motherhood in high-risk pregnancies?

Should we take our moral cues from a movement that—far too often—seems to love our children most before they're born?

Should we, in short, treat pregnant women as losers in God's—or nature's—lottery?

And, finally, should we tacitly support the GOP's war on reproductive rights because our preferred candidate did not win the Democratic nomination?

That question—like the others—should answer itself.

Long before the Republican convention, Trump had signed on for the full pro-life agenda.

The Sound and Fury of Donald Trump

APRIL 19, 2016

". . . it is a tale / Told by an idiot, full of sound and fury, / Signifying nothing."

The indelible phrase is from *Macbeth*, Shakespeare's drama of a regicide whose bloody ambition and untethered soul tears apart his country. But it perfectly captures Donald Trump's campaign for president—a howling hurricane of destruction whose core is as empty as the man.

For Trump, analogies to populists like Huey Long simply do not suffice. Such demagogues had a vision of the future, however distorted, that was grounded in more than the random or ephemeral. Nor does a comparison to Ted Cruz hold up. Cruz's obvious lies and deceptions have a consistent thread—tactical positioning—that makes him cognizable, even predictable, in the context of our politics.

Not so Trump. The unique danger he poses is his weightlessness. His Sturm und Drang emanates from the combustible combination of stupefying ignorance with a flippancy so vast that whatever he tells us, however inflammatory, has the half-life of a fruit fly. This profound detachment from the reality of the office he seeks—indeed, from other human beings—reduces his campaign to a psychodrama driven by the fleeting spotlight of the moment. One searches in vain for consistency or meaning.

There is none. Instead, Trump fills his own emptiness with a sound and fury meant to gratify his needs in the here and now.

His rallies are incitements to anger and division, barren of ideas and bereft of policy. He castigates the press and protesters—often minorities—then excuses acts of violence spurred by his provocations. He recites the names of young people killed by Mexican "illegals" and analogizes Muslims to snakes. He tells a story of General John "Black Jack" Pershing executing Philippine rebels—Muslims again—with bullets dipped in pigs' blood. He casts himself as the victim of an ever-shifting conspiracy in which all those who are "unfair" to Trump seek to rob his followers of a voice. He warns of riots in Cleveland if he is denied the nomination. He has no interest in consequence beyond the howls of his audience.

However bloody, the story is apocryphal.

After the convention passed without incident, Trump repeated this ploy by charging that the general election would be "rigged" against him.

For Trump, others exist only as an extension of himself. Thus his campaign manager Corey Lewandowski serves not as a tactician, but as Trump's thuggish doppelgänger. The result is unprecedented in the annals of our campaigns. Routinely, Lewandowski has threatened rivals and yelled obscenities at members of the press. Even more remarkably, he was caught on videotape collaring a protester and, days later, grabbing a female reporter by the arm to wrench her away from his master.

At the urging of his children, Trump later fired Lewandowski. But Lewandowski never stopped making trouble for his successor, Paul Manafort, who Trump eventually cashiered. Thereafter, Lewandowski reinserted himself as a voice in the campaign.

The latter incident showed the two men to be twinned by the lies, bullying, and slander that are endemic to Trump's character. The ultimate decision not to prosecute Lewandowski is in no way redemptive of his conduct—or Trump's. Denying the incontrovertible evidence of the tape, Lewandowski called the reporter "totally delusional," while Trump mocked her for complaining. When police charged Lewandowski with battery, noting the bruises on the woman's arm,

Trump asked reporters, "How do you know those bruises weren't there before?"

Startling in any normal candidate, Trump's behavior reflects the hollowness within. For Trump, truth is evanescent, reality ever-changing, the humanity of others of no concern. Nor does it surprise that he treated a woman with such contempt, for within Trump's void lurks a misogyny that borders on unhinged.

Indeed, Trump seems to have no inner mechanism to control it. Instead of trying to mime a would-be president, Trump marked his electoral victories by renewing what Fox aptly called his "sick obsession" with Megyn Kelly—in Trump's distorted view, a "bimbo" whose pointed question about his chronic disparagement of women, he implied last summer, emanated from menstruation. Remarkably, Trump never grasps that each new slur emblazons his misogyny on the public consciousness, suggesting a pathology that grows like kudzu.

Hence Trump's drive-by mauling of Heidi Cruz, about whom he threatened to "spill the beans"—a supposed reprisal for an ad featuring a semi-nude Melania aired by a Super PAC unrelated to Cruz. Undeterred by fact, Trump then compared the two women on the level he prefers, tweeting an unflattering photograph of Heidi next to one of his supermodel wife. In a candidate for president, one can but marvel at a compulsion so powerful that it obliterates all dignity or grace.

But the most comprehensive portrait of Trump's unwholesome nooks and crannies comes from Franklin Foer. Writing in *Slate*, Foer catalogs in detail the candidate's contempt for women.

No surprise that sexual boasting has been Trump's calling card since high school—a phase that seems never to have ended. But its flagrancy in adulthood bursts the bounds. Piqued at some on-air mockery by Tucker Carlson, Trump

Just how unhinged surfaced in October, in a videotape where Trump boasted of kissing and groping women without their consent—whereupon a number of women came forward to assert he had done this to them.

As noted, America later learned how true that was.

left Carlson a voicemail proclaiming that he—Trump—got more sex. On another occasion he called in to a talk show to inform a guest, "I've been successful with your girlfriend, I'll tell you that." This is not, it is fair to say, reflective of a presidential mettle.

But Trump's favorite indulgence is verbal cruelty to women themselves. When he judged contestants in his Miss Universe pageant unattractive, he ordered them to go stand with their fellow "discards," reducing some to tears. He sent Gail Collins a copy of an unfavorable column with her picture labeled, "The Face of a Dog." He demeans women with labels like "fat ass" and "slob" so routinely that the accumulation numbs.

As for the rest, I will spare you an ex-wife's account of sexual mistreatment—you can read the article yourself. Suffice it to say it is no surprise from a man who once told *New York* magazine, "Women, you have to treat them like shit."

This is the echo of sexual fury in the empty soul of a man who should never be president.

Whatever dwells in this wormhole distorts not just his sense of women, but of the larger world. His contract for campaign volunteers bars them from criticizing Trump, his family, his businesses, his products, or his campaign—for life. His balance sheet overstates his self-proclaimed "massive wealth" to a degree that smacks of fraud. Oblivious to the First Amendment, he proposes revising libel laws to facilitate lawsuits against those who criticize him. His chief adviser, he assures us, is Donald Trump.

And so the tale of sound and fury that is his campaign is, indeed, told by an idiot—the definition of which includes *ignoramus*. For only an idiot would be insensate to the boundless ignorance he so casually displays.

His moral void is matched by void of substance. His inner voice on foreign policy is the babbling of a fool.

In September, a former Miss Universe, Alicia Machado, described how Trump belittled her for gaining weight—calling her "Miss Piggy" and "Miss Housekeeping"—abusive behavior confirmed by a videotape of Trump dragging her to a gym to ridicule her in front of reporters. The nominee's demented response was to spend four days ridiculing her through Twitter and Fox News, urging his followers to look for a sex tape that did not exist.

Every now and then, one paused in amazement that Trump was getting away with this. The implications for the emotional health of the GOP electorate were alarming.

In October, confronted by a brace of women who accused him of assault, he suggested that several were too unattractive to warrant his attentions.

Every question is a surprise to him, something he has never thought about; every answer is meaningless, the transitory improvisation of an empty mind. The impact of his words is of no concern to him—if need be, he can simply change them. For Trump, tomorrow is not merely another day, but terra incognita.

The only constant is his indifference to anything a president should know. That the world is a dangerous place seems never to have occurred to him. He vows to rid us of an "obsolete" NATO, upending the balance of power with Russia. He prefers a nuclear South Korea and Japan to the expense of helping defend them, reversing a half-century of US foreign policy in the face of North Korea's burgeoning nuclear program.

He muses about using nuclear weapons against ISIS or in a European ground war. He advocates waterboarding and harsher forms of torture. He rejects all Muslim immigration, no matter how victimized refugees may be, portraying America to the world as racist, xenophobic, and mindlessly inimical to all Muslims. And, in doing all this, he becomes a dangerous propaganda tool for jihadists of every stripe.

Never once did Trump exhibit any sign of understanding the fight against ISIS. Yet another instance where his indifference to substance was profoundly disturbing.

He insults our most powerful European ally, Germany, asserting—falsely—that it has not stood up to Vladimir Putin. He insists that German society is "being destroyed" by "tremendous crime"—implicitly targeting the Muslims who are his universal scapegoat. He complains that the Iranian nuclear deal is causing American businesses to lose out to Europe on trade deals with Iran—wholly unaware that it is the Republican Congress, not the terms of the deal, that imposes sanctions on such trade.

But the mouse droppings of his mind accumulate apace. To make Mexico pay for his vaunted wall, he proposes cutting off all wire transfers from the United States to Mexicans, no matter how small—prompting President Obama to remark "good luck with that." He threatens China with a trade war that would dislocate the world economy. The grasp of geopolitics required from a president is alien to Trump. Nicholas Burns, an undersecretary of state under George W. Bush, puts the matter succinctly: "He doesn't understand diplomacy is not the zero-sum world of commercial real estate, hotels, and golf courses."

Heedless, Trump careens on, breaking diplomatic china as he goes. He touts the virtues of "unpredictability" in American foreign policy, an insight no doubt derived from listening to his own contradictory ramblings. His so-called team of advisers is composed of nonentities, several of whom he has never met. Little wonder that his prescriptions for our most dangerous foreign policy challenges change from moment to moment, like the stories of a child who keeps getting caught in lies. But not to worry: Trump promises to compel respect for America based on "the aura of personality"—his own.

That Trump substitutes himself for substance epitomizes his vacuity. For Trump, policy, like truth, is perishable and contingent, derived from nothing and meant to disappear. The Economist Intelligence Unit, whose mission is to think about such things, warns that as president Trump would seriously damage global growth—in part because his idiocy would stimulate global terrorism.

But his matching idiocy on domestic issues dispels the fantasy that there is any area where Trump knows what he is saying, or even remembers what he said the day before.

According to health care experts, his "plan" for replacing Obamacare is writ in vapor. But it is his pronouncements on the economy that completely displace reality as we know it.

Remarkably, he pledges to pay off our $19 trillion national debt "over a period of eight years." A leading budgetary think tank, the bipartisan Committee for a Responsible Federal Budget, took a pencil to this nonsense. The results provoke amazement. For Trump's proposal to become reality, he would either have to shrink the federal budget by two-thirds, or raise our annual growth rate—now projected

Even by the
standards of
Republican economic
voodoo, Trump's
proposals were
preposterous. But
the GOP's economic
nostrums had long
ago decamped
from fiscal reality,
paving the way
for Trump. For the
GOP's economic
conservatives,
embracing ruinous
tax cuts showed
that he was with
their program.

at 2 percent—to 46 percent. If one rules out cutting Social Security—which Trump does—he would need to slash the rest of the budget by 93 percent. Selling every asset the government possesses would not cover a fraction of his goal.

But his plan is even more hallucinatory than that. Remarkably, the tax cut he proposes would double the national debt, making the impossible twice as hard. Yet he promises to balance the budget, protect entitlements, and preserve essential services.

How? By cutting "waste and fraud and abuse," and abolishing the Department of Education and the Environmental Protection Agency. If you are struggling to construct a coherent picture from the puzzle pieces of Trump's thinking, so has every expert who has tried, only to discover that the task resembles reconstructing the theory of relativity from the detritus of a madman's brain.

Yet Trump topped all this by talking down the economy in a distinctly unpresidential way, predicting a "massive recession" caused by an enormous stock bubble. Fortunately, he tells us, there is one solution—electing him as president.

Before you jump at this opportunity, a small word of caution. In 2011, Trump predicted that Obamacare would cause unemployment to spurt above 9 percent. And in 2012, he forecast that Obama's reelection would cause oil and gas prices to go "through the roof like never before." One can get better advice from the crazy uncle who buries gold in his backyard.

Over drinks in the
early 1980s, Jerzy
Kosiński told me
that the fictional
Chauncey Gardiner
had come to be
embodied, to a
certain degree, by
Jimmy Carter. Jerzy
died too soon.

Here we should pause to stare into the abyss that is Donald Trump, for its full dimensions are difficult to grasp.

He is a unique figure in the history of America's major parties: not merely a demagogue, but one so completely unmoored that his world is a kaleidoscope of incoherence. There is no one home, and nothing in his head. He is Chance the gardener from Jerzy Kosiński's *Being There*, save that his inanity is not concealed by delphic ambiguities, but by banal bluster about magically making us great again. Never before have so many Americans considered electing a man so transcendently empty, so deeply disturbed, so utterly divorced from the gravity of the job he pursues, so completely determined to risk his country for his own solipsistic ends.

This idiot's tale, indeed, signifies nothing—no substance, no future, no hope. Nothing but another terrifying void—the black hole in our politics from which he emerged to seek the attention he so desperately needs in order to fill, at whatever cost, the vacuum within.

In the next two weeks, as predicted, Trump trounced Cruz and Kasich in the northeastern and mid-Atlantic states. He then wiped out Cruz in Indiana despite the fact that Cruz was supported by its governor, Mike Pence—who, nonetheless, tried to ingratiate himself with Trump. These victories clinched the nomination for Trump and drove his remaining rivals from the field. Not so incidentally, the results also left Pence looking for an escape route from Indiana, where his own run for reelection was flagging.

On this date, Trump beat Cruz in Indiana, cementing a foregone conclusion by driving Cruz from the race. And though Bernie Sanders would not yield for another month, as a matter of electoral mathematics there was no way he could catch up with Hillary Clinton.

Subsequently, a federal court of appeals struck down this law, saying that it disenfranchised African Americans with "surgical precision." By a 4–4 vote, on August 31, 2016, the US Supreme Court rejected North Carolina's appeal attempting to reinstate the law. But Chief Justice John Roberts and his three Republican colleagues voted to hear the state's appeal. The late Justice Scalia no doubt would have voted with them—reviving a law that the appeals court said selectively and deliberately targeted minority voters.

Closing Polls and Slamming Doors

John Roberts's Race-Based Agenda

MAY 3, 2016

A sharp bone of contention in the contest between Hillary Clinton and Bernie Sanders is who cares more about the lives of African Americans. One area of concern is minority voting rights—last week, a conservative federal judge upheld a repressive North Carolina voter ID law, passed by Republicans, clearly aimed at suppressing black turnout. This provides yet another pointed reminder of why the supporters of both candidates should unite come November—to stop Chief Justice Roberts and his allies from further gutting measures to protect minorities.

We should not mince words. The Roberts Court has not simply been racially obtuse—quite deliberately, it has dismantled affirmative action and diminished voting rights—upholding measures specifically designed to disadvantage Democrats by disenfranchising minorities, the poor, and the young.

Most recently, we have seen this in the Wisconsin primary, where a GOP-sponsored voter ID law kept an estimated 300,000 citizens from voting. That, not protecting the integrity of the ballot, was the law's sole and partisan purpose. So we need not discuss the current Supreme Court in the hushed and reverent whisper of tourists entering a cathedral.

With respect to issues regarding race, the Chief Justice has led the Court's conservative majority in a counterrevolution against the fruits of the civil rights movement. This is not a matter of happenstance, but a defining feature of his legal career.

For more than thirty years, John Roberts has pursued an aggressive campaign against programs that promote diversity and protect the voting rights of African Americans. Hence his famous rationale for this crusade: "The way to stop discrimination on the basis of race is to stop discriminating on the basis of race."

This excruciating platitude does not withstand exposure to the world as it actually exists—the excessive and often deadly use of force against blacks; laws passed to discourage black voters; laws that punish blacks more harshly than whites; continuing educational and economic inequities among the races.

Such banality is, perhaps, to be expected from a smug country clubber, smiling benignly at the black waiter who has just served up his favorite single malt scotch. But spoken by America's Chief Justice, it provides cover for rulings that serve the ideology and interests of the Republican Party at the cost of minorities.

Lest this seem too harsh, a bit of history well known to Chief Justice Roberts. In the wake of the civil rights laws of 1964–65, southern whites en masse deserted the Democratic Party—which they blamed for these laws—and embraced the GOP.

This was not because they suddenly discovered the charms of limited government as preached by Republicans: the engine of this tectonic shift from one party to another was race—and racial animus. Quite simply, millions of

Trump has been particularly insidious in suggesting that voter fraud by minorities would steal the election from him. In truth the only "rigging" is being done by Republican-controlled legislatures that, as the court of appeals found with respect to North Carolina, "impose cures for problems that did not exist."

whites feared and resented this potential sea change in political dominance and saw the Republican Party as their only hope of preserving the white power structure.

Abruptly, southern states became a key part of the Republican base. Cementing their allegiance, Richard Nixon adopted the GOP's "Southern Strategy," appealing to the widespread sense of white grievance. Under Ronald Reagan, this strategy ripened further—in 1980, Reagan kicked off his presidential campaign in Philadelphia, Mississippi, where, a decade and a half before, three civil rights workers had been brutally murdered.

This is not merely a racial dog whistle—it was more like a police siren.

Buoyed by his southern base, Reagan won by a landslide. And so Republicans seized the White House newly empowered to put into practice their antagonism to what, in their telling, was the Democrats' overconcern with racial justice.

Enter John Roberts. From the start, he was a political animal, his career nurtured in the precincts of the Republican right, his thoughts and actions attuned to the conservative ideology that facilitated his rise.

After clerking for the very conservative Chief Justice William Rehnquist—whose own early career included an unseemly antipathy toward integration—while still in his twenties, Roberts entered the Reagan Justice Department with a distinct hostility toward, as he put it in early memos, "race conscious remedies" that result in "reverse discrimination" against whites. More broadly, he evinced a consistent and profound distaste for policies—in the GOP's view wrongheaded—aimed at promoting racial justice.

He urged measures to advance "our anti-busing and anti-quota principles." He advocated resistance to broadening the Voting Rights Act of 1965 to facilitate the election of minority candidates. He scorned the Equal Employment Opportunity Commission as too friendly to claims of discrimination. He attacked affirmative action because, through his lens, it meant "the recruiting of inadequately prepared candidates."

And he consistently decried racial preferences intended to counteract de facto segregation.

It is, of course, reasonable to disagree about the efficacy, or even the wisdom, of such measures. But a studied racial insensitivity is something else—let alone a vehement dislike of race-based remedies so intense that it puzzles even judicial colleagues who agree with him.

It should not take much thought for people like me—and John Roberts—to appreciate that, by dint of sheer good fortune, we are the beneficiaries of the most successful affirmative action program in human history. We are white males born to educated and financially comfortable parents at the height of the American century, subject to all the advantages that conferred, and none of the barriers faced by women and minorities.

That is not guilt—it's simply fact. Compared to others, the comfortable white males of our era were born on third base. It is impossible to ameliorate every consequence of that, and foolish to try. But it is worse than foolish to deny that social inequities existed—and still exist today. And never more so than when such willful denial finds a home—indeed a weapon—in our nation's highest court.

This is not an attack on John Roberts the person, but an exploration of the damage done by John Roberts the Chief Justice. Former colleagues describe him as a nice and gracious man, albeit an unbendingly conservative one. Judging from his public statements, he seems genuinely concerned that the Court not be perceived as activist or partisan—rather more concerned, regrettably, with the perception than the reality that underlies it.

His seems to be the case of a top-drawer intellect hobbled by a narrow ideology and a deep political loyalty, aggravated by a limited ability to empathize with, or even imagine, lives different from his own. This is commonplace in private life. But in a Chief Justice, it can be very harmful indeed.

Take the Court's decisions with respect to voting rights.

The seminal case is the 2013 decision *Shelby County v. Holder.* At issue was a key provision of the Voting Rights Act of 1965, requiring that certain southern states with a history of voter suppression obtain federal approval of changes in their voting laws prior to enactment. The stakes were not abstract—pending at the time of the decision were a number of photo ID laws that, quite obviously, would disproportionately impact poor and minority voters.

There was—and is—no statistically significant evidence of in-person voter fraud that would justify these laws. Nor was their potential political impact obscure: as a matter of demographics, the majority of voters potentially affected were likely to vote Democratic.

Even if the evidence of these realities had not been put before the Court, it is simply impossible that they would elude a lawyer as politically sophisticated as John Roberts. Nonetheless, in a 5–4 majority opinion, the Chief Justice ruled that the "pre-clearance" provision for scrutinizing voter ID laws was unconstitutional—a dramatic evisceration of the law that had served as the chief protection for minority voting rights.

The essence of his reasoning was that racial progress in the South invalidated a requirement based on past racial history. In Roberts's formulation, the South in 2013 had changed so much that requiring pre-clearance of voting laws to protect minority rights was unfair to the states involved.

Really? Republican dominance in the South depends on the white vote and on resisting demographic change. Roberts surely knows this.

But, in fact, Roberts's distaste for pre-clearance had long preceded the history he claimed to rely on: thirty years before, as a Justice Department lawyer, Roberts had opposed the pre-clearance requirement. Plainly, the Shelby County opinion was less a matter of history than of the Chief Justice's preexisting—and fixed—ideology and beliefs.

Equally curious, in the private view of a distinguished federal appellate judge, was the uncharacteristic departure from the quality of Roberts's opinions outside the area of race. To this observer, his opinion in *Shelby County* is careless, disrespectful of precedent, and dishonest in its accounting of the record before the Court.

The evidence that Republican legislatures were poised to enact potentially discriminatory laws was staring Roberts in the face. Given all that, the Chief Justice's judicial critic reluctantly concludes that, far from being oblivious, Roberts knew exactly what he was doing—placing his finger on the electoral scales to help the Republican Party.

What is beyond dispute is that the states liberated from pre-clearance were run by Republican governors and legislatures. With unseemly alacrity, in the immediate wake of *Shelby* fourteen states—eight southern, all but one governed by Republicans—enacted or began enforcing strict voter ID laws. Texas did so within hours. And it was a case originating in Texas that gave the Chief Justice and his Court a glaring illustration of what the *Shelby* decision had wrought.

The case concerned a strict voter ID law twice blocked by the federal courts under the Voting Rights Act. After Shelby, the GOP-dominated Texas legislature promptly reenacted the law.

The Justice Department challenged it as discriminatory. After a lengthy trial produced an extensive factual record, a federal district judge struck down the legislation. Her findings were striking: the legislature had acted "because of and not merely in spite of the voter ID law's detrimental effects on the African-American and Hispanic electorate."

This could not put the issue more plainly—a direct and unequivocal conclusion that the law was racially motivated, specifically written to suppress minority voting. But on appeal a conservative panel of appellate judges decided that invalidating the law would disturb the voting process in Texas nine days before early voting started—in other words, that it was better to keep in place a law that, based on the evidence, could disenfranchise 600,000 Texas voters. Armed with this curious reasoning, the Fifth Circuit stayed the lower court's decision.

I did not attempt here to capture the shock this highly respected jurist expressed for, as he saw it, the transparent shabbiness of Roberts's "reasoning" in the Shelby County case.

Though if I'm right about the motivations of the Court's Republicans, that hardly matters.

The case promptly went to the Supreme Court. Ignoring the detailed finding of discrimination, the Roberts Court upheld the stay—effectively validating the suppression of minority turnout. In dissent, Justice Ginsburg wrote: "A sharply disproportionate percentage of those voters [affected by the law] are African-American or Hispanic," adding that "racial discrimination in elections in Texas is no mere historical artifact." But despite a decision by the entire Fifth Circuit to further review the law, just four days ago the Court allowed the stay to remain in place.

In June 2016, the Fifth Circuit struck down the Texas law as an unconstitutional denial of voting rights. In the months that followed, federal courts invalidated several other Republican voter ID laws.

"It is a sordid business," the Chief Justice had written in an earlier voting rights case, "this divvying us up by race." It is indeed. Just how sordid is exposed by Judge Richard Posner's evisceration of the voter ID laws protected by Chief Justice Roberts. Of all of the rebukes to Roberts's reasoning, Posner's is perhaps the most devastating.

Posner again, an honest man.

Circuit Judge Posner is a Republican, a Reagan appointee, and a renowned conservative legal scholar. He is this era's most eminent writer on the law and, according to one exhaustive survey, the most-cited legal thinker of all time. The occasion for his analysis of voter ID laws was an appeal wherein a conservative appellate court upheld laws passed by GOP legislatures in Indiana and Wisconsin—the latter of which has just disenfranchised 300,000 voters.

In a scathing dissent, Judge Posner demolished the pretense that these laws exist for any reason other than advantaging Republicans by choking off minority turnout.

First, he explodes the myth of voter fraud. Spelling out what any sentient observer knows, he affirms that "repeated investigations . . . show that there is virtually no in-person voter fraud nationally."

To the contrary, as Posner has stated elsewhere, these laws are "a means of voter suppression rather than fraud prevention." As he states in his dissent "there is only one motivation for imposing burdens on voting that are ostensibly designed to discourage voter-impersonation fraud, and that is to discourage voting by persons likely to vote against the party responsible for imposing the burden."

He then provides the proof. State by state, he surveys the nine states that have passed the most restrictive voter ID laws. All are governed by Republicans; all are politically conservative.

Finally, Judge Posner demonstrates why poor and minority voters are less likely to have IDs, such as driver's licenses—not because they are somehow scheming to perpetrate voter fraud, but because of lack of money, time, or easy access to the agencies that issue such forms of identification. The obvious effect—and intent—of such laws, Posner concludes, is to suppress voting among groups likely to favor Democrats.

This fact eludes their more comfortable fellow citizens, awash in ID to go with their credit cards.

Should any doubt remain, a participant in drafting the Wisconsin law has come forward to confirm the obvious—that the discussions among the Republican legislators focused not on concerns about voter fraud, but on how best to tilt elections toward the GOP. The ironic effect is to mirror the way voter fraud distorts democracy—instead of stuffing ballot boxes, Republicans are starving them.

This is the unique ugliness of the GOP effort to fight changing demographics—not by reaching out to minorities, but by disenfranchising them. Just last Friday, former South Carolina senator Jim DeMint trumpeted this strategy on conservative talk radio: Republican voter ID laws, he boasted, "are beginning to change elections toward more conservative candidates."

John Roberts cannot be ignorant of this. The facts of race-based voter suppression are glaring—and would be even were he not a politically sophisticated conservative Republican, which casts his "race-neutral" bromides in a particularly pitiless light.

Here we return to the most famous bromide of all—that the way to end discrimination by race is to stop discriminating by race.

The context is another Roberts bête noire: affirmative action. In this area, as well, his decisions are suffused with a single-minded focus on eliminating government plans that take any account of race.

His pioneer opinion was in the 2007 *Parents Involved* case. That case arose from efforts by Seattle and Louisville to preserve at least some racial diversity in schools affected by residential segregation. The plan that particularly offended the Chief Justice was Seattle's rather modest effort to use race as a factor in assessing applications to oversubscribed schools—wherein a student's ethnicity was one of several "tiebreakers" used to maintain a level of diversity roughly reflecting the city as a whole.

During oral argument, Roberts compared Seattle's efforts to promote diverse student bodies to the deliberate segregation by race barred by *Brown v. Board of Education*—simply because race, the sole factor in maintaining absolute segregation of blacks and whites, was also a factor in Seattle's effort to preserve some level of racial diversity. Morally and practically, this is intellectual perversity of a high order.

But in the judicial philosophy of John Roberts, any acknowledgment of race for any purpose—even a purpose consistent with Brown—abridges the Constitution. As for preserving racial diversity, Roberts flatly rejects this as an appropriate concern of government. No matter how racially segregated Seattle schools might become, in his view the Constitution prevents any effort to change this imbalance by directly considering race.

Indeed, Roberts's famous remedy for stopping discrimination was too much for Justice Anthony Kennedy, who countered that this pat formulation was "not sufficient to decide these cases. Fifty years of experience since *Brown v. Board of Education* should teach us that the problem before us defies so easy a solution. . . . To the extent that [Roberts's] plurality opinion suggests that the Constitution mandates that state and local school authorities must accept the status quo of racial isolation in schools, it is, in my view, profoundly mistaken."

Thus the conservative Republican Kennedy, no friend to affirmative action, felt compelled to disown this aspect of the Chief Justice's opinion, and concur on narrower grounds. One might hope that this would give John Roberts pause.

But Roberts's war on "racial preferences" continued apace. In 2014, he joined in the decision upholding Michigan's ban on affirmative action in public universities. This provoked a vigorous dissent from Justice Sotomayor, who characterized Roberts's signature bromide as "out of touch with reality." She went on to offer the Chief Justice her own formulation: "The way to stop discrimination on the basis of race is to speak openly and candidly on the subject of race, and to apply the Constitution with eyes open to the unfortunate effects of centuries of racial discrimination."

Undeterred, Roberts responded sharply: "It is not 'out of touch with reality' to conclude that racial preferences may . . . do more harm than good." Far from entertaining second thoughts, he was instrumental in an effort to review yet another program to raise diversity, a modest plan at the University of Texas to consider race as one of many "plus factors" in some student admissions decisions. But for the death of Antonin Scalia, court observers believe that the Roberts Court would have overturned the Texas plan.

Instead, the case is likely to be held in abeyance pending the appointment of a new justice. Left lingering in the air is Roberts's inquiry at oral argument of the lawyer for the university: "What unique perspective does a minority student bring to a physics class?"

This reductio ad absurdum exposes the fatuity of Roberts's campaign—not to mention the privileged thought bubble that isolates his philosophical abstractions from the reality of lives outside his own experience.

Does he really think this is merely about the principles of physics? What about the totality of campus life, and what

This may be where Kennedy began parting company with Roberts on race-based remedies. Note Kennedy's role in the University of Texas case, discussed here as well.

On June 23, 2016, the Supreme Court upheld the University of Texas by a 4–3 margin. Again, Kennedy was the swing vote; again, Roberts, Alito, and Thomas dissented. Justice Kagan recused herself because of prior involvement as solicitor general.

students of all backgrounds experience as part of a student body? Or the disadvantaged students—minorities and the poor—who are not sustained by the advantageous circumstances into which John Roberts was born? Absent the ability to ask such questions, politics and ideology can condemn even the smartest man to a callous mediocrity of thought.

The Chief Justice may not want to consider race, but voters can. Democrats can start by supporting whatever candidate wins the party's nomination and, therefore, has the hope of replacing Justice Scalia with an appointee of broader views. That would bring a measure of racial justice to the Court in the most elegant of ways—by making John Roberts, at least among his fellow justices, the member of a minority.

Instead, President Trump will reestablish a conservative majority by replacing Scalia with another right-wing ideologue. And given the age of several justices, his further appointments may mold the court for decades to come, transforming American law while diminishing individual rights and advancing the GOP's partisan interests.

Why Bernie Lost—and What to Do about It

MAY 10, 2016

The first part is simple. Hillary Clinton got more votes.

Three million more popular votes, to be precise. This margin will not significantly change between now and the end of the primary season. Nor will her margin in pledged delegates, close to three hundred, awarded proportionally state by state. By the normal metrics of any primary contest, Bernie Sanders has lost.

Why? This, too, is not hard to answer. The more vexing and important question we will save for last: What should Sanders and his dedicated followers do in November and beyond?

But first, let's take stock of what Bernie Sanders has accomplished.

For openers, he transformed the political dialogue within the Democratic Party, pushing his agenda to the forefront of our larger discussion. The impetus was his unrelenting focus on two broad areas of national dysfunction: the corrosive corruption of our campaign finance system, and the degree to which our politics abets, rather

Some of Trump's and Sanders's most fervent followers shared the belief that the deck was stacked against them—and their candidates.

By the end of the Democratic primaries, the margin was about 4 million.

than ameliorates, the economic inequity and dislocation that is killing off our collective sense of opportunity and hope.

Others have decried the barely veiled bribery that buys not just access, but outcomes. But only Sanders has done this with the clarity and ferocity that the issue deserves. The damage is not simply that money buys power, but that hanging out with wealthy donors distorts an officeholder's sense of the world.

This, no doubt, accounts for the power of Sanders's denunciation of Hillary Clinton's speaking fees. But that is simply emblematic of his larger and inarguable point: that our political process is slanted toward plutocracy.

Sanders's attack on income inequality has been equally telling. One can debate his prescriptions: reviving Glass-Steagall; opposing the TPP; an agenda that requires a dramatic raise in taxation and in the size of government. But he has relocated the discussion within the Democratic Party on his own turf, becoming the engine of a shift that has the potential to last beyond his candidacy. It is far more likely, now, that the plight of those left behind will be at the forefront of the Democrats' agenda.

His impact goes further still. By casting himself as a "democratic socialist," he has spurred Americans to consider anew how they view the role of government. He has made voters more class conscious, dispelling the myth of equal opportunity in an inequitable age. He has challenged the party to return to its roots as an advocate for the middle class, labor, and the poor.

He has separated the fear of globalization from xenophobia, denouncing trade deals while embracing immigration. He has rallied young people who want to rewrite the terms of the deal prior generations have handed them. He has won more states than most observers ever imagined he would, and he is going to the Democratic platform strongly positioned to call for change. And, remarkably, he has fought big money to a standstill by building a massive war chest from the modest donations of ordinary people inspired by his message.

But the very consistency of that message poses a conundrum—while arousing deep passion and loyalty, he did not broaden his appeal to key constituencies within the Democratic Party.

In the end, he came up against a truism of electoral politics—a following primarily composed of young people and white progressives, while substantial, does not in itself carry the party or the country. The difference between the Sanders and Obama challenges to Hillary Clinton is that Obama was able to take this base and add minorities, which, demographically, have become even more critical to Democrats in the last eight years.

As I wrote the previous October. The Sanders demographic never changed that much. Though no one doubted his commitment to minority rights, as a senator from Vermont his attention had gone elsewhere. In the black community he could never catch up.

Passion is an important ingredient in political success. But a passionate voter still votes only once. Many Democratic voters decided that Clinton embodies the knowledge, experience, and practical approach to making progress that they desire in a president. They may not turn out at rallies, but they get one vote too. It does not serve to condescend to them as docile, uninformed, or lacking vision or convictions.

The danger here is that real differences between the candidates mutate, among disappointed voters, into bitterness, which wrongly challenges the validity of the elections themselves. The argument that the popular margin won by Clinton is owed to a rigged system does not withstand a considered analysis.

No doubt that Wasserman Schultz was for Clinton. But her intrusions, such as they were, did not add up to 4 million votes. In any event, Russian hackers got her on the eve of the Democratic convention.

To start, the issues contested in these primaries were thoroughly aired. Granted, Debbie Wasserman Schultz put her thumb on the scales more than once, particularly with respect to debates. But, in the end, no observant voter could be left in doubt about what the candidates had to say.

Nor is it sufficient to complain that too many southern primaries came too soon. The calendar preexisted Bernie Sanders—far from a contrivance designed to derail his candidacy, the schedule has been like this for years. Granted that many of the Super Tuesday states are GOP bastions—though it is well to remember that Florida and North Carolina are purple, and that Georgia may go there soon enough. But the same day Clinton won those states she also won Massachusetts, home of Elizabeth Warren.

Before one wishes for a different schedule, consider that the first two states helped jump-start the Sanders campaign. Compared to the country as a whole, Iowa and New Hampshire have a disproportionately white populace, more fertile ground for Sanders. And the prevalence of caucuses early on, often a boon to Sanders, rewarded intensity over breadth of support, while making participation difficult for overworked and financially struggling people—frequently minorities—who cannot afford the time.

Beyond this, the core of Clinton supporters in the South—African Americans—are part of a nationwide Democratic constituency critical to victory in November. So, too, are Latinos—another group generally supportive of Hillary Clinton. No progressive, I am sure—least of all Bernie Sanders—would denigrate their role within the party.

Nor, whatever the peculiarity of voting in places like New York, can it be fairly said that Clinton's victories emanated from a voting process that, though conducted state by state, was pervasively flawed—let alone rigged across the country by malign forces in every state. There is no persuasive evidence that her 4-million-vote margin in the popular vote does not, overall, reflect the preferences of voters. This preference, not arcane rules, accounts for her decisive edge in pledged delegates who, after all, are awarded proportionally—if anything, this formula limited the impact of Clinton's success in garnering votes.

In explaining his shortfall, Sanders states that poor people vote in lesser numbers. But that fact, to the extent it is
one, cannot be blamed on Hillary Clinton. And for whatever
reason, Clinton fared well in states with the largest income
inequality.

Yet another problem for Sanders among Democrats was
his relationship to the party—specifically, that he has never
been a member.

Certainly, that should not—and did not—preclude
him from seeking the party's nomination. But political
parties do not exist simply to conduct plebiscites. Their
underlying purpose is to promote a sustained approach to
governance, which requires a cadre of people to keep the
party machinery running. Most often, these are not cynical self-promoters, but committed folks who believe that
their party's general philosophy is best for society. Superdelegates are people too.

Little wonder, then, that as a lifetime Democrat Clinton
draws more support from loyal Democrats than Sanders. But
the most committed Democrats care about winning—had
Sanders won more votes than Clinton, he would have garnered more superdelegates. And if the party simply elimi-
nated all superdelegates, as many Sanders supporters would
prefer, Clinton would have the clear majority of popular
votes and pledged delegates.

Ironically, Sanders's recent assertion that Clinton will
not garner the majority of all delegates before the convention rests on the existence of superdelegates, whose numbers
raise the mathematic ceiling for clinching the nomination.
This is where his logic turns on itself—one cannot complain
about the existence of superdelegates and then use their
existence to claim that the convention will be contested.
Indeed, if the party awarded superdelegates proportionally
according to the state-by-state results, which Sanders seems
to advocate, Clinton would maintain a comfortable majority of delegates.

Thus under any formulation, Clinton will have the clear majority of electoral votes and pledged delegates—not to mention superdelegates. The only conceivable way she could lose is for superdelegates to ignore the electoral results, and move en masse to Bernie Sanders. It would be hard to characterize that as either logical or consistent with any version of democracy one can conjure. And it directly contradicts Sanders's call for allocating superdelegates according to the popular vote in each state.

Finally, some complain that all Democratic primaries should be open to all voters or, at least, to unaffiliated voters not connected to the party. Some primaries are. But the fact that all are not has nothing to do with Bernie Sanders, and everything to do with maintaining a philosophically coherent party—including one that is not hijacked by candidates and voters who care nothing for its precepts.

Again, there is history here. A good way to render this more comprehensible is to invoke George Wallace, who sought the Democratic nomination in three different years—1964, 1972, and 1976—by attracting votes from racists of every political stripe, many of whom had no connection to the party. Wallace exemplifies why these rules exist in some Democratic primaries. Whether one agrees with them or not, they have a valid historic purpose, one which preceded this year's contest by decades.

But Sanders's defeat derives from more than demographics or electoral mechanics. Here, another paradox: the same proposals that created such excitement among some voters gave rise, among others, to doubts about their practicability or wisdom.

First, practicability. With unavoidable candor, Sanders acknowledges that his agenda cannot be enacted as matters stand. The only hope, therefore, is a "political revolution" that utterly transforms our body politic.

One need not be a cowardly centrist to believe this a daunting long shot. For deplore it as we may, by its very structure under the Constitution—embedded in the separation of powers—our governmental institutions resist tectonic change. From FDR to LBJ to Barack Obama, change has come incrementally, not from transformational rhetoric alone, but from pragmatism and patience. And in recent times our political process has become far more vicious and resistant—not only polarized, but Darwinian.

The basic facts are captured by Norman Ornstein in *The Atlantic.* Even should the Democrats recapture a Senate majority in 2016, they won't elect enough senators to break a Republican filibuster. And there is simply no chance of flipping a sufficient number of the one-sided and gerrymandered districts to retake the House. In short, a President Sanders would face the same miserable situation—a government hopelessly paralyzed by hostile parties—that Obama faced after the 2010 elections.

And, as with Obama, the Republicans would obstruct him without cease. Ornstein describes the grim terrain:

> Going over the heads of Congress has long been a staple of frustrated presidents, and it has almost never worked. . . . And these days, with most congressional districts resembling homogenous echo chambers—national public opinion has limited bearing on congressional leaders. Talk radio, cable news, social media and blogs mean more. And none of these outlets would be swayed or intimidated to create some huge populist uprising that would force Congress to bring up, much less pass, a sweeping populist agenda. The more Sanders pushed, the more there would be a sharp and vicious counter-reaction which would further tribalize the country.

One can but sympathize with Sanders voters frustrated by gridlock, polarization, and income inequality. But envisioning the passage of his agenda required a degree of magical thinking. Presented with the chance to hamstring Sanders, the congressional GOP would have made the Obama years look like the Age of Pericles.

Here, again, Obama holds a lesson. The fight for the Affordable Care Act nearly hollowed out his presidency.

Imagine, then, Sanders vainly trying to pass single-payer health care—a proven non-starter in a polarized and divided government—exhausting his political capital while destroying his effectiveness as president.

Prominent progressives have expressed these very concerns. Tom Hayden, a committed democratic activist since the 1960s, described in *The Nation* the agonizing reappraisal that caused him to switch from Sanders to Clinton. To Ornstein's list he adds this: that the Republican attack machine, which left Sanders alone as long as he was damaging Clinton, was simply waiting to launch the same merciless assault that Clinton has endured for years, redefining him in highly negative terms for general election voters. This, I know for a fact, is true.

Sam Brown, an esteemed activist since the era of civil rights and Vietnam, underscores all this with a hard-headed look at the electoral math. The reality is this: the turnout for Sanders, well below that for Clinton, does not presage the political tidal wave required to swamp reality as we know it.

Countering these forces to enact the Sanders agenda would seem to require not only entirely different conditions, but a different system—not to mention sheer political genius on a level unprecedented in any American president. Here, again, Sanders did not persuade enough voters that he could summon such a miracle.

To say that Sanders is a voice in the wilderness is not quite right—he was an effective and innovative mayor of Burlington, and he has used the amendment process in Congress to some effect. But his reputation as a loner and political purist, reflected in his limited legislative achievements, ran counter to the hope that he could be a uniquely transformational president in such fractious times.

After a quarter century of rising nastiness and paralysis, these concerns were not lost on Democratic voters. Whether one agrees or disagrees, they can hardly be blamed for not believing that the revolution Bernie Sanders says is necessary could, in fact, happen. Nor can they be faulted for believing that Hillary Clinton can more likely stave off the disaster of a President Trump, and then move the country as far toward progressivism as anyone can—and away from the nativism, negativism, and nihilism of the GOP.

As to substance, there was genuine doubt about the economic suppositions on which the Sanders agenda rests. That these fears were widely shared among the Democratic electorate is another reason Sanders fell short.

For many, the agenda itself is a stirring departure from the past. Breaking up the big banks. Free college. Health care for everyone, including undocumented immigrants. Mandating employers to provide new parents with three months' family leave. These proposals, and others, address a deep and unmet longing for a fair and inclusive society.

But, for others of good faith, the prospective cost is sobering. The price tag on health care alone—$1.4 trillion, more than the $1 trillion we pay out in Social Security checks every year—left many wondering about both theory and practice. The argument that the plan can offset this with $1 trillion in savings is, according to several experts, questionable without shortcutting medical procedures and services, as well as expenditures on new technology. God may not be in the details, but better health care is.

Overall, a number of analysts—including left-of-center economists not affiliated with Clinton—believed that the Sanders agenda, if ever enacted, would raise the size of the federal government and its spending by 40 percent. Aside from uncertainty about the economic impact of such a massive shift it is, politically, impossible.

Nor are its underlying premises free from doubt. Among the bases for the Sanders agenda is economic growth of 5.3 percent. When Jeb Bush offered a plan assuming 4 percent growth, he was widely ridiculed on the left. While gentler about Sanders, progressive economists are no less dubious.

Asked about the Sanders projections, Dean Baker, who writes frequently for HuffPost, opined that getting much over 2 percent is hard to imagine. Similarly, another regular, Jared Bernstein, described the assumptions behind the 5.3 percent figure as "wishful thinking." To a considerable extent, this same unease permeated the primary electorate.

Paul Krugman, no reactionary, expressed consistent bemusement at Sanders's proposals.

Other proposals added to this disquiet. Take free college. Among Democrats, there is wide agreement that college should be free—or, at least, very low in cost—for those who lack the resources to pay their own way. This would have the salutary effect of creating opportunity for those who need it, while enriching our society with their talents.

But, many asked, why spend our tax dollars on kids whose family can afford their education? Why not spend the money on infrastructure, job retraining, relocation of displaced workers, or our fraying social safety net? These are valid questions. Many concluded that we need to attack specific problems with maximum resources, helping the people who need our help, rather than transforming higher education for those who don't.

My point is this. Those who supported Clinton, and those who voted for Sanders, had valid reasons for doing so. Someone had to lose. But faced with Donald Trump there is little reason for lasting antagonism between people of goodwill who, in general, share much more philosophically than not.

So the question now is what Sanders and his most fervent supporters will do. And, as of now, there is reason to believe that many will refuse to support Clinton over Trump.

The evidence in cyberspace abounds. I'm not impervious to reader comments, and I'm grateful for any statement of appreciation or goodwill. But I have noted that in the rare instances I've expressed some skepticism about any aspect of the Sanders campaign, angry readers surface to accuse me of being a shill for Hillary or, horror of horrors, a Republican.

No complaints—and a modest price to pay for the privilege of writing for others. But this very passion reverberates in article after article, comment after comment, by those who say that they will never vote for Hillary Clinton—a sentiment reflected in an estimate that 25 percent of Sanders voters are disinclined to support Clinton in November.

For some, it is Iraq; for others, speaking fees; for still others, the varied explanations for the email controversy. Many question Clinton's true feelings about free trade agreements. For a segment of Sanders supporters, it is all of the above. A subsection goes even further—that given Clinton's perceived closeness to Wall Street, there is no difference between her and the Republicans.

I get this as a metaphor for the larger point that both parties are too enmeshed with the financial sector. It is particularly prevalent among those, including younger voters, who have no affiliation with the Democratic Party. But as a statement of fact it contravenes reality. The differences are too numerous, and far too critical, to ignore.

Here are a few. The Court. The environment. Reasonable regulation of Wall Street. Economic justice. Reproductive rights. Equal rights for minorities, women, and gays. A sane and effective program to counter terrorism, including nuclear terrorism. Job retraining. Affordable college. Improving Obamacare. Preserving Medicare and Social Security. Combating the fallout of globalization. And on and on.

And yet one hears repeatedly the Susan Sarandon school of political analysis—if Sanders voters abandon Clinton, and Trump wins, the revolution will come that much quicker.

How? She doesn't know. In what form? She doesn't say. At what cost? She has no idea.

The notion that Donald Trump would provoke just the kind of revolution Susan Sarandon wants is, in candor, hallucinatory. Far more likely Trump would drive us deeper into division, distrust, and despair, a downward spiral from which there will be no common idea of how to escape. I'm reminded of one of the more chilling chapters from the Vietnam War—when an American officer, having ordered his troops to decimate a hamlet and everyone in it, explained that "sometimes you have to destroy a village in order to save it."

No, thanks. We should save the village by making it better for all who live there.

Here, a word about third parties as a medium of self-expression. Certainly, one can vote any way one likes. But all that voting for Ralph Nader helped buy us was eight years of Republican rule. Can anyone look back at those years and say that President Gore would have made no difference? Only Ralph Nader, which captures the problem nicely. This is not the year for progressives to walk away—any more than 1968, when the disenchanted followers of Robert Kennedy and Eugene McCarthy helped elect their polar opposite, Richard Nixon.

Instead, the only realistic way for Bernie's legions to save the village is by continuing what they started. Keeping engaged with the Democratic Party—which, however imperfect, is the only realistic vehicle for positive change. Fighting for a platform that embraces progressive goals. Supporting candidates who reflect their values. Pressing for changes in the nomination process. Making themselves ever more important within, and to, the party. Holding it to its promises. Combating Super PACs and strengthening the role of small donors. Accepting that, in politics, one never gets everything one wants. And never forfeiting their purchase on power in exchange for impotent anger.

I could never fathom the idea, popular among third-party voters, that voting should focus on personal expression and moral purity. The point of voting, it seems to me, is to help achieve the best possible civic outcome.

As for Bernie Sanders himself, I believe that he will act on the truth he stated so clearly—that Hillary Clinton is infinitely preferable to Donald Trump. And so should those who look to him for leadership. Not simply because it's true, but because it matters to the future of our village.

In the fall Sanders spoke out strongly for Clinton over Trump, arguing that 2016 was no time for third-party voting.

PART III

*The Donald, Hillary,
Narcissism, Racism, Political Insanity,
and the Surprising Fatefulness
of Two Conventions*

BY EARLY MAY, A WOUNDED HILLARY CLINTON WAS SET to face off against a triumphal Donald Trump.

Breathless commentators forecast that the "candidate of change," however erratic, was set to defeat the tired candidate of the incumbent party, in a country that too many Americans believed was headed downhill. In this desperate fourth quarter of the mind, many argued, Trump was a political Hail Mary. And then portents swiftly accumulated that this construct was complicated by Trump's internal makeup.

For securing the nomination had not made Trump a statesman, positioning himself as presidential for the larger electorate awaiting him in November. Far from it. Trump seemed to have no second act at all—raising grave questions about what drove a persona he seemed unable to change. Particularly startling was his constant pursuit of petty personal grievances, his seeming addiction to the toxic tropes of bigotry, and the mendacious exploitation with which he responded to tragedies like the slaughter in Orlando. His inner world seemed to include no one but himself, forever looking in the mirror.

To me, all this marked Trump as a man far too damaged to become our 45th president.

So I set out to explain why—first pretty much on my own and then, abruptly, in the company of established journalists who came to believe, as I did, that avoiding the question of Trump's inner landscape was not responsible journalism, but its antithesis.

But the drama was far greater than one man's psychodrama. Trump had hijacked a major political party whose leaders, by and large, acted like hostages in thrall to a dangerous madman—parsing, rationalizing, enabling, and sometimes joining in as he dragged them ever deeper into the ever-growing fever swamp of racism, lies, and dishonesty that seemed calculated to sicken the country they purported to love. There was justice in this, for they had been tiptoeing in the very same swamp for years, and now were flailing in the quicksand beneath, shouting to all who would hear that Trump would save us from Hillary Clinton.

However damaged, Clinton was a different matter altogether. Having at last dispatched Sanders, she dusted herself off, took the measure of Trump, and set out to use him as a foil to fortify her candidacy and unify her party. It was an edifying sight. Relentless competence may not be heartwarming, but when the alternative is a thrill ride run by a man with attention deficit disorder, it is surely reassuring.

With good reason. Every time the chance for a breakthrough fell in his lap—notably the Clinton emails—Trump fumbled it. Clinton ground steadily on, the political equivalent of a football team playing on a muddy field, eschewing the long but risky pass for a punishing ground game.

Her steadiness kept paying off—in the consistency of her themes and in the method and even the predictability of her choice for vice president. In contrast, Trump threw fits of pique at petty targets, including other Republicans, and his selection of Mike Pence partook of farce. By the end of July, Trump needed a unifying convention to boost his chances; Clinton a humanizing convention to make her more acceptable to those devoted to Sanders or unsettled by Trump.

Even so, few anticipated that both conventions would provide such riveting spectacle.

Why Hillary Clinton

MAY 17, 2016

In Mario Cuomo's famous dictum, politicians "campaign in poetry and govern in prose."

While Hillary Clinton has effectively secured her party's nomination, her primary campaign has been difficult and distinctly unpoetic. By personality and inclination, Clinton is prose. Which, fortuitously or not, makes her a fit for the temper of these fractious times, where patience, pragmatism, and a mastery of policy count for more than soaring rhetoric and promises that cannot be kept.

Our politics is trench warfare. The Republicans are dug in, protected by a bulwark of gerrymandering and demographics that means that, out of 435 congressional districts, all but thirty-five or so are electorally impregnable. So, too, are roughly forty-five red state senators—not enough to make a majority, but sufficient to sustain a filibuster. And the machinery of polarization—including a media that tells right-wing voters what they want to hear—blocks transformational change.

We may not like it. But our quarrel is not merely with our current noxious politics, but with the founding fathers who, fearful of popular excesses, gave us political institutions ideal for dividing power and resisting change. Unwittingly, they embedded within our Constitution a system that is now exploited by a GOP mired in stasis and self-interest. The political front moves, if at all, by inches instead of miles.

In this environment things like single-payer health care are casualties of war. The question is how to carve out territory where progress, however incremental, is meaningful and lasting.

Take Barack Obama and the Affordable Care Act. Imperfect and incomplete as it may be, Obamacare has delivered health insurance to about 20 million Americans, with the greatest benefit to the poor, minorities, and struggling workers. Not only was this important—in the Hobbesian world of our politics, it was optimal.

From the day he entered office, Obama had to claw for every inch of political turf in the face of unrelieved opposition to any legislation he offered. Often, he had to stretch the limits of his executive authority to achieve anything at all.

In short, we elected a man who campaigned in poetry, and found that prose was writ in mud and paid for in partisan bloodshed. One doubts that today he would campaign quite as he did in 2008—indeed, he did not do so in 2012. Now Hillary Clinton is campaigning as she must govern—as a combatant, not an innocent, whose greatest weapon will sometimes be a veto.

She understands that progress in health care, infrastructure, financial regulation, tax reform, the environment, and limiting money in politics can only come through a mastery of detail and a keen sense of the potential, and limits, of presidential power. She is coming to the job prepared.

As a politician, she is like that congenital A student we all knew in high school—steeped in policy, enthralled by detail, and conscientious to a fault. Give her something to read, and she will read it and remember. When it comes to knowing her job, Hillary Clinton does not believe in faking it.

She has specific plans to improve the lot of embattled Americans, including women and their families. She has a well-conceived program to regulate the financial sector—a priority she spelled out a year before the crash of 2008. Indeed, there is no area of pressing need where she is not stocked with proposals that, mercifully, have an actual chance of moving forward.

Importantly, her agenda can be paid for without busting the budget, primarily by increasing taxes on the wealthy. One can quarrel with the details: certainly, it is easy to imagine more sweeping and ideal solutions than some that she proposes—indeed, Bernie Sanders often does.

What is impossible to imagine is passing them. And there is no reasonable doubt that a Clinton presidency will focus on building a fairer and more inclusive society. These things account, at least in part, for Clinton's decisive lead in the primary vote and pledged delegates: critically, Clinton enjoys broader support among Democrats than does Sanders—including from minorities who will be critical in November.

Then there is national security, an area where she must combat Donald Trump's empty bluster. To this task Clinton brings a sophisticated grasp of diplomacy, military strategy, and counterterrorism.

To be sure, the Iraq vote was a mistake that Trump, as has Sanders, will make her reckon with—it helped lead to a foreign policy disaster, and it will not suffice to say that she had lots of company. And, for some, Clinton is too inclined to interventions in the Middle East that, inevitably, have as many unintended consequences as those that we intend—assuming, of course, that we can realize even those.

But Iraq was fourteen years ago. And it is too easy to second-guess more recent decisions in a region where both action and inaction can be equally problematic—and which

It is hard to imagine anything much worse than Syria. As a humanitarian disaster it has created millions of dead, displaced, unemployed, and undereducated. And the wave of refugees threatens to destabilize Europe and create a lost generation vulnerable to terrorism.

ISIS uses as a launching pad for terrorism and terrorists. Over time, Hillary Clinton has acquired the knowledge to be president in a dangerous and ever-shifting global environment.

She has thought about this environment in detail and with care. Foreign leaders respect her. She is prepared to deal with issues as disparate as climate change, cyber warfare, and international drug cartels. Her plan for combating ISIS is thorough and considered. She understands counterterrorism and the threat of nuclear proliferation—including nuclear terrorism. She has the sophistication to maintain and build alliances, but also to understand their limits.

During their primary contest, Bernie Sanders has cited Iraq as proof that his judgment is superior, and that experience alone is not enough. But the latter truism is no substitute for an ongoing absorption in the complications of a complex world. That was never a priority for Sanders and, when it comes to picking a president, this matters. And being right on a single vote in 2002, however critical, is no guarantee of mastery of difficult issues in, say, 2018.

One can follow the Sanders campaign and hardly realize that ISIS existed. Foreign affairs and national security remained outside his wheelhouse.

In any event, the alternative to Clinton in November is not Sanders, but the ignorant, xenophobic, chronically offensive, Putin-loving moron Donald Trump. She is as fit to be president as Trump is not. The gap is daunting—the wrong result would be dangerous to America and the world. But to win Clinton must address her own weaknesses as a candidate, reflected in uncomfortably high negatives, and rooted in difficulties that cannot be wished away.

Some derive from twenty-five years of being pounded with lies, distortions, and half-truths, rooted in a pervasive double standard. In a way, this Darwinian experience is oddly reassuring. Hillary Clinton is tough—if she hasn't cracked by now, she never will.

But other problems are self-inflicted. In terms of credibility, the speeches on Wall Street cost her much more than she was paid, and her failure to perceive that suggests a certain tone deafness. Her reasons for not releasing the transcripts are so unpersuasive as to suggest discomfort with the speeches themselves. Similarly, the email problem has grown bigger with each shifting explanation.

Put simply, she does not excel at changing stories or admitting error. And, yes, Iraq truly is the gift that keeps on giving, especially when coupled with the suspicion that Clinton's positions are too often calibrated to suit the public mood.

> Clinton's problems tended to focus on defending her personal conduct, not her policy positions.

The latter, of course, is commonplace. That's how candidates get elected, and the flip side is the tactical flexibility needed to get things done. But, in Clinton, the air of contrivance is exacerbated by the fact that she is not, as events have compelled her to admit, a natural. Too often she exudes caution and, at times, wariness—understandable, to be sure, but unhelpful in conveying passion or authenticity.

All this feeds the perception, fair or not, that, in the immortal word of Congressman Kevin McCarthy, Clinton is "untrustable." There is irony here—by any reasonable measure of truth telling, Clinton's assertions during the campaign are, relative to other candidates, accurate and grounded in fact. But the perception has hurt her nonetheless—including among young women who have forgotten the hard and bitter fight that enabled a woman to run for president at all.

> When it came to talking about policy and issues, according to fact checkers Clinton generally hewed to the truth. Despite the common perception that neither was particularly trustworthy, an enormous gulf separated Clinton's generally responsible statements from Trump's chronic mendacity.

Another problem is that Clinton will need enthusiastic support from a Democratic electorate that is divided in a couple of different ways. One divide is between Clinton past—as examples, the crime bill and welfare reform of the '90s—and this Clinton in the very different present. Both Clintons are addressing this, and must continue to do so in a way that reaches progressives, minorities, and the young:

the alternative, after all, is not some beau ideal, but Donald Trump.

The second divide is between the pragmatic governing philosophy of Hillary Clinton, and the idealistic all-or-nothing populism of Bernie Sanders. Practicality is harder to sell than visionary phrases, and reality is not always a place where all voters want to live.

She cannot make these problems go away. What she can do is continue to remind voters that a president owes them reality, not fantasy—a critique even more apt for Trump than for Sanders. And then—through command, specifics, and an added dollop of passion—persuade the majority of Americans to trust her as president.

This is not the stretch that some might think it. In debate, she is smart, informed, unyielding, and even compelling—one can see her as our president in tough moments. That's a form of trust not easy to come by. And her mastery of policy will be a bracing contrast to Trump's abysmal ignorance. Part of her campaign must be focused on that—relentlessly disqualifying Trump on the issues and, critically, as the unpredictable and unstable megalomaniac that he is.

A second element is convincing Americans that behind her programs is a deep desire to make their lives, and the country itself, better—including a strong and persuasive indictment of the influence of big money in politics. She need not be Bill Clinton or Barack Obama—or, for that matter, Bernie Sanders. What she does need—and what many Americans still want from her—is an animating vision of the better place she wants America to become.

Given her immersion in pressing issues from college on, by now this should not be all that hard. Clearly she is thinking about this; so are others who want her to be president. By email Sam Brown—whose concern this has been since the civil rights and antiwar movements of the

For too many voters, Clinton's animating vision never materialized.

1960s—sketches a platform that, while not meant to be definitive, suggests a template for uniting Democrats and reaching Americans at large.

The basic vision it serves is that only a country that values all its people can be vibrant and strong—now and in the future. With a few additions, I venture it as a starting place:

> We believe that every student in America has the right to a debt-free college education. Because the voice of every citizen should carry equal weight, we support a constitutional amendment to stem the influence of money in politics.
>
> We believe that every American has the right to quality health-care regardless of their means. We believe in providing job retraining, education, and support for Americans dislocated by the forces of globalization.
>
> We believe in a society where opportunity is not defined by wealth. We believe that every American should bear their fair share of paying for our defense, rebuilding our infrastructure, and providing opportunity and security for all.
>
> We believe in protecting the equal rights of every citizen, regardless of race, gender, or sexual orientation. We believe in combating the scourge of gun violence through laws that protect the Second Amendment rights of law-abiding citizens, while keeping guns away from demonstrably dangerous people who would use them to kill others.
>
> We believe that it is imperative to protect our environment and combat climate change. We believe in addressing the complex problems of immigration and providing a path to citizenship for those who wish to be good citizens. We reject scapegoating of any kind, whether it be of Mexicans, Muslims, or those who wish to seek refuge from violence and oppression.

Is there any doubt that Hillary Clinton wants to lead that kind of country? Or that Donald Trump does not?

This was the campaign's goal in planning the Philadelphia convention—and, to a considerable extent, it succeeded.

Her task is to make more Americans see her as that leader—and to believe that our future is not a given, for good or ill, but a choice. If she succeeds, then she can bring this better country closer to reality.

Too Sick to Lead

The Lethal Personality Disorder of Donald Trump

JUNE 3, 2016

Try this as a thought exercise.

The year is 2005. Hungry for prominence, Senator Barack Obama resolves to jump-start his public acclaim. He hits upon a brilliant stratagem: calling Eugene Robinson at the *Washington Post*, he introduces himself as a press aide named John Miller. Recognizing Obama's distinctive cadences and turns of phrase, Robinson is stunned. Reflexively, he turns on his speakerphone.

"John Miller's" orotund voice fills the room, reminding Robinson of Obama's eloquent speech at the 2004 Democratic convention. "Miller" commences bragging about "Obama's" golfing prowess and "huge" book royalties. Though Obama is married, the faux flack then catalogs all the women who want to sleep with the junior senator from Illinois—"Angelina Jolie, for sure. But for a man like Barack Obama she's only a six.

"Beyoncé? She's absolutely desperate for him—it's kind of sad, really. Maybe I—I mean Senator Obama—will give her a break, move her up the waiting list. He's always had a fondness for the audacity of hope. Especially when a woman feels the fierce urgency of now."

In a piece written for The Huffington Post on May 24, with heady overconfidence I predicted that Clinton would carry the electoral college 347–191. Around the same time, the New York Times also forecast this precise number. In short order, Larry Sabato of the Center for Politics, the Cook Political Report, and the Rothenberg & Gonzalez Political Report landed on or near this forecast. The Times, Sabato, and I gave Clinton all the swing states Obama had carried in 2012, plus North Carolina.

(*continued*)

The major problem, it transpired, is that we had underrated Trump's appeal to blue-collar voters in Rust Belt states—Ohio, Michigan, Wisconsin, and Pennsylvania. Still, until the startling intrusion of FBI director James Comey into the race on October 28, I was pretty comfortable with foreseeing a Clinton win with well over 300 electoral votes. So were the overwhelming majority of prognosticators.

Pausing for breath, "Miller" adds in a confidential tone, "I'll tell you one thing—I've never seen anything like this guy. All the success, all the women. Look, I used to work for Denzel Washington and Daniel Craig, but they just don't 'measure up.'"

Stifling his gag reflex, Robinson endures a numbing fifteen-minute soliloquy of self that ends with "Gotta go. Jennifer Aniston just walked into the boss's office. Maybe this time he'll say what every woman wants to hear from him—'Yes, we can.'"

Silent, Robinson absorbs an experience that, mercifully, is unique in his career. Feeling the weight of his journalistic responsibilities, he begins checking to see if anyone else has received calls from Barack Obama pretending to be a staffer. One thing he knows for sure—the country can't afford to elect as president a man whose behavior suggests a serious emotional disorder.

Reading this, did you begin to cringe a little? Writing it, I sure did. And not just because, from Barack Obama, such tasteless and bizarre behavior would be unthinkable.

True, one of the many assets Obama brought to the White House is a peerless dignity and grace—not to mention a sanity grounded in, by the standards of politicians, a rare detachment from self. However one evaluates his presidency, these are among the attributes that should define the word "presidential."

But what moves this piece of fantasy from queasy to distressing is that it measures how precipitously our standards of seemliness and sanity have fallen, and how completely our mass media has failed us. For we are about to embark on a presidential race where one of the contestants is, beyond doubt, emotionally disturbed.

It is that disturbance—not the normal metrics of politics—that explains every aspect of Donald Trump's behavior.

Start with the all-too-real phone call that inspired my opening paragraphs.

In 1991, Sue Carswell, a reporter for *People* magazine, experienced a phenomenon familiar to her peers: calls from supposed PR guys named "John Miller" or "John Barron," gratuitously boasting about Trump's wealth, business success, and romantic prowess. Most bizarre, all agreed, was that the caller spoke and sounded exactly like Trump himself. But this particular call was immortalized on tape.

As others had, Carswell recognized the distinctive voice and accent. Distinctive, too, was the callousness and narcissism of an abysmal—and unbalanced—human being.

Trump was forty-four then, and living with his future second wife Marla Maples. Nonetheless, his boastful "representative" shared for public consumption that "Trump" had "three other girlfriends," detailing at length his alleged romance with Nicolas Sarkozy's future wife Carla Bruni. But not all women were so lucky—for the benefit of *People*'s readers, "Miller" described how Madonna stalked Trump at a charity ball before facing the ultimate devastation: "He's got zero interest that night."

But "Miller" could not stop over-sharing. Among the other women desperately seeking Donald, it turned out, was Kim Basinger. So at least for the moment, Carswell's caller confided, Marla Maples was out of luck—Trump's gift of a ring did not suggest that he would marry her. But Trump believed in "the marriage concept," his alter ego added, making sure that *People*'s readers understood the stakes: "When he makes a decision, that will be a very lucky woman."

Trump being Trump, Carswell also learned that "Trump" was doing "tremendously well financially." On one level, this incredible performance evokes being trapped in a bar with a twentysomething blowhard of a salesman, whose braggadocio becomes more appalling and preposterous with every rum and Coke.

But here's the thing that takes his performance from odious to pathological—Trump wanted a larger audience for his particular brand of self-aggrandizing swill, one in the millions, and was willing to assume a false identity to get it. It didn't matter if he was lying; he didn't care who got hurt. All that counted is what he needed in the moment.

Carswell played the tape for Maples who, after bursting into tears, confirmed that the voice was Trump's. But the reporter need not have bothered.

Trump's signature was in his words: gratuitously cruel, heedless of all but self, reckless in his lust for attention. Were he, say, Anthony Weiner, the call would have been another media-driven nail in the coffin of his public career, fresh evidence of an emotional disorder that rendered him unfit to be a third-tier congressman—let alone mayor of New York.

To meet his needs, Donald Trump wants us to make him president. To meet its own needs, the media—particularly cable news—is helping him.

It has been three weeks since this damning tape surfaced. The story vanished in a day. Confronted with the tape on the *Today* show, Trump told an obvious lie—"it was not me on the phone"—wrapped in his ineradicable narcissism: "I have many, many people who are trying to imitate my voice and . . . you can imagine that. . . . Let's get on to more current subjects."

The media complied.

Which was remarkable. The story is infinitely weirder—and more disturbing—than, say, Joe Biden's uncredited channeling of Neil Kinnock in a speech during his 1987 presidential campaign.

But there is nothing more "current" or important than Donald Trump's psychological fitness to be president. All the hyperventilation of the media—parsing his "positions," pontificating on his "strategy" and intuition—is a poisonous form of the "political correctness" he otherwise deplores, normalizing the abnormal by shoehorning him into the usual analytic boxes. And what it yields is, in great part, rubbish.

There is only one organizing principle that makes sense of his wildly oscillating utterances and behavior—the clinical definition of narcissistic personality disorder.

The Mayo Clinic describes it as "a mental disorder in which people have an inflated sense of their own importance, a deep need for admiration and a lack of empathy for others." This is bad enough in selecting a spouse or a friend. But when applied to a prospective president, the symptoms are disqualifying.

With Trump ever in mind, try these. An exaggerated sense of self-importance. An unwarranted belief in your own superiority. A preoccupation with fantasies of your own success, power, and brilliance. A craving for constant admiration. A consuming sense of entitlement. An expectation of special favors and unquestioning compliance.

A penchant for exploiting or disparaging others. A total inability to recognize the needs of anyone else. An incapacity to see those you meet as individual human beings. An unreasoning fury at people you perceive as thwarting your wishes or desires. A tendency to act on impulse. A superficial charm deployed to disguise a gift for manipulation.

A need to always be right. A refusal to acknowledge error. An inability to tolerate criticism or critics. A compulsion to conform your ever-shifting sense of "reality" to satisfy your inner requirements. A tendency to lie so frequently and routinely that objective truth loses all meaning.

A belief that you are above the rules. An array of inconsistent statements and behaviors driven by your needs in the moment. An inability to assess the consequences of your actions in new or complex situations. In sum, a total incapacity to separate the world from your own psychodrama.

Recognize anyone?

Then how, his admirers say, do you account for Trump's "success" in building a business and branding his persona? That's simple enough: in some areas of life, at least to a point, narcissism and self-aggrandizement serve success. All that is required is a certain intelligence and a sense of how a lack of behavioral constraints can overwhelm more normal folk.

As demonstrated by the fact that, having clinched the nomination, Trump kept repeating these behaviors.

Thus Donald Trump. If your life's work is building hotels and casinos, this pathology can work for you—especially if your dad has started you out with a few million dollars in chips. You can bully subcontractors, sue your enemies, and bury your misjudgments in a slew of bankruptcies and self-glorification. You can make Trump University sound like Harvard. You can use the media to create your own reality and sell it to the credulous. You can leverage your money to make your own rules.

The annals of business are filled with such people, some of whom wind up in jail, others of whom die rich. But however puissant they become in their chosen realm, their sickness of mind and spirit cannot ruin a country. That power is reserved for presidents.

Indeed, Trump's rise simply swells his unwarranted belief that he can stride the world like a colossus—naked of judgment, knowledge, temperament, or preparation. This reflects a fatal deficit in those who suffer this disorder—they cannot see themselves as they are.

To the contrary, their grandiosity is a defense against feelings of inadequacy too deep and painful to acknowledge. By the consensus of mental health experts, this emotional impairment has a last fatal ingredient—there is no cure. For a man like Donald Trump, life offers no lessons, no path forward save to continue as you have until, like Icarus, you fly too close to the sun.

This disability involves far more than a set of discrete character flaws, however grave, including those which suggest a lack of trustworthiness. We survived the dishonesty and paranoia of Richard Nixon, after all, albeit at considerable cost and only after forcing him from office.

But in many ways Nixon was well-equipped for the presidency, capable of navigating the larger world and understanding complex situations and people—as in China and its leaders. He did not reflexively substitute a grossly inflated sense of self for knowledge, strategy, or preparation. His

> Trump is the latest—and by far the clearest—demonstration that the idea that business success translates into presidential capacity is nonsense. Nor can our complex constitutional democracy ever be "run like a business."

tragedy, and ours, was that his crippling inner wounds out-stripped his proven strengths.

Donald Trump is altogether different—and infinitely more dangerous. He is afflicted with a comprehensive and profound character disorder that leaves no corner of his psyche whole. And this dictates—and explains—every aspect of his behavior.

Take his recourse to bullying and slander. "I'm a coun-terpuncher," he rationalizes. "[I]'ve been responding to what they did to me." Now we understand, Donald—your ene-mies made you do it.

Really? So Heidi Cruz made him ridicule her looks on Twitter? That handicapped reporter made him imitate his disabilities at a rally? His mockery of John Kasich's table manners was payback for opposing him? And who can forget Marco Rubio's sweat glands—"Little Marco" deserved it, after all, for standing in the way.

Or Megyn Kelly, whose question about sexist behav-ior forced him to accuse her of menstrual moodiness. Or the Republican governor of New Mexico—a Latina—who he trashed for failing to appear with him. Or any other Republican who won't climb on his bandwagon—like "that choker" Mitt Romney, a "stupid" man who "walks like a penguin." And on and on—the list of enemies he must demean is infinite.

A recent example typifies his psychological imbalance. Speaking at a rally in San Diego, he tried to shame an otherwise obscure federal judge in the city, who is presid-ing over a lawsuit against Trump University. Trump called the Indiana-born judge a "Mexican," a "hater of Donald Trump," and a "very hostile person" who had "railroaded" him. Heedless of his position or his audience, Trump wal-lowed in his personal grievances so long that his listeners grew restive. And so, yet again, the campaign for presi-dent descended into the poisonous murk of Trump's inner world.

Any second-rate politician who could pass a Rorschach test would have known better than to denounce the Khan family. That Trump could not help himself was a telling indication of his compulsions.

This astoundingly graceless and unpresidential behavior is far too pointless and indiscriminate to qualify as strategy or tactics. The common thread in all this lashing out—often at those who can't fight back—is that it has nothing to do with issues, or anything else one would expect from a normal candidate. It is another symptom of Trump's pathology—the visceral reflex to humiliate and degrade anyone who displeases him, no matter the context or situation.

Take the media. Where, one might ask, would Trump be without its constant and credulous attentions? But, like everyone else, the media can never do enough to feed his needs. He threatens the owners of newspapers with reprisals by the federal government, talks of changing libel laws to facilitate lawsuits for statements that affront him, proposes revoking FCC licenses of media that ruffle him. CNN is "very unprofessional"; like so many others, Fox has treated him "very unfairly."

He refers to the media that cover him as "scum." He singles out by name reporters who dare to challenge him. At rallies, he pens up journalists in areas they are not permitted to leave. A week ago, he used his rally to abuse reporters who had raised legitimate questions about his self-proclaimed contributions to veterans causes, calling one a "sleaze," and expressing anger that the media did not praise him. After all, Trump says, he's "fighting for survival"—ever victimized by hostile forces who fail to recognize his innate superiority.

Opposition of any kind enrages him. He incites reprisals against protesters. He threatened violence in Cleveland as payback for the GOP's "unfairness." He fuels anger against Latinos, Muslims, and other minorities that he perceives as inimical. And never—not once—does he take any responsibility for stirring these toxic pots. For one of the symptoms of his disability is an absence of conscience or accountability.

So what did women do to him, one wonders? The offense was obviously grave, for his misogyny is endless and, it seems, uncontrollable. One can but identify the same symptoms that drive his comprehensive impulse to demean—the need to dominate, displeasure at feeling thwarted, and, of course, a profound lack of empathy for anyone but himself.

But for Trump, ever beset, his empathy is boundless. His view of others vacillates wildly based solely on their deference to him—or lack of it. One hesitates to consider what would happen should Vladimir Putin, who Trump elevates for flattering him, challenge Trump as president.

Which brings us to a central problem of Trump's warped psychology—he believes that filling the presidency requires nothing but the wonder of himself. This gives the lie to GOP's most craven rationalization of its own capitulation: that a suddenly docile Trump will, as president, defer to a cadre of wise and experienced advisers drawn from the party establishment.

This is pernicious nonsense. Consistent with his character disorder, Trump proudly insists that his chief adviser is himself. Even were he so inclined, in order to learn from others he must know enough to discern good advice from bad. But such is his pathology that he feels no need to learn much of anything from anyone. And so, from the beginning, he has plunged us down the bottomless rabbit hole of his intellectual emptiness.

There was a certain grim amusement in watching Reince Priebus wallow in the mud bath of reality.

His ignorance and grandiosity form a lethal compound. He disowns NATO, unaware that he is playing into Putin's hands; blithely proposes nuclear proliferation in Asia; muses aloud about using nuclear weapons; and imagines negotiating one-on-one with North Korea's psychotic leader. He proposes a trade war potentially ruinous to the world economy. He abets ISIS and Al-Qaeda by scapegoating all Muslims at home and abroad. Oblivious to the appalled reaction around the globe, he promises to compel the respect of world leaders through "the aura of personality."

His equally spurious domestic "proposals," such as they may be, reflect nothing but the unreality of his own self-concept. His tax plan is absurd on its face. His astonishing proposal to trash America's credit by defaulting on our debt reveals an inability to differentiate between running a casino and running a country. His posturing for the NRA is as dangerous as it is dishonest.

But to talk of Trump in terms of issues is to flatter him. Most of what he says is provisional, ever subject to change, and based on nothing but his needs at the moment. After all, he tells us, "Everything is subject to negotiation, but I can't and won't be changing much, because voters support me because of what I'm saying and how I'm saying it."

Such is his imbalance that he cannot distinguish between a real issue, like combating ISIS, and exhuming the hoary and discredited conspiracy theories surrounding the death of Vincent Foster. When it comes to protecting the planet, global warming is a "hoax"; when it comes to protecting his seaside Scottish golf course, he cites climate change as the reason for demanding that the locals stem the rising tides with, naturally, a wall.

Disclose his tax returns? That's for lesser beings—like every other candidate in the modern era. Never mind that he excoriated Mitt Romney for not disclosing his; for Trump himself, it's "none of your business." Once again the unifying factor is the symptoms of this pathology: his need for adulation—for sure Trump is not nearly as rich as he claims; his lack of empathy—his charitable giving is no doubt paltry; and his compulsive rule bending—he likely paid little or no tax.

As for his excuse for nondisclosure—an audit—this is a transparent lie. But Trump lies and changes stories so routinely that we are becoming numb. The only constant is the gnawing hunger of Trump's misshapen psyche. What is most terrible to contemplate is investing his pathology with the power of the presidency.

One can forecast the inevitable day-to-day damage to our country—the lashing out, the abuses of power, the mercurial and confidence-destroying lies and changes of mind, the

havoc his distorted lens would wreak upon our institutions
and our spirit. But most dangerous of all is the collision
between a volatile world, a leader unable to perceive external reality, and the often unbearable pressures of the presidency. That Trump's judgment would crack time and again
is certain—the only question is how dangerous the moment.

So how have we fallen prey to a man who, by the damning evidence of his own behavior, is psychologically unfit to
be president? When did boasting top coherence; mindless
posturing become strength; a talent for ridicule supplant
experience or judgment; a gift for scapegoating surpass wisdom or generosity? Why must we even contemplate someone
with this stunted inner landscape as the world's most powerful person?

Much of the answer lies in a failure of our institutions—
governmental, economic, political, and social—to maintain
our trust. This has bred a popular flailing born of frustration
and despair: the desire to tear down those structures that, all
too many feel, have betrayed us. We can see it in the refusal
of Trump's followers to accept any criticism of their leader;
see it, too, in the cadre of Sanders supporters who insist that
electing Trump will unleash the chaos from which revolution
springs. For all too many, anger has drowned reason.

But two institutions deserve special condemnation.

First, the Republican Party. For too long it fed easy
scapegoats to the GOP's middle- and working-class
base—Washington, minorities—while the Paul Ryans of the
party contravened its voters' interests: pushing free trade,
reduced entitlements, and tax cuts for the rich. Trump is
what happened to the party when its electorate spat this
pablum out.

Even more contemptible is the party's embrace of Trump.
For we have reached, as David Brooks wrote, the GOP's
"McCarthy moment"—a turning point when concern for
country should override grubby pragmatism. Except this
reckoning is even more pressing—Joe McCarthy was not

running for president; Donald Trump is. We cannot—must not—invest him with this power.

Beyond peradventure, Trump's incapacities transcend issues or ideology, or the most vehement objections to the policies or persona of Hillary Clinton. It is one thing to preserve the party by fighting for its congressional candidates. But by pretending that Trump is fit to be president, the Republican Party has become the political and moral equivalent of a criminally callous auto manufacturer, willing to sell cars with defective airbags and exploding gas tanks.

Worse—for they are not selling us combustible cars; they are selling out the country. It is hard to put a name to their dishonor.

But, with honorable exceptions, the broadcast media has been even more shameful and complicit. Worst of all is cable news—in pursuit of revenue and ratings, they have given Trump $3 billion in free advertising, feeding his candidacy—and his ego—by spreading the mythology of his imperviousness and power.

Wallowing in self-interest, they have shrunk from saying what must be said: that Trump is unfit for higher office. Instead, they have breathlessly parsed his every move as if he were something grander, yet more normal, than a mentally disordered demagogue bereft of principles and starved for adulation.

Only lately have a few talking heads begun to notice, with perplexity and wonder, that Trump's behavior is, well, kind of strange. Really? They have countenanced lie upon lie; recast his disturbed behavior as strategic genius; marveled at the immunity from his own vacuity and vulgarity that they have helped create. Even more than Trump himself, they have thrust "Trump" upon a confused and vulnerable country. By doing so, they have disgraced themselves and betrayed their obligations to the rest of us.

One thinks of Edward R. Murrow's admonition when so many of his peers in television cowered before Joseph

McCarthy: "This instrument can teach, it can illuminate, and even inspire, but only if humans go to the extent to use it. Otherwise it is merely wires and a box." Or, now, something worse—a tool of disinformation and intellectual and moral degradation, turned over to a dangerously unbalanced man for whom this is the essence of his nature.

The Republican Party is beyond redemption. The media have five months left. Let them use it well.

An entire book could be written on how the media helped to elevate Donald Trump, especially during the primary season. And no doubt will be.

From Golden Boy to Fool's Gold

The Decline of Paul Ryan

JUNE 14, 2016

It is strange to see Paul Ryan looking like the subject of a hostage video.

This, of course, is the effect of being confronted by reporters with the existence of Donald Trump. But Ryan became a prisoner long ago—first, of the rigidity of his ideas; second, of his party's fratricide and incoherence. Beneath the narcissistic railings of a carnival barker Ryan surely hears the premonitory echoes of his own political demise.

True, Ryan has more going for him than the right-wing *lumpenproletariat* of the House Republican caucus, whose shrill rhetoric and dull intellect reflect the primitive world of gerrymandered districts, separated by talk radio from the reality that lies beyond.

He radiates clean living, with the pleasantly sharp-featured and sincere affect of a dedicated high school gym teacher. Buoyed by his Catholic faith and a secure and prosperous family, he endured losses while still young—the sudden death of his father, a grandmother afflicted with Alzheimer's. He became serious before his time, a hard worker in and out of school. He was marked for leadership early.

In this crowd, Ryan looks like Erasmus of Rotterdam. The reality is more second-tier Jack Kemp. Ryan's stated interest in the poor garnishes conventional supply-side thinking.

Politics does not seem to have changed his essence. He sleeps in his office, goes home to his family in Wisconsin as soon and often as he can. His pursuits are the same—hunting and fishing—and so are his friends from youth. By all appearances, he is as grounded as politics allows. And, more than his Republican peers, he has a passion for ideas.

But here, for many, lies the problem—those ideas, too, are rooted in his youth. Specifically, college—that heady time of imbalance between intellectual self-confidence and one's actual experience of life.

Most of us recover. But Ryan, perhaps, less than most. Thus his distressingly attenuated enthusiasm for the novels of Ayn Rand. Though the young Ryan was also devoted to the free-market abstractions of Friedrich Hayek and Ludwig von Mises, Rand became his intellectual wellspring.

For those whose short memories confer a certain mercy, a refresher course. In the estimate of critics, Rand's prose style is turgid and declamatory. But the real problem is her worldview.

In Rand's telling, altruism is a sham, social consciousness a cover for envy of one's betters, government the enemy of individual enterprise. Only the creative selfishness practiced by a small class of capitalist superpeople—the sole characters for whom Rand does not feel a withering contempt—can rise above our collective mediocrity.

This is social Darwinism run amok—a Hobbesian landscape in which, quite tellingly, no children appear to complicate her avatars' single-minded pursuit of wealth. It is a world that has never existed, and never will, save in the minds of readers privileged enough—and, in candor, white enough—to imagine it in safety.

To say the least, Rand's appeal to the political lab rats who comprise the Republican base—embattled white- and blue-collar folks—is roughly zero. But such has been Ryan's enthusiasm for Rand that, until it became an embarrassment, it seemed near-boundless.

Well into his congressional career, he credited Rand for inspiring him to enter public service; cited her as the source of his value system; and required his staffers to read her novels. "Ayn Rand," he asserted, "did the best job of anybody making a moral case for capitalism." Even now, his quarrel is not with her dystopian economics, but her atheism.

Thus the yawning gulf—too little noted for far too long—between the philosophy of Paul Ryan and the actual lives of Republican-base voters to whom he must appeal.

Start with the eponymous "Ryan Budget."

For lack of competition, Ryan has become the GOP's "serious thinker" on fiscal matters. In college, a friend recalls, Ryan's serious thinking centered on vigorous advocacy of trickle-down economics. Problem is, it still does.

In its various iterations, the Ryan Budget offers enormous tax cuts for the wealthy; eliminates taxation of capital gains, dividends, and interest; and abolishes the corporate income and estate tax. Some versions partially privatize Social Security; privatize Medicare; fund Medicaid through block grants to the states; and eliminate the tax exclusion for employer-sponsored health insurance. Other versions decimate Medicaid and eliminate Obamacare without anything to take its place.

In a time when many students are buckling under the weight of student loans, the Ryan plan tightens eligibility for Pell Grants, drastically reducing the potential beneficiaries while shrinking the amounts available. Student loans begin accruing interest while the students are still in school. And, ironically, Ryan champions the for-profit colleges which, in many cases, are an expensive consumer fraud paid for by looting Pell Grants.

None of these proposals addresses the needs of those embattled workers on whom the GOP depends. But Ryan advocates these measures as a grown-up effort to balance the budget. Far from it, for the plans are rooted in wishful thinking, calculated evasions, and lousy math. This is ideology, not budgeting. And it marks Ryan's besetting weakness: a preference for philosophy over fact.

Examples? Ryan's math depends on a hoary assumption that has been empirically disproven time and again—that tax cuts at the top increase economic growth and, like magic, generate more tax revenues. Thus Ryan skips over enormous revenue losses that will inevitably explode the deficit.

But his intellectual dishonesty is far more comprehensive. He proposes to eliminate tax loopholes and deductions—which remain nameless. And he assumes zero growth in domestic discretionary spending—which, according to *New York Times* columnist Paul Krugman, means a 25 percent cut, adjusted for inflation and increased population.

This would further slash spending on transportation, education, housing, health-related research, veterans' assistance, homeland security, the justice system, and environmental protection. Ryan spells out none of this.

Inescapably, the plan punishes the most vulnerable. It cuts down on food stamps, unemployment insurance, and, of course, entitlement programs that can be reformed in far less draconian ways. And virtually all the tax cuts go to the top 1 percent. Little wonder, then, that Ryan is a favorite of the Republican donor classes, including the funding circles of Paul Singer and the Koch brothers.

Little wonder, too, that students of the Ryan plan assert that it would markedly increase poverty and income inequality. With a few more tweaks, one could fairly call it the Ayn Rand Budget.

For edification and amusement, try Googling "Paul Krugman and Paul Ryan."

But reality has started gaining on Paul Ryan—fast.

In 2010, he and his House cohorts—Eric Cantor and Kevin McCarthy—recruited congressional candidates from the hard right by stoking Tea Party anger. But that same anger led to Cantor's humiliating primary defeat by an extreme right-winger. And then the trio's rageful janissaries brought down John Boehner and blocked McCarthy's bid to succeed him.

Desperate, the Republican caucus offered Ryan the speakership. His reluctance to accept this poisoned chalice was painful to watch. He knew too well the forces that awaited him—he had helped put them where they were, and now they were consuming their political parents. Only Ryan was untouched.

And so this man of ideas went from the safety of floating dubious budgets to presiding over a caucus beset by extremists. Worse, he assumed responsibility for one branch of a divided government, where the only alternatives to compromise are impotence or apocalypse—shutting the place down.

So far impotence is winning.

Ryan can't turn the "Ryan Budget" into law—if the Senate didn't block it, President Obama would. But too many in his caucus won't support a compromise, even one that achieves key Republican priorities. Indeed, some of his right-wing progeny will only follow Ryan if he jumps off the fiscal cliff—a political death spiral for his own career.

In short, the GOP's presumptive savior is being swallowed by his own ideas and those who believe in them most fiercely.

And now comes Donald Trump.

Ryan's dilemma was captured by his recent announcement of a plan to fight poverty and unemployment through block grants to the states. This proposal, at least, is interesting, though it requires an increase in funding that his caucus is unlikely to embrace. Moreover, it included a truly Randian proposal—repealing a new government regulation requiring that retirement advisers serve the interests of their clients, instead of profiting by steering them into high-cost investments. And the announcement itself—set in a struggling DC neighborhood—was overwhelmed by reporters' questions regarding the latest idiocy from Trump.

One problem with the GOP, a rueful Republican leader once told a journalist friend of mine, is that "too many in my party hate poor people."

This moment, too, was rich in irony. For the stark truth is that Trump is a political mutation spawned by Paul Ryan's "ideas."

Ryan has long stood for tax cuts for the wealthy; free trade; slashing entitlements; shredding the social safety net; reforming immigration to benefit employers; and other nostrums favored by the commercial interests that fund the party. So how have Ryan and the GOP sold this to their base?

They haven't, really. Instead the GOP offered diversionary scapegoats for their voters' economic insecurity: inefficient government, welfare recipients, and thinly veiled attacks on Democratic "interest groups"—i.e., minorities.

In his crude and opportunistic way, Trump ripped the party's mask off. He took the tacit racism of all too many Republican officeholders and made it overt—targeting Muslims, Latinos, and, with barely less subtlety, blacks. He said that free trade agreements betrayed American workers. He stood up against cuts in Social Security and Medicare. He questioned tax cuts for the rich. And, of course, he promised to build that wall.

In sum, he was everything that Paul Ryan is not. And the base loved him for it. Only Trump's historical illiteracy prevented him from narcissistically misappropriating Martin Luther King Jr. by telling his followers that, under "Trump," they would be "free at last"—in this case from Ryan and the Republican donor classes.

For them, Trump poses a hydra-headed problem. He has pretty well trashed their free-trade agenda: to the distress of Chamber of Commerce types, Trump is competing with Bernie Sanders for restive voters displaced by the global economy. In the process, he has turned the GOP's attack on identity politics into a defense of embattled white folks against the supposed depredations of a multiracial society.

Establishment Republicans were horrified. Though too intimidated to say very much, they knew that Trump's

Until Trump embraced them. For the general election, he turned over his economic thinking to ossified supply-siders like Larry Kudlow and Stephen Moore. This is how we learned that Arthur Laffer is still alive.

alienation of minorities was a demographic loser. And when racism stops whispering and starts screaming, polite Republicans begin squirming.

And so, yet again, they turned to Paul Ryan. Not only was he the party's highest-ranking elected official, but its defender of serious ideas—indeed, its very conscience. He became the GOP's St. Thomas More, its man for all seasons.

And so, like More, he dithered. Perhaps because he knows too well how the story ends, and dreads his own political beheading.

For weeks, he refrained from endorsing Trump, providing cover for worried Republicans while cloaking himself in principle. But for a man bent on preserving his own political life and, quite likely, running for president, this pose had a half-life of its own.

To pave the way for an endorsement, Ryan pretended to believe that the narcissistic casino magnate was buying into his serious ideas, facilitating their passage should Trump become president. But in the primaries Trump had kicked his agenda to the curb, and now was treating Ryan to condescension and veiled threats. And in Ryan's own caucus, nervous Republicans were pushing him to back their presumptive nominee.

At last he did so, penning a letter to his hometown newspaper that, it was clear, he wished were written in invisible ink. Promptly, Trump rewarded him by attacking the federal judge presiding over a lawsuit against the bogus Trump University—converting a respected Indiana-born jurist into a biased "Mexican" resentful of Trump's wall.

Confronted with this evidence of blatant racism—not to mention emotional disturbance—Ryan was compelled at the anti-poverty press conference to denounce Trump's virulence as "the textbook definition of a racist comment." And then this apostle of Republican inclusiveness reaffirmed his support for Trump—because, after all, he would be better than Hillary Clinton.

Really? Paul Ryan truly prefers that a narcissistic, igno-rant, ungovernable, unqualified, race-baiting, misogy-nistic moron becomes our next president? The *New York Daily News* captured the moment perfectly, tagging photos of Trump and Ryan with the lethal headline: "I'm With Racist!"

It will only get worse.

On Sunday, Trump reacted to the slaughter perpe-trated by a demented ISIS sympathizer at a gay nightclub in Orlando with the odious demagoguery that is his trademark, doubling down on his call for a ban on all Muslims from abroad, asserting that American Muslims at large "know what's going on" regarding terrorism, and congratulating himself on his supposed prescience in identifying thcse threats. He then topped this dangerous and irresponsible scapegoating—so damaging to our national security and national fabric—by implying that President Obama was complicit in, or at least tolerant of, terrorist violence against Americans. With every repugnant utterance from Trump, Paul Ryan becomes a little smaller.

And so, in the end, Ryan is not merely a captive in Trump's hostage video. He is a politician caught between his rejected ideology, and the racist pseudo-populism of an interloper who emerged from the political and moral void he and his party helped create.

Trump, of course, will lose. But he will leave behind a Republican *Titanic*, headed for an electoral iceberg that will shatter the party for years to come.

Ryan may survive as speaker by clinging to some piece of ideological flotsam—if only because no one else will want the job. But he will never rise above the waterline—not in 2020, or ever. The shipwreck is catastrophic, and its fatalities include the party's would-be savior, President Paul Ryan.

It did. With every extreme statement by Trump, Ryan tried to straddle disagreement and support, until he resembled a man with each foot on two separate icebergs that were drifting apart. As the straddle grew more painful, his stature diminished. In fairness, Ryan was stuck trying to protect the GOP majority in the House while attempting to manage contending forces in his own caucus.

Wrong again. Despite the GOP's fragmentation, Trump won—with James Comey's considerable assistance. This likely saved Ryan's job as Speaker. Left undetermined is how Trump's populism melds with Ryan's free-market ideology, and where the Tea Party fits in. The power struggle has just begun.

The 2016 Veepstakes
Who Will Trump and Clinton Choose?

JUNE 28, 2016

There is no surer sign that a writer has pundititis than to start picking vice presidential nominees. It's a God-given chance to be dead wrong in public—twice. And so I simply can't resist the temptation to reveal—with my usual uncanny accuracy—the identity of the next vice president of the United States.

Just so you know, my lens is cold-eyed realism—what is likely to happen, not who I'd prefer, or what might occur in a better cosmos. All I'm trying to do is make an informed guess in the context of current political realities as I perceive them, tested by conversations with smart insiders from both parties.

That said, here goes.

Democrats first. Maybe this is cheating. But it's always easier to make guesses when the nominee doing the choosing is, whatever you might think of him or her, sane.

In this case, Hillary Clinton. Not only is she in charge of all her faculties; she's experienced in politics and governance. Which makes her more predictable, and narrows the field of choices.

Let's start with the four basic templates for picking a running mate.

The first is trying to carry your choice's home state. This is more discussed than real: in the last ten election cycles, the vice presidential choice has given the ticket an average 1.1 percent bump in his or her state. As the latest example, the Romney–Ryan ticket lost Wisconsin.

The second is to add some assets to the ticket. Most recently, Barack Obama compensated for his lack of foreign policy experience by picking Joe Biden.

The third is to amp up some excitement. By selecting Al Gore, Bill Clinton sent a message of generational change.

The fourth, and perhaps the most widely honored, is to be sure the nominee—whatever else they might offer—doesn't do the campaign any harm. Here the best example is the train wreck that can happen when you don't take this into account—Sarah Palin.

So let's consider how all this fits with Hillary Clinton.

To start, she need not pick a vice president to help her navigate Washington, or to persuade voters that she has someone more seasoned to call on. So she is free to weigh the remaining criteria based on personal preference and practical political advantage.

Among other things, these potential determinants include a person with whom Clinton feels comfortable, and whose loyalty she can count on. A person who appeals to important party constituencies or, perhaps, might help pick up a state—though, as noted, the latter is less a factor than people think. A person unlikely to do harm.

One critical element is that the existence of Donald Trump gives Clinton greater leeway. Obviously, it would be quite helpful if Sanders voters felt enthusiastic about her choice. But the prospect of Trump as president will help consolidate many of them—though certainly not all. And Trump's gift for alienating minorities makes it less imperative that Clinton pick a Latino or African American.

As president, Clinton would like a Senate controlled by Democrats. This cuts against choosing a senator from a state with a Republican governor who would choose the replacement.

Finally, because Clinton has a problem with white guys, an appealing male candidate might help more than would a woman. Still, one way for Clinton to get a second look from voters who don't like her is to depart from stereotype by making a daring choice.

So let's start narrowing the field.

Bernie Sanders? The selection of Sanders would help cement support from the millions inspired by his campaign. But there are compelling reasons why this will never happen.

The biggest is that Sanders is simply not a vice presidential type. It is difficult to imagine him as a loyal messenger for Clinton, deprived of the freedom to advance his own agenda. Sanders should not want this, and it does not serve his interests.

For many of the same reasons, as well as the absence of personal closeness, Sanders would not be a comfortable subordinate for Clinton. And when the presidential nominee is in her late sixties, the heart that is one heartbeat away probably should not be seven years older. Sanders stays in the Senate.

Elizabeth Warren? More likely than Sanders, to be sure. She's principled, and shares many of those principles with Bernie. Nobody tears into Trump any better, or enjoys it more—it's as though God designed The Donald to embody every loathsome attribute that Warren despises in her bones. She would add fire to the ticket, and it's fun to think of Clinton countering Trump's misogyny by doubling down on the historic nature of her candidacy.

One of the curiosities of contemporary politics is the gap between progressive adoration of Warren and her private reputation as chilly and self-protective.

Their first joint appearance was surprisingly comfortable and devastatingly effective. Of the vice presidential prospects, Warren is easily the most electric, at least for the progressive left. All that raises her prospects of being chosen.

But Warren is not generally known for tractability, and she and Clinton do not have a close relationship. She's ambitious, inner directed, and would not happily share the stage with the two Presidents Clinton, current or former. Her history includes several sharp attacks on Clinton, and Wall Street doesn't like her—though that could cut both ways.

In all likelihood, her name is being floated to propitiate the Democratic left. But Warren could do her work as a surrogate almost as well outside the ticket. The speculation that Brexit ups the chances of a more populist candidate like Warren strikes me as overblown, the usual media over-reaction to the immediate in a campaign season with over four months yet to go. And a Republican governor would appoint her successor, albeit for a shorter time under Massachusetts law. All in all, it still seems unlikely that Warren will be chosen.

Cory Booker? Good for some excitement, though his tenure in the Senate has been unremarkable. A bit too young and unseasoned, perhaps. If Clinton tapped him, Chris Christie would put a Republican in his place. African Americans are with her already. And come the fall, America's premier black politician will be campaigning for Clinton as if his legacy depended on it.

Obscure white guys from swing states? This includes Senator Michael Bennet and Governor John Hickenlooper from Colorado, and Congressman Tim Ryan from Ohio. But trying to win a single state doesn't trump everything else, and Trump's problems with Latinos has likely given Clinton Colorado. Ohio is a bigger deal, but Ryan is not a bigger name.

Secretary of Labor Tom Perez? No one knows him. And there are other Latino officeholders who can bring more passion to the stump.

So here are my finalists.

Sherrod Brown. But for one not-so-small problem, Brown would be my odds-on pick. He's articulate, smart, and well regarded, a senator with genuine appeal to blue-collar voters.

Aside from Tim Kaine, the finalist turned out to be Perez and another well-respected white guy who did not figure in the early speculation—Tom Vilsack.

And he could help Clinton carry Ohio, a devastating blow to Trump.

Brown supported Clinton in the primaries, and she clearly likes him. But on many issues, such as TPP, Brown has more in common with Bernie Sanders—a good thing for the ticket. And less skilled politicians skate past their differences all the time.

So what's not to like? Simply this—John Kasich would appoint Brown's successor, jeopardizing the Democrats' chances of flipping the Senate. The question is whether Clinton prefers Brown so much that she would risk this—and all the pushback that would follow. Probably not.

Tim Kaine. For good reason, he's the walking definition of this year's conventional wisdom—a steady, likable, and capable if unexciting white guy. He speaks fluent Spanish. He has been a widely respected governor and senator from Virginia, a swing state, and a Democrat would appoint his successor. And as a former party chair, he knows every donor in the country.

If "first do no harm" is Clinton's chief criterion, Kaine is the obvious choice. But he would provide little in the way of spark, particularly for the Democratic left, who may remember his support for TPP. For those who perceive Hillary Clinton as overcautious, picking Kaine would be Exhibit A. Still, by tradition presidential nominees choose running mates who reliably hit singles, rather than hoping for home runs. That's Kaine.

Julián Castro. The secretary of HUD—smart, articulate, youthful, and Latino. Choosing Castro would link Clinton to our demographic future—he personifies the ways in which America is changing, and might attract some of the young people who found Sanders so compelling. As a matter of sheer optics, he and Clinton would make a good-looking ticket.

But Clinton has the Latino vote already. Castro can't help her carry Texas—no one could. He has not really been

A powerful senator close to Clinton told me that he had emphasized to her that controlling the Senate was the first priority, her preference in a running mate secondary. One suspects that this did Brown in.

Once chosen, he was steady and helpful. Singles count.

tested on the national stage. And he looks even younger than he is—a bit too young, perhaps.

Still, if the ongoing political dynamic persuades Clinton that the ticket needs some excitement, Castro is the safest exciting choice. In this way, he could be the ultimate beneficiary of the desire for sizzle stoked by Elizabeth Warren.

My pick? In order of likelihood, Kaine, then Castro, then Brown. If the nominee turns out to be someone I've never mentioned, even to discount, feel free to remind me.

So far, so good.

But for real fun there's always the Republicans.

Donald Trump adds that extra dash of excitement that only self-absorption can provide. It's not every election year that the choice of a vice president turns, not on political calculations that can be fathomed by the normal mind, but on the daily oscillations of a profound personality disorder that are, to put it mildly, elusive—perhaps even to Trump himself.

There is simply no book for handicapping the choices of a major party candidate whose narcissism eclipses the historic competition. This elevates the risk of punditry from walking through a cow pasture to navigating a minefield. There is simply no telling when something will blow up.

Were Trump not so riveted by Trump himself, he would give the qualities required in a running mate the most considered thought. Republican insiders swear that he has. In this telling, and occasionally in Trump's, he knows that he needs a "governing choice"—an experienced officeholder whose selection will help compensate for his own lack of, well, pretty much everything one might hope for in a president.

Given Trump, this is no small task. Sadly, those who might be up to it—say George Washington or Abraham Lincoln—are unavailable. And even were they at hand, who can say that The Donald would recognize their qualities as equal to his own?

For once, Trump followed advice—and appeared to hate it.

However, just last week he exercised the kind of leadership he showed on *The Apprentice*—he fired Corey

Lewandowski. So let's assume that he chooses a running mate with Paul Manafort whispering in his ear, rather than looking in the mirror and seeing Jesse Ventura.

The initial problem, then, would not be who he chooses, but who won't run screaming into the night from imagining four years of subservience to Donald Trump. And then there is a related problem—out of sheer self-respect, most credible prospects have been forced to utter some criticism of Trump. The Sun King, as we know, does not gratefully brook dissenters.

On both fronts, it would seem, John Kasich is disqualified. Even if Trump could overlook the fact that Kasich has yet to endorse him, the Ohio governor is just principled enough, and prickly enough, not to embarrass himself by running with a nominee so transcendently unfit.

More broadly, how many politicians with a future want to endure the shame and abuse of serving as second lieutenant on Trump's *Titanic*? Which opens up a frightening prospect: bereft of respectable choices, Trump falls back on his own instincts and gives us—God knows who.

Mike Pence came from nowhere. Part of the reason no one thought of him was that he was running for reelection for governor of Indiana. What went unnoticed is that he was in danger of losing and looking for a way out.

By trade, I'm a novelist, and for years exercised my imagination for a living. But channeling Donald Trump is where the standard powers of invention flag. All I can do is deal with the more or less conventional choices that might flit, like fireflies, through the shadowy recesses of Trump's mind.

So let's dispatch a few of the wilder possibilities.

Marco Rubio? Despite the vehemence of his last-ditch attacks on Trump, Rubio has one indispensable qualification—the political spine of a mollusk. But, ever ambitious, Rubio has reversed his supposedly ironclad pledge, and is running for reelection to the Senate.

Chris Christie? Last seen fetching Trump a hamburger, he has morphed from attack dog to lapdog—standing next to his master, he has a glazed look of a former mastiff who has undergone a prefrontal lobotomy. This may be Trump's most astounding achievement—shrinking Chris Christie.

His poll numbers in New Jersey are shrinking too. Put him down for Attorney General.

Rick Scott. I owe this speculation to reports that Florida's governor is on Trump's short list. But even mulling Scott pushes the swing state criteria to idiotic levels. In his prior life, Scott resigned as CEO of a health care company after it committed numerous felonies in overbilling the federal government. Not exactly the kind of business experience a dubious businessman would desire in a running mate.

Even as a parochial politician, Scott is mediocre—not articulate, not very popular, and certainly not smart. One cringes to think of him set loose under the klieg lights of a national campaign. He adds little in Florida, and nothing outside its borders. At best a wasted pick; at worst a terrible one.

Female governors? Sounds good, until you start to think about them.

Mary Fallin? Her major distinction is that she is the climate change–denying governor of a bright red state, Oklahoma. Sarah Palin leaps to mind. Perhaps Fallin could help Trump a bit with white women of modest discernment. But she adds no weight to the ticket, and any of the Democratic prospects for vice president would murder her in a debate.

Nikki Haley? Better, assuming that she would take it. But she, too, has not endured the rigors of national politics. And the experience of Sarah Palin has left the GOP terrified of the unknown.

Susanna Martinez? Better yet. But by excoriating Martinez in public, Trump blew his chances, proving only that he has the political and personal judgment of a deeply troubled toddler.

Any female at all? There's always Carly Fiorina, who would walk across ground glass for the chance to run with anyone. Her gift for political venom is unimpeded by fact. But the claim that she and Trump combine stellar business acumen would founder on an unfortunate fact—her

Forget that. The trial emanating from the Bridgegate scandal killed off Christie's chances. We can all look forward to Attorney General Rudy Giuliani.

business record, if it is possible, is even more execrable than his. So the fact that she has all the warmth of an anaconda is merely excess baggage.

Finally, John Thune. This one is a puzzler. The South Dakota senator is a conventional, presentable conservative, popular among his colleagues, and, as politicians go, unassuming. Recently, his name has surfaced in Beltway speculation. But he would seem to have little in common with Trump, personally or ideologically. And unlike his senatorial colleagues Bob Corker and Jeff Sessions, he is not known to have a relationship with The Donald.

In the past, Thune has pondered a run for president. Paying lip service to a narcissist while subordinating his own beliefs could well tarnish whatever national ambitions he still entertains. Given Trump's alternatives, Thune would certainly be a more than decent pick—though Corker seems a better one. But from the perspective of either man, especially Thune, it's hard to see why Thune would become Trump's choice.

So who does this leave?

Newt Gingrich. Granted, this requires a certain flexibility in defining "conventional"—if only because, between them, the two prospective running mates have been married six times. Here, again, age is a problem—Gingrich is even older than the seventy-year-old Trump. And if Trump is a Roman candle, the volatile Gingrich is at least a firecracker, likely to go off in your hand.

Among journalists looking for entertainment, Gingrich was the sentimental favorite.

No doubt he is a fountain of inventiveness. Bob Dole used to joke that he kept two file cabinets in his office—a tall one labeled "Newt's ideas," and a much smaller one labeled "Newt's good ideas." Still, Gingrich is smart, articulate, and ruthless in debate. Though he roundly criticized Trump's attack on Judge Gonzalo Curiel—to Trump's explicit displeasure—Gingrich would surely take the job. Which leads us to ponder questions of judgment and temperament that Donald Trump should avoid like Ebola.

Jeff Sessions. He is Trump's most faithful surrogate—indeed, apologist. Which is to say that he personifies the word "pinhead": inarticulate, nativist, narrow-minded, reactionary, and just plain dumb. Few senators are more lacking in stature. He's also short.

He would surely accept. Why not? But a Sessions choice would confirm the completeness of the disaster that is Trump—a hitherto unthinkable reflection of Trump's need for craven adulation, and the absence of a more respectable running mate who was willing to feed it.

Which brings us to the insiders' current favorite, Senator Bob Corker of Tennessee. Colleagues like him. He looks like a senator. He's sane. Unlike Trump, as chairman of the Foreign Relations Committee he does not require an atlas to navigate the world. He's steady and self-disciplined. Overall he meets the criteria for a sober choice that would suggest that Trump comprehends, at least in passing, the unease created by his very being.

Unlike Sessions, Corker is not insensate—a couple of weeks ago, he risked offending Trump by expressing dismay about his campaign. But, more recently, he compensated by expressing "excitement" when Trump materialized an actual rapid response team—just like a normal candidate! This gift for overstimulation suggests a man who wants to be vice president—one hesitates to envision Corker's rapture when Trump deigns to read from a prepared text.

Corker, too, felt uneasy. After a brief audition, he removed himself from consideration.

No one imagines a President Corker, so this is his shot at national prominence. And no doubt the establishment types will implore him to step up for the sake of party and country—not to mention the GOP's donor classes—providing a fig leaf for his more personal ambitions.

The question is whether pros like Manafort can persuade Trump that Corker serves his best interests. Which, of course, requires Trump to endure the staggering self-abnegation of actually listening to someone else. Still, even a blind squirrel finds an acorn now and then. And if there was ever a candidate who can't afford to screw this up, it's Donald Trump.

My finalists? Corker, Gingrich, and Sessions—in that order. And the implausibility of the latter two makes Corker look like Cincinnatus.

The finalists turned out to be Pence, Christie, Gingrich, and Sessions.

But put down John Kasich with an asterisk. If somehow the GOP's duennas manage to broker this shotgun marriage—perhaps by assuring Kasich that Trump has six months to live—Kasich has everything Trump could ask for: ordinary guy appeal, experience in Congress and as a governor, and a shot at taking Ohio. Everything save, perhaps, loyalty.

So who will become the forty-eighth vice president of United States?

One out of two ain't bad, I'm tempted to insist—even though Clinton and Kaine lost. But as the number of pundits who picked Kaine could fill a stadium, I can't take too much credit.

Tim Kaine. Thanks to Donald Trump, whoever Clinton chooses wins the lottery.

Kidnapped by a Narcissist

The GOP's Stockholm Syndrome

JULY 5, 2016

It is two months since Donald Trump clinched the Republican nomination, promising us a "Trump" who would now be "presidential."

So let's take inventory of the improvements.

He accused American soldiers in Iraq of massive stealing. He revived the absurd claim that Vince Foster was murdered; suggested that Ted Cruz's father was involved in the JFK assassination; and expressed doubt as to whether Mitt Romney was a "real" Mormon.

In the wake of the Orlando massacre, he insinuated that American Muslims knew about prospective acts of terrorism; renewed his call for the surveillance of Muslim communities; and intimated that President Obama sympathized with ISIS. He appeared as the guest of a lunatic talk show host who claims that 9/11, the Oklahoma City bombing, the Sandy Hook elementary school shooting, and the Boston Marathon bombing were either fabricated or perpetrated by the federal government—assuring this madman that "your reputation is amazing." All the while

Until this point, some argued that Trump was an unorthodox but clever tactician who tailored his pitch to the primary electorate and who, nomination attained, would turn "presidential." This imagined a level of self-control and self-discipline that is well beyond him.

he neglected the real work required of a general election candidate—organization and fundraising—preferring the roar of the crowd to the responsibilities of a leader.

This became an acute problem: by the measure of past presidential campaigns, Trump didn't have an organization.

Among GOP professionals, the light slowly dawned. The man who thrived in the hothouse of disinformation and resentment peculiar to Republican primaries was, ineluctably, a one-trick narcissist who has no second act.

Faced with their concerns, Trump told them to get over it. "Don't talk," he said of party leaders. "Please be quiet. [B]ecause they have to get tougher . . . they have to get smarter, and we have to have Republicans either stick together or let me just do it by myself." But left to his own devices, Trump refuses to learn; or to bone up on policy; or to listen to advice; or, in general, to do anything that suggests a sense of obligation to his party—let alone the country.

Trump is his own campaign and his only cause, obsessed with feeding the boundless need for admiration fueled by his psychic emptiness. He is not "off-message"—in his own mind, he is the message. Thus his disastrous trip to Scotland was vintage Trump; rich, as ever, in the self-infatuation that renders him oblivious to everything and everyone but the wonder who is "Trump."

He graced Scotland to, of all things, hype his renovation of the golfing resort at Turnberry—blithely ignoring the misgivings of party professionals racked with worry about the chaos of Trump's campaign. Despite arriving mere hours after the Brexit vote, he devoted his press conference to, no kidding, a long account of how he had "made Turnberry great again . . . built to the highest standards of luxury," capping this with a loving description of two hotel suites in a lighthouse. His numerous broken promises to the local community went conveniently unmentioned.

Pressed to address the small matter of Brexit on a day when markets were crashing worldwide, Trump cheerfully opined that a decline in the value of the pound would be

terrific for his business interests. After a few gratuitous shots
at David Cameron and some kind words for Vladimir Putin,
he proffered the remarkable suggestion that the prospective
breakup of the European Union was a good thing, intimating that—as, no doubt, everything does—it reflected the
influence of his own campaign.

With his usual inattention to matters occurring outside
his own head, he commended the Scottish people for "taking
their country back"—ignoring that over 60 percent of Scots
had just voted to remain in the European Union. Asked if
he had consulted about these matters with his foreign policy
advisers, he answered, "I've been in touch with them but
there's really nothing to talk about." Including, it seems, the
prospects of a global economic calamity.

As ever, oblivious. But no longer impervious. For the
media worm has very much turned.

Whether from professionalism, shame, or both, the
media has started covering him in-depth. For a mendacious
ignoramus who has no depth, this is deadly.

No longer can Trump lie or change positions with
impunity—reporters are checking facts and asking follow-
up questions, the building blocks of decent journalism. And
a few commentators dared to state what has always been
true: that the only explanation for Trump's behavior was a
disqualifying psychological condition—narcissistic personality disorder.

This analysis allowed reporters—and Hillary Clinton—
to assess Trump in terms of "character," "judgment," and
"fitness." And so, at last, the central question surfaced: "Who
is this man?"

Trump's answer was a blacklist of media banned from
covering him, tended by the man himself, supplemented
by verbally incontinent Twitter attacks. His spleen knows
no constitutional bounds—he has spoken of changing libel
laws so that he could more easily sue the media, and using
his power as president to target those that displeased him.

By August, the commentators who had raised this question in one way or another included David Brooks, Eugene Robinson, Robert Kagan, Joe Scarborough, and Peggy Noonan. In addition, a number of psychiatrists had defied professional norms by publicly discussing Trump's mental state.

All this was duly noted. So, too, was Trump's contempt for the rule of law in general. His assertion that judges could be disqualified based on their ethnicity. His prior attempts to disqualify judges who displeased him. His unconstitutional proposals to ban all Muslims from abroad and spy on Muslim communities at home. His ludicrous threat to go after the Professional Golfers' Association for moving a tournament from one of his courses.

This behavior evokes a tin-pot dictator from some banana republic—as rendered by *The Onion*. But Trump is the nominee of one of America's two major parties. So the press began to examine his one supposed qualification for the presidency—his business career. Which, it transpired, was marbled with dishonesty, self-dealing, and catastrophic failures of judgment for which others, but seldom Trump, paid the price.

A favorite tactic was using the Trump name to pitch courses that have no actual value, in which Trump played no actual role. One such scam was "Trump Institute," a supposed wealth-creation seminar for which Trump claimed "I'm teaching what I've learned." In fact, Trump had nothing whatsoever to do with the course, whose real operators used plagiarized materials and were trailed by numerous charges of fraud and deceit. In the words of one participant: "It was like I was in sleaze America. It was all smoke and mirrors."

Thus Trump University—a pastiche of shallow seminars to which Trump lent his imprimatur but, the sales pitch notwithstanding, no actual thought. He did not, as advertised, handpick instructors or concern himself with content, let alone provide "priceless information" to make his students wealthy. Instead Trump U was an exercise in hucksterism, in which salespeople pressured the economically vulnerable to enlist in his most costly form of worthless education—the "Gold Elite Program."

True, the Gold Elite Program is unavailable anywhere else—like Harvard. All this might be funny save for the pressure on students to incur often crippling levels of debt so that Donald Trump could get a little richer.

But preying on others has always been his modus operandi. In a devastating article, the *New York Times* explored Trump's history in Atlantic City. The short of it is this: he put in little of his own money. He borrowed excessively, at ruinously high interest rates. He shifted personal debts to his casinos. He collected millions in salary, bonuses, and expenses.

He took four trips to bankruptcy court. He stiffed investors, subcontractors, and suppliers, ruining numerous small business people. His casinos lagged far behind the competition. His only gift, it seems, was for self-enrichment at the expense of others. As an analyst remarked: "There's something not right when every single one of your projects doesn't work out."

Neither, when examined, would Trump's plans for the American economy.

Moody's Analytics, a respected research firm, studied the main components of his economic program: enacting large tax cuts slanted toward the rich; deporting millions of undocumented workers; and imposing tariffs on Mexico and China. Assuming that a President Trump got his wish list, Moody's forecast a deep and lengthy recession; a 2.4 percent drop in gross domestic product; and a rise in unemployment to 7.4 percent. Add to this a $9.5 trillion drop in the revenues over a decade; a ballooning deficit; and government borrowing at ever higher interest rates. Inevitably, inflation follows such disasters.

But then nothing in Trump's business background had ever suggested that he knew anything about managing the world's largest economy. Or, for that matter, a political campaign.

Trump's primary campaign, it turns out, was a political Potemkin village—understaffed, financed on the cheap, and sustained by the gift of free media in unprecedented amounts. In the small world of Republican primary voters, this was enough to overwhelm a feckless field of opponents too busy sniping at each other to go after Donald Trump.

A general election campaign is a different matter. So is Hillary Clinton. And Trump is monumentally unprepared to deal with either.

Belatedly chartered to build an organizational and financial structure, professionals like Paul Manafort are digging out of a very deep hole. Trump's campaign structure is skeletal. His minimal staff is, for the most part, short on experience. He has little or no infrastructure in key states. His super PAC is feeble.

Conflict within the campaign continues—new faces keep leaving shortly after being hired. Most recently, two members of Trump's surrogate team quit, one after having been publicly contradicted by Trump. Firing Corey Lewandowski solved nothing; the problem is Trump himself. And the primaries taught him nothing but what a narcissist will always believe: that Trump himself is enough.

He has raised virtually no money. He barely tries. He repels donors. Unsurprisingly, more than $6 million in campaign money has gone to Trump businesses or to reimburse Trump and his family for expenses. The situation got so bad that, as June began, his campaign had but $1.3 million on hand. And so instead of campaigning in battleground states, he was forced through a gauntlet of emergency fund-raisers in search of dollars to get up on the airwaves.

In the last week, we have seen yet another attempt—no doubt spurred by Manafort and company—to make Trump more sedate. As always, this effort was spotty—he responded to the tragedy in Istanbul by calling for waterboarding and more elaborate forms of torture. And when he read from a script, he trashed decades of Republican economic dogma,

In due course, Trump shouldered Manafort aside in favor of advisers who tried to channel a more disciplined version of the original Trump. Another problem for Manafort was his profitable connection with a thuggish, pro-Russian former leader of the Ukraine.

In subsequent weeks, he raised a more respectable amount, primarily from his base voters. But he did virtually nothing to help the party—to the contrary, he wanted the party to carry his campaign.

After becoming one of CNN's more controversial paid analysts, Lewandowski continued offering advice from the sidelines, knifing Manafort in the process.

excoriating NAFTA and the TPP, denouncing free trade in general, and promising a trade war with China.

Here, for the party, the problem was not that Trump was a text deviate but that, to the express horror of the Chamber of Commerce and other Republican pillars, he quite deliberately deviated from protecting their interests. The idea, of course, is that Trump can round up the votes of white working-class folks damaged by globalization. But this has its own problems.

As the self-proclaimed protector of American workers, Trump must, as often, confront himself. His clothing and furniture products are made in countries he identifies as the enemy, like Mexico and China, and in the past he has exploited undocumented laborers. And, within a day, he once more veered sharply off script, using a raucous campaign rally to lash out at former GOP rivals who have failed to support him, placing his personal grievances above all else.

As this was happening, the Clinton campaign was battering him in battleground states with millions of dollars in negative ads. The Trump campaign could afford no ads.

All this endangers Republican candidates in down-ballot races. To this Trump seems quite indifferent. Indeed, Trump has suggested that he will leave the work of organizing in swing states to the already overtaxed Republican National Committee, further draining its resources. Pity poor Priebus. Much like a Trump casino, his party is headed for Chapter 11.

Two months in thrall to Trump have taken a serious toll. Trump's poll numbers are slipping—every national poll shows Trump trailing Clinton. To the GOP's dismay, the race is shaping up as a referendum on Trump.

Not, for Priebus, a cheerful thought.

But the show must go on. The Republican national convention looms ahead—zombie candidate or no.

And what a show it promises to be. Trump boasts that his very own convention will reflect his gift for "showbiz." His main idea is for a "winner's night" of sports figures to speak on his behalf: Bobby Knight, who once physically attacked his own player; Ben Roethlisberger, formerly accused of sexual assault; and Tom Brady, who merely deflates footballs.

In reality, none showed up.

This is partly driven by necessity—even rising Republican politicians otherwise hungry for attention fear speaking at Trump's carnival in Cleveland. Such is the vacuum that Trump has proposed filling it with Sarah Palin, stretching nostalgia to the breaking point. So, like it or not, it's a fair bet that we'll be hearing from Trump's wife and kids. Indeed, at one point a Trump adviser suggested that The Donald himself might speak on all four nights.

Though he did not always speak, Trump appeared each night.

Faced with this, Apple joined a string of companies cutting or eliminating their financial support for the convention—oddly, they seem uncomfortable underwriting the coronation of a race-baiting demagogue. Indeed, some Republican delegates are so appalled by this prospect that they are mounting a desperate bid to block him that, while doomed, will surely add to the entertainment.

To head off open dissent, Trump and Priebus have allied, admonishing delegates that repudiating their pledge to Trump violates party rules, and threatening to deny speaking slots to prominent officeholders who do not endorse him.

Despite this Cruz was allowed to speak—a mistake.

The question is whether they can stifle opposition to Trump at whatever cost, reducing the convention to an ersatz version of the Soviet Comintern.

Mitt Romney describes the stakes. Electing Trump, he said, could change the character of the country, licensing "trickle-down racism," "trickle-down misogyny," and "trickle-down bigotry." Like Romney, the last two Republican presidents—the elder and younger Bush—have refused to endorse their party's rogue nominee.

So, too, have numerous Republican governors, senators, representatives, consultants, commentators, and foreign policy analysts. Whatever their more personal motives, these men and women are doing what is often discussed but little seen—putting country before party. The Republican dilemma throughout the convention and beyond is that Trump was chosen, with a truly disturbing enthusiasm, by the party's base voters.

And so most prominent Republicans have chosen to support him. Many barely mention his name. Instead they muster the most threadbare of excuses—that they owe it to the country to stop Hillary Clinton from becoming president. And so they hope, not without reason, that they can use political polarization to stem off electoral disaster—by adding to it.

It is hard to describe how contemptible this is. Even viewed through the most partisan lens—GOP accusations of dishonesty, venality, poor judgment, and bad policy choices—Clinton falls within the normal parameters of past major party candidates.

Not so Trump. In the history of presidential politics, he is a mutation—shockingly ignorant, unwilling to learn, indifferent to fact, addicted to lies, blindingly self-absorbed, reckless in his behavior, wholly unpredictable, and gripped by a profound personality disorder that renders him not merely unfit, but an existential menace to the country.

All the more shocking, then, is the GOP's Stockholm syndrome—the effort to persuade themselves, and us, that through some mystical process this terminally unstable pretender can be channeled for the national good. Yet the GOP has already seen his unruly harbingers in prior races—Sarah Palin, Michele Bachmann, Herman Cain. Here Republicans are captured in a black irony of contradictions: Trump is at once a nominee of unique and frightening incapacity, and the utterly predictable product of all the party has become.

To advance the economic agenda of its donors, ideologues like Paul Ryan contravened the desires of the base, embracing free trade, tax cuts for the rich, slashes in entitlements, and an immigration policy congenial to commerce. To secure the votes of its most embattled loyalists, they substituted scapegoats—government, minorities, welfare recipients, and the godless. Their product was anger—not hope, not inclusion, and not, in truth, much compassion for anyone but those who financed the Republican Party.

The party's trafficking in tacit racism is now overt. Its various factions are at war, their incompatibility exposed. Threadbare of credible ideas, the GOP has become a compendium of plutocrats, conspiracy theorists, free-market purists, climate change deniers, anti-tax fanatics, gun nuts, racists, nativists, protectionists, fundamentalists, and devotees of big oil, held together by dishonest rhetoric, diversionary attacks, and phony "facts."

As malignant as he is, Trump is but a symptom. The disease lies deep within the GOP. That is why the party will still be sick long after Trump loses, a dead weight on the country that it has helped make sick at heart.

The party will still be sick—babbling with incoherence, perhaps—but not before it has passed contagion on to the rest of us. Because I thought that so obvious should Trump become president, I still underrated the degree of polarization and alienation that, for so many, made the normal standards for appraising a candidate irrelevant. I felt this particularly strongly when his sexual predation emerged. It was not until James Comey's intrusion in late October that I thought Trump could win the electoral college even if he lost the popular vote. He did both.

The GOP Reaps the Whirlwind

Racism, Nativism, Xenophobia—And Donald Trump

JULY 12, 2016

The warning comes from the Hebrew book of Hosea: "Those who sow the wind will reap the whirlwind."

So it is with the Republican Party and Donald Trump.

True, Trump personifies a fear and hatred of "the other" embodied by some of our history's more frightening and despicable figures: Father Coughlin, Joseph McCarthy, George Wallace. These emotions spawned some of our most shameful chapters—lynchings, anti-immigrant violence, the internment of Japanese-Americans. Because such tragedies are so searing, we view them as unique.

But they do not arise from nowhere. Nor did Donald Trump. Those who are shocked by his success have given scant notice to the darker forces that stain our society and roil our politics. Or, more likely, they pretended not to notice.

Most deplorably, the Republican Party.

The terrible tragedies of last week have muted, for all too brief a moment, the racial politics that suffuse the Trump

It was a conceit among many Republicans of my acquaintance that Trump was a freakish "one-off"—a product of the celebrity culture with no antecedents who would leave no trace. Not only is this untrue, but it cloaks years of inattention and denial while absolving the party of its history—including with respect to race.

campaign. But they are there, and will persist. So there will never be a better time than now to examine how Trump became the Republican nominee.

From his entry on the political scene, Trump has left no doubt as to how he proposed to rise. He began by fomenting the birther hysteria against Barack Obama, neatly fusing racism—the fear of Blacks, nativism (Obama must be from Kenya), and xenophobia (our president is a closet Muslim). An avid audience awaited him within the white working-class base of the Republican Party—fearful of minorities, immigrants, and the tide of globalization. Even now, a near-majority of Republicans believe Obama to be a foreign-born Muslim.

Small wonder, then, that Trump secured the Republican nomination by targeting nonwhites—at home or abroad—as the preeminent threats to our way of life.

He labeled undocumented Mexican immigrants crimi-nals, murderers, and rapists. He promised to deport all 11 million, including children who grew up here. He pledged to build a wall on the border and make the Mexican govern-ment pay for it. When his rallies grew "a little boring," he bragged, "I just say, 'We will build the wall!' and they just go nuts."

Trump's amorality and manipulation, blatant in itself, was yet more evidence of something deeper.

Among Republican primary voters, his poll numbers shot upward.

In the wake of terrorist shootings, he started going after Muslims. He suggested registering American Muslims on a national database. He proposed monitoring Muslim neigh-borhoods and mosques. He promised to bar all Muslims from entering the United States—including refugees from the tragic slaughter in Syria. And he began winning primary after primary.

He fomented violence at rallies, once pledging to pay the legal fees of a man who assaulted a black protester. Ever the opportunist, he paid special attention to protest-ers from the Black Lives Matter movement. He falsely suggested that the greatest concentration of crime occurs in cities that, not so coincidentally, had a substantial African-American population. And, consistently, he used black demonstrators as foils.

In early May, he completely vanquished his last opposition, and became the GOP's de facto nominee.

To what, one wonders, did the Republican establishment attribute his astonishing coup?

True, he also inveighed against free trade agreements, and promised to impose tariffs on the Mexicans and Chinese. Even this, of course, had its ration of xenophobia. But no sentient Republican could miss that the predominant share of the GOP electorate had embraced Trump's war on nonwhite enemies.

Now he is forcing them to live with it—or not.

Though his offenses against tolerance have become notorious, it is worth taking inventory of what he has said and done since securing the nomination—not simply because of his venom and persistence, but because of the underlying meaning for the Republican Party and our society as a whole.

Not only has Trump continued scapegoating Mexican immigrants, but he gratuitously attacked a particular "Mexican"—the Indiana-born judge, son of immigrants, presiding over a lawsuit against the consumer fraud that is Trump University. Why? Because, in Trump's telling, "I'm building a wall. It's an inherent conflict of interest."

Being Latino, he means. It is merely an ironic sidelight that this particular judge, as a prosecutor, risked his life going after a murderous Mexican cartel that smuggled millions of dollars in narcotics into United States.

It is difficult to capture how deeply racist and perverse this is. Trump's argument is that Latino-Americans are uniquely biased against "Trump" by virtue of his own bigotry, and therefore incapable of functioning as jurists. By this logic, any member of an ethnic group attacked by Trump must be shunted to the sidelines.

If there is any doubt of that, Trump stated that a Muslim, too, would be disqualified to judge a case to which he is a party. It is, perhaps, not coincidental that the two judges Trump went after in a prior case were an African American and a woman.

It seems fair to conclude that Trump harbors a deep antagonism toward certain minority groups. One thing is certain: he is running for president by attacking our most precious, and sometimes most fragile, societal commitment— to treat all people with equity and dignity.

In a curious sidelight one of those judges, who was previously unknown to me, officiated at my youngest daughter's wedding in 2014. I subsequently learned that he had a long and distinguished record as a prosecutor and judge. Trump's lawyer later apologized for filing these motions to disqualify.

So it seems appropriate to offer as America's answer the response of Judge Leon Higginbotham, one of our first black federal judges. Faced with an argument that blackness made him biased, Higginbotham answered: "I concede that I am black. I do not apologize for that obvious fact . . . However, that one is black does not mean, ipso facto, that he is anti-white."

Nor is Trump, ipso facto, a racist and a bigot. In this way, if no other, he's a self-made man.

But there is nothing like a tragedy to expose the racist underbelly of Trump's dank soul—Paris, Brussels, San Bernardino, and, most starkly, Orlando.

On learning that a homophobic American Muslim had slaughtered forty-nine LGBT fellow citizens, Trump's first reaction was to congratulate himself for being "right on radical Islamic terrorism." He then proceeded to trumpet his proposal for banning Muslim immigrants by—as is his practice—lying about the immigration process.

Muslims were the targets for several of Trump's most noxious lies.

Conjuring an imaginary horde of Muslim migrants, he asked: "Can you imagine what they'll do in large groups, which we're allowing now to come here?" Claiming that, "there'll be nothing, absolutely nothing left" of America, he warned: "We cannot continue to allow thousands upon thousands of people into our country, many of whom have the same thought process as a savage killer. We're importing radical Islamic terrorism into the West through a failed immigration system and through an intelligence community held back by our president."

Nor did he stop there. Of immigrants, he claimed. "We have no idea where they come from, we have no idea who the hell they are. We know they believe in certain things that we don't want to believe in." Two weeks later he once again concocted a fictional invasion of Syrian refugees: "We're letting tens of thousands of people come in from Syria, and we don't know who they are, and many of them are from ISIS."

All of which was demagoguery riddled with lies, racism, and xenophobia.

Since 2011, we have admitted under 5,000 Syrian refugees. Immigrants are carefully screened, and the government keeps detailed records on their numbers and origin. The FBI, Homeland Security, the State Department, and national intelligence agencies painstakingly check refugees' data against security databases.

All this takes eighteen months to two years. The screening process for Syrian refugees is particularly arduous. And as journalist Peter Beinart points out: "Since September 11, the United States has accepted 784,000 refugees, not a single one of whom has committed a terrorist act in the United States."

But let's be fair to Trump—he casts the same careful eye on Americans of a suspect color or religion. American Muslims, he claims, "know what's going on" regarding terrorism. For these disloyal Americans he has a warning: "They have to cooperate with law enforcement and turn in the people they know are bad. They know it. They have to do it, and they have to do it forthwith."

In case we missed their treachery, he added, "They're not reporting people. They have to do that." Given that this particular group of Americans threatens the rest of us, Trump renewed his call for a blanket surveillance of Muslim communities.

But Trump also targeted another strategically placed nonwhite American—the president of the United States.

Here too, after all, Trump had been prescient—six years before, he had relentlessly questioned Obama's religion and national origin. So it was completely in character when Trump claimed that Obama "continues to prioritize our enemies over our allies and, for that matter, the American people." Indeed, he asserted that our own president may well be a double agent: "Look, we're led by a man who either is not tough, not smart, or he has something else in mind."

And what might that be? Despite the fact that Obama has taken out Osama bin Laden and numerous leaders of Al-Qaeda and ISIS, Trump charged that when it comes to terrorism "he doesn't get it or he gets it better than anybody understands—it's one or the other, and either one is unacceptable."

In other words, our first black president is either incompetent or aligned with terrorists who want to kill Americans. Here Trump crosses from racism to a deep sickness of mind and spirit.

The silence of most Republican officeholders as to these attacks speaks for itself—and to the pervasive sentiments within the party to which they were acquiescing.

In this rancid environment, the racial dog whistles routine to his campaign have gone almost unnoticed. They should not, for they are endemic to Trump's appeal.

Just last week, one day after the Baton Rouge police shooting, a local sheriff serving as a warm-up speaker for Trump again stoked the embers of anti-black feeling. As reported in the *Washington Post*, "Jones asked the crowd if they would feel safe walking down the sidewalk in Chicago, Baltimore, or Washington. Each time, the crowd bellowed: 'No!' Jones called for a crackdown on illegal immigration and said that he wishes he could deport some of the 'homegrown criminals' in his country. He praised Trump as someone who is going to 'take our country back . . .'"

From whom, precisely? The answer is all too obvious. To put it mildly, in an age of police shootings and racial violence—tragically underscored in Baton Rouge, St. Paul, and Dallas—a presidential campaign that promotes further antagonism is the very opposite of what this country needs. Any decent candidate would disclaim such talk forthwith.

Trump said nothing. Indeed, he said nothing whatsoever about the death of black men in Baton Rouge or St. Paul until the tragedy in Dallas. This was the very culmination of the horrors of race hatred—police monitoring a peaceful protest while protecting the protesters, only to be killed by a lone gunman bent on his own grotesque version of "revenge" against whites.

The murder of five white police officers by a black man spurred Trump, at last, to issue an anodyne statement that noted, without apparent irony, that "racial tensions have gotten worse, not better." A fair example of why this is so came from Corey Stewart, a Republican candidate for governor of Virginia and Trump's state chairman: "Liberal politicians who label police as racists—specifically Hillary Clinton and Virginia Lt. Gov. Ralph Northam—are to blame for essentially encouraging the murder of these police officers tonight."

In any event, Trump's attempt at grace in the wake of tragedy was predictably short-lived. Speaking as a leader should in such an anguished national moment, Barack Obama called for mutual understanding, suggesting that Americans were not as divided as some suggest. Promptly, Trump reverted to the moral low road of demagoguery and exploitation.

The president, he brayed, is "living in the world of the make-believe." He then intimated that Obama and Hillary Clinton bore some unspecified responsibility for the tragedies themselves: "Look what is happening to our country under the WEAK leadership of Obama and people like Crooked Hillary Clinton. We are a divided nation!" He said nothing, of course, about his own strenuous efforts to become America's divider-in-chief.

So what have the leaders of the Republican Party had to say about Donald Trump?

Confronted with Trump's various bigotries some, like Kelly Ayotte and Pat Toomey, took to scampering past reporters. John Cornyn invoked a vow of silence until election day. And many of those who spoke became so mired in hypocrisy that it lent scampering and silence a certain grace.

Paul Ryan denounced Trump twice—calling his attack on Judge Curiel racist and objecting to his anti-Muslim rhetoric as contrary to Republican principles. And then continued to support him.

With respect to Curiel, Mitch McConnell said "I couldn't disagree more." Newt Gingrich called Trump's attack "inexcusable." Bob Corker said of Trump "he's going to have to change." Senator Tim Scott, a leading black Republican, called Trump's statements "racially toxic."

All continue to support him.

Their behavior is, to say the least, telling. As William Kristol put it: "Official position of the leadership of the Republican Party: Trump is an inexcusable bigot, and Trump should be our next president."

But really, is this all that surprising?

It shouldn't be. For half a century now, beyond doubt or ambiguity, the GOP has trafficked in coded bigotry.

This began after the civil rights legislation of 1964, when the party recast itself as the defender of the South's established racial order. Whether couched in terms of "states' rights," "local control," or "law and order," this appeal triggered a mass migration of millions of Southern whites to the GOP.

They had not suddenly discovered, through some blinding and simultaneous stroke of insight, the virtues of a party that they and their ancestors had collectively despised since the Civil War began. Like that war itself, this historic turning point was, preeminently, about race.

It transformed voting patterns—and the Republican Party. The GOP's "southern strategy" elected Richard

Nixon. So, too, Ronald Reagan, who opened his 1980 campaign in Philadelphia, Mississippi, where, barely over a decade before, three civil rights workers had been brutally murdered. This otherwise puzzling choice was hardly inadvertent—once in office, the Reagan administration assiduously cut down on affirmative action and the overall enforcement of civil rights laws.

But racial friction was hardly confined to the South. As George Wallace demonstrated, a toxic brew of prejudice, economic insecurity, and fear of crime could spread the politics of racial antagonism nationwide. Historically, the Republican Party had been a strong proponent of civil rights. But over time, and with many honorable exceptions, the party made room for voters, and politicians, who were indifferent or antagonistic—however they couched it—to the concerns of black Americans.

Republican support was critical to the passage of the civil rights acts of the 1960s.

This gave rise to a vicious cycle: the more hostile the party became to African Americans, the more African Americans voted against it. And so the GOP mined fear of minorities with ever greater zeal, hoping to gain an ever greater share of the white electorate.

In the 1990s, this trend began incorporating anti-Latino sentiment. This started with California governor Pete Wilson's crusade for a ballot initiative to deny undocumented immigrants public education, non-emergency healthcare, and other government services. Among white Californians, Wilson's pyrrhic victory was followed by a popular reaction against Latino immigration in general; a second ballot initiative that prohibited public universities from giving preferences to racial and ethnic minorities; and a third initiative that cut back on bilingual education.

The same chain reaction began occurring nationwide. Politicians like Tom Tancredo, Joe Arpaio, Jeff Sessions, and Steve King made anti-immigrant rhetoric a centerpiece of their appeal. Over time this permeated the party—since 2006, the GOP has blocked proposals to expand legal avenues to immigration, focusing exclusively on hardening physical barriers on the southern border.

There is, of course, a vast difference between controlling our borders, and trafficking in racial stereotypes that demean a particular group. The latter was epitomized by Congressman King: for every Mexican valedictorian crossing the border, he declared, "there's another 100 out there who weigh 130 pounds—and they've got calves the size of cantaloupes because they're hauling seventy-five pounds of marijuana across the desert." And so, too often, the debate over borders became about race.

As more Republican voters became hostile to immigration, both legal and illegal, more Latinos became hostile to the party. Caught in a demographic death spiral, the GOP became ever more dependent on a shrinking share of the electorate—white voters.

Over the last two decades, the GOP in California has grown increasingly moribund.

All this was accelerated by the ravages of globalization. America's financial elite—the Republican donor classes in particular—embraced free trade as a key to prosperity. Whatever the larger truth of this, globalization caused dislocation among the American working class. But instead of trying to ameliorate this through retraining or reeducation for the new economy, many Republican politicians cast minorities and immigrants as a cause of working-class travails—often shrouded in rhetoric about the "takers" who robbed America's "makers."

And so appealing to racial fears became essential to the glue that held together constituencies with conflicting economic interests. By accident or design the Republican Party had morphed into a political sorcerer's apprentice—it had conjured the demons of race, and now could not break the spell among its aggrieved base voters. Our long and painful grappling with race had come to divide the two parties—not simply because minorities were trending Democratic, but because racial attitudes among party loyalists in general—including among whites—were sharply different.

Increasingly, the GOP became the home of white voters driven by racism, nativism, and xenophobia. Hence the party's fervor for voter suppression laws calculated to keep minorities from voting—as racial animus distorted the party, the party began distorting the law. Too late did Republican professionals, foreseeing doom in presidential races, call for demographic outreach. As a party, the GOP was addicted to racism.

Thus the telling silence of most Republican officeholders when young black men were shot by police under questionable circumstances or, like Trayvon Martin, by self-appointed vigilantes. Decency did not demand that they prejudge the particular case, or reflexively condemn police tasked with a difficult and dangerous job. But it did, at the least, require prominent Republicans to express concern for justice—including a genuine interest in whether the toxins of race might have fueled these incidents, and how we as a society should respond.

The need for such an inquiry has long been painfully obvious. One must start by acknowledging all the good police who risk their lives to protect the rest of us, and by deploring all violence—and threats of violence—directed against police. But any white American who knows a black male likely knows someone who has been stopped by police for no good reason. And if that African American has a black son, he will have cautioned that child about how to act if confronted by police, warning that a misstep might be fatal.

Any white American who does not know these things has never asked. Let alone asked himself to imagine the divided soul of a black policeman who faces dangers like those that erupted in Dallas, yet must warn his own son against the dangers posed by bad or careless police.

One role of a genuine leader is to ask such questions for all of us, not least in the wake of tragedies like those in Louisiana and Minnesota. But among Republican officeholders, there has been precious little of that. One can but conclude that too many erstwhile leaders chose to tacitly profit from racial polarization by maintaining a timid silence in a political environment where, all too often, complex and painful questions of race are—literally and figuratively—reduced to black and white.

So it is distressing, but unsurprising, that the Republican Lieutenant Governor of Texas blamed the Dallas shootings not just on the shooter, but on the peaceful protesters the police were protecting, and on Black Lives Matter protesters in general. By doing so, he deepened the tragedy of the murders, and of racial division writ large, by further subtracting from our well of common humanity and understanding.

Donald Trump did not start any of this—far from it. His perverse genius was to see what the Republican Party had become, and to exploit this among the party's base without ambiguity or shame.

If he had any doubt, it was resolved by the GOP's response to the blatant nativism and racism of his birther attack on Barack Obama—the muted demurrals, the cringing silence, the odious evasions, the crafty exploitation. Trump simply built on this by stressing attacks on Muslims, proffering another scapegoat to an all-too-willing audience of Republican primary voters.

This, too, was hardly novel within the GOP. Even before his rise, Republicans in Congress blocked administration efforts to take in more refugees from Syria. And in the wake of Orlando, House Republicans proposed to ban all refugee resettlement absent congressional approval, echoing Trump's call for a ban on Muslim immigration. A party that had lost its political and moral core was, at last, ripe for a man like Donald Trump.

And so he has summoned the whirlwind. Where before the party spoke of race in whispers, Trump embraced racism with a full-throated roar. It is the Republican nominee—not Latinos nor immigrants nor Muslims nor aggrieved black protesters—who threatens American values.

But among too many Republicans, his offense is against decorum. The GOP had already become the home of bigots and bigotry, all dressed up for a garden party. Only now they are fearful of the help.

It is time for the GOP to face the truth, or face extinction.

The GOP is not extinct yet. But they secured the White House by becoming the party of white people—a demographic divide exposed by the November election. This short-term victory is a shortcut to societal disaster.

Leading the Lemmings

The GOP's Idiot King Marches on Cleveland

JULY 19, 2016

On the eve of their convention, the erstwhile chief counselors of the GOP had, at last, comprehended the horror that is Donald Trump.

There is comedy in this. One imagines the ministers of some obscure Ruritanian monarchy, awakening to discover that their new king is the idiot former crown prince, who combines congenital feeblemindedness with preposterous vanity, irrational willfulness, unpredictable outbursts of rage, the attention span of an infant, and a frightening ignorance of statecraft. In short, the not-so-good King Drumpf.

If only Peter Sellers still lived.

Regrettably, this is not a movie set in Moldavia. It is an American presidential campaign, and the idiot king is the Republican nominee—which is way too serious to serve as farce.

Still, one must grant its farcical aspects—not least in the two weeks prior to his coronation in Cleveland.

A chief source of drollery is what happens when his counselors cannot control him, which is pretty much all the time. The pluperfect example of which is his meanderings in the wake of a political gift from God—FBI director James Comey's root and branch critique of Hillary Clinton's email practices.

Leaving nothing to chance, his aides gave him a script dedicated to Clinton's demolition. He read it for a while before, abruptly bored, throwing it away. What followed was that which his handlers most feared—lint plucked from His Donald's all-too-woolly mind.

Never good. Even less good when, as often, Trump begins reciting his grievances. He attacked Chuck Todd and savaged CNN. He complained that the media had (accurately) reported his baroque praise of Saddam Hussein for supposedly killing terrorists—which Saddam never did—and then repeated it, cementing Saddam's place along with Vladimir Putin and Kim Jong Un as the despots Trump admires for being "strong." But even worse was his irrationally perverse revival of an incident that raised the specter of anti-Semitism.

The controversy began with yet another tweet—this passing on material from a white supremacist website. Small wonder, then, that the site made its point about Clinton's supposed venality by imposing a Star of David over a pile of money. Not subtle. So when the media pointed this out, Trump's tweet patrol covered up the star before deleting the image altogether.

To the normal mind, mere damage control, and high time to move on. Not Trump. He was outraged—at the media for reporting the origins of the tweet and, remarkably, at his campaign for taking it down. For Trump, this was a matter of principle—and his chief principle is that "Trump" is never wrong. And so, bizarrely, he complained that the whole thing amounted to "racial profiling" by the media—directed at Donald Trump.

In itself, this performance was nothing new. His entire primary campaign was one rally after another stuffed with ignorance, insults, lies, boasting, inflated poll numbers, and

Republican professionals were appalled by Trump's failure to pursue the most obvious attack lines. But his obsession with petty personal grievances should have enlightened them long before.

moronic bits of apocrypha snatched from God knows where. His policy statements were less positions than attitudes—a certain mindless machismo supplemented by an alarming obliviousness to known reality, and cemented by constant complaints that the media, his opponents, the GOP, and pretty much the entire world were being grossly and inexplicably unfair to Donald Trump.

But somehow the panjandrums of the GOP told themselves this was all okay. It was only the primaries, after all, and the party had been selling a milder version of this bilge for years. Surely, sobered by his anointment, Trump would listen to their advice.

And so, for them, his latest burst of mania was a bit like looking up from a belated reading of the *DSM*, scales falling from their eyes, to discover that their leader was not the unpredictable but canny operator they imagined, but flat-out nuts.

Which, given that he is in the grips of a profound personality disorder, is true enough. Trump's entire life has been a self-centered exercise in self-branding that blinds him to all else. Thus his campaign has been a hall of mirrors in which he sees nothing but himself. And he brings nothing to the quest—not self-discipline, self-knowledge, or any interest in learning.

His egotism and inattention repel the advisers he needs most. He shows no appreciation, or even awareness, of the awesome responsibilities imposed on America's president. In sum, his quest for power is a rolling disaster that but augurs the disasters that would follow should he attain it.

By August, an impressive number of GOP foreign policy thinkers had turned against Trump, many endorsing Clinton.

Potentially disastrous, as well, for Senate Republicans battling to maintain their majority. Trump's gift for repelling Latinos, women, and millennials is potentially lethal—for Republicans in swing states, he is the political equivalent of the Zika virus.

In 2016, only in Nevada, which elected the first Latina senator.

One would think, then, that he would approach this endangered species with at least a trace of faux humility, as behooves a man with an exceptionally impressive 70 percent disapproval rating.

Not our Donald. In a calamitous meeting with Republican senators, he began by asking a prominent dissenter, Ben Sasse, if he preferred Hillary Clinton. This provoked Jeff Flake to introduce himself as "the other senator from Arizona—the one who didn't get captured," adding that, to date, things like Trump's remarks about Latinos had kept him from being supportive.

A lesser man might have attempted to mollify a senator concerned about an important voting bloc. Instead, Trump retorted that absent an attitude adjustment he would make sure that Flake lost his seat in November. This menacing threat was reduced to the merely astonishing by the fact that, apparently unknown to Trump, Flake is not up for reelection.

But the idiot king did not reserve his bile for those present. In a particularly gratuitous attack, His Petulance labeled Mark Kirk of Illinois "dishonest" and "a loser." This did not go over well: if Kirk, indeed, turns out to be a loser, a principal reason will be Trump himself. Not that the man cares all that much. Asked by a reporter whether retaining a Senate majority meant anything to him, he answered, "Well, I'd like them to do that. But I don't mind being a free agent, either."

Kirk lost. Even for an amateur, Trump's ignorance of politicians and their world was always stunning—until one considered who he is.

Having treated senators to a glimpse of a brave new era in congressional relations, Trump breezed on to a meeting with House Republicans. This, mercifully, was more pacific, if not altogether reassuring. Asked for his understanding of the powers of Congress under Article I, King Drumpf assured his minions that, as a "constitutionalist," "I want to protect Article I, Article II, Article XII"—adding, with a monarch's grandeur, five nonexistent articles to the current seven.

Afterwards, His Superbity pronounced the meeting a howling success. But just to ensure that his new subjects expressed the appropriate appreciation, Trump gave them a script for the press: "It would be great if you could say we had an unbelievable meeting. 'Trump loves us. We love Trump.' It's going to be so good. Okay? You gotta say great things."

As an expression of Trump's worldview, if not reality, it was perfect.

Of course, the essence of Trump is a vast internal emptiness, a void of curiosity, a penchant for lying, a lust for attention, an infinitesimal attention span, a stunning deficit of self-awareness, and yet, paradoxically, a monomaniacal absorption with self. Combine this with the need to dominate, an indifference to consequence, the complete absence of conscience, and an awe-inspiring lack of empathy for other human beings, and you have a would-be satrap who stiffs small contractors, stints on charity, treats women like serfs, and scams the credulous; whose business career is larded with fraud, bullying, and mendacity; and whose mode of inspiration is to talk about himself.

This is the man with no soul against whom journalists have begun to warn us. Depicting his internal wasteland—not parsing tactics or handicapping horse races—is political journalism as it should be. Over time such portraits take their toll, as truth often does.

Granted, the bar for Trump remains astoundingly low—all too often, the media still treats his stray scripted moments of simulated sanity as revelatory of the statesman within. But as more reporters capture the real man, more voters take notice, including a cadre he desperately needs: the college-educated whites who boosted Romney within shouting distance of Obama. For every blue-collar white entranced by his persona, there is a more prosperous Caucasoid Trump repels. Instead of redrawing the electoral map, he may well be sticking the pencil in his own ear.

But this demographic divide also reflects a fault line within the GOP itself. To appeal to blue-collar workers, Trump rejects the free-market dogma of the party with an imperious flick of his hand. Not for him the "financial elite,"

By this time such delusions were wearing thin. Behind a teleprompter Trump was unhappy and unconvincing, often reverting to type.

In the end, enough college-educated Republicans came home for Trump to win.

"powerful corporations," and "Wall Street funders," who have "rigged the system for their benefit." Not for him the politicians—and that means you, Paul Ryan—who practice "economic surrender" to the forces of free trade.

Not for Trump, indeed, is the global economy as we have come to know it.

No, the new King promises a very old deal—a call for protective tariffs that harks back to the eighteenth century. Like any satrap without sense, Trump proposes to repeal reality, throwing the engines of globalism into reverse. How? Simple—he will magically restore manufacturing jobs that began vanishing years ago by exhuming the protectionism of centuries ago. Let lesser men—or women—propose job retraining for workers dislocated by the new economy. King Donald will simply abolish the new economy.

This was the core article of faith he clung to after the supply-siders had largely rewritten his economic plan.

Never mind that automation has transformed manufacturing: it's not American products that it disappeared—it's American jobs. And so Trump's promises are the economic equivalent of bread and circuses.

The sans-culottes he has awakened are a restive bunch. Trump's blandishments may be fantastical, but their suffering is real. And the one thing they know for sure is that the apostles of "limited government" and "economic freedom" don't give a damn about them. Indeed these privileged grandees, in Trump's telling, are the very mustache-twirlers who "are moving our jobs, our wealth, and our factories to Mexico and overseas."

Which, for the GOP, is a problem. For what Trump is proposing is to swap the politics of distraction for an outright fraud. When the bread is eaten and the circus disappears, his subjects will still be starving.

So what are party traditionalists to do? Some schemers fantasized about a coup. Others imagined that, in time, their dimwitted leader would revert to looking in the mirror while they replaced his "policies" with their own. One might call this Ryan's Hope.

Given His Vacancy's vacancy, this is always possible. But he may well have gelded Ryan and his honor guard, the free marketeers. For one thing, the blue-collar base has routed their program. And Ryan's own principality, the House of Representatives, is so riven by GOP factionalism that the speaker can't even pass a budget. One looks at Ryan and, in moments of sympathy, imagines Prince Charles.

Trump rolls merrily on, racial animus bubbling in his wake. Compelled at last by the murders in Dallas to issue a limpid statement of sympathy, Trump shortly reverted to type, declaring himself the "law-and-order candidate" and, with his keen historical and sociological insight, blaming America's racial divide on Clinton and our first black president. And so the GOP arrived in Cleveland as the party of bigots and bigotry.

Not to mention fundamentalism. Here, yet again, Trump's regal inattention to detail had consequences: a platform that sprang straight from the heads of the furious fundamentalists who—rejected again and again by our society writ large—came to Cleveland to stake their claim to the party's soul.

Left unsupervised by the Trump campaign, the GOP's cretinous creationists doubled down on denunciations of abortion, same-sex marriage, and gay rights in general. The Bible, we discovered, is not merely a text for Christians but should be taught in public schools. Particularly ironic then, is the party's large-spirited definition of "religious freedom": the freedom to refuse service to gays.

One can but admire its principled stand against tolerance and diversity—social or religious—and its firm rejection of those enemies of society: women, minorities, and the young. If only in the way one admires a herd of lemmings headed for Lake Erie.

In the meanwhile, tragedy struck again: the slaughter in Nice—in Trump's world, a marketing opportunity. He responded with his usual gaseous bluster, calling for a

> Trump's victory now makes it likely the GOP will pass something like the Ryan budget—big on tax cuts for the wealthy, which, though the GOP won't acknowledge this, will surely swell the deficit. But there are signs that Trump will sell out his blue-collar base. As one example, the right-wing House is not attached to infrastructure programs to create jobs. To secure one, Trump would have to make common cause with Democrats. We'll see.

> This was striking—as the country headed one way, the GOP headed another.

congressional "declaration of war" against ISIS while offering no actual solutions to the multi-faceted problem of transnational terrorism. And so one was grateful for a moment of comic relief—the King's audition of crown princes or, before she fled in horror, a princess.

The most prominent possibilities regarded this prospect less as a glass slipper than a political cement shoe, rooting them to the bottom of the lake as they expelled their last air bubble. They sought dry land in droves: John Kasich, Rob Portman, Scott Walker, Kelly Ayotte, Nikki Haley, Brian Sandoval, Susanna Martinez, and pretty much anyone else with hopes of a better life.

Lesser lights endured the seriocomic, compelled to audition for the king by praising him to gatherings of subjects and, as a reward, to seek the blessing of his kids. Fresh from his ordeal, the erstwhile establishment choice, Bob Corker, declared that he was otherwise employed. Joni Ernst too declared her fondness for the Senate, though her prior experience as an Iowa farm girl—spent neutering pigs—seemed ideal for any woman forced to work under Donald Trump. The four stragglers who remained were a perfect reflection of the party's plight—second-tier white guys with nothing to lose.

The two most gifted were, politically, extinct volcanoes: Newt Gingrich and Chris Christie. The third, Jeff Sessions, was qualified only by that which was utterly disqualifying—the actual belief that Trump should be president. And the fourth, Mike Pence—faced with a potentially career-ending loss for reelection as governor of Indiana—seemed to view becoming Trump's lackey as the political equivalent of the witness protection program.

True to character, Trump treated his quartet of bobbleheads with the whimsy of a monarch and the empathy of a puppeteer. Invoking the slaughter in Nice as a pretext, he kept his prospects dangling by canceling his stated announcement date of 11:00 a.m. on Friday, as the rumored selection, Pence, flew to New York in anticipation of a joint press conference, only to be left twisting in the ever-shifting winds of King Donald's public musings. In this messy inter-regnum, conflicting rumors issued from inside the campaign; Gingrich and Christie publicly angled for the slot; and Pence faced a legal deadline of noon on Friday to withdraw his candidacy for governor.

As hours passed, decorum dissolved, replaced by a dispiriting glimpse of palace intrigue in the court of an idiot king. Trump took to the airwaves to deny choosing anyone; Gingrich launched a scene-stealing denunciation of Muslims; and Pence silently suffered the stature-shrinking role of puppet-in-waiting. Angry at the leaks from within naming Pence as his choice, Trump began looking for a way out.

Filled with hope and desperation, both Gingrich and Christie pleaded with the monarch for his favor. Reports buzzed that Trump regarded Pence as a drag on his "brand," another tired iteration of the also-rans he had kicked around in the primaries. But Pence was the choice of party regulars because he was precisely that—just like they are. And so the professionals surrounding Trump were reduced to begging for Pence's life as if it were their own.

Then, abruptly, Trump popped his announcement—in a tweet. Bypassing the risky personae of Gingrich and Christie, he at last anointed the humdrum but compliant Pence, a standard-issue evangelical conservative with all the fascination of a tire leak.

Pence's principal distinction is his stalwart opposition to abortion and gay rights in any form, most recently as champion of Indiana's anti-gay "religious freedom" statute. But while Pence buys Trump nothing outside the airless antechamber of the right—save, of course, the potential for further alienating young people, women, and social moderates—the Sun King can be confident in the infinity of his gratitude. Not to mention his capacity for enduring all the humiliations to come.

Their strained and tepid debut as a ticket augured their relationship. There was zero electricity in the room or chemistry between the candidates, and Trump looked like he had just committed an unnatural act—taking advice.

Introducing Pence, Trump spoke glowingly and at length about . . . himself. "Back to Mike Pence," he said at long last, then forgot Pence altogether. After several minutes of this a certain fascination settled in—how often, one wondered, would references to Pence interrupt Trump's song of self. Rarely, it turned out.

Finally, he summoned Pence, treating America to a middling Republican cheerleader, speaking as though to persuade a crowd of Rotarians that Trump was, contrary to the evidence of their senses, one of them yet also their salvation. His hit parade of provincial pieties—God, country, family, freedom, Reagan, and the diabolical threat of Hillary Clinton—culminated in a church organ recitation of his Majesty's mythic virtues. With enough huffing and puffing, one thought, Pence might inflate himself sufficiently to resemble the last vice president from Indiana—Dan Quayle. Nostalgia did not ensue.

As for the coronation in Cleveland, it, too, boasts those special touches worthy of a rump regime in Ruritania. One particularly charming feature may turn out to be armed Republicans—a redundant phrase, perhaps—brandishing assault weapons outside the convention hall to dramatize their support for an armed America. Some stalwart delegates, thwarted by the Secret Service in their desire for a convention bristling with handguns, plan on packing heat at satellite events. As one delegate explained, "I think it's part of Republican values, American values, to be responsible for our own safety."

Good luck with that. Under Ohio's open carry law passed by Republican legislators, other upstanding Americans are also free to carry weapons outside the hall. Less enthusiastic

One of the campaign's small dramas was Pence's efforts to retain a scrap of dignity while serving as Trump's apologist. Given Pence's stature, this never rose to tragedy. He succeeded only in proving that he was small enough to be Trump's vice president.

are the Cleveland police, hoping not to be caught in the crossfire.

Mercifully, the convention passed without significant violence.

Should they make it inside, those delegates willing to brave the combat zone unarmed could anticipate a no doubt tasteful exploration of Bill Clinton's sex life. Further intellectual sustenance is being provided by Rudy Giuliani; practitioners of mixed martial arts; several border patrol agents; The Donald's third wife; and four of Trump's kids.

This Z-list of luminaries is intended to compensate for the absence of the last two Republican presidents; the two prior presidential nominees; the entire Bush family; a brace of Republican senators whose alternate plans include getting reelected; the governor of the host state, John Kasich; and pretty much every GOP officeholder who ran against Trump save for the ever-charming Ted Cruz. The chief difference between purgatory and four nights in the court of King Donald is that the latter may feel like forever.

But day one was merely what this year has taught us to expect. As demonstrators gathered outside the convention hall, Trump blamed the murder of three Baton Rouge police officers on Barack Obama's "lack of leadership." And on Monday night we learned from various hectoring speakers that the poisons of terrorism, race, and racial violence—fed, in their telling, by a black man and a white woman, Obama and Clinton—will vanish if we but license Donald Trump to "make America safe again."

But that was not all. Not content with victory, Trump's campaign manager picked a pointless fight with John Kasich. Clumsily if briskly, Trump's housecarls put down a rebellion on the floor, an unwelcome reminder of discontent in the realm. Then a cadre of brave or emotionally wounded men and women appeared to pillory Clinton—one, the mother of an American who died in Benghazi, to accuse her of lying and worse—while certifying the strength and patriotism of a man who had pretzeled himself to avoid military service.

Good enough for a night's work, one would think. But though a would-be nominee has never spoken before his actual nomination, Trump could not deny his followers the balm of his presence. And so The Donald appeared from a cloud of blue smoke to introduce his wife—for a brief, crazy moment, the imagination struggled to substitute Mitt and Ann Romney before accepting that the GOP as we knew it was, indeed, smoldering embers in a dumpster fire.

To the surprise of those who have never read from a script, Melania affirmed that Drumpf is every inch the king we never knew him to be—a caring friend to women and minorities, the spirit of American inclusiveness. Even by the standards of conventions this was, to say the least, a bold reinvention.

But though Mrs. Trump delivered it well, her text was oddly impersonal, without a trace of emotion or anecdote to attach it to the man she lives with. No accident, it turns out—whoever wrote her speech appeared to have plagiarized whole chunks from the 2008 convention speech delivered by, of all people, Michelle Obama. Thus the evening ended on a bizarre if not disastrous note, evoking the hollow panoply of a craven court, assembled to clothe its naked emperor's ravenous ego in empty praise and cynical falsehoods designed to gull the masses.

And so they have hunkered down in Cleveland: a once great party that now stands for little but racism, fundamentalism, and AK-47s, led by a bombastic narcissist with no program but self—leaving the rest of us with nothing but the hope that, like lemmings, they will save the country by drowning in November.

The amateur status of the campaign was evidenced by its belated explanation—Melania had junked a speech written by professionals in favor of one written by, well, an amateur.

A Tale of Two Conventions

Hillary Versus the Man on Horseback

JULY 26, 2016

Seldom have our national conventions provided such enlightenment.

Usually these quadrennial talkfests are mounds of verbal tapioca, as riveting as a four-hour walking tour of your own living room. Their ostensible purpose is to unify the party and burnish the candidate, launching the campaign with a burst of enthusiasm that swells the hearts of voters. But this year's conventions sharpened our divisions and exposed one candidate's craving for adoration and submissiveness, provoking waves of uncertainty and fear.

The Republican convention was notable for its emptiness—of vision, ideas, or even hope. Its singular aim was to frighten us into entrusting our future to a demagogue.

The strategists for Donald Trump have concluded that stoking anger and division is their only way to win. An opening night dedicated to the theme "Make America Safe Again" became a hymn of hatred against Hillary Clinton. The second night was more venomous yet, its centerpiece

Chris Christie's indictment of Clinton as delegates shouted "Lock Her Up!"

Indeed Clinton, not Trump, was the central figure of both nights. Bereft of credible reasons why Trump should be our president, the party resorted to hysterical reiterations of why Clinton should not.

A grieving mother of a son lost at Benghazi essentially accused Clinton of murder. A state representative from New Hampshire said she should be "shot for treason." And the inimitable Ben Carson revealed that Clinton is the handmaiden of Satan himself.

Like Lucifer, we discovered, Hillary Clinton is responsible for all evil in the world. Thus Paul Manafort's revelation that Melania Trump's plagiarism—a stunning example of organizational ineptitude—had become an issue only because of Hillary Clinton's war on other women.

And what of Paul Ryan, the GOP's erstwhile man of big ideas? His presentation was largely Trump-free. To tepid applause, he assured those assembled that unity is everything and Hillary must go—truly a program for the ages.

To whom, one began to wonder, are they appealing beyond partisans who are as beyond reason as Pavlov's dogs? Even the assembled loyalists began evincing a certain fatigue of spirit.

So they seemed resuscitated by Ted Cruz—whose remarkable achievement it was to give them someone other than Hillary Clinton to hate. Specifically, Cruz himself.

True, inspiring loathing is his greatest gift. But your own party's convention is a unique opportunity, and Cruz did not disappoint.

Like the legion of others who can't stomach Trump and have ambitions of their own—John Kasich leaps to mind—Cruz could have stayed away. Instead he delivered a self-satisfied paean to principle that ran fifteen minutes overtime, which he capped by imploring conservatives to vote their conscience in November. He might as well have said that any conservative with a conscience should never vote for Trump.

Transparent as ever, Cruz was positioning himself for 2020, betting that Trump would lose decisively. He still may go after Trump on the grounds that he is a failed president. His pitch will be that, to win, the GOP must pick a true conservative. Guess who?

True enough. But delegates booed the apostate vociferously. So visceral was the atmosphere that Heidi Cruz had to be escorted from the floor.

Were Cruz not the epitome of oleaginous opportunism, an observer might have seen his moment of payback as simple justice. It was Trump, after all, who mocked Cruz's wife's appearance in a tweet, and who linked Cruz's father to the JFK assassination—low points even in a year where The Donald dragged our politics into the primordial ooze.

But where the two antagonists so richly deserve each other, we were left to ponder why Trump allowed yet another night to veer from any sane person's idea of a message—especially given that Trump's people knew what was coming well beforehand. Compelling us to wonder yet again whether Trump is stupifyingly incapable of running a convention, a campaign or, God help us, a country, or whether his idea of a successful liftoff stems from WWE.

And so Mike Pence's moment in the sun became an afterthought. Though he proved himself a serviceable attack dog, his speech was standard right-wing boilerplate that had little to do with anything Trump purports to believe.

This raised a question—had Trump indeed taken over the party or, in the minds of its establishment, was he merely a veneer on the same old stuff that had gotten the GOP in such trouble with its base? A companion curiosity is whether Trump even noticed.

But the ostentatiously Christian Pence recycled another familiar trope—lying. Invoking the deaths at Benghazi once again, he declaimed, "It was Hillary Clinton who left Americans in harm's way in Benghazi and after four Americans fell, said, 'What difference at this point does it make?'"

This was no casual lie. Quite deliberately, Pence wrenched Clinton's response to a question about the attacks during a congressional hearing completely out of context, converting her comment on the question itself to an expression of indifference about four tragic deaths.

The GOP makes much of Clinton's supposed character flaws. But Pence's self-proclaimed Christianity, it seems, does not preclude slander and mendacity in the service of ambition, especially when Pence is forging a personal relationship with his political savior—not Jesus Christ but, regrettably, Donald Trump. Even more lamentable is that his master has made such smears so routine that his acolyte's emulation went widely unremarked.

As for Trump himself, there was no mistaking the meaning of his acceptance speech.

It introduced a GOP without pride or principle, an empty soundstage in the service of Donald Trump. As David Brooks put it, "This is less a party than a personality cult." And the personality it serves is that of a demagogue who stampedes the electorate with lies and fear in order to serve himself.

His speech was a remarkable moment in our political history. As a matter of intellectual rigor, I routinely deplore the facile references to fascism and its progenitors that the left too often deploys as shorthand for leaders or movements they detest. I will try to do better here.

But first, a confession. When Trump appeared on stage, I began wondering where I had seen those mannerisms before—the semi-comical strut, the pursed lips and look of self-satisfaction, the self-preening tendency to present his profile for the crowd, first left, then right. Then the original came to me: film clips of Benito Mussolini.

You can't say this in a column, I admonished myself at once—it's too glib, too cheap, and, ultimately, explains nothing. Then Trump started speaking. And so honesty

Pence operated as a standard-issue political hack, defending Trump while mouthing the usual right-wing attacks and platitudes. But his utter lack of distinction was obscured by Trump's vulgarity.

In subsequent weeks, a montage of photos pairing Trump and Mussolini was widely circulated. Their similarity of expression and physiognomy was more than a little startling.

requires me to acknowledge the historical antecedents for Trump's performance—all the more so because far too many in the media have normalized this speech beyond its due.

Its components were classic and quite simple.

First, fear.

Relentlessly, Trump painted a dystopian America, for Obama and Clinton are killing off our safety and our future. Best to simply quote examples:

The irresponsible rhetoric of our president, who has used the pulpit of the presidency to divide us by race and color, has made America a more dangerous environment than, frankly, I have ever seen.

Not only have our citizens endured domestic disaster, but they have lived through one international humiliation after another.

I have embraced crying mothers who have lost their children because our politicians put their personal agendas before the national good.

Decades of progress made in bringing down crime are now being reversed by the administration's rollback of criminal enforcement.

Nearly 180,000 illegal immigrants with criminal records . . . are tonight roaming free to threaten peaceful citizens.

But to this administration, their amazing daughter was just one more American life that wasn't worth protecting. One more child to sacrifice on the altar of open borders.

This is the legacy of Hillary Clinton: death, destruction, terrorism, and weakness.

And on and on, depicting America as too dangerous to place in the hands of a woman who "wants to essentially abolish the

---

While some commentators underscored the darkness and dishonesty of the speech itself, many praised its political effectiveness without any real analysis of its contents. This was another example of the media's indulgence of Trump, and the way in which he garnered benign coverage simply by reading from a teleprompter.

Second Amendment"—in order, we learned, to deprive Americans of their means of self-defense against the barbarism that she and our first black president have unleashed.

Second, lies.

With respect to crime, Trump deployed falsehoods as a fear-enhancer in order to depict a violent country swamped by a rising tide of murder.

In truth, since 1991 the rate of violent crime has been cut in half. Trump's assertion that the murder rate for police has risen by 50 percent this year is a blatant lie. And his claim that decades of progress in reducing crime are being reversed—a lie in itself—also throws our federal system and Constitution on the trash heap of mendacity.

As a matter of basic civics, the federal government is not responsible for law enforcement in American cities. Either Trump does not know this or, far more likely, does not care. In this area, as in so many others, Trump's America is a fiction conjured to serve his grasp for power, here enhanced by a peculiar irony—the suggestion of a federal takeover of law enforcement that abridges the GOP's commitment to local control.

Trump's dire economic portrait is also daubed in lies. His claims about black unemployment and Latino poverty—virtually his only effort to address minorities—are blatantly untrue. He doubled the unemployment rate for black youths, and ignored that the percentage of poverty among Latinos has declined. His assertion that household incomes are down more than $4,000 since year 2000 is based on stale numbers from 2014, and ignores that incomes have risen substantially in the intervening years he so conveniently omits.

His claims about taxes are equally deceptive. His charge that Clinton "plans a massive . . . tax increase" ignores that 95 percent of Americans will see little or no change. His promise of the "largest tax reduction" proposed by any candidate this year ignores that virtually all of the benefit goes to the very wealthy. And it omits another inconvenient

truth—that according to non-partisan experts Trump's proposals will explode the deficit by $10 trillion in a decade.

Ditto Trump's appeals to xenophobia. As one example,
he asserts that there is no way to vet the Syrian refugees who,
in his telling, threaten our lives. In truth, the thorough vetting process that already exists takes eighteen to twenty-four
months. And of all the immigrants admitted since 9/11, not
a single one has committed an act of terrorism. Here, as elsewhere, one marvels at Trump's shamelessness and cynicism,
the harbingers of an utter lack of conscience.

But the most disturbing element was his only solution to
the problems he conjured from fear and lies—himself.

Throughout, the speech was naked of concrete remedies.
All he offered us was the authoritarian promises of history's
man on horseback, a malign fairy tale told to children with
no power to reason or even to think: that his mere presence in the White House—and only his presence—would
become both ends and means, our last hope of salvation
from all the forces that beset us.

Again and again, Trump invoked the magical power of
himself. And, again, only quotation will suffice:

Nobody knows the system better than me, which is why I alone
can fix it.

On January 20, 2017, the day I take the oath of office, Americans
will finally wake up in a country where the laws of the United
States are enforced.

I have a message for every last person threatening the peace on
our streets and the safety of our police: when I take the oath of
office next year, I will restore law and order to our country.

I have made billions of dollars in business making deals—now I'm
going to make our country rich again.

I'm going to bring back our jobs in Ohio, in Pennsylvania, in New York, in Michigan, and all of America.

I am going to turn our bad trade agreements into great trade agreements.

We're going to defeat the barbarians of ISIS. And we're going to defeat them fast.

How will he accomplish these wonders? He certainly doesn't know, clearly doesn't care, and never even pretends to tell us. Why should he? He is not like other men and women—he is Donald Trump. And because no claim of uniqueness is complete without forging a mystical personification of a people in the leader who will determine our fate, he assures us: "I am your voice."

A very loud voice. Trump shouted most of his speech in the tone of a man bent on compelling fear and hatred—of all those who oppose him, and all of the enemies he promises to crush on our behalf. There was little warmth or humor, little effort to be likable. Such variations in tone do not befit a national father.

Nor did Trump display any real interest—in tone or substance—in reaching beyond his base of angry and disaffected whites. There was no recognition of diversity, no appeal for support from people of color. There was no uplift, no indication of any high or noble purpose in the American spirit. Demographically and spiritually, Donald Trump's America is as small as the man himself.

I should be clear. America is not Italy in the 1920s. We have a Constitution, and our traditions are democratic, not authoritarian. Trump cannot transform our institutions by himself; one doubts that he's even considered the difficulties. Still, as president this man on horseback can do America great harm.

He can overreach, provoking a Constitutional crisis. He can mire us in a dangerous drift caused by his own incompetence and incomprehension of our institutions. He can use the levers of government to intimidate the media and harass his host of enemies, real or imagined. He can plunge us into disaster through ignorant and impetuous decisions. He can deepen the violence and severity of our racial divide.

Quite possibly, he would do them all. And his failure to make good on his magical promises would surely create further anger and alienation among his followers, fracturing our society in a way that threatens our stability and our capacity for self-governance.

No responsible political party would give us this man.

Yet the GOP left Cleveland bearing the stamp of Donald Trump—the party of white identity and populist economics, led by a demagogue on horseback. That, sadly, is likely sufficient to rally most Republicans in such fearful and polarized times. The party's soulless gamble is that the souls of enough other Americans have shriveled sufficiently to drink from its poisoned chalice.

It is Hillary Clinton's job to persuade them they should not. And so she came to Philadelphia needing the very good convention that she is quite capable of putting on—one much more positive in tone and substance than the Republican festival of rage.

In this disturbing and volatile season, Clinton has the aura of experience and competence to reassure an electorate that, in the words of public opinion expert Peter Hart, is not "aspirational . . . but one that would just be satisfied to find peace and quiet." But twenty-five years of relentless partisan attacks, accentuated by her own missteps, have planted misgivings about her trustworthiness.

Part of her difficulty is that after two terms of a Democratic president, Clinton embodies the status quo for those who desire change. But the email controversy has become a magnet, attracting iron filings of other doubts and

---

In the wake of the convention, these fears became more widespread among the electorate at large.

July marked Comey's debut as a force in the 2016 election. Having absolved Clinton of criminal conduct, he made a remarkable—and highly unusual—public statement criticizing her handling of classified material. This allowed the GOP to complain that she should have been indicted while using Comey's critique to keep the issue alive.

discontents, its power reinforced by James Comey's damaging exoneration.

The act at its heart was never indictable, but its incaution was a serious mistake. And her shifting explanations provide an echo chamber for the further controversies that dog her, like Benghazi, long after the central question has been resolved in her favor.

This curse cannot be exorcised by November—the narrative that she is careful with the truth is too deeply embedded, a GOP mantra. So she must find alternate avenues of trust, including to younger voters, and this convention is where she must start.

One theme is to remind voters that she cares about issues that are important to them, and has for decades. Another is that she actually has solutions that—unlike Trump—she can describe in a credible and persuasive way. Still another is that, as a senator, she enjoyed good and productive relationships with Republicans, and that she cares to do so as president.

A convention is the ideal setting for expert witnesses—Barack Obama, Joe Biden, and Elizabeth Warren—who can vouch for her as a caring and capable leader. Here Bernie Sanders is critical. She needs his voters, and they need to be reminded of all the ways that she has embraced the themes of his campaign. And Sanders needs to say repeatedly and emphatically, as he did last night, that Trump should never be president.

Another crucial partner is Tim Kaine. Here Trump was helpful—his selection of a garden-variety evangelical conservative as his running mate helped free Clinton's hand to make a pragmatic choice.

In this context, Kaine was a smart and solid pick. While the left is riled by Kaine's support of financial deregulation and the TPP, Trump's Halloween convention should help consolidate progressive support. And Kaine's record as a civil rights lawyer, opposition to the death penalty, advocacy of gun control, and strong relationship with the

Among media observers, there was widespread bemusement about why Clinton did not simply take her lumps and move on, as best she could.

The convention was largely successful in advancing these goals, while reinforcing Clinton's image as an experienced leader.

black community in Virginia commend him as a liberal of conscience.

His résumé bristles with attributes. He has been a mayor, governor, and senator. He is widely respected and universally liked, with a reputation for integrity and good judgment. He speaks fluent Spanish. He knows foreign policy. He can help carry a swing state. He is a former chairman of the DNC. And, critical to a candidate who cares deeply about governance, Kaine is qualified to serve as president.

Finally, he is an affable white guy from a modest background—an observant Catholic whose idea of religion was doing missionary work in Honduras instead of, like Pence, burning gay rights and reproductive freedom at the stake of theocracy. He can appeal to the center in a way that Pence does not.

In a bracing contrast to Trump's botched unveiling of Pence, Clinton's rollout of Kaine was a ten-strike. Trump spoke about himself; Clinton took pride in reciting Kaine's qualifications to be president. Trump seemed indifferent to his running mate; Clinton and Kane displayed an easy camaraderie. Trump vanished after introducing Pence; Clinton's smiles throughout Kaine's speech underscored how terrific it was.

In fact, a bit of a revelation. Though his presence is unimposing, he combines a likable, everyman appeal with the sense that he knows his stuff. Even when attacking Trump—which he did to great effect—Kaine's verve did not obscure a pleasing amiability, a sense that he is quite human and accessible. He explained what he cares about, and why, with unforced passion. He made his family—parents, wife, and kids—come alive. He spoke in Spanish, firing up the crowd. And far from seeming rote, his account of Clinton's qualities humanized her claim to leadership.

One could not watch him without appreciating Clinton's choice, and the care with which she had made it. Which was the biggest contrast of all—Clinton looked like a president; Trump like a petulant fool who rued his most crucial decision.

And so, unlike the GOP, an upbeat spirit carried the ticket into Philadelphia.

But on the eve of the convention, vexing fissures suddenly reopened, threatening to roil the proceedings: emails from within the DNC suggesting an anti-Sanders bias; renewed calls for Debbie Wasserman Schultz to go; discontent on the left with Kaine; a divide over superdelegates that lingered from the campaign; a progressive protest march that dramatized these grievances.

The immediate solution was obvious to all but Debbie Wasserman Schultz. Obama himself was forced to request her resignation, and for a time she insisted on speaking to the delegates—a prescription for further discord—oblivious to the reality that, Ted Cruz aside, supporting actors are not entitled to a divisive soliloquy. But at length she relented under public pressure, and the next challenge for the campaign was to minimize divisions at the convention itself.

In the meanwhile, a CNN poll showed Trump with a bounce from the GOP convention. And the email controversy had so revived the bitterness of Sanders delegates that, in the morning, a gathering booed Sanders himself when he urged support for Clinton. All this made last night's opening session yet more critical, the speech by Sanders most of all.

It turned out to be modest and transient, and was erased altogether by the Democratic convention.

It began badly, with a hard-core cadre of protesters booing speakers from the floor. It took, of all people, comedian Sarah Silverman to lance the anger—a Sanders supporter, she admonished the dissidents "you're being ridiculous" to considerable effect, and then asserted that she was proud to vote for Clinton. While this did not fully tamp down the outrage, it changed the atmosphere for the speeches to come.

Here the Democrats had the advantage. The GOP convention was so bare of star power that it relied on Trump's children to give polished, but curiously impersonal, testaments for their father. But the high-voltage Democrats who took the stage for

Clinton were important not only for who they were and what they said, but what they symbolized.

Cory Booker gave a fiery speech that evoked the one given twelve years before by another young black senator, Barack Obama. The first black first lady, Michelle Obama, summoned a stunning star turn that framed the case for Clinton in terms of her own kids—and everyone else's. Another woman, Elizabeth Warren, reminded her audience that the alternative to Hillary Clinton is an ignorant misogynist. All acknowledged our challenges; all summoned the hope we can surmount them. In words, but also by their example and their presence, they captured the difference between the parties, and between Clinton and Trump.

Then, Sanders.

Unlike Ted Cruz, he came as a rival whose mission was to unify. He did so in full voice. He reminded his adherents of all they had accomplished—not least in moving the party, and Hillary Clinton, in their direction. With clarity and passion, he spelled out how contrary a Trump presidency would be to the spirit he had helped inspire. So when he said that he was proud to stand with Clinton, the cheers drowned out the dissent.

Dissent remained, and a core of bitterness lingered in the hall. But Bernie Sanders had done all he could. And so for that evening, at least, the tide of anger had subsided a bit, subdued by a spirit more generous and inclusive than anything seen in four angry nights in Cleveland. By November, that may make the difference.

America Meets Hillary Clinton

JULY 29, 2016

Who is Hillary Clinton?

For twenty-five years now, an infinity of ink and air-time has been expended on that very question, reverberating in cyberspace until it overwhelms us. But the Democratic convention asked us to consider a remarkable proposition: that a woman we thought we knew well—for some, too well—would turn out to be, as president, the best blind date we ever had.

Getting there was no small thing. The convention opened in the sour spirit of imminent divorce, with the email crisis serving as a last bitter quarrel before someone called a lawyer. Indeed, Sarah Silverman was forced to remind the combatants to remember the kids. Even then, it took the gracious neighbor, Michelle Obama, to invoke what the kids could be, and gruff Uncle Bernie to spell out the horrors awaiting them in the custody of Donald Trump.

But though Monday ended far better than it began, the sour spirit of schism lingered.

Then, on Tuesday, this was overcome by hope, humanity, and even, at times, joy.

The airing of differences—a roll call vote much dreaded in the hall—became a celebration rather than a protest, honoring all that Bernie Sanders and his supporters had achieved. And so when Sanders rose to confirm Hillary Clinton as the nominee, the mood of the convention was more festive than schismatic.

What followed was a political masterstroke: a sequence of testimonials to Clinton's qualities, delivered by witnesses that only a churl would shout down.

The mothers of young black men wrongfully killed pleaded for the lives of other young men—and for the lives of police. Of Clinton, one said: "She isn't afraid to bear the full force of our anguish. She doesn't build walls around her heart."

A young woman enslaved by three years of human trafficking said: "Before there were laws to identify and protect victims . . . Hillary Clinton was fighting to end modern slavery." A young man afflicted by dwarfism recalled how a first lady had held him while promising the care he needed and, when she held him again two years later, noticed that his back brace was gone.

The convention used this kind of humanizing detail to great effect.

A cop who had choked down toxic air from 9/11 reprised how Clinton had worked to get health care benefits for affected police and firefighters. A woman horribly burned in those attacks described Clinton's calls and visits. A congressman who lost a firefighter cousin spoke of how Clinton had helped the city recover—noting, in a lethal aside, that Donald Trump had claimed $150,000 from a fund Clinton had established to help small businesses rebuild.

One waited for an acknowledgment of these trials that never came—a grace note that, to many, seemed like the thing to do. But his speech was nonetheless effective.

In all the political debris surrounding Hillary Clinton, such stories get lost. Which made them new and, for that, more telling.

So it was time for Bill Clinton.

This testimonial was, by far, more complicated, inevitably invoking the public trials of their marriage. But only he could recall for us the young woman he met well before the country did.

One doubts that most people knew that the young Hillary Clinton had worked to get disabled kids access to school; or helped register migrant workers in Texas; or investigated segregated academies in the South; or started a legal aid clinic in Arkansas; or worked for the Children's Defense Fund instead of going to Wall Street. It's a rare American who knew all these things—perhaps only Bill Clinton. Yet this was what Hillary Clinton had decided to do before anyone else was watching, or judging.

Suddenly Clinton was a three-dimensional woman, fleshed out by anecdote—a person wholly unlike the Donald Trump we were treated to in Cleveland, a hologram from an Ayn Rand novel.

Now the former president could confront the bloodless and calculating Hillary Clinton of GOP lore.

In truth, like most of us, she is many things, and one could regret that years of political warfare have made her the cautious public figure we have come to know. But her husband reminded us not to judge her by the malign shorthand of politics, or even by her own mistakes. The Republican version is, indeed, a "cartoon"; the "real" woman Bill Clinton introduced is real too.

That woman, he reminded us, had a gritty lifetime of working for change—often against the odds and in the face of determined opposition. "Life in the real world is complicated and real change is hard . . . She is the best change maker I've ever known."

The evening ended with a reminder of one way that is true beyond doubt—a montage of the forty-four presidents who came before her, followed by Clinton herself. Lest we forget, the images said, history had just materialized before our eyes. No one there would object to that.

And so, on Wednesday, the Democrats offered what the GOP could not: a compelling sequence of expert witnesses who could tell us, from their own experience, what kind of president this historic figure would be—and why electing Donald Trump would be a mistake of historic proportions.

Former defense secretary and CIA director Leon Panetta—Obama and Clinton's partner in taking out bin Laden—began the ongoing theme of compare and contrast. Clinton was knowledgeable and able; Trump an irresponsible amateur who, just that day, had asked the Russians to hack us in order to help him become our president.

Then came Joe Biden. Everyone knew Joe's story. For forty-five years, he had connected the party to the struggles of ordinary men and women. And he had suffered setbacks of his own, some quite terrible. He had lost part of one family to a tragic accident; helped meld the survivors into another close-knit clan. He had twice run for president and lost, suffering embarrassment along the way. Yet he had persevered, becoming an esteemed and able vice president. And just when he imagined reaching for the prize one last time, the death of his beloved son stole his heart for the chase.

So he stood where he had imagined speaking for himself, and spoke for Clinton in the way only he can: "If you live in the neighborhoods like the ones Jill and I grew up in, if you worry about your job and getting decent pay, if you worry about your children's education, if you're taking care of an elderly parent, then there's only one—only one—person in this election who will help you . . . That's Hillary Clinton's life story."

But "[t]hat's not Donald Trump's story . . . He is trying to tell us he cares about the middle class. Give me a break . . . He has no clue what makes America great. Actually, he has no clue, period." Including about our safety: "No major party nominee has ever known less or been less prepared to deal with our national security."

When Biden left the stage, he was bathed in warm and poignant applause. For everyone knew this about Joe, too—it was his final star turn in elected office, and he had given Hillary Clinton his all.

The counterpoint to "middle-class Joe" was a billionaire who is all Trump is not—Michael Bloomberg.

As an independent, Bloomberg affirmed, he does not adhere to either party. But he knows Hillary Clinton to be capable, caring, and collegial—even when they disagree, she always listens. He does not doubt her fitness to be president.

Then he tore into Trump's only claim to leadership. "New Yorkers know a con when they see one. Truth be told, the richest thing about Donald Trump is his hypocrisy." "I built a business, and I didn't start it with a million dollar check from my father." "Trump says he wants to run America like he's run his business. God help us." And then he raised perhaps the most crucial issue of the campaign: Trump's glaring personality disorder. "Let's elect a sane, competent person," he implored us—a stinging contrast between Clinton and Trump.

Then Everyman appeared again in the person of Tim Kaine—but with a résumé that suggests that he can spot a leader. He got right to it. Evoking his son, a Marine newly deployed overseas, he said, simply, "I trust Hillary Clinton with our son's life."

As for Clinton's life, he argued that we should judge a political leader by a simple but telling criterion: whether they had a passion for lifting others well before seeking office. Then he drove home the message of Tuesday night—Hillary Clinton has a lifelong passion for helping families and kids.

In contrast, Kaine told us, "Donald Trump has a passion for himself." As one pointed example he asked, "Does anyone here . . . believe that Donald Trump paid his fair share of taxes?" Then he catalogued all the ordinary people Trump has victimized in business—an impressive list, to be sure.

Thus far every speaker had added to the cumulative force of endorsement and indictment. But it was left to Barack Obama—once Hillary Clinton's rival—to close the evening on her behalf.

One interesting aspect of the campaign was how Clinton and her advocates chose to frame the increasingly widespread perception that Trump was mentally unstable.

He did so in a way that evoked the best of convention speakers, Ted Kennedy and Mario Cuomo. And, perhaps, surpassed them.

The best such speeches speak to the best of us. Obama did that.

His Scotch-Irish grandparents, he recalled,

> didn't admire braggarts or bullies. They didn't respect mean-spiritedness, or folks who were always looking for shortcuts in life. Instead they valued traits like honesty and hard work. Kindness and courtesy. Humility; responsibility; helping each other out . . . True things. Things that last. The things we try to teach our kids.
>
> They knew these values weren't reserved for one race . . . They knew these values were exactly what drew immigrants here, and they believed that the children of those immigrants were just as American as their own . . . America has changed over the years. But these values my grandparents taught me—they haven't gone anywhere. They are as strong as ever; still cherished by people of every party, every race, and every faith. They live on in each of us.

The best such speeches link these qualities to the party's nominee. Obama did that:

> That's the America I know. And there is only one candidate in this race who believes in that future, and has devoted her life to it; a mother and grandmother who'd do anything to help our children thrive; a leader with real plans to break down barriers, blast through glass ceilings, and widen the circle of opportunity to every single American . . . And no matter how daunting the odds; no matter how much people try to knock her down, she never, ever quits.
>
> That's the Hillary I know. That's the Hillary I've come to admire. And that's why I can say with confidence there has never been a man or a woman more qualified than Hillary Clinton to serve as president of the United States of America—not me, not Bill, no one.

The best such speeches contrast the nominee with her opponent. Obama did that, too—with devastating irony.

And then there's Donald Trump. He's not really a plans guy. Not really a facts guy, either. He calls himself a business guy, which is true, but I have to say, I know plenty of businessmen and women who achieve success without leaving a trail of lawsuits, and unpaid workers, and people feeling like they got cheated.

I was later told that Obama's advisers excised several passages in which the president filleted Trump to withering effect. The reasoning was that Obama should save some of his best material for the fall. He did.

He took on not just Trump, but Trumpism:

He's just offering slogans, and he's offering fear. He's betting that if he scares enough people, he might score just enough votes to win this election . . . [H]e's selling the American people short. We are not a fragile or frightful people. Our power doesn't come from some self-declared savior promising that he alone can restore order. We don't look to be ruled . . .

America has never been about what one person says he'll do for us. It's always been about what can be achieved by us, together, through the hard, slow, sometimes frustrating, ultimately enduring work of self-government.

And then came an arrow to the heart of Trumpism:

Anyone who threatens our values, whether Fascist or Communist or jihadists or homegrown demagogues, will always fail in the end.

But there was yet more, for he ended by placing his hopes for America in Clinton's hands:

Time and again, you've picked me up. I hope, sometimes, I've picked you up, too. Tonight, I ask you to do for Hillary Clinton what you did for me . . . This year, in this election, I'm asking you to join me—reject cynicism, reject fear, to summon what's best in us; to elect Hillary Clinton as the next president of United States, and show the world we still believe in the promise of this great nation.

Once again, we had seen the very best of Barack Obama on center stage—the easy command, the interplay of wit and a deep seriousness, the incandescent smile, the soaring appeal to hope over fear. And then a classic moment of political theater—suddenly Hillary Clinton appeared beside him.

The place erupted. All that was left—all that now mattered—was Clinton's acceptance speech on Thursday evening.

Or so one thought. On Thursday Khizr Khan—a Muslim immigrant whose army officer son had been killed in Iraq—provided one of the most stunning moments of any convention in recent memory.

With his wife beside him dressed in traditional Muslim garb, Khan spoke movingly of their grief and loss. Then he rebuked Donald Trump for betraying all his son had died for:

"Donald Trump, you're asking Americans to trust you with their future. Let me ask you, have you even read the United States Constitution?" Pulling out his own pocket edition, he said, "I will gladly lend you my copy."

Asking Trump if he had ever visited Arlington National Cemetery, he instructed: "Go look at the graves of brave patriots who died defending the United States of America. You will see all faiths, genders, and ethnicities."

"You have sacrificed nothing and no one."

The quiet power of that statement still lingered in the air when it was time for Clinton to speak.

A terrible moment for Trump. But what stupefied is that he extended the damage for a week, belittling the Khans—Mrs. Khan in particular—while complaining that they had "viciously" attacked him.

Even by the harrowing standards of her public career, this was a daunting challenge. In coming to her aid so powerfully, Obama had set the bar sky-high—while a serviceable public speaker, by her own reckoning she lacks the rhetorical gifts of the last two Democratic presidents.

More difficult, perhaps, was to embody the human and caring Hillary Clinton summoned by the last three nights, and yet capture the historic moment with a resolve that reassured her fretful and suspicious countrymen in a fractious time. All that, and still more: the delegates had passed through conflict to a communal sense of promise it was now her purpose to sustain.

It was of much benefit, then, that she was introduced by a final witness to her life, her own daughter.

Since childhood, Chelsea Clinton had lived in her parents' harsh spotlight. At times, this must have felt unendurable. But she had endured it, and more, and now this served her mother well.

With ease and warmth, Chelsea spoke of "my wonderful, thoughtful, hilarious mother," telling anecdotes of Clinton's deep pleasure and engagement in being a mother and grandmother. A political commonplace, perhaps. But it was obvious that, unlike Trump's kids, Chelsea actually knew her mother as a parent, because her mother had actually been one. And done it well.

At last it was Clinton's turn.

She met the moment with an air of confidence. And, more than usual, she spoke of what lies beneath her sometimes opaque surface: "The truth is, through all these years of public service, the 'service' part has always come easier to me than the 'public' part. I get it that some people just don't know what to make of me."

But she, too, had a story—a modest family, a mother who was abandoned by her parents as a young girl, whose first grade teacher saw that she had nothing to eat, and brought extra food to share. "The lesson she passed on to me years later stuck with me: no one gets through life alone."

She remembered that, Clinton told the delegates, when she met a young girl in a wheelchair on the back porch of her house, prevented by her disability from attending school. "I couldn't stop thinking of my mother and what she went through as a child. It became clear to me that simply caring is not enough."

Thus her work with the Children's Defense Fund to ensure that kids with disabilities have the right to go to school. "But

One of the myths of the campaign was that Trump's children proved what a great father he was. By most accounts, he was a distant and uninvolved parent who left child rearing to their mothers. And no one ever seemed to ask why these supposedly self-actualized adults worked for Trump instead of carving out separate careers.

how do you make an idea like that real?" she asked rhetorically. "You do it step by step, year by year."

That experience, she asserted, underlies her reputation as a bit of a grind: "I sweat the details of policy. Because it is not just a detail if it's your kid, if it's your family. It's a big deal. And it should be a big deal to your president."

This adeptly humanized one of Clinton's acknowledged strengths—that she knows her brief.

She did not need to mention Donald Trump.

Instead she spoke of her plans to make the lives of Americans better. Unlike Trump, she has a lot of them. Appointing justices who will get money out of politics and expand voting rights. Fighting climate change, and creating clean energy jobs. Comprehensive immigration reform to grow the economy and keep families together. Profit-sharing for workers.

Raising the minimum wage to a living wage. Equal pay for women. Investing in infrastructure. Making college affordable for all. Education and job retraining to help those displaced by the global economy. Easing credit for small businesses.

And what of ISIS? As president, she promised, she would strike their sanctuaries from the air, support local forces on the ground, and strengthen our intelligence to prevent attacks at home. "It won't be easy or quick," she allowed, "but make no mistake—we will prevail."

Here, at last, she got to Trump. Quoting him to lethal effect—"I know more about ISIS than the generals do"—she told him, "No, Donald, you don't."

This was one of her best lines, touching on questions of temperament which resonated throughout the campaign. Advertising along these lines soon followed—the Clinton brain trust was adept at pairing message with media.

Then she went to work disqualifying him as commander in chief: "Donald Trump can't even handle the rough-and-tumble of a presidential campaign. He loses his cool at the slightest provocation. When he's gotten a tough question from a reporter. When he's challenged in a debate. When he sees a protester at a rally.

"Imagine him in the Oval Office facing a real crisis. A man you can bait with a tweet is not a man we can trust with nuclear weapons."

Nor did she neglect Trump's hypocrisy. "Please explain to me what part of America First leads him to make Trump ties in China, not Colorado. Trump suits in Mexico, not Michigan. Trump furniture in Turkey, not Ohio. Trump picture frames in India, not Wisconsin.

"Donald Trump says he wants to make America great again—well, he can start by actually making things in America again."

But then Trump, she argued forcefully, is antithetical to the spirit of America itself: "Americans don't say 'I alone can fix it.' . . . He wants us to fear the future and fear each other."

As for Clinton herself, she quoted her mother's Methodist credo: "Do all the good you can, for all the people you can, in all the ways you can, as long as ever you can." By the testament of others, spelled out in the four nights of the convention, her public career was built on such an effort.

Then the speech was over, and history made. Smiling, for long minutes Clinton basked in the celebration—the cheers and tears and balloons falling—and also, it seemed, the relief and satisfaction of a job well done.

By most observers' reckonings, it was. The speech lacked Obama's eloquence—that is not her gift. But it did its work, and so did the convention. The idealistic young woman Americans had met at last now lived within the battle-tested candidate who, perhaps, they finally knew a little better.

Advantage Hillary Clinton.

PART IV

*Russian Hackers, a Media Awakening,
Videotapes, Charges of Groping, Claims of
Voter Fraud, Three Debates, a Dogged Democrat,
and a GOP Candidate Cracking Up Until an
FBI Director Throws Him a Lifeline*

BY AUGUST 2016 THE CONTAGION WAS SPREADING, AND the fever swamp was consuming us all.

The storylines were as compelling as they were heretofore unimaginable. It was no surprise that Barack Obama came from the wings to center stage, using all of his gifts to boost Hillary Clinton and savage Donald Trump. But then a confluence of events gave Michelle Obama one of the single most riveting moments of the campaign—a denunciation of Donald Trump unprecedented for any first lady, one which spoke to any woman who had ever been harassed or assaulted by a man.

With grit and doggedness, Hillary Clinton endured fresh questions about her emails and the Clinton Foundation while, remarkably, the Russian government siphoned stolen emails through WikiLeaks in an effort to bring her down. Her antagonist, Donald Trump, accused her of being corrupt, inept, sickly, and, quite possibly, brain-damaged—not to mention calling her an enabler of her husband's own behaviors.

Yet she pushed on with a rare determination that masked, one sensed, a steely anger. Under pressure, her mettle became more obvious, her stability and confidence ever more reassuring. But by the time of the first debate, the mutual loathing between the two candidates was palpable.

As ever, the agent of contagion was Trump. So erratic was his behavior that serious journalists begin questioning his mental stability—a break with tradition, if not a breach of journalistic decorum. So incessant were his lies that sober institutions like the *New York Times* began calling them out. And so rabid were his followers that they viewed any criticism as part of a conspiracy against Trump—and them—perpetrated by worldwide elites.

No matter what, they believed him. They believed him when he claimed that America was flooded with ISIS operatives from Syria; that thousands of illegal aliens were poised to vote against him; that statistically non-existent voter fraud was rampant; that America's electoral machinery was rigged. They believed his incredible denials when a growing list of women accused him of sexual predation. And when he departed from all tradition by refusing to commit to honoring the election results, they applauded.

Trump was no longer running a campaign—he was dividing the country by driving a stake through the heart of our civic traditions. A candidacy that began as farce was ending as tragedy, with an outcome—and a cost—as yet unknown.

Then, at the eleventh hour—eleven days prior to the election—FBI director James Comey gave Trump a priceless deus ex machina.

And everything changed.

Coming This Fall

The Sublime Revenge of Barack Obama

AUGUST 9, 2016

Most presidential campaigns are freighted with drama: colliding ambitions, revelations of character, pivotal moments that arrive without warning. But the drama of 2016 involves much more than a clash of two candidates. For it also turns on the ideals and ambitions of America's first black president, and how the trials of his tenure—indeed, of his life—have permeated not only the national consciousness, but his own soul.

True, much of the resolve Barack Obama will bring to electing Hillary Clinton is about legacy. But it is also about the kind of man he is, and what he wants this country to be. And that is inexorably intertwined with the entirely different man who is Donald Trump.

First, legacy.

It is not my purpose here to make the historic case for Obama's presidency. But his accomplishments bear at least some resemblance to those of Franklin Roosevelt in the early days of the New Deal, or of Lyndon Johnson before he crashed and burned in Vietnam.

He ameliorated the worst economic crisis since the Great Depression. He saved the auto industry. He extended health

One of the truly melancholy aspects of this election is that Barack Obama will be succeeded by Donald Trump. Knowing how that feels to so many of us we can sense, also, how it must feel to Obama. He and the First Lady brought eloquence, passion, and grace to supporting Hillary Clinton and, by extension, to their effort to engrave the accomplishments and spirit of his tenure on the years that followed. However one feels about their time in the White House, they are exceptional as people, and as models of behavior.

care to millions of Americans. He put two capable and progressive women on the Supreme Court. And he did so in the face of unprecedented partisanship and polarization.

In the area of foreign policy and national security, he took out bin Laden and decimated Al-Qaeda. He negotiated the Iran deal, and opened a new relationship to Cuba—controversial acts that, in the end, will likely be vindicated by history. And he helped design and negotiate an international treaty to combat climate change.

It is in foreign policy, as well, that the principal criticisms of his tenure lie. It can be argued that he left Iraq too soon, entered Libya too precipitously, and abandoned his red line in Syria for too little. But it is surely true that in the Middle East the consequences of action or inaction are as difficult to forecast as they are severe.

In the margin: *Sadly, Trump and the GOP have pledged to gut his legacy—including the Affordable Care Act, the Iran nuclear accord, the multinational agreement to combat climate change, and, effectively, the president's efforts to promote tolerance and diversity. As a conspicuous example, Trump's principal environmental advisor is a climate change contrarian.*

In the end, there is little doubt that history will view Barack Obama as a very consequential president—perhaps even, some may argue, a great one.

That verdict lies ahead. More salient, for now, is to consider what kind of man he is.

I can't claim to know him—I don't. But four years before he became president I got at least some insight, which the trials of his presidency bore out.

The occasion was the morning after his breakthrough convention speech in 2004—overnight, it seemed, he had become a prominent and potentially unique national figure. The circumstances of our meeting aren't important. But for roughly forty-five minutes, my wife, Nancy, and I visited with him alone.

For a number of reasons, he made a deep impression on us both. Part of this involved the difference between Obama and the numerous other political leaders I've known over time—not to mention Donald Trump as all of us have come to know him.

Our conversation was just that—a genuine conversation. He listened closely, attentive to nuance. It became obvious that Obama had a deep curiosity, and knew great deal about a great many things. But where another politician might work overtime to show his knowledge of whatever most concerned you, more striking were his questions and how much he took in.

My concerns were those of a more or less typical white progressive—no surprise, then, that a smart guy like Barack Obama had mastered those subjects. But then he began probing Nancy's work as an educational consultant in underdeveloped countries—a subject about which most Americans, including our politicians, know even less than they imagine.

Not Obama. Again, he asked great questions. More surprising, it gradually became apparent that he knew quite a bit about the context for Nancy's efforts. This, then, was not a matter of professional necessity, but genuine curiosity.

With this came a nice sense of detachment from self. Later on that summer, we went to a fund-raiser for his Senate campaign. Based on our prior acquaintance, the three of us were having an amiable and nonpolitical conversation when the representative of a women's group shouldered us aside, claiming the space to assure Obama that her group had been pivotal to his rise.

As we watched, Obama responded with polite appreciation. At length the woman departed. With mock gravity, Nancy put a hand on Obama's shoulder and said, "For my part, Senator, I want to assure you that I've had absolutely nothing to do with your success."

Many a candidate would squirm at such an irony. Obama grinned, then broke up altogether, eyes alight with real amusement. Here was a politician who got the joke—including his role in it.

Needless to say, Donald Trump never would.

But the awareness of self and surroundings was surely bred in Barack Obama from early on. To appreciate this, one need not know him—one need simply pause to imagine his life, and what went into becoming the man who became our forty-fourth president.

Imagine being a multiracial kid whose Kenyan father abandoned him young. A kid whose peripatetic mother moved him to Indonesia to marry her Asian second husband before divorcing him. A kid returned to a distant outpost of America, Hawaii, to be largely raised by his white grandparents. A kid separated from the history and heritage of the African Americans with whom America would group him. A kid who knew that every time he stepped into a room, others would see him as a different version of "the other."

Imagine, then, the sense of caution, the gift for observation, the feeling of solitude, the awesome self-reliance the young Barack Obama would need to navigate the world. Imagine the stunning realization that, in ways few could understand, he was a person unto himself. Imagine the sensitivity to difference through which he learned to deal with differences.

Then, perhaps, we begin to imagine the man we came to know. The truly extraordinary understanding he brought to speaking on race when that necessity was thrust on him by Reverend Jeremiah Wright. The experience of becoming a human Rorschach test who, simply by aspiring to leadership, symbolized our psychic response to race—for most of us, of racial progress; for a fearful minority, of displacement within a society that threatens them.

Imagine, too, the awesome forbearance it took to remain stoic in the face of the racist birtherism stoked by Donald Trump. Or the criticism of African Americans who believed that he should speak first and foremost as a black man. Or the racist rudeness of a white southern congressman shouting "liar" at a black American president. Or the ceaseless Republican obstruction underwritten by racial animus. Or political enemies trying to convert his own wife to that racist stereotype—angry black woman—fueled by their own subliminal guilt and unease.

Imagine, further, the burden of knowing that, though you personified the best of America to the world, millions of your fellow Americans hated you because of your race.

Imagine all that, and wonder at the extraordinary grace Barack Obama brought to the ceaseless task of both leading and representing us. Feel gratitude, as well, for a man who gave us an administration that was high in ethics, and a family so consistently admirable in leading such a uniquely unnatural existence.

But we have been lately reminded, yet again, that for any president—but particularly this one—race is a minefield, all the worse because of the ongoing trials of black Americans, to whose experience too many whites are oblivious, and who look to Obama to express their frustration and pain.

The tragedies in Baton Rouge, St. Paul, and Dallas captured his dilemma. Blacks asserted that he had been too slow to condemn police shootings of other blacks; irrational and angry whites held him responsible for deaths in Dallas simply because he expressed concern about the deaths in Baton Rouge and St. Paul; the despicable Trump accused him of dividing the country. As a fatalist, he must surely have anticipated this, just as, surely, it must have taken a toll.

And yet throughout his term, as he did again in Dallas, he has comported himself with admirable balance, speaking for all Americans without retreating from his identity as a black man, whether stating the stark and simple truth that Trayvon Martin could have been his son, to leading the mourners in Charleston by singing "Amazing Grace."

Graceful, indeed—and hard.

So imagine how Barack Obama must feel about Donald Trump.

Some of those feelings are surely personal—and wholly justified. Trump is the odious gasbag who tried to humiliate our first black president by feeding the racism, nativism, and xenophobia of the bogus birther movement. The moral cipher who, simply to get attention, assaulted Obama with groundless lies. The opportunist who ultimately compelled our president to release his birth certificate to quell the fevered suggestion that he was not, somehow, legitimate.

Thus it was pleasing to watch Obama dispatch Trump at the White House Correspondents' Dinner, turning the man's bloviations to sport for our national amusement. But his disdain for Trump is far more than personal, for the bilious billionaire is the antithesis of everything that Obama wants America and its president to be.

Obama prizes reasoned dialogue; Trump is an ignorant demagogue. Obama strives to make judicious judgments; Trump's sputterings are mindless to the point of danger. Obama speaks to inclusiveness and generosity; Trump to suspicion and divisiveness. Obama is a man of dignity; Trump a narcissistic buffoon who would degrade our public life.

Obama is ever conscious of his responsibilities; Trump feels no responsibility to anyone or anything but his own all-consuming ego. Obama is the president who made the brave and risky decision to go after Osama bin Laden; Trump is the draft dodger who questions his loyalty and spine.

And here's the core of it. Obama has surmounted the toils and trials of race, and asked us to do the same. Trump is a practicing racist.

Trump's offenses against decency are legion. He targets blacks with racist dog whistles; Mexicans with demeaning stereotypes; American Muslims with insinuations that they are, collectively, a fifth column for terrorists. And, in doing so, he tears at the fabric of that which is most precious, and often most fragile, in our society.

Every fiber of Barack Obama must want to banish Donald Trump from public life. And, at last, his opportunity is at hand.

We have already seen the preview. In the wake of the slaughter in Orlando, Trump shamed himself by spewing self-congratulations combined with demagoguery, lies, and practical and moral idiocy—scapegoating Syrian refugees and every Muslim abroad; suggesting that American Muslims at large were complicit in terror; labeling Obama's careful effort to distinguish between terrorists and all Muslims as weak; and, perhaps most loathsome, questioning the president's loyalty.

With palpable contempt, Obama eviscerated all this. He then reminded us that "we don't have religious tests here" and that "we've seen our government mistreat our fellow citizens, and that has been a shameful part of our history." And, by doing so, he reminded us of the ways in which Donald Trump would not only undermine our security, but our values.

But that response was the grim duty of a president faced with tragedy. At the Democratic convention, we got a glimpse of how Obama will eviscerate Trump—for the emptiness of the man, and the stunted prism through which he views America. And after Trump demeaned the Khan family, Obama used the moral authority of his office to challenge Trump's fitness to hold it.

Come the fall, Barack Obama will be free to mount an argument in his own time and way, giving everything he has to make sure that the next president embraces, not destroys, the values he has brought to the office. And, by doing this, he will exact his well-earned reprisal on Donald Trump, dispatching him from public life with the back of his hand.

Perhaps that is the best part. Barack Obama's ultimate revenge is not simply that he will do that, but how—with a grace and elegance beyond the power of a man like Trump to summon, or even imagine.

Sublime.

Obama proved to be an aggressive and devastating surrogate, savoring each moment as he vouched for Clinton, rallied his coalition, and lanced Trump for every aspect of his disturbed and disturbing behavior. But the power of Michelle Obama on the stump was stunning—especially when speaking for women after Trump's predation surfaced. Together they held back nothing.

The Fateful August of Donald J. Trump

AUGUST 30, 2016

In the month since the conventions, the jittery surface of the twenty-four-hour news cycle has been roiled by crosscurrents, its avatars trumpeting each new event as more dramatic than the last. But beneath there is a sickly stillness of a candidacy mired in the swampland of Donald Trump's own mind, creating a numbing ennui seeping through the electorate like encephalitis in slow motion. Too many Americans have realized who he is.

The contrast between the dystopia of Cleveland—four midnights in America—and the competence of Philadelphia left him trailing. But something worse had happened to Trump himself: instead of provoking excitement, he was inducing fear and stupefaction.

True, his lies come so quickly that none has meaning in itself. But the larger meaning comes through—Trump's every statement has no meaning but Trump himself. To call him a liar is to assume deliberation in a man who cares nothing about the words he speaks beyond whether they serve him in the moment. Such people are not merely frightening—they are exhausting.

With ten weeks to go, he seems no more thoughtful or capable than he did during the primaries, when all he had to

According to polls, Trump's negatives remained the highest recorded for any major party candidate in history—well over 60%. But in the campaign's stunning final days, even that was not enough.

do was inflame a plurality of inflammable Republicans. The only difference is that, fearful of defeat, he reads more often from a teleprompter, proving nothing but that he has the basic literacy to recite the simplistic sentences others write for him. He may have changed his management team, but he cannot change himself.

The larger audience of the general electorate is on to this, and it worries them. They sense that the real man—the only man Trump values—resides in his spontaneous utterances. And those betray the stunted soul who lives within Trump 3.0.

That is why his attack on the Khan family—a far more egregious and persistent lapse than Mitt Romney's 47 percent moment—lingers in the mind. His stunning lack of empathy, particularly for Mrs. Khan, was bad enough. Add lack of judgment—a normal man would not disparage the parents of a dead American soldier. And, even worse, throw in his whiny claim that he was "viciously attacked."

He kept after this for four days, asserting on his own behalf that his pursuit of billions "involved a lot of sacrifices"—though not, perhaps, quite as wounding as losing a son or, even more precious, his own life. But we swiftly learned that Trump was never at risk of this, having secured a medical deferment during Vietnam—a safe harbor he falsely attributed to a high lottery number. Another man might have maintained a graceful silence.

But then another man would not try to recover his footing by accepting a Purple Heart from a veteran, then braying that this was a "much easier" way of acquiring one than actually getting wounded in the service of his country.

As with all the months before, August was replete with such defining moments. The difference is that more Americans are watching Trump more closely. And what they see disqualifies him—not just as a leader, but as a man.

Instead of reaching out to Republican officeholders worried about his candidacy, he disparaged them. But this was as nothing to the several days he spent insisting that Barack

Obama and Hillary Clinton were the "founders" of ISIS, praising himself as a "truth teller" before retreating, under pressure, to the claim that he was merely being "sarcastic." Whatever he was being, it was not presidential.

Asked about sexual harassment, he opined that should his own daughter be victimized, "I would like to think she would find another career or find another company . . ." Startling—until one remembered that Trump defended Roger Ailes against charges of serial harassment worthy of Bill Cosby, questioning the motives of some of Ailes's accusers.

But this is standard fare, for Trump's search for the bottom is bottomless. Having begun the month by attacking the Khans, he ended it by exploiting the separation of Hillary Clinton's aide, Huma Abedin, from the troubled Anthony Weiner—suggesting that Weiner had access to classified information from the State Department. His grounds? There are none. For Trump, gratuitous cruelty to others is just another opportunity to get the attention he craves.

This ugly verbal incontinence has a way of turning sinister. Hence his suggestion that "the Second Amendment people" could find a way to prevent Hillary Clinton from appointing judges they don't like—a casual recycling of the violent right-wing trope that "Second Amendment remedies" may be needed to address some imaginary federal overreach.

Thus, too, the rancid undertone of his commentary on race, religion, or ethnicity.

Speaking in Maine, he offended locals of all races by groundlessly portraying peaceful Somali immigrants to the area as sources of crime and potential terrorism. Even his purported outreach to African Americans—delivered to a crowd of white folks in an obvious effort to mollify white suburbanites—was riddled with condescension and inaccuracy and suffused with racial stereotyping: "You live in your poverty, your schools are no good, you have no jobs,

It was not until October, when Trump defended himself in a similar way against charges of sexual assault, that his defense of Ailes fully resonated. In the interim Fox had paid a handsome sum to settle a sexual harassment suit involving Ailes.

Or so I thought. Eleven days before the election, while investigating Weiner for sexting a fifteen-year-old girl, the FBI discovered that the disgraced Congressman's computer contained emails between Clinton and Abedin. Though neither he nor anyone else in the FBI knew at the time what was in those emails, FBI Director James Comey wrote to Republican committee chairs in Congress that the FBI had new information

(continued)

58 percent of your youth is unemployed. What the hell do you have to lose?"

One can start with any hope of a responsible dialogue about race. Trump's "alt-right" view of African Americans—so effectively skewered by Hillary Clinton—decamps from reality. By any historic measure our cities are safer. Despite the stubborn scourge of our racial history, more black Americans are doing better, and few recognize their communities—however grave their difficulties—in the bleak "war zones" that Trump describes. To be sure, the devastating portrait he paints is about something real: not the lives of black people, but about how Donald Trump has always seen black people.

To the extent that he sees them at all. Over the weekend, the cousin of NBA star Dwyane Wade was randomly killed in Chicago by gunfire while walking her baby. Trump responded with a particularly odious tweet: "Just what I have been saying. African Americans will VOTE TRUMP"— neatly exemplifying his insensitivity to personal tragedy and to black Americans as a whole.

Among increasing numbers of Americans, the overall effect is boredom and fatigue—akin to listening to a cretinous uncle, deep in his cups as he spoils Thanksgiving dinner, spouting ignorant racial theories made even more dispiriting by the certainty that he shares them with his friends. All that jolts one out of stultitude is that Trump wants his friends to make him president.

Equally noxious is his appeal to racism as a means of delegitimizing the general election in advance. "I'm telling you," Trump forecasts, "November 8 we'd better be careful because that election is going to be rigged." On this pretext Trump is proposing voter suppression vigilante-style: encouraging squads of supporters to show up at polling places to identify suspect voters. One need not be a cynic to appreciate that the means of identification will involve pigmentation.

But just as corrosive is Trump's cynical effort to excuse defeat by eroding confidence in our electoral process because

potentially relevant to Clinton's use of a private server. Comey was widely criticized for this introduction of a potentially game-changing discovery so close to the election, and his actions allowed Trump to crow about his prescience and display his grasp of modern history by claiming it to be the "biggest political scandal since Watergate."

"the other" has stolen the election. The residue could transcend the birther movement in its damage to our societal glue—the feverish belief among a subset of Americans that Hillary Clinton is not a legitimate president.

A particularly disturbing compound of lies, stupidity, self-delusion, and self-interest fuels Trump's vacuous commentary on Vladimir Putin. Start with the foundational falsehood: Trump's stunning claim in 2014 that, "I was in Moscow recently and I spoke, indirectly and directly, with President Putin, who could not have been nicer." Or his assertion in a November 2015 GOP debate that, "I got to know [Putin] very well because we were both on *60 Minutes*."

Six-year-olds are allowed to conjure imaginary friends. But not presidential candidates. It is beyond dispute—as Trump has now been forced to admit—that he and Putin have never met or even spoken. Even more bizarre is that Trump seems to imagine that the rest of us share his incapacity to separate fiction from reality—and thus that no one would notice, for example, that *60 Minutes* taped its interviews with Trump in New York and Putin in Moscow.

But his obsession with Putin transcends the merely fantastical, raising serious questions about our national security. He publicly encouraged the Russians to hack Hillary Clinton's email. And, quite clearly, he is the intended beneficiary of hacking against the Democratic National Committee performed, experts believe, by Russian intelligence, resulting in emails siphoned through WikiLeaks to damage Clinton's campaign. One must wonder why Putin takes such an apparent interest in making Trump our commander in chief.

Could it be, just maybe, that this serves Putin's interests?

Trump's ignorance surely does. Questioned by George Stephanopoulos as to why the GOP platform softened its stance on defending the Ukraine against Russian aggression, Trump said of Putin, "He's not going into Ukraine, okay, just so you understand."

In October his lies about voter fraud reached a crescendo and then their unprecedented apotheosis—his refusal to commit to honoring the election results.

Astonished, Stephanopoulos rejoined, "Well, he's already there, isn't he?," compelling a clearly mystified Trump to fudge with, "Okay, well, he's there in a certain way . . ." That certain way, as any Ukrainian could tell him, includes the annexation of Crimea and insinuation of Russian troops and military hardware into that part of the country that remains.

But not to worry, Trump said—"From what I've heard [the Crimeans] would rather be with Russia than where they were." The origins of this insight went unmentioned, though one possible source is his erstwhile campaign manager, Paul Manafort, who has raked in millions advising a pro-Russian autocrat who was formerly president of the Ukraine. Elsewhere, to Putin's larger benefit, Trump has declared NATO to be "obsolete," and questioned the principle that an attack on one member state is an attack on all.

Indeed, Trump's partiality for Putin partakes of callousness—and not just toward Russia's external victims. He described Putin to Joe Scarborough as a "leader, unlike what we have in this country," fusing fondness for his imaginary friend Vladimir with an unseemly taste for authoritarianism. When Scarborough countered that Putin "kills journalists that don't agree with him," Trump blithely responded, "Well, I think our country does a lot of killing also, Joe."

Of journalists? Such moral and intellectual vacancy is a boon to cold-blooded men like Vladimir Putin.

But perhaps, by pandering to Putin, Donald Trump is also looking out for himself. I have it on good authority that Trump can no longer get financing from American banks. There is no doubt that, under Putin's auspices, he could do much better in Russia—if he has not done so already. Which may be one reason, among many, to conceal his tax returns.

Whatever the case, highly placed Russian officials have openly welcomed the prospect of a President Trump. No mystery here—if anyone knows how to exploit ignorance and egotism, it is surely Vladimir Putin. Which is why

Michael Morell, a former acting director of the CIA, has characterized Trump as an unwitting agent of Russia.

Given the cacophony surrounding Trump, his affinity for Putin has stolen but imperfectly into the national consciousness. Still, it is already seeding doubt. And August is the month when more Americans became fearful of Trump as commander in chief.

Nowhere is presidential latitude broader, and the risks greater, than in the conduct of foreign policy and the exercise of military power. The opportunities to take ill-advised and unilateral actions are legion—abandoning allies, scrapping treaties and trade deals, arbitrarily barring all immigration from friendly European countries, and, of course, lighting the powder keg of the Middle East. The latter threat, at least, is something that Americans get. But nothing focuses our collective mind like the specter of nuclear war.

Thus it is striking that the prospect of President Trump has provoked a broad discussion of the chief executive's power to go nuclear. The alarming consensus is articulated by nuclear expert Franklin C. Miller: "The president and only the president has the authority to order the use of nuclear weapons." Perhaps the most effective ad run by the Clinton campaign in August addresses the danger of Trump's stubby fingers on our nuclear codes. And given his behavior—this month, and every month—more Americans are recoiling from the thought.

That is lethal. Because August is the month when concern about Trump's mental state went mainstream. For the first time in recent memory, a candidate's pattern of behavior—sustained for fourteen months now—made his psychological health the subject of serious and considered public discussion.

For a good while, those of us who raised this directly were a distinct minority of commentators, running afoul of the understandable journalistic reluctance to speak to a candidate's emotional stability. For many, this was a matter of ethics. But, at last, Trump's behavior swept all that away.

And so in August, in varying ways, some of our most prominent pundits across the ideological spectrum expressed fears about Trump's mental fitness to be president: David Brooks, Eugene Robinson, Charles Krauthammer, Peggy Noonan, Joe Scarborough, and Robert Kagan. And, with annihilating thoroughness, Keith Olbermann spelled out in *Vanity Fair* how perfectly Trump's otherwise inexplicable conduct matches up with the symptoms of narcissistic personality disorder.

Americans as a whole do not keep the *DSM* at their fingertips. But they do have instincts that, unlike Trump's, stem from their experience in noticing other human beings. August was the month that a critical mass of Americans noticed that Donald Trump notices nothing but himself.

So, given all this, why didn't Clinton win? Analysts will argue about this for years: It was a change election. It was the emails; the Clinton Foundation; unfair press coverage; twenty-five years of abuse from the right wing. She's not a natural. She's too cautious, or too moderate. James Comey cost her the election (which I tend to believe). But I also remember a preeminent Democrat strategist asking me last winter, "When will she get a message?" What he meant was a clear vision, clearly articulated, about how Clinton would improve our lives and our future. Many argue that one never really gelled—a serious failing in these restive times, when a majority of the electorate thought America was heading in the wrong direction.

Trump 3.0

Pivoting in Quicksand

SEPTEMBER 6, 2016

As most Americans enjoyed Labor Day, Donald Trump found himself staring into the political abyss.

Imagine his surprise and disappointment. The new Donald was pivoting! He had a message—Hillary Clinton is bad. His new campaign manager gave him new words to read from a teleprompter. He was the candidate of change—any change. He was reaching out to black people to impress white people. He might even allow a few undocumented immigrants to linger—though maybe not. And after fourteen months of lying, some polls even said that he was still more "trusted" than Clinton—though not so much.

Why am I still behind, Trump must wonder, when those emails are sticking to Hillary's shoes like chewing gum? Sometimes she even stepped in it herself. What did she think Colin Powell was going to say—that he begged her to use a private server? And so what if none of the emails actually show political corruption? Millions of Americans believed him when he called the Clinton Foundation "the most corrupt enterprise in political history"—especially the ones who have never heard of Richard Nixon. And who the hell cares about Caligula—whoever he was.

Plus, The Donald had a great new team to help him appeal to women—Stephen Bannon, Roger Ailes, and Julian

Assange. After all, those domestic violence charges against Steve were twenty years old. No one had actually accused Roger of rape, just being a tough negotiator. And those rape charges against Julian are entirely unproven, just like his connection to those helpful hackers in Russian intelligence who keep siphoning him Hillary's emails.

World-class recruits, one imagines Trump thinking. And that Kellyanne Conway is tougher than any man, or even Rachel Maddow . . .

But enough. Sorry, readers, I just can't keep this up—trying to think like Donald Trump is too exhausting. So instead I will try to explore why, come November, none of these changes will save him from himself.

It all seemed so logical—which, perhaps, was my analytic failure. I certainly persuaded myself.

True, the seemingly infinite supply of emails will dog Hillary Clinton until Election Day, and some of her wounds are self-inflicted. But despite all the media piety about the "appearance of impropriety" with respect to the Clinton Foundation, the substance of these emails contains a paucity of the improper. One strains to find a flyspeck of wrong-doing in the dunghill of reportage.

And whenever things get bad, Clinton—or Trump himself—has proven adroit at shifting the subject to Trump's biggest weakness: Trump himself. That is why her linkage of Trump with the bigoted "alt-right" was so devastating and persuasive—Trump himself has seeded the ground with his designation of the head of Breitbart.com, an "alt-right" website awash in racism, as his campaign's CEO.

Of little help was his drive-by photo op in an African-American neighborhood in Detroit, accompanied by the extraterrestrial Ben Carson. Its essence was foreshadowed by a comedic prelude: the revelation of a script for a taped interview wherein Trump would be queried by a black pastor. Not only did the Trump campaign provide the questions—it had written out answers to be memorized by their clueless candidate.

This drove home a devastating truth—without help, Trump has nothing to say to black Americans. Briefly visiting Carson's childhood home, Trump resembled a tourist entering a foreign country. And when he appeared at a black church, he read a few scripted sentiments so obviously alien to his thinking that every word must have come as a surprise—to Trump himself.

Nowhere did he acknowledge any words or actions—in this campaign, or ever—that might have offended his audience. But given that he did not know his audience, save as interchangeable props in his dystopian view of black America, perhaps he had no language for this. To imagine Bill Clinton in his place, joyfully immersed in the spiritual life of the parishioners, is to capture the shallowness of Trump's performance. It did not last long.

Equally hollow was his recitation of "policy speeches" meant to dress him up in substance.

His prescriptions for the economy combined the worst of two worlds. First, he caved in completely to the GOP's hoary economic dogma: a budget-busting combination of tax cuts for the rich and corporations, with a special tip for the donor class—a total repeal of the estate tax that would benefit the wealthiest .02 percent of Americans. Reversing course, he then doubled down on his potentially ruinous economic populism, pledging to kill trade deals and slap tariffs on the Chinese. One cringes to think what this schizoid Donald would do to our economy.

Never did Trump concede that he cannot exhume jobs killed by automation and the global economy. Nowhere did he promise struggling Americans the one thing that could help—retraining, education, and help in relocation for those displaced by the new economy. Instead of substance, the whole thing smacked of fraud.

Similarly, his speech on fighting ISIS interspersed new absurdities among the old ones. He would bar immigration from countries that breed terrorism. Who? Germany, France, Belgium—or all three? He promised "extreme vetting" of immigrants—including probing inquiries as to whether the applicant believed in things like honor killings, presumably prompting a wave of confessions from guilt-stricken would-be terrorists. He pledged to evaluate other countries based solely on their help against ISIS, ignoring a host of areas—such as global warming and nuclear proliferation—where we need the assistance of governments with interests of their own.

To this he added a few incendiary old favorites—like approving of torture and seizing oil fields in the Middle East. All in all, Trump succeeded only in reducing counterterrorism to a video game, proving that nonsense is not improved merely by reading it from a teleprompter.

But nothing captured Trump's intellectual and emotional twitchiness better than his multiple feints on his core issue, immigration.

In the primaries, that was how he made his bones—as a wall-building, Mexican-deporting, America First hardliner. And he loved it—so much that he conjured a "deportation force" to perform the impossible task of kicking out all 11 million undocumented immigrants. And anytime a rally became too decorous to sate his need for adoration, he would put up the wall again and demand to know who would pay for it, provoking his rapturous fans to feed the beast by shouting "Mexico!"

But that, sadly for Trump, was then. In recent weeks his new campaign team broke the news that a lot of voters thought his policies more than a bit inhumane—not simply Latinos and other minorities, but the suburban whites he would need to have a prayer of becoming president. Maybe, just maybe, he ought to soft-pedal the stuff about shipping out every last grandmother, wife, and kid.

For Trump, this must have been hard to take. He'd only been having fun, after all—and it was lots of fun! Still, the idea of getting slaughtered was surely painful. So what was an egotist to do?

No one seemed to know—not Trump, not his team. In one semi-incoherent day Trump suggested that he was "softening" on mass deportations, then appeared to reverse himself. At length it was announced that Trump would clarify all in a speech to be given in Phoenix.

For the next few days, his surrogates implied that he would focus on expelling criminals instead of the entire undocumented population. The TV commentariat exhausted itself—and the rest of us—in wondering whether this newly empathetic Trump would mollify white suburbanites or alienate his hard-core base. Breathlessly, we awaited his debut.

Abruptly, on the day of his speech Trump flew to Mexico to meet with President Enrique Peña Nieto who, to the mystification of all, had agreed to serve as a prop for Trump's campaign. In the joint appearance that followed, Trump excited awe and wonder by reading his speech in a normal tone of voice. Even more striking, in the view of many, was his diplomatic avoidance—at least by his own account—of raising with Peña Nieto the subject of who would pay for his wall. And so for the next several hours, cable news proclaimed the advent of a statesmanlike Donald on the world stage, authoring a masterstroke of geopolitical theater.

As often, the effect was tarnished by a Twitter war—precipitated, in this case, by the Mexican president's insistence that he had told Trump that his country would never pay for the wall. This was accompanied by bitter tweets from all quarters of Mexico, condemning the hapless Peña Nieto for meeting with Trump at all. By the time Trump landed in Phoenix, theater was descending into farce, and the diplomat had morphed into a demagogue hungry to whip up a crowd.

And so the red meat flew. Trump was building that wall, and Mexico was paying for it. Mexican immigrants were murdering Americans and taking their jobs. His deportation force was going after the hordes of Mexican criminals first, but no one was safe from deportation, and any hope of legal status was out the window. The only nuance, if it was one, was his failure to address the subject of purposeful mass deportations—in the hope that voters for or against would see Trump as their champion.

Thus, after all of the confusion, obfuscation, and hints of a new direction, nothing much had changed—not the tone, nor the appeals to racial resentment, nor the insatiable craving to foment mass anger and frenzy. The GOP's die was cast: their candidate was unwilling, or unable, to kick the hard line that had won him the primaries and that, in all likelihood, would precipitate his defeat in November—killing off other Republicans in the bargain.

Their conundrum grows ever more excruciating—and embarrassing. Party leaders like Mitch McConnell and Paul Ryan remain determined to ride out the hurricane by patching up Trump's leaky boat, hoping to reach dry land after he drowned in November. The price has been a series of verbal contortions in which they distance themselves from his most offensive effusions, while invoking Clinton as a reason to support him. They might look small now, the reasoning went, but their party would be grateful to those who steered the boat to safety.

This, too, is the plight of Reince Priebus. And so Priebus struggles to save his House and Senate candidates by buttressing the man who threatens to bring them down, all the while pretending that Trump is fit to be president—at least until it becomes exigent to ditch him in all but name.

Such are the burdens of collective responsibility. Sustained by the rationale that preserving their fractious party served the larger good, these men have put political courage and even decency on hold. This has earned them widespread scorn. But perhaps more should have noticed that many Republicans who disowned Trump, however sincerely, had little but their own interests to think of, and even less to lose.

Take the Republican senators who have disowned or explicitly distanced themselves from Trump. Susan Collins, Ben Sasse, Jeff Flake, Lindsey Graham, and the inimitable Ted Cruz are not up for reelection. Still, their collective

It is still stunning to consider how completely Trump violated every paradigm for a successful candidate. Any one of his endless mistakes would, in any other candidate I can think of, be disastrous. One can imagine all the politicians whose careers were ruined by a single misstep watching him with envy and amazement. Everything bounced off him—including sex, lies, and videotape.

critique is a telling reminder to white-collar Republican voters that Trump is not a normal nominee.

The same is true of the fifty Republican national security experts who declared that Trump "would put at risk
our country's national security and well-being." Or the 100
past or present GOP officials who implored Priebus to stop
supporting Trump. Or the conservative intellectuals who,
by rejecting Trump, hope to advance a new agenda that
addresses the struggling middle class and poor. Together,
these voices become part of the background noise of the
campaign, helping to leach support where Trump needs it
most—his own party.

Another problem is that Trump's serial sackings of his
campaign team further undermined his managerial preten-
sions. The aversion of Republican pros left him dependent
on a scurvy sequence of deputies. Corey Lewandowski
proved thuggish and abrasive. Paul Manafort, it transpired,
had raked in millions from a pro-Russian ex-president of
the Ukraine, casting a dubious light on Trump's passion for
Vladimir Putin.

Not to mention Trump's disinterest in character and
indifference to vetting. Fresh from departing Fox News
after multiple charges of sexual harassment, Roger Ailes
signed on as an adviser. Trump's new campaign CEO, Steve
Bannon, comes trailing charges of domestic violence and
falsely claiming residence in Florida. Only his latest campaign manager, Kellyanne Conway, is capable and experienced, evoking rapture from the media desperate for a
familiar face.

For those delving the murky recesses of Trump's mind,
Bannon rewards particular attention.

His website, Breitbart.com, is financed by another dubious character, Robert Mercer. Mercer is not exactly a man
of the people: an ultraconservative billionaire and alleged
tax cheat, he was last seen conducting his war against
the IRS by supporting Ted Cruz. Now a fanatic Trump

In the end, Trump survived because so many Americans in these polarized times disliked Clinton—fairly or not—and because, for an angry plurality, the importance of the message they were sending transcended the quality or qualifications of the messenger. Many of those people, of course, identified with him on a visceral level as a voice shouting down the elites they despised.

supporter—a fact no doubt related to Trump's tax cuts for the rich—Mercer commended Bannon as just the man to sharpen the candidate's message.

Indeed. Breitbart.com is home to what a writer for the conservative *National Review* called "the racist, moral rot at the heart of the alt-right," including white supremacist rhetoric and articles like those recently cited by Hillary Clinton: "Birth Control Makes Women Unattractive and Crazy"; "Would You Rather Your Child Had Feminism or Cancer?"; and "Hoist It High and Proud: The Confederate Flag Proclaims a Glorious Heritage." Not to mention this gem—"Gabby Giffords: The Gun Control Movement's Human Shield." For Bannon, as for Trump, words don't matter—venom does.

Which makes Bannon the perfect enabler. Under his auspices, we can safely expect Donald Trump to achieve new lows in what is already the most vile campaign in modern history.

Hillary Clinton will not simply be untrustworthy, unwise, ethically challenged, and wrong on the issues—she will be traitorous, corrupt, immoral, criminal, bigoted, sickly, and brain damaged. There resides Trump's sole hope of victory—turning out his base in a low turn out election so repugnant that millions of potential voters will recoil in disgust, thereby degrading the country he proposes to lead.

Here's the only good news—it's too late for anything else.

If anything, the demographic fundamentals for Trump have gotten a bit worse. Except for white males, where his support is eroding, Trump is losing in virtually every key demographic.

Clinton is slaughtering him by potentially historic margins among nonwhites, whose loathing he has so richly earned. She is beating Trump among women as a whole, and gaining ground with Republican women. Unlike Romney, Trump is losing the Catholic vote decisively—suggesting,

Trump proceeded to degrade the country. But some of his worst behaviors—his Twitter war with a beauty queen and, more damaging, gamy video tapes and charges of sexual assault failed to repel as many women as polls predicted.

perhaps, that feuding with the Pope was not a brilliant notion.

Among college graduates, traditionally helpful to the GOP, Clinton has opened a lead. Her margin among young voters is close to three to one. And the bulk of Sanders voters are now Clinton voters. For all the talk that Trump would change the demographic map, it seems more likely that Clinton can challenge him in states like Georgia and Arizona.

Trump's dilemma is that his base—modestly educated whites—is shrinking, the groups he repels expanding. And Republicans are losing their fight to defend the voter suppression laws through which they hoped to diminish nonwhite turnout.

Unlike Trump, Clinton is running a steady campaign, and she has largely succeeded in making him the issue. Most voters harbor deep-seated doubts about his temperament, not to mention his fitness to be commander in chief. What keeps him in the game is that roughly as many voters doubt that Clinton has been transparent or even candid in addressing her personal conduct—a serious weakness reinforced by the constant drip of emails that, if nothing else, resurrect her bad decision to use a private server.

Still, Trump has the bigger weakness—himself. Whatever her problems with trust, a great many voters trust Clinton to be competent and prepared. For many voters, this is the ultimate test—who can they imagine as president—and only Clinton passes it. In this environment, a greater proportion of Republicans than Democrats may cross over or simply stay home.

Nor is the vaunted black swan event—some transformational occurrence—likely. Terrorism? Voters question Trump's judgment. Some terrible email? We haven't seen one yet, nor do we have a reason to believe that such a phantasm exists. Trump trouncing Clinton in debate? Really? Obama couldn't do it in 2008, and he actually knows his stuff.

On election day, the candidates' relative turnout was exactly as Trump planned. Trump attracted more white voters than expected; Clinton did not turn out blacks, Latinos, and young people to the degree that her campaign hoped—and worked hard to get. In this sense, Trump defied demographic trends.

The black swan event—unanticipated and unprecedented—was James Comey's letter of October 28.

I don't foresee a rout. Chances are that dislike for Clinton will combine with political polarization to close the margin in the popular vote. But if anyone will be redrawing the electoral map, it's Hillary Clinton—leaving Trump with the dregs.

He will have earned every one of them—and a great many of the votes for Clinton, as well.

In the event, Clinton took the popular vote, but Trump rearranged the electoral map in Rust Belt states. Again, turnout.

Public Disservice
The Media and Hillary Clinton

SEPTEMBER 13, 2016

For over a year, stories about Hillary Clinton's emails have dominated the coverage of her campaign. But an equally important story is the coverage itself—and, more broadly, whether campaign reportage in the modern era adequately informs the electorate about its choices.

The answer, I believe, is no.

This did not begin with Hillary Clinton but, I would suggest, with Richard Nixon.

The investigative journalism that unhorsed Nixon exemplifies why we need a free and independent media. But it also created a template for ambitious reporters—uncovering a scandal. It's showy and, at times, easier than analyzing the impact of policies or programs.

So what makes a "scandal" scandalous, something that truly affects the public interest? And who defines the difference between actual wrongdoing, and merely suggesting its possibility in the absence of genuine proof?

Asserting the "appearance of" or "potential for" impropriety is easy enough. But at its worst it can become a kind of polite McCarthyism, dressed up in the First Amendment, where the gravest insinuations rest on little or nothing in the way of facts. Journalists are no more free from error or ambition than politicians or prosecutors, and the power they wield—for good or ill—can be as great.

We should care deeply about whether our politicians are ethical and honest. But we should also care about whether such issues are honestly reported, as well as whether the press gives sufficient attention to the impact of what our leaders do and say with respect to the issues—national security, the economy, the environment—that indubitably affect us all.

And what subject matter makes for a scandal? Things like corruption, influence peddling, and unethical behavior are easy. But "judgment?" Sure, when it affects a politician's conduct of his or her public responsibilities. So what about sex?

Yes, if the conduct involves assault, predation, or harassment. But what of adultery involving consenting adults? And what is the difference between private character, which does not affect the rest of us, and public character, which does? No one suggests that FDR was a model of marital rectitude; no one suggests that Jimmy Carter was not. And there is little doubt who history judges to have been the better president.

Which brings us to lying. When the president lies about his consensual sex life, reflecting the self-protective behavior of millions of his fellow citizens, how does that harm us? We can be as pious as we like about "role models" but, in our public officials, we should be far more concerned when they dissemble about matters of public import.

Indeed, this raises another question—why does the press waste its attentions, and ours, on the sex lives of politicians? The answer is obvious: the story is easy enough to get, and it sells.

A loftier journalistic distraction is, ironically, more often decried—the "horse race" coverage of presidential campaigns.

Rightly so. A campaign is, for sure, a race. Who is winning, and why, is a legitimate subject of political coverage. But the proliferation of polls has made the coverage of poll numbers an end in itself, crowding out more substantive reporting. Covering numbers is far easier than analyzing substance, and infuses our campaigns with a constant churn of mini-dramas.

This near-obsession with polling has transformed political reportage. In short order the narrative of a campaign begins resembling a *Rocky* movie—who is up or down, surging or in freefall, gaining or losing ground, or, best of all, making a dramatic comeback. The rhythm of reportage, too, partakes of Hollywood—to keep the drama going, the story needs changes in momentum. What results is often fiction supplied by its authors, the press.

If you think I'm kidding about this, I invite you to watch the next eight weeks of reportage on Hillary Clinton and Donald Trump, and see how this model plays out. If it comes to dominate the coverage, far more salient subjects will suffer.

Then there is the problem of the so-called metanarrative: a fixed notion about the character of a candidate. As the extreme example of Trump demonstrates, this is hard to avoid. I can offer myself as Exhibit A, in that I've strenuously argued that a serious personality disorder is the unifying explanation for most of Trump's behavior.

But the reflexive recourse to metanarratives can distort coverage of a candidate, causing reporters to dwell on or slight information depending on whether it conforms to this fixed characterization. If the undeniably intelligent Bill Clinton had misspelled *potato*, no one would remember. But Dan Quayle? I need not go on.

Like everyone else, journalists have a herd mentality. In the twenty-four-hour news cycle, this creates an echo chamber of received, if dubious, wisdom, which reinforces the metanarrative about a candidate.

Finally, there is the profit motive. I must emphasize how many great journalists ply their often underpaid profession with honesty, distinction, and all the considerable objectivity they can muster. You don't need to go to China to appreciate how valuable this is—a trip to Great Britain will do nicely.

But the organizations our journalists work for are not public utilities. They are for-profit corporations. This is a good thing in itself—it breeds competition, and who would want to rely on a state-run press?

But, of necessity, our media outlets exist to make money—at least enough to survive—which requires building and maintaining an audience. In the modern age, all too often that means reporting "news" that has entertainment value, no matter its value to an electorate making choices about our future.

This reinforces everything else: the focus on scandal, the horse race reportage, the metanarrative. As they say, that's entertainment. And it badly distorts coverage of the presidential campaign and the major candidates, Hillary Clinton in particular.

You don't have to take my word for it. How this dynamic played out during the run-up to the 2016 primary season has been exhaustively documented in a study by Harvard's Shorenstein Center on Media, Politics and Public Policy. Instead of focusing on cable news, often cited as ratings-hungry and overheated, the study analyzed coverage from eight major print and broadcast media: CBS, Fox, the *Los Angeles Times*, the *New York Times*, *USA Today*, the *Wall Street Journal*, and the *Washington Post*.

Its conclusion? Contrary to the general perception of a "liberal media," Donald Trump was the runaway beneficiary of positive media coverage throughout 2015. As for Hillary Clinton, she drew the most negative coverage of any candidate in either party.

Equally telling as this conclusion are the reasons for it. Propelling the tsunami of coverage for Trump was his

Despite this, Trump chronically complained about all the "dishonest" media outlets that were treating him unfairly. This reflected his psychologically skewed response to any critical reporting—including threats of lawsuits.

entertainment value. Instead of following his rise in the polls, this coverage preceded—and drove—that rise. Here the report is detailed and unsparing:

> Journalists seemed unmindful that they and not the electorate were Trump's first audience. He exploited their lust for riveting stories. He didn't have any other option. He had no constituency base and no claim to presidential credentials. If Trump had possessed them, his strategy could have been political suicide, which is what the press predicted as they showcased his tirades. Trump couldn't compete with the likes of Ted Cruz, Marco Rubio, or Jeb Bush on the basis of his political standing or following. The politics of outrage was his edge, and the press became his dependable if unwitting ally.

As Trump ascended, the press served as his megaphone—the source of $2 billion of free media in the primaries alone. Among his competitors in 2015, Trump received 34 percent of all media coverage compared to 18 percent for the runner-up, Jeb Bush. Broken down by category, 34 percent of this coverage related to his events and activities, 27 percent was classified as "other," and 21 percent reported on polling. As for substance, only 12 percent of the coverage concerned issues or philosophy, and a mere 6 percent dealt with his personal character.

As for tone, the great majority of Trump's coverage was deemed positive or neutral, from 63 percent in the *New York Times* to a whopping 74 percent in *USA Today*. Increasingly, this fed what became the dominant story—that Trump was winning the horse race, driving yet more coverage. It seems highly doubtful that, without the benefit of extensive and favorable coverage through the primaries, Trump would be a general election away from becoming president.

Compare this to Hillary Clinton. In all but one month of 2015, the study found, her coverage was overwhelmingly negative. Remarkably, its tone was 84 percent negative. By contrast, after an initial dearth of coverage, the reportage about Bernie Sanders was overwhelmingly favorable. In turn, this drove negative "horse race" stories about Clinton's failure to overwhelm Sanders.

As part of this picture, the study identified "more than a few anomalies" involving the coverage of Clinton. While reporters frequently referred to her past history, her tenure in the Senate—in which she earned bipartisan praise—was rarely mentioned. Nor, in general, was the substance of her performance as secretary of state—as opposed to, I would note, the intense focus on issues like emails or Republican allegations regarding Benghazi.

No doubt such issues are newsworthy. But this selective focus, the study showed, helped feed the metanarrative about Clinton as described in the report: that she is calculating, or cautious, or untrustworthy, or a mediocre candidate, or simply hard to like. In short, the metanarrative seemed to shape the coverage.

Thus the Hillary Clinton metanarrative requires a closer look. Its essence is that Clinton is lacking in character or candor. Thus questions about her email practices, Benghazi, or the Clinton Foundation fit, and feed, this narrative. But what are its deeper causes?

It is hard to find a definitive answer. But some tributaries are clear enough. Over the years, both Clintons have endured numerous investigations driven by their political opponents. Though none has resulted in findings of corruption or criminality on behalf of Hillary Clinton, their very existence was newsworthy. A moment of absolution cannot undo months of inquiry. In the minds of many, charges become fact.

One does not have to assert that such charges are always politically inspired to know that they are politically useful—as GOP house leader Kevin McCarthy admitted with respect to the Benghazi inquiry. Among the GOP base, it is an article of faith that the party must keep Hillary

Beyond doubt, relentlessly negative press coverage was a factor in Clinton's defeat. Coverage of her email problems was incessant; attention to her policy positions fairly scant.

This point is perfectly illustrated by the nine days between Comey's first letter regarding the existence of the Abedin emails, and his second letter acknowledging that they contain nothing of import. In those nine days incessant media speculation dominated the campaign—and it was lethal to Clinton.

Clinton from ever becoming president. This helps ensure her status as a lightning rod for controversy.

But remember when Barack Obama arrived in 2008, that breath of political fresh air who would sweep away the toxicity of the Clinton era? In 2016, after nearly eight years of partisan trench warfare, his 50 percent approval rating is considered near-miraculous. The agent of toxicity, it turns out, is political polarization and—like or not—the media has become its carrier.

So it is hardly surprising that, as numerous academic observers have found, Hillary Clinton is most unpopular as a candidate—negative advertising works, including when waged through the media. Whether sexism—discomfort with an ambitious woman—helps drive this political rancor I will leave to the social scientists. But as an officeholder, whether in the Senate or as secretary of state, Clinton fares considerably better than when she is seeking office.

The obvious fact that attacks on a candidate's character, whatever their basis, serve partisan political purposes does not mean that they should never be reported. But the media should examine its role as amplifier: after all, emails, Benghazi, and the Clinton Foundation are exactly what Republicans want voters to think about—and think the worst of. No surprise, then, that another Republican congressman, Jason Chaffetz, is demanding another investigation into Clinton's email practices. By attenuating the GOP's central campaign theme, this also feeds the metanarrative about Hillary Clinton.

This environment makes the role of the media all the more important, and raises critical questions about its coverage of Hillary Clinton—both in itself and as compared to other candidates.

Here, the veteran reporter Jonathan Allen provides an interesting perspective. In an article for *Vox* entitled "Confessions of a Clinton Reporter: The Media's Five Unspoken Rules for Covering Hillary Clinton," Allen tackles the questions raised by the Shorenstein Center. His central diagnosis is blunt:

> [The campaign is] an essential frame for thinking about the long-toxic relationship between the Clintons and the media, why the coverage of Hillary Clinton differs from coverage of other candidates for the presidency, and whether that difference encourages distortions that will ultimately affect the presidential race.
>
> The Clinton rules are driven by reporters' and editors' desire to score the ultimate prize in contemporary journalism: the scoop that brings down Hillary Clinton and her family's political empire. At least in that way, Republicans and the media have a common interest.

As a reporter, Allen has been tough on the Clintons, and there is no reason to believe that he has suddenly gone soft. So his critique deserves attention. Briefly summarized, here is how he describes the unspoken premises that drive the coverage of Hillary Clinton:

Every charge against the Clintons, no matter how ludicrous-sounding, is worthy of a full investigation by federal agencies, Congress, and the media. Every allegation, no matter how ludicrous, is believable until it can be proven completely false—even then, the conservative media keeps it alive. The media assumes that Clinton is acting in bad faith until there is hard evidence to the contrary. Everything that the Clintons do is newsworthy. And everything Hillary Clinton does is fake and calculated to serve her political benefit.

This dynamic, Allen suggests, creates a particularly vicious cycle—because Clinton distrusts the media, she tries to keep it at arm's length, deepening its antagonism and distrust. As demonstrated by the questions about her health following her feeling faint on Sunday, this serves neither Clinton nor the press—nor the public that depends on the media for information. With respect to the campaign, Allen describes the impact on Clinton as he sees it:

> The emphasis on a candidate's flaws—real or perceived—comes at the cost of the candidate's ability to focus his or her message and at the cost of negative attention to the other candidates . . . [T]hese double standards are an important thing to keep in mind when judging [Clinton] against her rivals for the presidency. Whether they're fair or not, the Clinton rules distort the public's perception of Hillary Clinton.

In short, Allen believes that the media is predisposed to look for, or believe in, purported scandals damaging to Hillary Clinton—causing extensive and negative reportage regardless of the merits of any particular allegation. Moreover, he suggests, this predisposition warps coverage of Clinton's campaign, and impedes her ability to communicate her policy proposals to the electorate. So let's gauge Allen's analysis against recent coverage of the campaign.

The single dominant story—by far—involves Clinton's email practices as secretary of state. Beyond doubt, this is a legitimate area of concern. It raises questions about the protection of confidential information, whether Clinton deviated from good practice for personal convenience, and whether her actions were careless and imprudent.

Nor is there doubt that her email practices, including the use of a private server, were a serious mistake—as she has been compelled to concede. In estimate of many, she has further damaged herself by being far too lawyerly, too prone to offering a series of excuses rather than a simple mea culpa. Even if one attributes this defensive reflex to the hostility surrounding her, a different response would have served her better—here, and arguably elsewhere.

But, by now, the central points about the emails are clear. Though FBI director Comey condemned her practices as careless, he made the straightforward judgment that they fell well short of the standard for criminal intent. With whatever reluctance, Clinton has admitted error, and pledged not to repeat it.

After over a year of inquiry and reportage, that's pretty much it. The American public can make its collective judgment and move on.

But even last Wednesday, during the national security forum, Matt Lauer consumed one third of Clinton's time by reprising the email issue yet again. And a considerable segment of the media has turned to questioning Comey's judgment and integrity. One does not have to be a Clinton partisan to conclude, as did the *Washington Post*, that "[t]he story has vastly exceeded the boundaries of the facts."

This search for a scandal nourishes another media staple—the horse race. The more plentiful the reportage on the email problem—regardless of substance—the more Clinton's poll numbers flag and her unfavorables rise, all duly reported to confirm that Americans don't trust her. And so, in due course, more Americans question her trustworthiness—leading to yet more reportage. It is one thing to question a candidate's honesty, another to help create a feedback loop that shapes the answer.

The avalanche of reporting involving Clinton's role in Benghazi also stemmed from a serious issue—whether she was responsible for the security conditions that led to the death of four Americans. But it is, as well, another example of the media abetting a Republican effort to feed the metanarrative, regardless of the facts.

Again, the bottom line is plain. After eight investigations related to Benghazi, and hours of congressional questioning of Clinton herself, one cannot conclude that Clinton is responsible for the conditions in Benghazi. But this has been lost in the cacophony surrounding the assertions themselves—both before and after the inquiries.

Most recent was the revelation of thirty supposedly "deleted" State Department emails regarding Benghazi. All were innocuous; all but one, it turned out, had surfaced previously. Yet the taint of wrongdoing was refreshed yet again.

Abetted by a post-Comey change of momentum, Trump edged out Clinton in all four states—plus Michigan and Wisconsin.

Along with pressure from Republicans in Congress, this drumbeat in the media may have helped precipitate Comey's fateful and ill-judged letter of October 28.

Finally, the Clinton Foundation. Various media outlets have cited another trove of emails to intimate a pattern of "pay to play"—that large donors to the foundation influenced the activities of the State Department under Hillary Clinton.

Serious, if true. But despite the media-generated firestorm, there is no sign that it is.

The major ingredient was a story from the Associated Press, preceded by its breathless announcement that: "More than half of those who met Clinton as cabinet secretary gave money to the Clinton Foundation." There was one not-so-small problem with this: the AP's math left out all officials of foreign governments, or our own.

That rules out almost everyone Clinton met with as secretary of state. The relatively minute sample remaining included, among others, a man awarded the Nobel Prize for his services to the poor, and representatives of a charitable foundation interested in a public-private partnership to combat AIDS. Other supposedly questionable emails included a request that diplomatic passports be given to aides accompanying Bill Clinton on a trip to secure the release of journalists by North Korea. As for evidence of wrongful "pay to play," none has surfaced.

None of which prevented a host of commentators from going down the rabbit hole of unsupported conjecture—"the appearance of" or "potential for" unknown and unspecified improprieties, based on the gauzy assertion of "preferential access." When these outlets include the *New York Times*, the line between speculation and truth blurs in the public mind, creating the aura of a "scandal" without any proof of one. Thus a recent poll shows that six of ten Americans believe that Clinton granted special favors to foundation donors.

All this conjuring of would-be misconduct not only nourishes the metanarrative involving Hillary Clinton, but shows how that narrative influences—or distorts—the coverage of Clinton's campaign.

It is perfectly reasonable to scrutinize the Clintons as part of rigorous political reporting—for instance, their relationship to money, personal and political. As one example, Hillary Clinton's acceptance of large speaking fees from Goldman Sachs was a bad idea, and her stated reason for not disclosing the speeches—that other politicians don't—evades the point: Who else was getting paid like that? But the standards of fairness that apply to any public figure—including that suspicions should be rooted in substance—should apply equally to Hillary Clinton.

Which brings us back to Donald Trump.

As compared to the ephemeral speculation about the Clinton Foundation, the recent story about the Trump Foundation involves hard facts suggesting the existence of "pay to play." At a time when the Florida attorney general's office was investigating charges of fraud against Trump University, Attorney General Pam Bondi solicited and received a $25,000 campaign contribution from Donald Trump. Bondi claims not to know what her office was investigating; Trump asserts that they never discussed the matter.

But the contribution itself was channeled through the Trump Foundation, effectively obscuring its origins while violating IRS regulations. Trump says that all this was an oversight, not intended to conceal an effort to influence the investigation. Perhaps this is so; perhaps the fact that the Attorney General's office subsequently dropped the investigation is another instance of happenstance. But if one cares about "pay to play," the sequence of events deserves a good look.

It did get some attention. But a recent article by a Clinton supporter asserts that, to date, there were thirty-four times more articles about the Clinton Foundation than the Trump Foundation's illegal gift. One need not check the numbers to observe that the volume of the media reportage was, with respect to the two foundations, in inverse proportion to the known facts. This becomes more curious in light of several

When, in October, Russian hackers fed the speeches to WikiLeaks, they showed—unsurprisingly—that Clinton is favorably disposed to free trade and global investment and, subject to meaningful regulation, to Wall Street. While this was not catnip for the Sanders-Warren wing—as the Russians obviously grasped—no bombshells surfaced. Thus her secretiveness was more damaging than the speeches themselves.

prior instances where Trump concealed political donations or circumvented campaign finance laws.

Whatever the reason for this disparity, it cannot be Trump's reputation for honesty. The *New York Times* and *Washington Post* have done good work in reporting a number of questionable business practices. This history includes casino bankruptcies where Trump protected himself at the cost of his investors; nonpayment of contractors; allegedly fraudulent educational or self-improvement programs directed at vulnerable consumers; charges of housing discrimination; and use of undocumented workers. A handful of other articles have documented sworn depositions where Trump told numerous and demonstrable lies.

Trump's business record is his basis for seeking the presidency—indeed, it is the only credential he has. Yet his record of dishonesty in business has received scant attention from the media as compared to Clinton's emails. Once more, the metanarrative that Clinton is untrustworthy has obscured on important question—whether the hard evidence of a lifetime shows Trump to be pervasively dishonest. And so, according to polls, voters continue to believe that—at least in relative terms—Donald Trump is more honest and trustworthy than Hillary Clinton.

This seems all the more anomalous when one considers the candidates' statements during the campaign itself. Fact checkers consistently find Clinton to be much more truthful in her assertions than most candidates, while crediting Trump with historic levels of mendacity. But given the nature of the coverage to date, these findings have not penetrated the public consciousness. However one feels about Hillary Clinton, her complaint that the media writ large has helped create a false equivalency must be taken seriously.

But this raises an equally important question: In casting about for scandal, calling the horse race, and focusing on the Clinton metanarrative, has the media slighted the most important subject of all—the candidates' preparedness to hold the most powerful, and potentially most dangerous, office in the world? Has it, in other words, become a weapon of mass distraction, detracting from its efforts give us the information we most need?

To be sure, the scrutiny of Trump's statements and qualifications since the primary season is far more intense than the generally indulgent coverage that preceded it. In the last month, especially, the media is looking hard at his veracity, his behavior, and his positions with respect to important issues. But Clinton has always received such attention—often with the utmost skepticism—and much work remains for the media's examination of Trump to catch up with the man himself.

With full-throated fury, Trump cited this as evidence of a media conspiracy against him—claims that the "conspirators" duly reported.

For on matters of substance, too, the double standard lingers on.

Perhaps by inadvertence, CNN's Dana Bash identified one reason. Asked about the debates, she said, "I think the stakes are much higher . . . for Hillary Clinton because the expectations are higher for her because she's a seasoned politician. She's a seasoned debater." By comparison, Bash continued, "Donald Trump . . . is a first-time politician," concluding, "[m]aybe it's not fair, but that's the way it is. The onus is on her."

But is "the way it is" the way it should be? If anything, should not the media be especially zealous in exploring the positions and qualifications of a candidate with so little relevant experience? Yet, all too often, Trump gets outsized credit when he reads canned speeches, with scant exploration of the content or the knowledge behind them. To the extent this occurs, it involves more than a double standard—it is a fundamental failure to seek the information voters need.

And want. Polls show that the issues that most concern Americans are the economy and national security. The press should focus on what the candidates propose in these areas, all the more so in case of Trump, about whom so little is known—including what he actually knows. The same is true in critical areas like the environment, race relations, and nuclear proliferation. Yet the media spends far too little time exploring these issues.

Even Trump's remarkable embrace of Vladimir Putin, though widely reported, requires much more probing. What are Trump's commercial relationships in Russia? Why is his leading military adviser, Michael Flynn, so closely tied to Russia and its government? What plans, if any, does Trump have to counter Russian expansionism? How does Trump view Russia's role in Syria? What is Trump's understanding of Putin's suppression and even murder of dissidents? These questions, and more, deserve at least some of the energies expended on Clinton's emails.

This is also true of Russia's role in hacking emails. What do our intelligence analysts know about this? Why has Russia targeted Democrats for hacking? Why have they hacked electoral records in several states? And is there a concrete reason to believe that Russia is conducting these activities to tilt the election in favor of Donald Trump? That these questions must be handled sensitively and responsibly only enhances the need for responsible journalists to explore them, for they go to the heart of the stakes in this election.

By October, our intelligence agencies publicly opined that the Russian government was directing the hacks. The overwhelming consensus was that Russia and Julian Assange were colluding in carefully timed leaks in order to assist Trump's campaign.

Beyond doubt, the stakes are serious. The choice of a new president occurs at a critical juncture, in which we face grave challenges both at home and around the world. And yet the common metanarrative about this crucial decision is typified by a tweet from Chris Cillizza of the *Washington Post*: "This election is about voters choosing the least worst candidate. That's where we are in our politics."

This is glib, and it is lazy. This election is about far more than that. And the media must do far more to spell that out.

They can start with a more intense and probing inquiry about the issues—including, critically, in the debates. One can only hope this happens. For, thus far, the Clinton meta-narrative has consumed too much space, throwing the coverage off balance.

Whatever her strengths and weaknesses, as a candidate for president, Hillary Clinton deserves better. More important, so do we.

Clinton vs. Trump

Black Swans and Perfect Storms

SEPTEMBER 20, 2016

Supporters of Hillary Clinton have long feared the "black swan"—that cataclysmic event that gives Donald Trump more than a puncher's chance to knock her out. But more discerning worriers conjure a perfect storm of circumstances that, coalescing at just the wrong time, dismantle her edge in the electoral college.

Two weeks ago the skies seemed clear enough. The month started with a more comfortable candidate taking questions from reporters, giving good and measured speeches, and dismissing the feverish rumors about her health with a few amusing quips. She was reaching out to disaffected Republicans while attacking Trump with an air of presidential confidence. The most concrete concerns focused on turnout and demographics and, even here, her superior ground game gave her several paths to 270 electoral votes.

Still, it was possible to imagine a demographic breakdown that, although unlikely, would place her on the razor's edge between victory and defeat.

In theory, Trump's gift for repelling blacks, Latinos, women, young people, and college-educated whites gave her a daunting advantage. So why were the polls tightening?

The simplest answer was Trump's massive lead among whites without a college degree—particularly working-class men. Here, Trump's attacks on free trade and immigration, and promises to preserve entitlements, gains him a larger and more loyal following than Mitt Romney enjoyed in 2012.

True, this demographic is shrinking as opposed to those where Clinton leads. This gives her the potential to overwhelm Trump's narrower base. But, in itself, changing demographics means much less than intensity of support—who actually shows up to vote. Thus a gifted pessimist can imagine a scenario where, despite her organizational advantages, turnout goes absolutely haywire.

Start with what appears to be a passion gap. Polling shows that more than 60 percent of the registered voters who support Trump are following the campaign closely, and more than 90 percent say that they are certain to vote. Clinton voters are less attentive—45 percent—and a full 20 percent are less committed to voting. Thus polls of likely—as opposed to registered—voters erase Clinton's edge.

There are reasons to question this model, and it overlooks the distribution of votes in the electoral college. Still, to win comfortably Clinton must reassemble the Obama coalition: the minorities and young people—otherwise disinclined to vote—who turned out to elect and reelect America's first black president. So far, it seems, she is falling short.

Obama is working this demographic hard, and the Clinton campaign is deploying Michelle Obama, Bernie Sanders, and Elizabeth Warren to help. But millennials, particularly blacks but also other minorities, seem less drawn to Hillary Clinton than to the president, and young African Americans are harder to reach than their parents and grandparents. The question is less who they vote for than whether they vote at all.

A depressed turnout among her potential supporters would jeopardize Clinton in crucial swing states where the race has tightened, leaving her more vulnerable to defeat.

At this point, roughly seven weeks before the election, I began to see a possible path to a Trump victory. But given his grave and self-inflicted problems in the interim, it was not until the Comey letter that I believed he had a real chance.

And a less enthusiastic voting base leaves her vulnerable to unforeseen events—as this weekend's bombings reminded us yet again.

Even so, to have a chance of winning, Trump needs to turn out a bunch of less-educated white Americans who almost never vote. Here, too, passion is important, and events may matter—these otherwise disaffected people have to believe that Trump can win and that, as president, he would be a human Powerball ticket, transforming their lives for the better. While a massive influx of new voters seems unlikely, it is not inconceivable—as Trump's recent rise in Ohio suggests.

Still, this alone is not enough. Trump also needs more Republicans to come home—including suburban and college-educated whites. To some degree, polls suggest that this is already occurring. Indeed, given that our politics are polarized, our candidates polarizing, and our information compartmentalized, the grip of old loyalties will only intensify. But to garner all the Republican-leaning but wary voters he needs, Trump needs to look normal or, more accurately, to create the illusion of normality.

Finally, there is the impact of third-party candidates—Gary Johnson and Jill Stein. Trump not only needs them to outperform expectations for such political outliers, but to drain disproportionate support from Clinton. And, as of now, polls suggest that third-party candidates are hurting her more than Trump. The question is how many, and how much?

But suppose all that happens: overwhelming blue-collar support for Trump; depressed turnout for Clinton; a host of new Trump voters; a massive restoration of party loyalty among Republicans; and third-party damage to Clinton in key states. Further assume that virtually every important event between now and November breaks Trump's way—including, contrary to right reason, the debates.

It then becomes possible to imagine a Trump electoral college victory, of necessity based on winning Florida, Ohio, North Carolina, and, least likely, Pennsylvania. Or even that nightmare of improbabilities: a 269–269 electoral college tie. That would throw the election into the House of Representatives, which could give us President Trump.

This is the sequence of horribles that worries Democratic pros. For with the economy still flagging for too many Americans, the GOP should have the advantage of a "change election." What they need is for their candidate to become thinkable for a sufficient plurality of Americans.

This is why thoughtful Democrats have started sweating the polls, near even despite an overwhelming advertising assault by the Clinton campaign. They fret that all the negative media about emails and the Clinton Foundation, however skewed, is tarnishing the positive image of Hillary Clinton that emerged from her convention. They wonder if her campaign has focused too much on denouncing Trump instead of inspiring voters. They fear the unknown that is yet to come.

For this reason, Russian hacking of emails caused the Clinton campaign real consternation—no one knew for sure what was out there.

Then stuff started happening.

The first warning shot was fired by the moderator who couldn't shoot straight—Matt Lauer. During back-to-back appearances at a forum devoted to military matters, Lauer consumed much of Clinton's time aggressively relitigating the email controversy. In embarrassing contrast, he allowed Trump to deliver a series of lies and idiocies with his usual bluster, largely unimpeded by any references to reality.

This drove home some pitfalls awaiting Clinton in the "debates"—a word to be used advisedly. First, the quality of discourse depends greatly on the skill and resolve of the moderator. Second, absent a determined interlocutor to call him to account, a self-assured ignoramus like Trump can appear "presidential" while reciting nonsense. Given that the expectations for Trump are so low, in such a permissive environment he might be deemed the "winner" if he simply completes most of his sentences.

Then Clinton made an unforced error that confirmed the existence of a double standard—one for Trump, the other for everyone else. Speaking at a donor event—ever a fallow ground for folly—Clinton tossed half of Trump's followers in "the basket of deplorables"—the "racist, sexist, homophobic, xenophobic, Islamaphobic—you name it." A pretty effective list of adjectives if directed against the man himself. But against a chunk of the public, not so much—at least if you're running for president.

Such verbal slips are nothing new. Obama described a Republican base "clinging to their guns and religion"; Romney told a gaggle of rich folks that 47 percent of their fellow citizens were moochers. They both paid—Romney in particular, because it fit his caricature as a heartless plutocrat.

To some degree, so will Clinton pay. For those Democrats keeping score, it was a reminder that this year's playing field is far from level—Trump spouts far worse things with such metronomic regularity that nothing he says seems to stick. Except, ironically, to Hillary Clinton.

Potentially more worrisome was her literal stumble at a Sunday event to commemorate 9/11. On Friday, it transpired, she had been diagnosed with pneumonia. Given the rigors of campaigning, this was no surprise. But her decision to "power through" her schedule without disclosing her illness led to a ruder surprise—an alarming piece of film followed by several hours of delay before the campaign fronted her pneumonia.

This created two problems, both predictable. For a moment, at least, it fueled all the health hysteria fomented by the Trump campaign—including that she is suffering from cerebral damage. More lasting, it fed the usual trope about Clinton's lack of "transparency."

Her campaign has put out more health information—which, along with steadiness during the debates, should help put this to rest. It also appears that, as he did with the aptly named Dr. Oz, Trump will continue to vamp about his own superlative health, rooted in the benefits of Big Macs and insomnia. Still, this incident was another unpleasant reminder that, in presidential campaigns, surprises happen—whether or not provided by the Russians in October or, as just occurred, by terrorists from New Jersey. And it kept her off the stump for a few precious days.

They did—particularly Clinton's three strong and assured debate performances. By the end of each debate it was Trump who seemed winded.

As vexing, for once Trump did not stumble over himself to squander an advantage. His response to Clinton's illness was, for him, positively demure. Instead, almost like a normal candidate, he seized on Clinton's "basket of deplorables" to deplore her condescending cruelty to Americans who long to make their country great again.

Smart—this no doubt energizes his base and, quite possibly, could rally more nonvoters to Trump. Those DEPLORABLES FOR TRUMP T-shirts are on their way. And the last thing Democrats need is a deepening class war with blue-collar whites—they've been on the wrong end of this one for years.

They swiftly appeared. A particularly clever version proclaimed LES DEPLORABLES.

Perhaps fearful of humiliation, Trump has allowed his new campaign team to impose greater discipline. He is hewing more to prepared texts; blurring some of his most controversial positions; veering less into his own grievances. His attack lines, however outrageous, are more focused on Clinton. And he is finally up with attack ads of his own, placed strategically instead of at his whim. The Clinton camp can no longer count on Trump to help them—at least not quite so often.

Still, late last week, Trump provided fresh evidence of his own transcendent squalor. With chilling carelessness, he falsely accused Hillary Clinton of wanting to "destroy" the Second Amendment, and suggested that her Secret Service protectors "disarm" so that we could "see what happens to her." This followed the latest episode in his five-year history of spearheading the birther movement—a "press conference" that spotlighted his own mendacity and, more important, renewed fundamental questions about the media's responsibility in covering his campaign.

Pressed by his brain trust to at last abandon birtherism, Trump created drama by promising a major announcement. He then kept the media waiting for an hour, tying up cable news outlets, before appearing to promote his latest hotel. He capped this with a thirty-second statement that he now believed that America's first black president was born in the United States.

He did not explain how, after years of falsehoods, he had now divined the truth. Nor did he apologize. Instead, he praised himself by offering still more lies: "Hillary Clinton and her campaign of 2008 started the birther controversy. I finished it."

In fact, the Clinton campaign did not indulge in birther rhetoric. Its principal agent was Trump himself. Nor, despite his statement, did he accept Obama's birth certificate when the president made it public—to the contrary, he questioned its validity. Never once, until last Friday, did he disown any part of the racist lies and insinuations that paved his entry into political life, and inspired the widespread belief among Republicans that Obama is a foreign-born Muslim.

For once, the combination of his contempt for truth, and for the media, inspired a swift reaction. Several cable commentators expressed embarrassment that he played them; major newspapers documented the litany of statements promoting birtherism that showed Trump, yet again, to be a liar. And, in the wake of this performance, important outlets—particularly the *New York Times*—analyzed the impact on our politics of a candidate whose recourse to lies is so comprehensive and unconstrained. Here, as well it should have, the press at large refused to serve as conduit for a shameless and amoral con man.

The unanswered question arising from this incident is whether the media will, at last, cover Trump with the sustained rigor his candidacy deserves—including on substance. It is not hyperbolic to suggest that, on matters of policy, Trump is a crank candidate—Lyndon LaRouche with money. Never has a major party nominee been so inexperienced, uninformed, behaviorally erratic, intellectually dishonest, and pervasively untruthful. His ideas about the economy, foreign policy, and national defense are routinely inconsistent, contradictory, incoherent, and tinged with nonsense from the fringes of political thought.

His statements on taxation are, in the main, self-canceling gibberish. On the day of his birther announcement, Trump backed away from a promised $1 trillion tax cut for small businesses, before his campaign assured one interest group that Trump was still behind it, then promised another that Trump was not. In the last year, he has praised and denounced Janet Yellen and the Fed so many times that but one thing is clear—he has no grasp whatsoever of monetary policy. As for critical matters of science, he is an utter crackpot, whether the subject be global warming or vaccination.

And what of counterterrorism? Trump's renewed denunciations of Muslims, intemperate attacks on Hillary Clinton, and promises to be tough may resonate with voters, especially in the wake of the bombings in New York and New Jersey and the stabbings in Minnesota—the kind of unpredictable occurrences that worry the Clinton campaign. But it is not sufficient for the media to speculate about the electoral impact of such events. The real question is what Trump's "toughness" actually means in terms of policy and effectiveness, and how this compares to Clinton's proposals to combat terrorism at home and abroad.

The fact that, unlike LaRouche, Trump is a major party candidate whose entertainment value provides the media with millions of eyeballs means that—unlike LaRouche—he could actually become president. Thus what he proposes to do as president is of the gravest consequence, and should be to those who cover him. And if Trump is the proverbial naked emperor on matters of policy, that must be rigorously explored.

Substance still suffered. But this press conference was something of a watershed. Major media outlets like the *Times*, the *Post*, CNN, and MSNBC began labeling his lies as such, and there was more probing reportage of his character, behavior, and shallow grasp of issues. This was a salutory departure from the artificial strictures of "he said, she said" reporting where journalists passed on without comment whatever Trump said. But truthfully reporting Trump's lies made the media his antagonist, feeding his claim that journalistic conspirators were rigging the election. Such were the unique difficulties of covering a behaviorally erratic candidate with no regard for truth.

But there hasn't been nearly enough of this—and likely won't be. One of the most prominent excuses comes from the public editor of the *New York Times*, Liz Spayd.

(*continued*)

The media's reluctance to critically examine Trump's policy positions, she suggests, stems from the standards of objective journalism. Those who claim that the media is mired in "false equivalency" between Trump and Clinton are calling for "a partisan explanation passed off as factual judgment." Thus the media should not be concerned that coverage of Clinton's emails is excessive, lest they go down the "slippery slope" of covering the emails too little. In Spayd's view, what critics "really want is for journalists to apply their own moral and ideological judgments to the candidates."

Really? Or do they simply think that the media should be something more—and better—than a megaphone for unexamined claims on issues of the utmost public importance? Objectivity is different than vapidity.

Yet here we are. And so we await the first debate, perhaps the single most important moment of this campaign. As much as on the candidates, its outcome depends on whether the moderator, Lester Holt, asks Clinton and Trump the hard questions a president must answer.

For the candidates, that's only fair. For the rest of us, it's essential.

Turning Point

Judging the Great Debate

SEPTEMBER 27, 2016

So how do we judge last night's debate?

Before we get to what actually happened, we should start with what history—from past years and this year—tells us about how to view it.

First, audience. The number of Americans watching no doubt dwarfed the viewership for any prior debate—including for the legendary first meeting between John F. Kennedy and Richard Nixon. Given the closeness of this contest, and the widespread doubts about both candidates, last night's affair could be unusually influential in determining the outcome.

Second, these events often turn less on substance than on memorable moments—the gaffe or zinger—endlessly replayed on our screens. Who of a certain age can forget Dan Quayle's gaffe in comparing himself to the martyred President Kennedy, followed by Lloyd Benson's zinger: "I knew Jack Kennedy. Jack Kennedy was a friend of mine. Senator, you're no Jack Kennedy."

To merely quote these lines does not fully capture this moment of devastation. For those too young to recall it, a quick trip to YouTube will prove worthwhile.

Third, never before have two candidates had such contrasting styles. Hillary Clinton tends to be lawyerly, resolute, and well prepared. Donald Trump customarily relies on insults, outrage, and serial mendacity, breaking all rules for normal political decorum. The question was whether the format, and the moderator, would reward substance or bluster.

Fourth, as a result Lester Holt's role was critical. Would he be prepared to call out falsehoods? Would he probe the candidates' grasp of issues, the basis for their prior statements or changes in position, the means by which they make crucial judgments? In short, would he help the audience—at least the more discerning—take the contestants' measure as potential presidents?

Fifth, many of the undecided viewers were no doubt low information voters, unequipped to assess the policies debated in terms of specifics, yet wary of both Trump and Clinton. Their response was bound to be more visceral. The question is who more of them liked better and trusted more, and on what basis.

A last question summarizes all the rest: How well did each candidate do in addressing their weaknesses? Clinton's task was to seem more likable and trustworthy or, at least, to persuade more Americans to trust her as president. Advantaged by a bar so low it was almost subterranean, Trump merely had to make "President Trump" more thinkable, especially to a critical mass of undecided voters unprepared to be critical thinkers.

As to all this, prior first debates—four in particular—have much to tell us about the dynamics of picking last night's winner.

The first televised debate proved the centrality of expectations and appearances. As compared to Richard Nixon, the incumbent vice president for eight years, John F. Kennedy was a lesser known senator of scant accomplishment. Their debate, it was widely anticipated, would dramatize this gap. Instead, Kennedy came off as crisp, confident, and deeply informed, Nixon's equal as a prospective president—a draw that, because it surprised, advantaged Kennedy.

But even more telling was how they looked. Kennedy was tan, rested, and attractive, the candidate as movie star. Nixon had just spent time in the hospital recovering from an infection and was drawn, pallid, and sweaty—without makeup and cursed with a five o'clock shadow, he looked more like a shifty-eyed character actor in a crime movie. Even his suit didn't fit; the patrician Kennedy, as ever, was impeccably tailored.

Even for would-be presidents, optics matter. Those who watched television gave Kennedy the edge; by a small margin, the radio audience favored Nixon. But Kennedy had exceeded expectations—and looked better doing it. He gained an edge that he never lost.

The presidential debate of 1980 had similar dynamics, but may be even more instructive in assessing Trump's performance. Polls showed a close race between President Jimmy Carter and Ronald Reagan. But in itself that spelled trouble for Carter. He was widely regarded as a failed president—what gave him the edge was pervasive doubts about Reagan's knowledge and judgment. Which made Reagan the combatant with much more to gain.

What transpired was that rare debate that may well have flipped the outcome. In what was widely viewed as a gaffe, Carter cited his adolescent daughter Amy's advice that nuclear weapons were the most important issue—reinforcing a sense of fecklessness. In contrast Reagan was not only an experienced actor but, as a two-term governor of California, a gifted political performer. He looked confident and at ease, dispatching one of Carter's attacks with a practiced zinger—"There you go again"—delivered with an indulgent chuckle.

Once again, low expectations had served a candidate's smoother performance—a surprise to many. For millions watching, Reagan had become thinkable as president. He never looked back.

As in prior years, the first debate of 2000 presented an experience gap. Al Gore was the sitting vice president; many voters questioned George W. Bush's acumen and experience. One wildcard was that a considerable segment of the media, while questioning Bush's substance, harbored an intense dislike for Gore—as the story line went, he was stuffy, or disingenuous, or unresponsive to their inquiries. As the media has tender feelings, this is never a good thing.

Nonetheless, in the immediate wake of the debate the journalistic consensus was that Gore had won. The next morning I went to visit a friend—a highly placed Republican professional—and voiced the same opinion. The gist of his response was this: you may think that now, but wait until we finish spinning the result.

It turned out that Republican operatives had spliced together a tape of Gore, sighing at Bush's answers with showy exasperation. It was, indeed, a lethal affectation, serving the trope that Gore was a pompous stuffed shirt, and swiftly became all the press could talk about.

Gore's win evanesced in an avalanche of changed perceptions. With help from the media, the GOP had snatched at least a standoff from the jaws of defeat. We all remember what happened in November.

The Bush–Gore debate also underscores the media's role in shaping public perceptions of who won or lost. That is particularly salient in 2016, where the omnipresence of social media increases this influence exponentially, ensuring a flood of instantaneous opinion. The question was whether a media consensus would emerge, and how that compared with the first reaction of viewers.

Finally, there is a contradictory example—the first debate of 2012. To the surprise of many, President Obama turned in a lackadaisical performance. Sharp and well prepared, Mitt Romney walked away from any number of his prior positions, an acrobatic series of flip-flops for which he was never called to account. The near-uniform consensus was that Romney had seriously dented Obama's lead.

Not so much. Obama recovered nicely in the second and third debates. Perhaps more instructive is that, by 2012, our politics was so polarized that Romney's victory seemed to change few minds. Winning the first debate wound up counting for almost nothing.

So, given these precedents, who won last night?

It was the kind of night Hillary Clinton needed. Though this debate will not transform the poll numbers, historians may conclude that it was critical in preserving her electoral advantage.

That this is so owes much to how both candidates performed.

In terms both of substance and optics, Clinton did well. Her responses were crisp, coherent, and well considered. On the economy, she spoke directly to middle-class voters and effectively tied Trump to trickle-down GOP economics. She navigated the thicket of race relations clearly and effectively. And, in particular, she addressed foreign policy issues in a measured and knowledgeable way, effectively contrasting her experience with Trump's intemperate bluster.

Perhaps more critical, she looked calm, confident, and unruffled throughout. The brand of trust she needs to establish is that America would be safe in the hands of President Hillary Clinton. Her manner last night served that goal. And though Trump interrupted her frequently, she maintained her poise, leavened at times by a hint of amusement.

Clinton also succeeded in bringing out the Trump in Trump, hitting him with barbs and attack lines that pierced his sensitive skin. As his responses descended into interruptions and irrelevancies, he looked less like a president than an obnoxious ex-husband.

That was the key. Even more decisively than Clinton won, Trump lost.

He started well enough, attacking Clinton on trade and casting himself as an agent of change who would sweep away the failed policies she supposedly represents. Regrettably for Trump, there were seventy-five minutes left.

What began as a slow-motion train wreck gained speed as Trump reeled to the end. His answers became increasingly garbled, defensive, and pointlessly self-referential—as usual, he forgot that the campaign is supposed to be about other people. He made all the same old mistakes; lying about his original position on Iraq; clumsily evading his five-year embrace of birtherism; repeating his dystopian portrayal of black communities. None improved with repetition.

It turns out there is only one version of Donald Trump, and it does not wear well over ninety minutes. He was woefully unprepared, unable even to pretend that he knows more than he does—which, quite evidently, is very little. It was a telling window on a man too self-absorbed to look any better than he is. And he looked even worse when, after he jibed at Clinton for taking time off to prepare for the debate, she responded that she also believed in preparing to be president.

But then Trump looked pretty bad throughout. He grimaced, twitched, sniffed, gulped water, and, toward the end, seemed too weary to make much sense even by his own elastic standards. By then he was an easy mark for Clinton's jabs about his history of sexism, racial discrimination, and dubious business practices. The alpha male was at risk of becoming a human piñata.

For Trump, this was a lost opportunity on an epic scale. All he needed was to exceed America's very modest expectations, and more independents and wavering Republicans might have come his way. He succeeded only in speaking to the already converted, at most solidifying a base that is too small for him to win.

Among the mistakes that I and other analysts made was underrating Trump's ability to turn out his base without a conventional political machine. Another thing we missed was that the Obama coalition was not so much a Democratic property as it was the president's personal property.

For Trump is no JFK, Reagan, or George W. Bush, underrated candidates who showed their mettle. Trump proved that he was not underrated at all—except, perhaps, in his own mind. What too many voters saw was a pretender who proved himself worthy of their wariness and unease.

Perhaps the ripest moment came near the end. Asked by Lester Holt to explain his remark that Clinton did not have the look of a president, he said that she lacked stamina—an unfortunate remark from a man who was beginning to resemble a beached flounder. Clinton's response was perfect—when Trump has visited 100-plus countries, as she did, he should get back to her. One expects that this remark resonated in the souls of more than a few hard working women.

As for Holt, on a couple of obvious occasions he challenged Trump's statements. But in general he did something far more damaging—he let Trump speak. Much of the time Trump had nothing much to say, and he said it badly. The audience, on this night, was well served by Holt's light hand. And so a consensus emerged among the media and in early surveys of viewers: Clinton had done well; Trump had not.

As the Obama–Romney debate suggests, given our polarized politics a win in debate does not presage a dramatic shift in voter sentiment. But Clinton likely stabilized her support, while opening some minds among undecideds, wavering Republicans, and potential third-party voters. By doing so, she took one large step closer to becoming president.

For one night's work, it was more than enough.

In the end, it appears that Clinton's historically strong debate performances counted for less than the degree to which Comey's letter amplified her preexisiting negatives.

Losing It

Donald Trump's Public Crack-Up

OCTOBER 4, 2016

One of this campaign's most unnerving aspects is that Donald Trump's perpetual biliousness has numbed us to the mania fueling his vulgarity. But last week those not yet insensate could absorb an appalling reality: the presidential candidate of a major party was focused on accusing Miss Universe 1996—falsely—of making a porn film. This singular digression marked the moment when Trump retroactively turned a bad debate into a calamity, warning us yet again of his pervasive instability.

In itself, the reason for his poor performance exposed his mental and emotional unfitness to lead. Faced with the most important moment in his political life—the chance to persuade his fellow Americans to entrust him with the presidency—Trump prepared by doing almost nothing. Aides charged with prepping him privately revealed that he was unwilling, perhaps unable, to pay attention.

This is a stunning incapacity: a failure to summon, or even to appreciate, the seriousness of mind and spirit required of a leader at such a public crossroads—suggesting that there is nothing, ever, that can penetrate Trump's surreal

This was a classic illustration that one can lose a debate—or worsen a defeat—after the debate is over. Sometimes it takes a while for the post-debate analysis to permeate the public consciousness. But here, again, Trump did something unique—by working overtime, he tuned a cringe-making debate moment into a rolling disaster, in the process dramatizing his imbalance.

self-absorption. But as revealing of his psychological deficiencies was his aides' apparent inability, even in the wake of his miserable showing, to suggest ways in which he could improve.

Trump, it emerged, insisted that he had beaten Hillary Clinton and would not hear otherwise. Unable to advise him, his minions were reduced to communicating with their leader through leaks to the press, stressing his need for preparation before the next debate. A man who cannot absorb the reality that surrounds him, and renders his advisers fearful of addressing it, is frightening to contemplate as president.

For Trump, the reality of the first debate was devastating. His defeat on Monday night did not stem from a gaffe, or one bad answer. Rather, so comprehensive was his failure in both substance and style that presidential historians could not find its equal.

Ninety minutes of exposure revealed that he has little grasp of—or interest in—the subject matter of the presidency itself. Instead the subject that absorbed him was . . . himself. And Trump as he conceives himself is superior to those other humans for whom, individually, he shows no more regard than he does for society at large.

He was, as ever, self-referential, whiny, and defensive, blaming others for his problems, whether with individuals or the IRS. Baited by Clinton, the hereditarily wealthy Trump recast himself as a self-made billionaire, and offered such practices as profiting from the 2008 housing collapse, employing multiple bankruptcies, and paying no income tax as evidence of his savvy. As for habitually stiffing contractors, by Trump's solipsistic account their work was habitually substandard.

Widely perceived as a chronic liar, he lied still more—often and detectably. This was particularly damaging with respect to accusations of misogyny: instead of expressing regret about past slurs against women, he denied uttering them at all. And, in the end, it was his sexism that greased the skids of his self-destruction.

Here, too, he should have been prepared—surely by now someone, perhaps Kellyanne Conway, has revealed to Trump that millions of Americans deem him hostile to women. Indeed, before the debate Alexandra Petri of the *Washington Post* tweeted, "Finally, the whole country will watch as a woman stands politely listening to a loud man's bad ideas about the field she spent her life in."

A lesser man would have taken the hint. Instead, Trump interrupted Clinton constantly and, with his own endurance and concentration clearly flagging, chose to deride her stamina. While Trump may not have been prepared, Clinton was.

After reprising Trump's insults to women, Clinton went for the jugular: "And one of the worst things he said was about a woman in a beauty pageant . . . [H]e called this woman 'Miss Piggy.' Then he called her 'Miss Housekeeping,' because she was Latina. Donald, she has a name. Her name is Alicia Machado." As Trump interrupted yet again, Clinton finished, "She has become a US citizen, and you can bet she's going to vote this November."

A grim moment, made worse when Trump defended himself by gratuitously offering that Rosie O'Donnell, previously unmentioned, "deserves" his prior insults. But no one—except, perhaps, the Clinton campaign—could imagine what Trump would do next. Liberated from his handlers, he turned his "Machado moment" into an attenuated display of his profound emotional disturbance, kicking off the most disastrous and disturbing week a modern presidential candidate has ever inflicted on himself.

The subject dated back to 1996, when Trump ran the Miss Universe contest—and was potentially incendiary. In an earlier interview, Machado asserted that Trump's psychological abuse about her weight contributed to her anorexia and bulimia, a claim she repeated on camera after the debate. A normal man would grasp the number of women who, repelled by body shaming, would find this assertion sympathetic.

Worse for Trump, the abuse itself was captured by a scarifying video—for once, he could not lie about his conduct. In a series of excruciating filmic moments, Trump shepherded the teenaged Machado to a gym, where she exercised in front of dozens of reporters and cameramen. Trump himself provided the color commentary. "This is someone who likes to eat," he informed his audience, adding that, "the way she's going, she'd eat a whole gymnasium."

In my first piece on Trump, I posited that old videos would start coming back to bite him. The pity is that we had to wait a year.

Quite obviously, a sane candidate would leave this dreadful incident behind or, better, find a way to apologize. Not Trump. The Tuesday morning after the debate, he took to Fox News to belittle Machado and defend his disparagement of her appearance. "She was the winner and she gained a massive amount of weight, and it was a real problem. Not only that—her attitude. And we had a real problem with her."

No doubt to his surprise, commentators and much of the public reacted with revulsion and even shock: Trump was echoing his prior attack on individuals like Judge Curiel and the Khans, this time in a way that, perhaps, was even more unseemly. But with the deranged grievance of a man who forever imagines himself the victim, Trump relentlessly made things worse.

For three more days he persisted in demeaning a former beauty contestant. And in the early hours of Friday morning, he issued a series of manic tweets further disparaging Machado—after suggesting that Clinton helped her become a citizen, he urged his followers to "check out" a sex tape featuring Machado that seems not to exist. So, once more, Trump had reduced the campaign to a reality show in which he played a slanderous bully with no grasp of his own poisonous psyche.

Obviously, Machado did not materialize from the ether. She was Clinton's weapon of choice, ready for deployment, and her past included unsettling, if unproven, accusations—driving a getaway car for a boyfriend who had just attempted murder, then supposedly threatening a judge. But the proof of Trump's abusive conduct toward her was there for all to see, and his senseless attacks on yet another woman proved his inability to govern—even himself.

Thus when Clinton remarked that "his latest Twitter meltdown is unhinged, even for him," she spoke for many more people than herself. After all, Clinton noted, "Really, who gets up at three o'clock in the morning to engage in a Twitter attack against a former Miss Universe?"

No one but Donald Trump. By doing so, he demolished the scripted persona his latest brain trust had scripted for him, buttressing Clinton's assertion that he is "temperamentally unfit to be president of the United States." Even Republican professionals felt the kind of muted horror expressed by Ohio State Chairman Matt Borges, "Can this thing just end—please?" The sharp GOP strategist Ana Navarro was more emphatic: "Forget being president. This guy isn't fit to take care of a puppy."

One doubts that Trump can take in what he's doing to himself. Increasingly, he is enabled by a soulless palace guard led by Rudy Giuliani, who now resembles a vicious and demented elder, screeching and flailing as his keepers administer sedatives. "Republicans," Giuliani opined with his now habitual sneer, "are a bunch of frightened rabbits." Giuliani's better idea is to use Bill Clinton's sexual history to tear down his wife.

Never mind that, based on their own scurvy behavior toward women, Giuliani and Trump should avoid the subject like, well, scurvy. Giuliani's advice appeals to Trump's worst instincts—the only instincts he has. And so he has segued from Machado to a personal attack against Hillary Clinton almost as ill-advised: that she was her husband's enabler. To which he adds this stunning assertion: "I don't even think she's loyal to Bill . . ."

And so, as America watched, his descent into madness accelerated. The public crack-up came Saturday night.

Its predictable predicate was the kind of humiliation to which Trump, predictably, responds by losing control. His poll numbers—as ever his chief measure of success—were flagging. The media was dwelling on his floundering debate, accentuated by his irrational actions in its wake. And a leaked page from his tax returns in 1996 strongly suggested that, due to staggering business losses, he has paid no income tax for the last twenty years.

The result was a frightening foretaste of what a Trump presidency might portend. At a nighttime rally in Pennsylvania he went completely off the rails, the very portrait of a man cracking under pressure. Best simply to report, without elaboration, the events described by Jenna Johnson in the *Washington Post*.

Ignoring the script his handlers had prepared for him, he veered from one tangent to the next. He implied that Hillary Clinton was adulterous. Evoking his prior mockery of a disabled reporter, he imitated her loss of equilibrium at the 9/11 memorial service. He suggested that Clinton is "crazy." He opined that she should be in prison.

He wondered if he should have done another season of *The Apprentice* instead of running for president. He blamed his debate performance on a defective microphone, intimating that it was sabotaged. He invited the crowd to jeer the moderator, Lester Holt. He attacked "the dopes at CNN."

He again raised the specter of election fraud that would cheat him of the presidency. He invited his mostly white crowd to visit polling places in "certain areas" on Election

Day, suggesting that they "watch" to see who was voting. "I hear too many bad stories," he informed them, "and we can't lose the election because of you know what I'm talking about."

Finally, this. After warning that Clinton was giving away the jobs of hard working Pennsylvanians to please her wealthy donors, he said, "You're unsuspecting. Right now, you say to your wife: 'Let's go to a movie after Trump.' But you won't do that because you'll be so high and so excited that no movie is going to satisfy you. Okay? No movie. You know why? Honestly? Because they don't make movies like they used to—is that right?"

This is not a joke—it actually happened. One quails at the thought of Chief of Staff Rudy Giuliani saying, "Right, Mr. President."

No doubt one engine of this meltdown was the mortifying revelation about his taxes, fusing his seamy self-aggrandizement with his incompetence in business. To say the least, this ran counter to Trump's narrative. Tax avoidance, he asserted at the debate, "makes me smart." And after the *New York Times* revealed just how "smart" he had been, the craven Giuliani suggested that Trump had been unduly modest: "He's a genius—absolute genius."

Not so much. In the early 1990s, it turns out, Trump reported business losses so massive that they could shelter him from income taxes on nearly $1 billion. As a former head of the Congressional Budget Office remarked, "It's either a unique combination of bad luck or he's a terrible businessman or both. I don't understand how you can lose $1 billion and stay in business."

Here's how. Trump used the tax and bankruptcy laws to turn an epic series of business disasters into a tool of personal survival—perhaps at the edge of legality—while his contractors went unpaid and his investors lost their money.

His avoidance of taxation is not evidence of acumen, but an undeserved reward for selfishness and ineptitude.

With this, a core truth about Donald Trump was confirmed at last. He is not a master builder who would make America great again—he is a child of our corrupt tax code, stacked to insulate wealthy real estate developers from the consequences of failure. Genius did not save him— loopholes and bankruptcies did, and at a cost to everyone but Trump. Little wonder that his tax proposals for America are designed to treat developers like Trump even better. In the words of another venal developer, Leona Helmsley, "Only the little people pay taxes."

Including the little people of Florida who happen to be Cuban. In mid-September, Trump courted anti-Castro Cubans by attacking President Obama's "one-sided deal" to normalize relations with Cuba. Last Thursday, a mere two weeks later, a well-documented report in *Newsweek* asserted that, in 1998, a Trump business enterprise had spent money in Cuba exploring business opportunities—a violation of the legal embargo lifted by Obama.

The Trump campaign's evasive response was merely one more piece in a week-long mosaic depicting Trump's inner landscape. The last piece fell into place just yesterday—an action by New York's attorney general against the Trump Foundation.

The foundation has already been exposed for the sham it is—a source of illegal campaign donations whose charitable impact is minimal and that, for the past eight years, has not been funded by Trump himself. Now, it transpires, the foundation is violating state law by soliciting donations without proper registration, enabling it to avoid the rigorous audits otherwise required by New York law. Wherever Trump goes, pathology follows.

But some venues are far more dangerous than others. That is the larger point dramatized by the events of last week—Trump's deeply disturbed behaviors most of all. The man who would be our president is a liar and a charlatan, devoid of conscience or empathy for others, alive to nothing but his own ungovernable desires, and beset by multiple pathologies that metastasize under pressure. The chapters of history are filled with such men, and they do not end well.

Again, for his followers the actual facts about Trump seem to barely matter. For them, he was an imaginary person, a larger-than-life character being smeared by vicious opponents. The dynamic began to partake of one of those bad summer movies about superheroes.

And so conservative newspapers have started shouting across the divide that separates Trump's supporters from reason. The *Cincinnati Enquirer* has supported Republicans for nearly a century; the *Dallas Morning News* since before World War II; the *Houston Chronicle* traditionally leans Republican. Citing Trump's temperament, all have endorsed Hillary Clinton.

In its thirty-four years, *USA Today* never endorsed a presidential candidate. After the events of last week, its editorial board wrote that Trump is "unfit for the presidency." They offered a bold-faced litany of disqualifications:

> He is erratic. He is ill-equipped to be commander in chief. He traffics in prejudice. His business career is checkered. He isn't leveling with the American people. He speaks recklessly. He has coarsened the national dialogue. He's a serial liar.

Seems like enough. But the morning after Trump's debate debacle, when the *Arizona Republic* endorsed a Democrat for the first time in its 126-year history, its editorial director cut to the quick of why: "There is something extraordinary about this Republican candidate that was making us all break from our history."

Whatever their reservations about Clinton, he explained, she "treats the office with respect. And Trump has no respect for the office that he seeks. If the leaders of our country don't respect our important institutions, no one is going to respect them. That's why he scares us."

Trump's conduct last week, frightening in itself, indelibly captured this difference. Hillary Clinton is not only competent, but eminently sane. Trump is neither.

He is not merely unqualified, though that is more than enough. Nor is he merely a dreadful human being. He is a very sick one, fighting to become the most dangerous man on Earth.

Beyond Debate

The Squalid Meltdown of Donald Trump

OCTOBER 11, 2016

The second presidential debate occurred on Sunday, October 9, five days after the sole vice-presidential debate.

How badly did Donald Trump lose on Sunday night?

As The Donald would say, bigly—the climax of a week capturing all that is odious about Trump, and the party that is trying to make him president of the United States.

Though this was lost in the disasters that followed, he started losing the night Mike Pence debated Tim Kaine. For throughout the week, the sanctimonious Pence served as a human weathervane, whose maneuvers unerringly pointed to the stages of Trump's calamity and, ultimately, to the disgrace of the Republican Party.

The post-debate commentary praising Pence elevated manner over mind. No doubt Kaine was so eager to deliver his lines that he tripped over his opponent, the moderator, and himself. As a former talk show host and self-professed man of faith, Pence excels at dispensing extreme unction coated in molasses. Advantage Pence.

But to what end? Or, more precisely, in whose interests?

That was the key to decoding the debate. Kaine served Hillary Clinton's interests in 2016; Pence served his own interests in 2020. Trump's interests were roadkill.

Heretofore, Pence had shown a craven willingness to shill for Trump—who, after all, had rescued him from the prospect of an embarrassing defeat in Indiana. In the debate, Pence was a soothing presence for party-line Republicans who find Trump unnerving, singing verities from the GOP hymnal in a church organ voice. But Trump had the base already—the core tenet of their theology is that Clinton is the anti-Christ. Serenity in the voting booth adds no votes.

This helped Pence's future far more than Trump's present. For Trump, the principal benefit of the debate was that it happened, providing a break from his prior miserable week. And so Trump seized the moment by praising himself for picking such a sterling subordinate.

But rumor had it that Trump was unhappy. This was hardly surprising. For a man like Trump, it is unbearable to hear that your underling outperformed you—especially when he did so without trying too hard to make you look good. That was the story of Tuesday night's undercard: every punch Pence ducked struck Trump square in the face.

Repeatedly, Kaine hit Trump's slurs on women, immigrants, Blacks, Muslims, John McCain, a former Miss Universe, and, not least, Barack Obama. Time and again, Kaine cited Trump's failures to apologize for any of these offenses, wondering aloud if Pence approved.

Between counterpunching, Pence resorted to a defensive crouch. At one point, nettled, he groused, "Senator, you've whipped out that Mexican thing again"—an unfortunate lapse that launched a blizzard of tweets from Latinos. Most often, he evaded the Augean stable of Trump's verbal manure by bobbing and weaving, interspersing flat-out denials of reality with squints and shakes of the head, as if hoping that Kaine would punch himself out without doing Pence too much harm.

Perhaps this was the best Pence could do—certainly for himself. But, by the end, the dominant figure of the debate was neither of the combatants, but Tim Kaine's version of Donald Trump. And such excuses as Pence offered for Trump's statements were so patently false that, in retrospect, they sullied his own performance.

Kaine also made his points on Social Security, the environment, and Trump's tax cuts for the wealthy. While the overall menu was catnip for the base, it also was serviceable for the less committed. And by invoking Ronald Reagan's concern about some madman armed with nuclear weapons, he drove home the theme that Trump is too unstable to be president. By the end, he had offered a decent account of Clinton's worldview—and a dire account of Trump's.

Pence had his own hit parade: the "war on coal"; emails; the Clinton Foundation; the "basket of deplorables." But he seemed to contradict Trump on Syria, Putin, and how to deal with Russia. Overall he had less to say; what he said was less connected to Trump.

And so the ostensibly loyal Pence left Trump where he was that morning—a solitary figure in a deepening hole. By comparison, Kaine had helped sustain the greater enthusiasm for Clinton—particularly within the Obama coalition, and among independents—after she trounced Trump in the first debate. In the wake of Kaine versus Pence her edge persisted, notably in key battleground states Trump needs to carry. The message was clear: only Trump could salvage Trump, and Sunday night's debate might be his last chance to do so.

This was a lot to ask of a seventy-year-old with the self-awareness of a seven-year-old. While his large core of supporters will never leave him, the voters Trump had to reach on Sunday—particularly college-educated women—needed to see a different Trump in both style and substance. And Sunday's format made self-transformation no easier.

Town halls pose a very different challenge than moderator-driven debates. Audience questions favor candidates with a broad and detailed grasp of policy, and it does not do to act dismissive of an interrogator who is an ordinary person. In particular, this format favors candidates who can offer—or at least fake—a respectful interchange derived from genuine interest in the question and the questioner.

What it does not reward is personal attacks that the audience deems excessive. Yet, going in, Trump had signaled his resolve to turn Bill Clinton's sexual history against his wife. Given the sensitivity of the subject and the volatility of their candidate, smart Republicans were holding their collective breath in fear of Sunday.

They did not have to wait that long. On Friday, Trump's aggressive misogyny sprouted a toxic toadstool—an eleven-year-old videotape in which, among other excretions, he boasted of being such a "star" that he could grab women's genitalia at will. All that surprised was that Trump's bottomless vulgarity could still surprise. But the timing of his sleazy celebration of sexual assault spotlit his repugnance: his third wife, Melania, who he had married eight months prior, was pregnant.

More videotape. But this one was truly historic. One could argue that, in its graphic immediacy, this was the most fateful political moment of 2016. At least until James Comey decided to write Congress.

His "apologies" were classics of sociopathy. His first effort expressed regret "if" anyone was offended—suggesting that, among many millions of Americans, Melania had once more slipped his mind. He then sealed his offense by asserting that "Bill Clinton has said far worse . . ."

This left Trump knee-deep in a mass revulsion he lacked the decency to grasp. His handlers, who did, spent the next ten hours imploring him to do better. Shortly after midnight, a palpably angry Trump gave us ninety seconds read from a teleprompter.

Dismissing the videotape as a "distraction," Trump allowed that "I said it, I was wrong, and I apologize." But not so much. After all, he went on, "Bill Clinton has actually abused women, and Hillary has bullied, attacked, shamed, and intimidated his victims."

For some Republicans this was—at last—too much. What followed was a mudslide of revoked endorsements and pleas to withdraw. Notably, Paul Ryan disinvited Trump to a unity rally in Wisconsin—upon which it was announced that Pence would take his place.

Despite this, Trump carried Wisconsin in November.

This moral awakening was particularly loud among endangered Republicans in down-ballot races. And so, like lieutenant in Casablanca, all were shocked by the astonishing revelation that such an obvious creep had been captured on tape in his obviousness.

And what of Trump's decorous toady Sancho Pence? His initial reflex was to recycle the lines he had used for all of Trump's prior offenses, most recently regarding Alicia Machado. "They'll say this time they got him," he proclaimed, but 'they' would again discover that "Donald Trump is still standing stronger than ever . . ."

But 'they,' it turned out, were about to have good Christian company. A day later, the ostentatiously pious Pence discovered that his moral compass was pointing toward 2020. Abruptly canceling his appearance in Wisconsin, he issued a statement that suggested his political antennae had been born again.

"I do not condone his remarks," Pence said of his erstwhile leader, "and cannot defend them." Particularly rich was the unctuous blather he invoked to flee the scene: "We pray for his family, and look forward to the opportunities he has to show what is in his heart when he goes before the nation tomorrow night." With this Pence disappeared from public view, presumably to spend the interregnum praying for his own survival.

Or, perhaps, his immediate accession. Among panicky Republicans, a fantasy developed—Trump would resign, and Pence would take his place. And so Pence began playing a double game, leaking word of his moral anguish while avoiding the announcement of further public appearances. The message was clear enough: Pence would judge Trump's performance, at the ready to resign from the ticket—or to answer his party's call. In the process, Pence descended from righteous role model to palace schemer.

Trump reacted to all this with predictable fury, attacking restive Republicans as "self-righteous hypocrites . . . more concerned with their political future . . ." One could certainly see his point, starting with his would-be vice president. But Trump came to Sunday's debate a man alone—stripped of cover from his party, having stripped himself of the moral authority to lead.

The overture to the debate was fitting. More tapes of Trump's misogyny emerged, hours of repulsiveness adduced by Howard Stern that underscored his contempt for women. His oh-so-presidential counter—a press event, staged an hour before the debate, with alleged victims of Bill Clinton's prior sexual behavior—presaged another tawdry chapter in his degradation of our political life.

It began with his "defense" of the appalling videotape. His apology, so perfunctory as to be meaningless, was followed by diversions that epitomized his barren psyche. First, why were we concerned with his behavior when ISIS is beheading people? Second, why are people talking about him when he's placed the women who complained about Bill Clinton right here in the audience? Watching, one could only be grateful never to have met him.

He then proceeded to cement his own doom in a way that exposed his party's bankruptcy. He did nothing to reach the unconvinced. Instead, he resorted to the red meat of unreason through which he, and the GOP, have reduced their hard-core base to the human equivalent of Pavlov's dogs.

He promised to prosecute Hillary Clinton. He threatened her with jail. He accused the moderators of bias. He repeated his dystopian view of black America. He raised the specter of disloyal American Muslims. Having spewed his own venom, he said that Clinton "has tremendous hate in her heart."

Instead of offering new proposals, he recited old grievances—Obamacare, emails, the nuclear deal with Iran. He recycled the lies his followers love to hear, asserting, as one example, that Syrian refugees are coming here by the "tens of thousands." This reached an apex of moral idiocy when he claimed that the Syrians, Russians, and Iranians are our allies in fighting ISIS—when, in fact, they are slaughtering the Syrian opposition to the murderous Assad in a volume so horrendous that it constitutes a war crime.

Frequently, Trump blurred the line between mendacity and ignorance. Asked about the refugee crisis in Aleppo, he stumbled into a morass of misinformation before retreating into a jumbled critique of military tactics in Iraq. And one day after the US government definitively stated that Russia was hacking American electoral systems, he suggested that there is no evidence of hacking—whether by Russia or anyone else. No one not already a loyalist could credit his alternate reality.

And, as ever, he was graceless. This reached the point of cruelty when he suggested that Captain Khan would still be alive had Trump been president, drawing a rebuke from Khan's family. Nor did he neglect Pence. Asked about his running mate's call in the debate for a harder line against the Russians in Syria, Trump said coldly, "He and I haven't spoken, and I disagree."

In late August Khan's father exacted his revenge: an ad in which he asked whether Trump would have allowed his immigrant son to come to America as a child. Clinton ran it in battleground states.

His presence was equally off-putting. He made no attempt to engage with his audience. He did not address the concerns of women or minorities. His entire focus was attacking Clinton.

The result was a debate depressing in tone and, often, substance. At times Clinton looked off-balance when confronted with hard subjects—her emails and Wall Street speeches. But overall she turned in a solid if lower-key performance, engaging with her questioners, offering policy proposals on taxes and the economy, and giving knowledgeable responses on issues like Obamacare, Syria, and ISIS.

The impact was unsurprising: the two scientific polls taken after the debate showed her winning by a decisive margin and, among women, by a landslide. Trump had blown his last chance by being the worst and only thing he could be—himself.

But the GOP was stuck: by stunting his appeal to the voters that he, and the party, so desperately needed, Trump had rallied the base. Any effort to push him aside at the eleventh hour would stoke their fury to new heights, tearing the party apart. The GOP had become like a man in a catatonic trance—conscious of everything around him, but unable to speak or move.

The best evidence of this was the craven tweet through which the pusillanimous Pence tried to clamber back on board: "Congrats to my running mate . . . Proud to stand with you as we #MAGA." Standing with Trump, Pence once again looked as small as he is, a walking rebuke to those who had seen him as the party's last hope.

Reappearing the next morning on talk shows, the ever adaptable Pence granted Trump absolution: "He showed humility and he showed strength and he expressed genuine contrition." And then, in imitation of his once and future master, Pence attacked Bill Clinton over Monica Lewinsky. While not an uplifting testament to the power of prayer, this was a vivid testimonial to the dangers of temporal ambition in a man too small to contain it.

Not to mention the dilemma of Republican leaders who, in contrast to Pence, are burdened with actual integrity.

After the debate Paul Ryan had, at last, seen enough. In a conference call Monday morning, Ryan informed House Republicans that he would no longer defend Trump—instead, he would dedicate himself to preserving control of the House. His recompense for this pragmatism was fierce attacks from his own caucus for abandoning the base. In miniature, this captures the dysfunction of a GOP

Some of his critics would not even commit to retaining Ryan as speaker.

After the videotape emerged, a number of Republican legislators retracted their endorsement of Trump. After his base erupted in fury, many retracted their retraction. The spectacle was too morally pathetic to evoke laughter. Given Trump's sense of grievance and taste for reprisal, it will be interesting to see how he treats Republicans who were less than slavish in his defense.

In fact, the GOP carried Trump all the way to the White House. Given his nature, this is potentially more ruinous to the party than his candidacy threatened to be.

caught in the rhetorical trap it had set for voters—who repaid it with Donald J. Trump.

Never has a political party so richly earned its plight. For months the GOP insisted that this comprehensively ignorant, mentally unstable, narcissistic, racist, and misogynist moral midget would save us from the horror of Hillary Clinton. But the real horror is theirs alone, and it is too late for them to escape him. This is not merely poetic justice, it is outright operatic—a soulless, choiceless party forced to carry its stillborn candidate to term.

Apocalypse Soon

Imagining President Trump

OCTOBER 18, 2016

This year's presidential campaign is awash in bogus claims. But, to me, the worst is that it makes no difference whether we elect Hillary Clinton or Donald Trump.

The reasons for this assertion vary: disgust with the system; dislike for both major candidates; a craving for transformational change; the need to rationalize staying home; the desire to cast a protest vote. Perhaps the recent exposure of Trump as a serial groper will vitiate this sentiment. But the national polls remain uncomfortably close, and the claim itself betrays a profound failure of imagination about who Trump is, and the power he would have to impose his toxic vision.

Only one of two candidates can win. Only one is an emotionally unstable narcissist. Only one is possessed by malice, ignorance, and impulse. Only one could, by his very being, endanger America and the world.

Anyone who argues otherwise should pause to imagine President Trump.

Imagine him issuing executive orders unimpeded by Congress. He can renounce the Iran nuclear deal or the Paris Agreement on controlling greenhouse gases. He can start a trade war with China. He can unleash the Justice Department on his political enemies. He can turn ICE loose on

Mexicans or order surveillance of American Muslims. Take your pick. But it's his choice, not ours.

It will be harrowing to see how many of these possibilities come to be.

Imagine his appointments to the Supreme Court: anti-choice; anti-LGBT rights; pro-NRA; pro-corporate; pro-Citizens United; pro-expansive executive power in the hands of Donald J. Trump. Every new Justice—every new federal judge—would be his choice, not ours.

We do not have to imagine his contempt for freedom of speech and the rule of law. He threatened Hillary Clinton with prosecution. He said that a critical commentator should be barred from television. He threatened the owner of the *Washington Post* with prosecution by the IRS. He threatened Judge Curiel with investigation. He repeatedly violates the laws regulating charitable foundations. He advocates changing the libel laws so that he can sue his enemies. For Trump, there is no law but his—not ours.

Nor need we imagine his misogyny. His contempt for women and obvious predation are appalling and, in a presidential candidate, shocking. But it is well to imagine what electing such a man would say to the new generation of American women.

His racism is equally blatant. He rose by attacking the legitimacy of our first black president. He portrays black neighborhoods as undifferentiated hellholes. He implies that minorities will perpetrate massive voting fraud. He deputizes his followers as racist poll monitors. He tars undocumented Mexicans as criminals. His road to power is paved with bigotry.

President Trump would be bigotry in action—a prescription not just for injustice, but violence. Hillary Clinton denounces systemic racism; for Trump, racism is a law enforcement tool. The discredited tactic of stop and frisk policing would be merely a down payment. Trump has elevated racial dog whistles to a fire alarm that would precede the fire—racial divisions stoked to conflagration by an American president for the wider world to see.

Equally incendiary is the prospect of mass deportations. That is what he has promised his followers—and it is central to sustaining President Trump. So imagine America as an anti-immigration police state. A growing deportation force. Using IRS files to hunt down undocumented immigrants. Diverting more state and local law enforcement to raid suspect workplaces. Expanded internment centers for apprehended immigrants. All this is within his power—his choice, not ours.

Another promise to his base was profiling Muslims and spying on Muslim neighborhoods. This is not simply racist. It is stupid: counterterrorism experts agree that alienating loyal Americans will promote terrorism, not stop it. And it is dishonest: Trump's claim that "political correctness" prevents law enforcement from investigating suspect Muslims is a poisonous lie. Only one candidate would, as president, drive a dangerous wedge between American Muslims and their country.

His environmental policy is just as clear—and it is an existential threat to us, to our children, and to the globe. Clinton advocates clean energy policies at home and cooperation abroad. Trump says that climate change is a hoax perpetrated by the Chinese. He would gut the EPA and pull America out of world efforts to stem global warming. Only President Trump would be an agent of global oblivion.

Not to mention economic ruin. No doubt Americans ravaged by automation and globalization need our help. But economists of all stripes agree that Trump's "solutions"—protectionism and trade wars—would trigger a recession so deep that it would wipe out millions of jobs.

Trump's tax plan would deepen our financial collapse and threaten our fiscal future. The non-partisan Tax Policy Center estimates that his tax cuts for the wealthy would explode the deficit by $4 trillion in a decade. By comparison, Clinton's proposals provide tax relief for everyone else, while increasing revenues by $1.4 trillion. Only President Trump

Five days before the election, *Mother Jones* reported that a former senior intelligence officer for a Western country working as an opposition research consultant had provided the FBI with information regarding a long-term Russian plan to co-opt and assist Trump. According to the article, the FBI thought the information credible enough to request the spy's sources and further materials. As reported, among the spy's more arresting assertions is that Russian intelligence had "compromised" Trump during his visits to Moscow and, therefore, could "blackmail him." Whatever the truth of this, it is a fact that throughout the campaign Trump and his foreign policy advisers spoke positively about Putin, ignoring his brutality at home and abroad.

The flood of emails continued until the end, a blatant effort to assist Trump by damaging Clinton.

would gut our budget and shred our social safety net for the sake of people like Trump.

This captures something fundamental: the degree to which President Trump would eviscerate our sense of community. Clinton calls for a commitment to national service to help revitalize our states and cities. Trump shows no interest in a sense of common citizenship or communal compassion, whether realized through government or Americans helping each other. Instead, he turns Americans against each other to advance his own ends. A president who cares nothing for others would—by his actions and his example—diminish what binds us together.

So imagine President Trump as our face to the world. He calls for a wall between United States and Mexico. He advocates torturing suspected terrorists and murdering their families. He disdains our alliances and scorns the Geneva Convention. He shuns refugees from the horrors of Syria. He speaks blithely of nuclear proliferation and of using nuclear weapons. He scares our allies and emboldens aggressors like Vladimir Putin. Never has America elected a president so ignorant, so careless, so dangerous to us and to everyone else.

His attachment to Putin evinces his unfitness to serve. American intelligence agencies have briefed him on Russian hacking—not just of the Democratic Party, but of our electoral system. Yet in the latest presidential debate Trump blatantly lied, suggesting that the idea of Russian hacking might be a ploy to discredit him. Only this is true: Russian hacking discredits him.

The pattern of leaks in October is clear. Putin does not simply imagine Trump in the White House—he is trying to put him there. Never before has a foreign leader invaded our electoral process for his own ends. Only Vladimir Putin, and only to help Donald Trump.

It is easy to imagine why—it is easy to manipulate an ignorant narcissist. So beguiled is Trump by Putin that he excuses Russia's involvement in war crimes that have horrified the world. Only Trump could claim that the mass slaughter by Russia and the Assad regime of the Syrian opposition—as well as of relief workers and innocent men, women, and children—is, contrary to fact, directed against ISIS.

But then Trump comprehends nothing about ISIS, Iraq, Syria, the Middle East, or any of the geopolitical dangers a president must navigate. Of these, the most dangerous of all is the threat of nuclear war.

So imagine that only the judgment and stability of President Trump stands between us and a nuclear holocaust.

That sentence is not framed to frighten—it states what is true for every American president. Under the Constitution, the president is the commander-in-chief of our military. His orders are final and, in our time, presidents have used this power to launch strikes and start wars. There is nothing in the nuclear chain of command that would stay a presidential order to use nuclear weapons. We depend on a president's wisdom and restraint, for that is all we have.

In this arena, as in so many others, Hillary Clinton and Donald Trump are not the same. Far from making no difference, which one we choose to be president will make every difference.

Donald Trump is unstable, unbalanced, and devoid of prudence, empathy, or concern for anything but his needs of the moment. He lacks the basic attributes of a normal human being—let alone a president.

Hillary Clinton has those attributes, and many others. To compare her with Donald Trump is not simply false equivalency—it is willful blindness. But let us assume for the moment that Hillary Clinton is not the flawed but able leader reason shows her to be, but the venal caricature painted by her most hysterical political enemies.

I am reminded of the race for governor of Louisiana in 1991. The Democrat was Edwin Edwards, as personally corrupt as they come. But the Republican was a vicious

demagogue, racist, and anti-Semite. A man named David
Duke.

As governor, Duke would not have been a threat to the
country, or the planet. But he was a threat to the reserves of
decency in the state of Louisiana, and the only electable alternative was Edwards. So Duke's opponents crafted a bumper
sticker. It read: VOTE FOR THE CROOK—IT'S IMPORTANT.

This was not a joke, nor was it flippant. It was a profoundly moral statement—a rejection of false parallels,
social irresponsibility, and self-pity that one's choices were
disappointing. It was an adult acknowledgment that those
choices were very different, with different consequences, and
that only one made sense. It asked voters to imagine, and to
choose, the best alternative at hand—and to imagine the
price of inaction.

In 1991, voting for Edwin Edwards was the only way to
keep David Duke from becoming governor. The voters of
Louisiana did so. In 2016, Americans face a far more consequential choice: the only way to keep Donald Trump from
the White House is to vote for—and elect—Hillary Clinton. There is no doubt that Trump's supporters will turn out
for him on November 8, no matter what more we discover.
So the rest of us must consider the consequences of how—or
whether—we choose to vote.

Imagine President Trump.

Making America Hate Again

Trump's War on Civil Society

OCTOBER 25, 2016

Has it been only five paranoid, divisive, dishonest, self-pitying, conspiracy-filled, societally degrading days of Donald Trump since Wednesday night's debate? Hard to believe. For Trump has made the last two weeks feel like an excruciating journey to a country we should never be.

The comprehensive damage he has inflicted on our national spirit is unprecedented in a presidential candidate. As sordid as it is, his behavior toward women is but a symptom of his pervasive contempt for the traditions of decency and civility that bind us together as Americans. Still, it is well to start there, for his disdain for women epitomizes his disdain for everyone and everything but Donald Trump himself.

Despite his mendacious whining, through videotape and interviews Trump painted his own self-portrait as an emotionally stunted serial groper who forced himself on women, intruded on naked beauty contestants, and saw attractive females as prey. As of this writing, eleven women have now come forward to allege that Trump is precisely the tongue-thrusting, genital-grabbing Peeping Tom he boasted of being.

Their accounts are detailed, credible, and, in several cases, conform to what they told friends at the time. Trump's response is pathological: everyone involved is a liar—not only all eleven women but Trump himself. This is worse than unbelievable, though it is surely that. Our would-be president is claiming that, when describing himself as a sexual predator, he was lying to enhance his image.

This particular irony—that Trump's "defense" rested on calling himself a liar—went widely unremarked. This was yet another sign that Trump's perpetual mendacity had dulled reportorial reflexes. In the same debate, Trump asserted that he did not know Vladimir Putin, having claimed months before that they had a cordial relationship. Again, hardly anyone blinked—exhausted, the press had stopped cataloguing the times where Trump identified his own lies.

Equally demented, he has threatened the women with lawsuits and intimated at rallies that two of his accusers are too plain for his predation. Of one, he said, "She would not be my first choice, that I can tell you"; after calling the other a "liar," he added, "Check out her Facebook, you'll understand." To this he added a sexist jibe at Hillary Clinton: "And when she walked in front of me [at the second presidential debate], believe me, I wasn't impressed."

Finally, having humiliated his wife, he pushed her in front of the cameras to recite his storyline: his boasts were false; his victims are lying; the media is "so dishonest and so mean." A phrase better used to describe her husband.

Another woman, Michelle Obama, spoke for countless others. Trump's self-description, she said, "has shaken me to my core . . . It's like the sick, sinking feeling you get when you're walking down the street minding your own business and some guy yells out vulgar words about your body, or when you see that guy at work that stands a little too close, stares a little too long so you feel uncomfortable in your own skin."

Her candor and eloquence reminded us of how unthinkable it would be to replace the Obamas with the Trumps. And, perhaps, made it a little easier for women to cope with, and speak of, their experiences with men like Donald Trump.

But our national experience with Trump is hardly over, and it is coming at a very high price. Unhinged by adversity—a disqualifier in itself—he is turning the death throes of his campaign into a scorched earth attack on our civil society.

Instead of reaching out for voters, he is rallying his base with lies, vitriol, and paranoia. In Trump's account he, and they, are victims—of the government, the media, minorities, a crooked electoral system, a corrupt international conspiracy to advance Clinton, an American elite that views his followers with contempt, any woman who accuses him of sexual assault, and every American who does not see the world as they do. All critics of Trump are lying to them; they can believe no one but Trump. He is no longer advancing an argument; he is shredding our social fabric.

Every fusillade of lies is like a Rorschach test, meant to separate his true believers from the rest of us. The *New York Times*—having reported on his accusers—is a cog in the conspiracy to elect Clinton run by Mexican billionaire Carlos Slim. In Trump's telling, this evil cabal will stop at nothing:

> Anyone who challenges their control is deemed a sexist, a racist, a xenophobe, and morally deformed. They will attack you, they will slander you, they will seek to destroy your career and your family, they will seek to destroy everything about you, including reputation. They will lie, lie, lie, and then again they will do worse than that, they will do whatever is necessary. The Clintons are criminals, remember that. They're criminals.

The vapor trail of his incitements is like a field guide to mass insanity: Hillary Clinton should take a drug test before the final debate. Clinton "meets in secret with international banks to plot the destruction of US sovereignty in order to enrich those global financial powers . . ."—a gamy resurrection of anti-Semitic tropes. His accusers have made up stories fed them by the conspirators. The conspiracy presumably includes the CIA: despite the fact that intelligence professionals briefed him on Russian hacking, Trump says, "Maybe there is no hacking."

But there is no lie so misshapen that Trump will not utter it. The most corrosive of these is his attack on our electoral process.

In-person voting fraud is so rare as to be statistically nonexistent. Numerous studies have shown this. As the *Washington Post* reports: "One of the most comprehensive investigations into voter impersonation found only thirty-one possibly fraudulent ballots out of over 1 billion votes cast between 2000 and 2014."

Despite this, Trump and his campaign inflame his followers by repeating a series of enormous lies.

Trump asserts: "Of course there is large-scale voter fraud happening on or before Election Day. Why do Republican leaders deny what is going on?" His campaign claims without evidence that there are "recent voting irregularities across the country from Pennsylvania to Colorado and an increase in unlawful voting by illegal immigrants." Trump again, throwing in a dollop of racism: "I hear too many stories about Pennsylvania. Certain areas. We can't lose an election because you know what I'm talking about. So . . . go check out areas."

More Trump: "People that have died ten years ago are still voting. Illegal immigrants are voting. So many cities are corrupt, and voter fraud is very, very common." Newt Gingrich: "To suggest that . . . you don't have theft in Philadelphia is to deny reality." Trump yet again: "It's one big fix. This whole election is being rigged." All this in the service of his insinuation that hordes of minority voters will commit election fraud.

Thus he focuses his fictions on cities with substantial African-American populations. One day before the debate, he proclaimed: "Voter fraud is all too common, and then they criticize us for saying that. But take a look at Philadelphia, what's been going on, take a look at Chicago, take a look at St. Louis. Take a look at some of these cities, where you see things happening that are horrendous."

This is grotesque. The Pulitzer Prize–winning fact-check site PolitiFact rates Trump's lying as "Pants on Fire": "More people are struck by lightning or attacked by sharks than are accused of voter fraud." Ohio's Secretary of State, a Trump supporter, says flatly: "Any time your comments draw into question the legitimacy of the elections process, they cross the line. Particularly if you can't back it up with evidence."

Trump does not even try. But his naked lies have made his followers believe that voter fraud is rampant—just like, polls show, a majority of Republicans. When Trump loses, millions of Americans will believe that he was cheated out of victory. This is exactly what he intends: to delegitimize Hillary Clinton as president—as he once tried to do, through the birther movement, to Barack Obama. But this time not before, quite possibly, inciting race-based intimidation or even violence at the polls.

So where was the leadership of the Republican Party? In hiding, mostly. They no doubt fear Trump and his legions, to whom he described Paul Ryan as "weak and ineffective." So Ryan confined himself to a tepid statement expressing confidence in our electoral process; Mitch McConnell said nothing. So much for leadership—or integrity.

But then Trump was piggy-backing on shabby falsehoods that the GOP concocted long ago. For it is Republicans, not minorities, who have tried to rig the vote—by excluding minorities. How? By advancing bogus claims of voter fraud to justify voter ID laws calculated, as a Court of Appeals recently held, to target "African-Americans with almost surgical precision." Trump is not an aberration; he is the GOP's hideous offspring, turned back against them at the head of a peasant army of rebellious Republicans.

By and large, the party's erstwhile leaders are a pitiful sight. Willfully ignoring Trump's character, they imagined that he could be tamed. Now they cower in the face of his excesses. The most recent, most pathetic, examples were the officeholders who abandoned Trump over his abuse of women, only to crawl back on board when the base howled in protest. Like the evangelical eunuch Mike Pence, they dare not speak for decency, or even for themselves.

Barack Obama got this precisely right: Republicans are now caught in the "swamp of crazy that has been sold over and over and over and over again"; Trump is the nominee you get when your appeal is "based on lies, based on hoaxes." He should know. Some of their lies and hoaxes—including Trump's—were directed at America's first black president.

Now they are his vehicle for degrading our national life. In the *Washington Post*, Michael Gerson described his party's nominee and where he is taking us. Trump is "frighteningly unstable under pressure." He is "easily baited—hyperbolic and vengeful." His advisers are "feeding his manias." He is "completely unmoored from restraining influences, and would be as president."

He is the champion of "crackpot conservatism—an alt-right rage against a vast, scheming establishment that includes the liberal media, global financiers, and a growing list of women making accusations of sexual assault." He "has no commitment to the American political system." He "is perfectly willing to delegitimize democratic institutions as a campaign tactic, squandering a civil inheritance he does not value." His "descent into ideological psychosis has tainted the reputation of all who were foolish enough to associate with him."

What else did the GOP expect from an obvious bully, narcissist, ignoramus, liar, and cheat, a man for whom nothing—and no one—exists but himself? It created the fever swamp in which he has thrived. Now, day by day, he is degrading our political life and, by his example, our society. In the words of Daniel Patrick Moynihan, he has made America "define deviancy down" to accommodate his worst instincts—and nourish ours.

So Wednesday's debate, moderated by the estimable Chris Wallace, represented a final reckoning. For Trump, it was one more chance to call Clinton sickly, incompetent, and corrupt in front of a massive audience. But in return Trump would have to respond in real time to hard questions about real issues. In short, this debate was sanity's last shot.

Thanks to Wallace, sanity prevailed—until, thanks to Trump, it didn't.

For a good while, Wallace's skillful questioning produced the miraculous, a debate involving Donald Trump that seemed almost normal. Issues materialized from nowhere: the Court, nuclear weapons, taxes, the economy, Syria, ISIS. While woefully uninformed, for a time Trump hit his right-wing talking points like a kid reciting from memory. One could not help but think that his mom, Kellyanne Conway, was beaming with pride.

Still, there was no missing the adult in the room. On issue upon issue Clinton was confident, crisp, and comprehensive—a president in waiting. At times, she dodged uncomfortable subjects like emails and her position on free trade. Nonetheless, with respect to substance, she was clearly winning on points, the predictable outcome of a cage match between a policy wonk and an incurious dunce.

But Clinton was not content. Like the heroine of a political revenge movie she turned on her thuggish tormentor, sticking sardonic sound bites like darts into his very thin skin, served with extra relish.

When she was helping black kids in the South get better schooling, she reminded him, the government was suing Trump for racial discrimination. When he was building Trump Tower, this enemy of illegal aliens exploited undocumented workers. When he built his signature hotel in Las Vegas, this proponent of a trade war with China used Chinese steel. This wall-building enemy of NAFTA and exporting jobs shipped jobs to Mexico. This master of the universe constantly whines that everything—even the Emmy Awards—is rigged against him.

When Clinton was involved in taking out bin Laden, Trump was hosting *Celebrity Apprentice*. When the Clinton Foundation was combating AIDS, the Trump Foundation "took money from other people and bought a six-foot portrait of Donald"—a dart to which Clinton added, "I mean, who does that?" Under Clinton's plan to fortify Social Security, "my payroll contribution will go up, as will Donald's—assuming he can't figure out how to get out of it."

At this, the erstwhile Übermensch—the very same guy who called her criminal, incompetent, corrupt, and a liar; the same guy who brought several women to the prior debate to highlight her husband's indiscretions—snapped "such a nasty woman." Given that she had previously catalogued his alleged serial abuse of women, this rejoinder was, to put it mildly, ill-considered.

Trump had already elicited gasps from the audience by claiming: "Nobody has more respect for women than I do. Nobody." One could only share their amazement: by then he had labeled nine women's detailed accounts of sexual predation as lies "probably started by [Clinton] and her sleazy campaign"; denied the slighting comments about two of them immortalized on tape; asserted—falsely—that the women's accusations had been debunked; and claimed—incredibly—not to know anyone on a list of accusers that included women he had previously admitted knowing.

But given ninety minutes Trump can lie a lot. He lied about suggesting that Japan, South Korea, and Saudi Arabia should have nuclear weapons. He claimed that the United States was inundated with ISIS operatives from Syria. He falsely asserted that "Hillary Clinton wants to double your taxes." Despite having been briefed by our intelligence agencies, he denied knowing about the Russian hacking of the DNC and the Clinton campaign.

So far, so squalid—the numbing new normal to which Trump has reduced us. By this time, I was developing a

certain fascination with the split screen. I have a novelist's
sensibility, I'll admit. But the close-up of Trump struck me
as a merciless psychic x-ray. With every look of anger and
contempt, every moment of thin-lipped, squint-eyed fury,
I imagined his gargoyle soul becoming graven on his face.

A flight of fancy, perhaps. But then he turned his pathology on America's civic traditions, political precedents, and
rules of presidential behavior.

Citing Trump's claims of widespread voter fraud, Wallace asked whether he would accept the result of the election.
Unlike any major candidate in our history, Trump refused
to commit.

"What I've seen is so bad," he asserted, claiming that
there were "millions of people that are registered to vote that
shouldn't be registered to vote." He then blamed the media
for stacking the election against him, having, for good measure, charged that Clinton "should never have been allowed
to run for the presidency based on what she did with emails
and so many other things."

Reminding Trump with obvious incredulity that one
of the "prides of this country is the peaceful transition of
power," Wallace asked again, "Are you saying you're not
prepared now to commit to that principle?" Dismissively,
Trump replied, "What I'm saying is that I will tell you at the
time. I'll keep you in suspense, okay?"

There it was. In a single moment, Trump had illuminated the depth and danger of his pathology—a nihilistic
contempt for everything that matters.

For values: Truth. Integrity. Principle. Decency. Civility.
The rule of law.

For others: Women. Minorities. Muslims. The physically
challenged. His fellow citizens. His own family. Anyone—
and anything.

Even his country.

Never before had a candidate challenged the legitimacy
of a presidential election before it was held. As Michelle

Obama said, Trump "is threatening the very idea of America itself."

So what happened next?

His base applauded. His party cowered. Ryan and McConnell remained silent. Pence contorted himself in support. In the wake of their cowardice, for the first time millions of Americans questioned the honesty of our electoral process. And our sense of decency and community, to which Trump has already done such grievous harm, diminished still more.

And Trump? "Hillary Clinton," he proclaimed the next day, "is the most dishonest person ever to run for president."

It is impossible to know whether Trump would have conceded the election, let alone with anything like the grace that Clinton managed, or the civility with which Obama honored the tradition of an orderly transition of power.

Hillary Clinton's Final Test

NOVEMBER 1, 2016

On Friday, some believe, FBI Director James Comey changed the dynamic of this election. But before we assess the Comey effect, one must consider its political context. For until Comey's bizarre intrusion, the last weeks of a mean and grueling campaign had yielded a surprising new candidate—a buoyant Hillary Clinton.

One sensed a woman who felt liberated—or, at least, relieved. Her last debate with Donald Trump was in the rearview mirror, leaving Trump as rhetorical roadkill who, like a cartoon character, ran himself over after she mowed him down. When she spoke of him, her contempt was leavened by a trace of amusement, as though he was just another chauvinistic blowhard in life's parade of fools.

Her strengths in the home stretch—Comey notwithstanding—continue to reflect who she is. Her campaign organization is disciplined and deep, sustained by money she labored assiduously to raise. Her get-out-the-vote operation is driving early voting. They, and she, are working hard in swing states to choke off Trump's path, while expanding the map in places like Arizona and Georgia.

Her advertising is sharp and multifaceted—and running everywhere it matters. Her surrogates—Barack and Michelle

For several days, the contrast between Clinton before the Comey letter and afterwards were striking. After becoming unusually upbeat and relaxed, she seemed to be grimly soldiering on. The letter had given Trump control of the narrative and a massive cudgel to beat her with. For a candidate who had entered the last days of the campaign with the wind at her back, this was a walking nightmare.

Obama, Joe Biden, Elizabeth Warren, Bernie Sanders, and of course, Bill Clinton—are more talented, ubiquitous, and well deployed than ever seen for any presidential candidate. Her campaign is worthy of a president; Trump's campaign is worthy of no one but Trump.

The debates proved to be pivotal—adding up to the best performance by any candidate in the three-debate format. Clinton was tough, self-possessed, thoroughly prepared, and on top of the issues. She carried out a well-conceived plan of attack, which drove home her message in every debate and in the days that followed.

With well-timed thrusts, she exposed Trump's ignorance and, as lethal, his emotional volatility and gracelessness under pressure. She exploited his misogyny without mercy. She spotlit their differences on critical issues in this environment, race relations, climate change, gun violence, income equality, tax and economic policy, and, of course, experience. Her relentless competence inspired its own form of trust—whatever the electorate's misgivings, she looked up to the job.

So she began talking about the future she hopes for alongside the damage Trump would do to it. According to polls, she was drawing away support from third-party candidates. In the process, she had reawakened voters to the historic nature of her candidacy—we would not just be electing another familiar face, and a Clinton at that, but a woman with her own hard-earned credentials.

As always, Trump helped. His performance at the Al Smith dinner was a classic of solipsism. At a charitable event meant to feature the candidates' gifts for self-deprecation and good-natured needling, Trump resembled a boorish dimwit who, having consumed a few beers, wandered into a comedy club by accident and was pushed onstage. Like any amateur, he drew few laughs and was roundly booed at several points during his standup routine. Still, it is no easy trick to turn a black-tie crowd feral—every time you wondered how bad things could get worse, Trump supplied the answer.

It was like watching a malign spirit inhabit his body—somehow, despite the obvious hostility of the crowd, he failed to grasp that a charity event featuring Cardinal Dolan was not, unlike a Trump rally, an ideal forum for attacking a woman. The horrors accumulated. His signal achievement was to make the appearance of Hillary Clinton seem like the advent of an angel of mercy.

But not entirely merciful. After pointing out—pointedly—that the Statue of Liberty represents a nation that welcomes immigrants, she suggested that Trump "looks at the Statue of Liberty and sees a 4. Maybe a 5, if she loses the torch and tablet and changes her hair." Having evoked The Donald's decree that a flat-chested woman can never "be a 10," she cheerfully added, "Come to think of it, you know what would be a good number for a woman? 45."

That, of course, is her serious point: her campaign is not simply about electing a particular woman, but about the elevation of all women. And Trump's self-exposure as a serial groper has made him, at last, a kind of everyman—as in, every man who ever pawed a woman without her consent. When Clinton goes after him she is in a sweet spot millions of other women share—not least Elizabeth Warren, for whose righteous loathing Trump seems specially engineered. This is no longer merely political or ideological, but personal: for Clinton, for Warren, and for an important slice of women who will vote their own experience and aspirations.

Empowered by her successes, Clinton began pressing for a governing mandate: a bigger electoral majority, and down-ballot victories that would give the Democrats control of the Senate and a more robust minority in the House. This was not overconfidence; she was reaching for the tools to do the job and, in the process, to eviscerate Trump's claims of a rigged election.

Essential to this strategy was tethering Trump to Republicans like a large and very dead cat. Those adhering to Trump are morally unfit to serve, the message goes; those

distancing themselves are weak-kneed trimmers who, fearful
of defeat, claim to have discovered what they already knew.
So even as Republicans were desperately paddling to stay
above water, Clinton and friends were pushing their heads
under while Trump pulled on their legs.

Barack Obama was especially trenchant in asserting that
Trump is the Republican Rosemary's baby, spawned by the
groundless conspiracy theories and mindless partisanship
the party has trafficked in for years. The Republican base,
Obama said, "actually began to believe this crazy stuff. Donald Trump didn't start this. He just did what he always does,
which is slap his name on it, take credit for it, and promote
it. Now, when suddenly it's not working, suddenly that's a
deal breaker. Well, what took you so long?"

In between gasping for breath, Republicans had a few
talking points. Just when Trump had forgotten Obamacare,
a rise in premiums came along to remind him. And while
every leaked Clinton email was, by itself, a mosquito bite,
a few hundred bites can induce some serious scratching—
especially those that, while they contain no evidence of "pay
to play," link fund-raising by the Clinton Foundation with
the Clintons' family finances.

But Trump has a mosquito's attention span. Handed a
speech proclaiming his intent to "drain the swamp" that is
our nation's capital, he instead commenced by threatening to
sue his female accusers from a dais at Gettysburg. Speaking
to a highly receptive crowd of people on his payroll at his
Mar-a-Lago estate, he asserted that "all of my employees are
having a tremendous problem with Obama care"—only to
discover that few, if any, are actually on Obamacare. This
gives mere inattention to detail a good name.

But then, as Obama famously said, "Donald is not a
details guy." Clinton is certainly not a guy, but she's hell on
the details that count.

Among them is fund-raising. Like it or not, that is part
of a candidate's do or die—for the party's sake as well as

her own. Clinton knows that; Trump neither knows nor cares. So he has taught the GOP what others learned long ago—that a man who cares for no one and nothing shafts everyone but himself.

His indifference to fund-raising has left the GOP and its candidates short of cash and strength on the ground. His campaign claimed that he was focused on bringing his message to voters. But it is Clinton who was delivering a clear and confident message; Trump campaigned like a man who, obsessed with personal grievances, was searching for scapegoats instead of votes. Her campaign was a political symphony focused on Americans at large, his a dreary and interminable song of self.

Indeed, before Comey intervened, Trump's campaign resembled a self-indulgent concert tour, awash in whining, excuses, and attacks on the army of imagined conspirators who have stacked the decks against him. He was, as ever, the victim—of a "rigged election," massive voter fraud, "phony polls," the "disgusting" media, and all the Republicans who have betrayed him. His bright spot? While Clinton was campaigning in the pivotal state of Florida, Trump was opening an eponymous hotel in Washington, DC, by slicing a ribbon with a giant pair of golden scissors.

And so dyspepsia was spreading in his wake. Rudy Giuliani was picking colors for Hillary Clinton's prison jumpsuit. Newt Gingrich was picking an on-air fight with Megyn Kelly: when she asked, quite reasonably, whether the questions involving Trump's conduct toward women had contributed to his slippage in the polls, Gingrich accused her of being "fascinated with sex"—a cringeworthy charge.

More seriously, Trump's claims of victimization have driven some of his followers past the bounds of reason. On television, one of his supporters strongly suggested that he might assassinate Clinton. At a rally in Colorado Springs covered by a *New York Times* reporter, attendees asserted, variously, that only a rigged election could defeat Trump; that

Hillary Clinton intended to confiscate their weapons; that her accession might require them to defend themselves through violence; and that the solution might be violence against Clinton herself.

The contrast with the real Hillary Clinton continues to be stark. The America Trump describes at his rallies is a dystopian place that he alone can save. Clinton's America remains the best country on Earth, capable of seizing the future through a shared resolve to strengthen our national community. Appearing together in North Carolina, Clinton and Michelle Obama spelled out the gulf between the two campaigns.

Together, they presented a historic tableau—the first African-American first lady and, quite possibly, our first female president. The theme of the rally was "turn out to vote"; the large and enthusiastic crowd was young, multicultural, and multiracial, the very voters Clinton needs. If their cohorts' commitment to voting remained in doubt, they nonetheless formed a mosaic of America's future, symbolizing the demographic and cultural headwinds buffeting Trump and the GOP.

By this time, the Clinton campaign perceived that low turnout among the Obama coalition could be a real problem. Their hope was that deploying the Obamas themselves could lessen the shortfall.

By voting, Clinton told them, they could define that future. The stakes were high: voting rights; marriage equality; combating climate change; equal pay for equal work; affordable college; student debt relief; support for veterans; immigration reform and a path to citizenship; and yes, "dignity and respect for women and girls is also on the ballot."

As Clinton presented it, this was more than a laundry list of policies, framed as a partisan argument. It was the path to a more compassionate, inclusive, and open society. "All our kids," Clinton said, "must know that America has a place for you."

One could still remember 2008, when Barack Obama's more rancorous opponents cast Michelle as an angry black woman with no love for America. But when they went low, she went very high indeed. Now she was more beloved than her husband—and the most charismatic non-candidate around, a woman whose love of country impelled her to speak out for Hillary Clinton.

Clinton and her opponent, Michelle said, have dramatically different visions of America. His is "grounded in hopelessness and anger." His America is "weak and divided" and filled with "communities in chaos." His "campaign of fear" asks us to "fear our fellow citizens."

An American president, Obama said, "is the most powerful role model in the world." So we must ask "what do all our children deserve in our president." Her answer: A "unifying force" who "sees our differences not as a threat, but a blessing"; who "honors and values women"; who "understands that this nation was built by people who came here from all corners of the globe"; who "sees the goodness in our communities, not just the brokenness"; a president "who takes this job seriously, and has the temperament and maturity to do it well."

Hillary Clinton, Obama argued, wants to build a better world for our children. But her opponent is "trying to make this election so dirty and ugly that you don't want any part of it." Firmly, Obama concluded: "No one is going to take away our hopes."

Meanwhile, in Ohio, Trump proclaimed that the Clintons were the most corrupt political figures in our history; that Obamacare was ruining Americans' household finances; that only he could fix Washington, DC; and that the comprehensive conspiracy against him was without historic precedent. To his supporters' relief, he was more or less back on message. But compared to Clinton and Obama, the message seemed as small as the man.

It still is. But then on October 28—a mere eleven days before the election—James Comey bolted from the wings to hand Trump a stool and a megaphone.

The FBI Director's intrusion into the race was as perplexing as its source was strange. A federal investigation into

Anthony Weiner's alleged sexting of a fifteen-year-old girl had led to the confiscation of, among other devices, a computer that contained emails sent by Weiner's now-estranged wife, Huma Abedin, a principal aide to Hillary.

That was it. The discovery was not related to the investigation of Clinton's email practices. The FBI had not reviewed the emails, and no one knew what was in them; whether they contained anything of consequence; which, if any, had been sent to Hillary Clinton; and, if some did, whether they were duplicates of emails already reviewed. There was no suggestion that Clinton or the State Department had withheld them from the FBI. In sum, this discovery did not suggest any impropriety or that, when examined, the emails would materially add to the public record.

Nonetheless, Comey wrote Republican committee chairmen in Congress reporting that these emails existed, and that they were potentially relevant to the bureau's investigation of Clinton's private server. His letter said no more—because he had no more. In an internal memo to FBI employees, Comey acknowledged that he could not assess "the significance of this newly discovered collection of emails" and that, as a result of his letter, "there is a significant risk of being misunderstood."

No kidding. Within minutes, the letter was leaked—no doubt by Republicans. At once the media, particularly cable news, inflated it into a "bombshell," "crisis," "potential game changer," and "firestorm"—an "October surprise" that could transform the dynamic of the race. For the next three days, there was no other story.

Hysteria took leave of fact. With his usual respect for truth and reason, a freshly energized Trump said variously: "I think it's the biggest story since Watergate"; "I think this changes everything"; that Clinton was "corrupt on a scale we have never seen before"; and that "we must not let her take her criminal scheme into the Oval Office." From all quarters, Republicans trumpeted the latest evidence of Clinton's

supposed criminality, throwing around words like "indictment" and "impeachment" in an effort to make it the focus
of the race.

All that, responsible reporters noted, because of an
unspecified number of emails that no one had even read—
Comey had wreaked political havoc over, as far as he knew,
nothing.

But this was lost in the suffocating mudslide of reportage, speculation, and partisan exploitation conjured by his
letter. Calling his judgment "appalling," Senator Dianne
Feinstein said that "Director Comey's announcement played
right into the political campaign of Donald Trump."

For that very reason, we soon learned, senior Justice
Department officials had implored Comey not to send the
letter—citing department guidelines cautioning against
actions that could influence a pending election. As one
former senior official told Jane Mayer of *The New Yorker*:
"You don't do this. It's aberrational. It violates decades of
practice." The obvious reason, he added, is that "it impugns
the integrity and reputation of the candidate, even though
there is no finding by a court, or in this instance even an
indictment."

By ignoring these warnings, Comey had changed
the momentum of the campaign, with consequences yet
unknown. In the immediate aftermath, all that Clinton
could do was ask the FBI "to release all the information that
it has." But having thrown Trump a political lifeline, Comey
had nothing more to offer. And the public was assaulted by
a story with no substance.

Given all that, there was severe and widespread criticism
of Comey from law enforcement professionals of both parties,
for intruding on the campaign and damaging the reputation
of the FBI. Democrats were equally critical: Clinton herself
called his actions "unprecedented" and "deeply troubling."
In response, officials at the Justice Department pledged the
resources necessary to review the emails swiftly—an effort

to address the damage done by Comey, which nonetheless kept the story alive and the public waiting for more.

As we wait, the political crosscurrents keep swirling. Bereft of new information, Trump nonetheless has a new theme that, for the moment, keeps him focused on making Clinton's trustworthiness the issue. Reprising Clinton's use of a private server while she was Secretary of State, he asserts repeatedly that she is guilty of criminal conduct—clearly hoping to rally Republicans and estrange wavering voters from Clinton. Trump's campaign is not shy about the strategy: mobilize his base and suppress turnout among likely Clinton voters in every way they can, whether through negative information, voter ID laws, or intimidation at the polls. It's the only way that Trump can win.

Even before October 28, the polls were tightening, most likely because of Republicans coming home. In states that Trump must carry, like Ohio and Florida, he may have regained the edge. But the Clinton campaign is driving early voting, in which she appears to be doing well, and the electoral map tilts very much in her favor. The question is whether, when the polls close for good, Clinton's superior ground operation will have turned out the voters she needs.

The last seven days will no doubt be eventful—Hillary Clinton's final test. WikiLeaks will keep releasing hacked emails. The Clinton campaign will try to retake the narrative. The Obamas will give Clinton their all. More gamy revelations about Trump may emerge. His rhetoric will grow ever more mendacious and ugly. The battle for the Senate will tighten. Polls will oscillate. Each campaign will make tough judgments about which states deserve more resources.

Through all this will run the Comey effect. More questions will emerge about his refusal to sign off on a statement saying that the Russian government was meddling in the presidential election—on the ironic grounds that the statement would come too close to the election. And the FBI's mysterious discoveries among Weiner's emails will hang

For the Clinton campaign, turnout was an ever-increasing concern. A particular worry was that early voting revealed a falloff in turnout among African Americans—another reason for Obama's hectic campaign schedule. The problem was exacerbated in the pivotal state of North Carolina by Republican efforts to strike residents of black areas from voter rolls, and to make early voting in those areas more difficult.

In yet another oddity, seven days before the election the FBI released documents related to its 2001 probe into Bill Clinton's

(continued)

over the campaign unless, and until, their contents become public.

The irony here, logic suggests, is that the emails are of little significance—that Comey placed his thumb on the scales without reason. Perhaps voters will perceive that. More likely, Comey's potentially historic misjudgment will not be enough to upend the fundamentals of the race. By now too many voters have made up their mind.

Trump, after all, remains Trump. And so does Clinton. Whatever the obstacles, she will continue to do what she always does: work hard, work smart, and stay focused to the end. Those are the qualities of a president and, as her campaign has shown, only Clinton has them.

controversial pardon of fugitive financier Marc Rich. The reason for this curious timing was not immediately clear. Though the documents contained nothing of particular interest, their release deepened the sense among Clinton supporters that, in the words of David Axelrod, the FBI had become the "Federal Bureau of Intervention."

PART V

*The Last Very Scary Days,
an Election Filled with Dread,
and an Extremely Sober
National Reckoning*

IN THE AFTERMATH OF JAMES COMEY'S OCTOBER 28 LETter it became clear that he had transformed the final days of the campaign.

The subject of Clinton's emails again commanded the news; polls narrowed, both nationally and in key states; the candidates' messages, advertising, and travel schedules changed in reaction; and the expectation that Clinton was cruising to an electoral college mandate evanesced. By reanimating the subject of Clinton's biggest weakness, Comey's letter had sown fresh doubt among independents and other persuadable voters. And it had transformed Trump from a floundering, failing candidate to a full-throated demagogue whose line of attack dominated the campaign's final days.

With the renewed focus of a man reborn, Trump kept repeating the same grotesque lie: that Comey's letter made it certain Clinton would be indicted, convicted, and imprisoned for the crimes revealed in Abedin's emails. Never mind that no one knew what was in them—in Trump's hands, Comey's Delphic letter was a blank slate for slander, the perfect means for turning the page past Trump the misogynist groper. "Her election," he blared from screens across America, "would mire our government and our country in a constitutional crisis that we cannot afford."

And it was working. Polls showed that restive Republicans were returning to the fold; that the enthusiasm gap between Trump and Clinton voters had widened; that a majority of undecided voters considered Comey's letter to be a factor in determining their vote. There was a significant increase in early voting among whites more likely to vote for Trump. And, at long last, Trump's handlers had managed to separate their man from his suicidal Twitter account, reportedly by changing his password without his knowledge.

The dynamic had shifted. In an effort to refocus attention on Trump, Clinton went back on the attack, muting the positive message she had intended to stress in the campaign's final week. Barack Obama felt compelled to break his silence by sharply criticizing Comey's decision to go public ahead of the facts, later adding that law enforcement "should not be used as a weapon."

There was much to criticize, and not just Comey's decision to disregard specific admonitions from the Justice Department that he was disregarding department guidelines. Almost immediately, more questions surfaced regarding Comey's judgment in so hastily sending a letter that would so obviously impact the campaign.

The *New York Times* reported that, in the summer of 2016, the FBI had decided not to take steps in two politically charged investigations that, in the view of Justice Department officials, would make them public too close to the election. One involved Trump's former campaign chairman, Paul Manafort, and his undisclosed business dealings in the Ukraine. The second concerned the implications, if any, for State Department policy stemming from contributions by foreign entities to the Clinton Foundation.

In both cases, the Justice Department and the FBI—presumably at Comey's direction—decided to wait until after the election. Combined with Comey's refusal to associate the FBI with a statement regarding Russian meddling in the election, this made his October 28 letter all the more astonishing.

For by sending it, Comey had authored the most consequential October surprise in the history of presidential politics.

Why, one wondered?

Some defenders argued that he had no choice—that having reported to Congress in the summer about the Clinton email matter, he was compelled to update them when these other emails appeared. But about what, exactly? At the time he sent the letter, he had no idea what was in the Abedin emails—the FBI had not yet obtained a search warrant to review them. Given that the FBI had refrained from taking any steps that would disclose other politically sensitive inquiries, it was exceedingly strange that Comey would make such a disclosure so close to the election.

Other explanations for his startling intrusion involved self-interest: that he had placed his reputation for personal probity above Justice Department guidelines; that he was a sophisticated political player who deployed that reputation to advance his own interests; that he was a partisan Republican who disliked Hillary Clinton. Or all of that.

But a proliferation of reporting in the campaign's final days suggested deeper causes. The starting point was that conservative FBI agents hostile to Clinton, concentrated in the New York office, were the source of leaks about the FBI investigation of the Clinton Foundation—which they were eager to pursue immediately regardless of, or perhaps because of, its potential impact on the election. The same group, the reportage had it, would have leaked the discovery of the Abedin emails had Comey not come forward.

In short, the FBI itself had begun wallowing in the fever swamp. The suspicion that rogue FBI agents were politicizing the Bureau for Trump's benefit was effectively confirmed by his principal surrogate, Rudy Giuliani. Hours after Comey sent his letter, Giuliani attributed Comey's action in a radio interview to "the pressure of a group of FBI agents who don't look at it politically."

As quoted by Wayne Barrett in *The Daily Beast*, Giuliani claimed inside knowledge: "The other rumor that I get is that there's a kind of revolution going on inside the FBI about the original conclusion [not to charge Clinton criminally] being completely unjustified and almost a slap in the face to the FBI's integrity." Added Giuliani, "I know that from former agents. I know that even from a few active agents."

Another comment from Giuliani suggested that the Trump campaign was expecting Comey's letter—and, perhaps, had spurred the rebellion that pushed Comey to act. Two days before Comey sent the letter, Giuliani volunteered on Fox that "I think [Trump's] got a surprise or two that you're going to hear about in the next few days. I mean, I'm talking about some pretty big surprises." Asked for details, Giuliani responded, "We've got a couple things up our sleeve that should turn this thing around."

It was easy to start connecting dots. As Barrett reported, Giuliani has strong connections to the FBI's New York office. These began when he was a federal prosecutor, and deepened when his law firm represented an association that includes 13,000 former and current agents. One is James Kallstrom, the former head of the New York office, with whom Giuliani is particularly close.

Both Giuliani and Kallstrom were vociferous critics of Comey's decision in July not to recommend criminal charges against Clinton in the email matter. Through the media, Giuliani claimed that numerous past and present agents were outraged—including Kallstrom, a strident public critic of the Clintons. Joining the chorus on Fox News, Kallstrom claimed that agents he knew were "basically disgusted" by Comey's performance. One sensed a pincer movement ratcheting up the pressure on Comey—one pincer in the media, the other within the agency—connected to Trump's most ferocious public backer.

But the real stunner came three days before the election. Appearing again on Fox, a cackling Giuliani (yes, he seemed increasingly mad) triumphantly acknowledged that he had anticipated Comey's letter three to four weeks before he sent it to Congress—based, he said, on conversations with former agents.

This appeared to be a clear admission that, directly or indirectly, Giuliani had been communicating with agents within the FBI who sought to help the Trump campaign in this extraordinary way. No surprise, then, that Congressman Elijah Cummings cited Giuliani's statements in demanding an investigation into apparent misconduct. Nor was it a surprise that Giuliani then backtracked, carefully denying specific advance knowledge of Comey's letter.

One could not know what role all these pressures played in Comey's decision to write the letter. But their existence helped explain his anomalous behavior—and there was no doubt that Comey had given Trump exactly what he needed in the campaign's final days.

Publicly, the Clinton campaign tried to suggest that business was as usual. But the change in the electoral map was striking. By November 3 a dire Clinton fund-raising letter depicted a Trump path to victory that, while unlikely, was no longer implausible. First, Trump had to take the states that Romney won in 2012, including North Carolina—a total of 206 electoral votes out of 270 needed. Next, Trump had to win three states where polls showed him winning or statistically tied—Ohio, Iowa, and Florida—bringing him to 259.

The letter then suggested several paths for Trump to pick up the last eleven electoral votes. One—winning Pennsylvania—at this point seemed unlikely. Another involved taking Colorado and Nevada, two states with substantial Latino populations in which, despite this, polls showed tightening races post-Comey. The third involved winning Colorado and adding New Hampshire—a state where, according to the latest polling, Trump had drawn even.

Under this calculus, everything would have to break just right for Trump—and his campaign clearly knew that. So they dedicated both the candidate and resources to blue states where, heretofore, no one had had imagined them winning— New Mexico, Michigan, and Wisconsin. Unlikely, and the polls said as much. But the addition of any one of them to Clinton's nightmare scenario could put Trump over the top.

Abruptly Clinton, too, was appearing and spending in Michigan and Wisconsin. It was difficult to tell whether the campaign was truly worried, or shoring up their firewall to cut Trump off.

A lot depended on turnout. In the age of cell phones and disappearing landlines, polling is ever more imprecise; a good get-out-the-vote operation is worth an extra point or two. Only Clinton had one, and the sophisticated data to go with it—including what issues move which voters, and what different subgroups exist within a wider demographic. Only Clinton had the capacity to turn out early voters. All that was money in the electoral bank.

Still, the Comey effect was a tricky thing to read. To find out what was happening beneath the surface, I reached out to people who knew—one at the heart of Clinton's campaign apparatus; one with close connections to her campaign; and one who has spent four decades in presidential politics as a preeminent Republican operative. Nothing you tell me will see print until after the election, I assured them, and I will never use your name. With this proviso they described what those on the inside were seeing.

The long and short of things was that Comey's letter had transformed the inner workings of both campaigns.

The tightening of the race, all felt, was too dramatic to attribute to the partisan habits of a polarized electorate or, though it was helpful to Trump, to bad news about Obamacare. Post-Comey, the revelations about Trump's behavior toward women—which, in their estimate, had given Clinton an artificial lead—had been overtaken by an overwhelming, and overwhelmingly negative, focus on Clinton.

This was denying her votes she might have had—particularly from independents and Republicans who had seen too much of Trump. As recycled hourly by the media, the mere existence of the letter became a force multiplier, reminding such voters of all they disliked about Clinton. Some would stay home; others, in the end, would gravitate to Trump.

Within the Clinton campaign, her estimated chances of winning had dropped by roughly 10 percent. That number, like their confidence in grinding it out, still remained high—around 84 percent. But Comey had thrown their message into reverse.

After all the bitterness, Clinton had planned to end the campaign on a positive theme, reaching out to voters with a promise of hope and inclusion. Prior to the letter, the campaign's advertising mix had shifted to 80 percent positive, a bid to assemble a convincing electoral mandate by reaching any voter who remained persuadable. Now the mix was almost 100 percent negative, attacks on Trump focused on turning out base voters in key states.

On the stump, Clinton's message had changed accordingly—she was back to spending much of her time running against Trump. Something precious had been lost, and the campaign knew it. They were intensifying polarization, turning off some voters in order to rally those they needed most. The act of winning would make it harder to govern.

But her campaign was propelled by demographic logic— the imperative of turning out the Democratic base. Clinton was still lagging among key components of the Obama coalition, black people and young people. This would be offset, the campaign believed, by outperforming Obama among the growing Latino vote that Trump had repelled beyond redemption—helping Clinton in the battleground states of Colorado, Florida, North Carolina, and Nevada, as well as in traditionally Republican Arizona.

And Clinton was continuing to lead Trump among white college-educated women. Those advantages, they judged, would help deliver the key states they needed—a sense confirmed over the final weekend before the election by a surge in early voting among Latinos.

But both campaigns were looking at the same map, and it kept changing before their eyes. A 350-electoral-vote victory for Clinton, a real possibility pre-Comey, now seemed remote. A shift in voter enthusiasm that favored Trump made it harder for Clinton to flip states like Arizona and

Georgia, or to take closely contested battleground states. The map had become a chessboard—the key for Clinton was cutting off every path Trump might have to victory.

Before the Comey letter the Clinton campaign believed that they would win every battleground state that Obama had won in 2012, squeezing out the closest of them, Ohio and Iowa. Now Trump appeared to be leading in both, closing in on New Hampshire and Florida, and moving up in North Carolina.

He needed all five—a daunting task, the Clinton campaign thought—plus Nevada and Colorado. But if the change of momentum delivered all seven states to Trump, he would become our next president.

This scenario looked a lot like the electoral dystopia conjured by Clinton's fundraising letter. But despite its alarums, her campaign remained confident that a large Latino turnout would secure Nevada and Colorado—which, it seemed clear, the Trump campaign suspected as well. If so, Trump's presumptive path to victory was short one state—a blue state at that—to replace Colorado and Nevada.

I finished writing this piece one day before the election. On election day, propelled by the Latino vote, Clinton carried both Colorado and Nevada.

That was why Clinton and her ad money had suddenly popped up in Michigan and Wisconsin, followed in Michigan over the weekend by her husband and Barack Obama. Absent Pennsylvania—the Republicans' quadrennial equivalent of Charlie Brown and the football—winning one of those two states, rich in blue-collar voters, was Trump's last path to a winning majority of 270 electoral votes.

A mere week earlier such a conversation would have been preposterous. This was one measure of the Comey effect.

Bernie Sanders had beaten Clinton in the Michigan primary—in the wake of Comey, the Clinton campaign was no longer taking the state for granted. And my Republican source noted that, however blue Wisconsin had been in presidential elections, it was the one GOP target state where Trump's abysmal organization did not matter. The ground game needed to win was already in place—Paul Ryan and

Reince Priebus were both from Wisconsin, and its Republican governor, Scott Walker, had assembled the machinery to win two exceedingly nasty races.

Skeptical, I questioned whether this translated in a high-turnout presidential election. Ordinarily, he acknowledged, Republicans coming home to the party were not enough for a winning coalition. But the post-Comey world was a crazy place to be—with momentum on their side, the Trump campaign thought they could win, and he put their chances at 50–50.

The Clinton campaign shared my skepticism. Pre-Comey, Trump was getting 77 percent of Republican voters; in 2012, Romney had garnered 92 percent. Even post-Comey, they doubted that Trump could make up all of the difference.

Still, the guru of electoral statisticians, Nate Silver, was now giving Trump a 35 percent shot. It was all about turnout, after all—in senatorial races, too.

My sources agreed that Comey had made it harder for Democrats to retake the Senate. This was particularly true in red states like Missouri and Indiana, where a bigger margin for Trump could defeat down-ballot Democrats—including the promising Jason Kander in Missouri, representative of the new generation Democrats need so desperately.

Even Russ Feingold was sweating it out in Wisconsin—a promising sign for Trump—and New Hampshire, North Carolina, Pennsylvania, and Nevada were now toss-ups. In Florida, the restless void that is Marco Rubio was poised for reelection, no doubt primed to embrace right-wing obstructionism as his latest path to the White House. That the GOP would maintain control of the House—albeit with a smaller, but more toxic, majority—was a mortal lock. A Hobbesian Congress loomed before us—much like the current one, but worse.

One could see this in the last days of the campaign. On the stump, the candidates and their surrogates scrambled across the map in an effort to turn out their base and, in

On election day, the Democrats lost the Senate contests in both Indiana and Missouri, as well as close races in Wisconsin, North Carolina, and Pennsylvania. By a wider margin, Marco Rubio won in Florida. With these victories the GOP maintained control of the Senate.

Trump's case, flip a state—including, remarkably, deep blue Minnesota. In the meanwhile, a *New York Times* poll showed that eight in ten voters said the campaign had repulsed them.

No great surprise. In the supposedly disastrous event of a Clinton presidency, Trump and his fellow Republicans promised us indictment, impeachment, investigations, and the perpetual obstruction of Supreme Court nominees. To break the monotony, they quoted from emails hacked by the Russians. Only half kidding, Barack Obama told a crowd in North Carolina, "I hate to put a little pressure on you, but the fate of the republic rests on your shoulders."

Not if they can't vote—other forces were at work. That morning, the state's NAACP was in court attempting to stop three counties from throwing African-Americans off the rolls—including, in Obama's telling, a one-hundred-year-old woman who had lived at the same address and voted regularly ever since she had the right. When it came to turn-out, the GOP was leaving nothing to chance—though, on Friday, a federal judge intervened to block its efforts to suppress voting in North Carolina.

Over the weekend, one could sense that the fundamentals of the race were beginning to reassert themselves, and Clinton was about to go up on the airwaves with a strong positive ad. The most respected commentators, pollsters, and statisticians remained confident that she would ultimately prevail. And then, on Sunday afternoon, Comey dispatched another letter to Congress.

It was, in its own way, as remarkable as the first. The FBI had now examined all the emails on Abedin's computer. "[B]ased on our review," Comey reported, "we have not changed our conclusion that we expressed in July with respect to Secretary Clinton."

The gravity of Comey's misjudgment was now clear: he had transformed the campaign and potentially changed its outcome—over nothing. In the nine days of uncertainty between his gratuitous initial letter and its tardy successor millions of votes had been cast; millions of words printed and spoken; countless charges hurled about Clinton's criminality. The proliferation of baseless speculation fed by Republicans conjured imminent indictments and shocking new discoveries. It was too late for Comey to undo what he should never have done.

Why, one was left to wonder, didn't Comey simply take those nine days to find out what the facts were? His letter did not say. Nor did it change Trump's behavior in any way.

Quite the contrary—the Trump campaign accused Comey of caving in to political pressure. According to Trump, his opponent was looking at the prospect of a criminal trial, and Comey was effectively perpetuating a cover-up. "You can't review 650,000 new emails in eight days," Trump brayed at a rally. "Hillary Clinton is guilty. She knows it, the FBI knows it, the people know it, and now it's up to the American people to deliver justice at the ballot box on November 8."

Watching this, I thought again of what one of my sources had said about the impact of Comey's letter.

It wasn't just that Trump could actually win. Gaming out the electoral map, he saw a scenario that rendered a tie in the electoral college—or, almost as bad, an unresolved outcome that turned on recounts and disputed ballots, bringing Trump's prediction of a rigged election to corrosive life. What then would happen, he asked me, to public faith in our democracy?

That was the state of the race when on Monday morning I sent in my final pre-election piece to The Huffington Post—written with a sense of urgency informed by, among other things, what I had heard but could not yet write.

The Imperative of Voting for Hillary Clinton

NOVEMBER 7, 2016

What kind of country do you want?

That is the question each of us must answer tomorrow. Many millions of our fellow Americans will answer "Donald Trump." This column is for everyone else.

First, reality. The only way to defeat Trump is by voting for Hillary Clinton. One can no longer assume that she will win—James Comey's unprecedented and unwarranted intrusion in the election, though belatedly exposed as worse than pointless, may nonetheless alter its outcome.

Indeed, millions of Americans have already voted under the influence of Comey's misjudgment—his letter of correction, stating that the Huma Abedin emails contain nothing new, came ten days too late. For voters to stay home tomorrow or cast a protest vote may well enable the most unstable and unqualified presidential candidate in American history. With respect, that is not a rational choice.

I appreciate that many voters wish their choice were different. Some question Clinton's honesty and candor. Some wish she were more progressive or less tied to established institutions. Some want a political party that embraces their political beliefs without compromise or ambiguity. Some on the right think her too reliant on centralized solutions. Some object to the dynastic implications of electing a former first lady. And some flat-out just don't like the Clintons.

One's moral purity is not on the ballot tomorrow. Nor is one's personal vision of a perfect world. The stakes are far more profound—in an imperfect world, what choice is best for us, our children, and the future all of us share.

In that light, only one choice makes sense.

For progressives, the issues are enough. Only a President Clinton will work to combat climate change, reduce gun violence, reform the immigration system, and fight terrorism with reason instead of xenophobia. Only Clinton supports pay equity for women, raising the minimum wage, making public colleges and universities tuition-free for all but affluent students, and reducing the crushing burden of college debt. Only Clinton will appoint progressives to the Supreme Court.

Only Clinton proposes to lower the price of prescription drugs. Only Clinton promises to rebuild our infrastructure. Only Clinton supports LGBT rights. And only Clinton pledges to secure our fiscal future by taxing those who can most afford it, rather than plunge us into further staggering debt through tax giveaways to the wealthy.

For progressives, this may not be perfection, but it is surely a down payment. And achieving a meaningful part of this agenda will require all the support she can get.

Moderates may view that agenda with misgivings. And some traditional Republicans, including principled conservatives, may believe that it cedes too much to government and grants too little credence to local and individual initiative.

Let me simply suggest that your recourse is to congenial candidates in down-ballot races—not to President Donald Trump.

Because of Trump, this is no ordinary year. He is certainly no moderate or, by any reasonable definition, a conservative. On issues, he is an ignorant creature of impulse who calls climate change a hoax; embraces an economic plan that would explode the deficit and, in the opinion of experts, throw us into a recession; lacks even a primitive understanding of counterterrorism or the uses and limits of military power; and speaks cavalierly about nuclear proliferation and nuclear weapons. Pick any issue—all are potentially existential.

But as disqualifying as these positions are, they are mere signposts of a personal and psychological unfitness so profound that he would do the country that all of us care about—regardless of our philosophical preferences—terrible harm.

A frequent rejoinder from those who oppose Clinton is "she's no better." The basis for this flat assertion may involve careless handling of emails; or an overlap between the Clinton Foundation and the Clinton's personal finances; or a supposed absence of candor regarding Benghazi; or a general belief that she is calculating, above the rules, and, when it serves her, untruthful. Or all the above.

For critics, these are more than sufficient grounds for objecting to Clinton as a candidate. But what then? For to assert a moral equivalence between Clinton and Trump is to substitute emotion for a mature comparison of what we know about both.

First, Clinton. Over twenty-five years she has been so battered by partisan charges that one tends to forget that the charges themselves came to little or nothing. This creates a remarkable dynamic—each new charge creates a presumption of guilt unjustified by the underlying facts.

The Abedin emails are but the latest example. One can deplore Clinton's use of a private server, or conclude that the Clinton Foundation—whose many good works are indubitable—is too closely linked to the Clintons' private business activities. But there is no evidence of "pay to play"; no sign that she subordinated her work as secretary of state to personal interests; no objective evidence that the Republican

FBI director, Comey, failed in his duties when, in July, he called her email practices careless, not criminal.

Here Comey's reckless and precipitous letter of October 28 is the perfect illustration. Having enabled Trump to cite his letter as evidence of Clinton's criminality without a shred of proof, Comey now reports that the actual contents of the Abedin emails were innocuous—as logic always suggested they were.

In casting their vote, Americans are left to sort all this out. But, in doing so, it is well to consider a few other things. A record of service to the underprivileged well before Clinton rose to prominence. Her deep preparation for the presidency. The skill, stamina, and knowledge she displayed in debate. Her steadiness under pressure. Her ability to surmount adversity. Her record of bipartisan cooperation as a senator. And, unlike Trump, a general disinclination to complain about criticism.

All that adds up to the inner resources and emotional balance one would want in a president. And Trump?

Abysmally ignorant. Chronically narcissistic. Emotionally unbalanced. Temperamentally unstable. Indifferent to our political traditions and institutions. To his core, morally repellent.

Any sane consideration of his disabilities places this election in a category all its own. This is not a choice between philosophies or parties. It is a profoundly moral choice for every voter—whether to enable, or oppose, the election of a president who will endanger and degrade us in every conceivable way.

He is a risk to our national security. He is a demagogue who divides us by race, religion, and ethnicity, turning Americans against each other. He traffics in scapegoating and xenophobia. He is a misogynist who, by his own account, revels in groping and abusing women. He slanders those who displease him and threatens to turn the power of the presidency on his critics. He has no regard for the rule of law.

He lies incessantly. He concocts bizarre conspiracy theories. He plucks his information from the darker recesses of the Internet. He advocates torture. He refuses to commit to respecting our election results. He tells his followers that American democracy is rigged against him. He tried to delegitimize our first black president with racist lies. He bragged about conversations with Vladimir Putin that never occurred.

His inner world is barren of any concern but self. He cares nothing for others—not family, party, or country. He judges people based on whether they satisfy Trump's need for adulation. He is so susceptible to manipulation that an antagonistic foreign power—Putin's Russia—has siphoned thousands of hacked emails through Wikileaks in order to elect him.

Despite all this, polling suggests that a significant, perhaps critical, number of Americans—including millennials—will stay home or cast a protest vote. This deserves the most serious consideration: in a close election, votes that are effectively cast aside may decide the winner by default. And so a word for potential third-party voters or non-voters, particularly in closely contested states.

In themselves, their sentiments are easy to grasp. Some are disappointed that Bernie Sanders fell short; some are drawn to Gary Johnson or Jill Stein; some believe that America is stacked against social justice in favor of the wealthy; some distrust our societal institutions. Some feel all that at once.

Understandable, surely. But should one allow such frustrations, however deep, to impel what amounts to casting half a vote for Donald Trump? When the future of our country is at stake, does conscientious objection at the polls suffice?

Consider Sanders and Elizabeth Warren, who are working hard to elect Hillary Clinton. The path of reason, they argue, lies with electing the best—and only real—alternative to Trump, in order to advance the policies they believe in.

In several states, the third-party votes exceeded the margin by which Trump beat Clinton. It is sheerly speculative to guess at where these votes would have gone between the two major party candidates and whether they would have made a difference in the outcome. But the risk of that was, quite obviously, very real—as was the profound difference between Trump and Clinton.

This is not the year, Sanders says, for third-party voting. As Warren puts it, "I understand the frustration, but channel that frustration into making government work, not into throwing away your vote . . . [T]he answer is to seize the system and make it work for the people, not to just turn it over to the bigots and billionaires."

They are right. A vote for Johnson or Stein may best express one's core beliefs. But, in the worst case, casting such votes in battleground states could elect Donald Trump.

For what purpose, in this year, does one take such a risk? And, in addition, the reality that third-party candidates will lose may insulate some protest voters from considering in depth who, or what, they are voting for. So it is well to ask what abstract moral principles such voting represents.

Start with Gary Johnson. By now, it is widely known that Johnson has little grasp of foreign policy. Less known is his disinterest in climate change, his call for abolishing the Department of Education, his plan to phase out the progressive income tax, and his opposition to gun control.

If one is going to vote on principle alone, best to find better principles—unless these are the principles one thinks America needs more of. In which case, one must ask oneself whether they are worthy enough to risk electing Donald Trump.

Which brings us to Jill Stein, whose candidacy is more likely than Johnson's to help Trump by siphoning votes from Clinton—particularly crucial in states where the outcome is in doubt. For there is no doubt that the Green Party has a consistency of vision that results in a consistent level of support: just enough, among many other factors at work in 2000, to give George W. Bush the state of Florida and, as a result, the presidency.

My Green Party friends argue they should not be blamed for a system that, in their view, revolves around choosing the lesser of two evils. I respect this feeling, and their point is fair enough if stated in a vacuum. But what if one of the two electable choices in 2016—Trump—is monstrous? So let us pause to consider whether, despite this, those drawn to the Green Party must feel morally compelled to cast a vote for Jill Stein that effectively helps Donald Trump.

For those to whom the answer is not clear, Stein herself deserves the scrutiny one applies to the remaining candidates. To start, she's a bit of a political eccentric who encourages vaccine skeptics and opposes the Green Party's call for universal broadband on the theory that wireless signals could damage kids' brains. More broadly, her appeal rests on a call to political and moral clarity in the service of progressive principles.

As a candidate, she denounces without compromise the banking industry, Wall Street, defense contractors, the pharmaceutical industry, big tobacco, and energy companies that contribute to global warming—and, in her narrative, the major parties for representing them. As she puts it, "I've long since thrown in the towel on the Democratic and Republican parties because they are really a front group for the 1 percent, predatory banks, fossil-fuel giants, and war profiteers."

As a private citizen, however, she invests in those very same industries. As *The Daily Beast* reported, her financial disclosure statements reveal that much of her considerable wealth is invested—directly or through mutual funds—in big oil, the financial industry, major pharmaceutical companies, the tobacco industry, and defense contractors. In extenuation, she says, "Like many Americans . . . my finances are largely held in index funds or mutual funds . . . Sadly, most of these broad investments are as compromised as the American economy—degraded as it is by the fossil-fuel, defense, and finance industries."

It is true that the mutual funds, not Stein, direct her wealth to the industries she attacks. It is also true that she could put her money in other investments—such as socially responsible index funds or clean energy funds—more consistent with the moral stance through which she seeks our votes. Despite this, she asserts that "I've not yet found the mutual funds that represent my goals of advancing the cause of people, planet, and peace."

God save Hillary Clinton should she ever say such a thing.

My point here is not to single out Stein. Candidates are people, not saints, and inconsistency between their public positions and private conduct is hardly unknown in politics. But when Stein's political reason for being is uncompromising moral clarity, her personal contradictions make the protest vote she asks for less morally meaningful than she suggests—even in the abstract.

But the moral and practical consequences of this election are far from abstract. Yet Stein argues that it makes no difference who we actually elect—and, therefore, that she represents our only chance to vote against the corporate malefactors she invests her wealth in. Says she, "I will have trouble sleeping at night if Donald Trump is elected. I will also have trouble sleeping at night if Hillary Clinton is elected."

This pat assertion of equivalency is not an adequate response to the threat posed by Donald Trump—or even to his claim, anathema to all that Stein espouses, that climate change is a "hoax" concocted by the Chinese. Nor, I respectfully suggest, is voting for Jill Stein a practical or morally adequate response—at least in battleground states—to an excruciatingly close election where the wrong choice could have devastating consequences for our country.

Beyond all this, there are additional matters of moral principle that impel a vote for Hillary Clinton—and against Donald Trump. One is to defeat his bogus claims of vote-rigging and his embrace of voter suppression, whether through intimidation or laws crafted to keep minorities from voting. The right of all Americans to vote is too essential to allow Trump to succeed.

Another is the damage he is doing to our social fabric by stereotyping blacks and scapegoating Latinos and Muslims. For them—and for our collective sense of decency—countenancing the election of Donald Trump would be nothing short of tragic. All of us owe them better.

Still another is to consider the difference between electing a self-styled sexual predator and our first female president. What, one must ask, is this country saying to women—including the next generations—if we choose Trump over Hillary Clinton? Electing a woman empowers women; electing Trump rewards a man for treating women with contempt. Regardless of one's politics or misgivings about Clinton, that alone makes enabling Trump close to inexcusable.

In its simplest terms, this election presents a binary choice. It is not simply a choice between competing policies, and it is certainly not one between aspirants whose qualities are comparable. In 2016 our choice is between a candidate who is qualified to be president, and an ignorant and unstable demagogue who endangers our institutions, our compassion for each other, and, beyond that, our common future.

This is an existential and moral choice. It may not be, for many of us, the ideal choice of candidates. But, far beyond any election in memory, the only sane choice is clear.

Hillary Clinton.

Where Does America Go Now?

A Farewell Letter to My Readers

NOVEMBER 9, 2016

For the last fourteen months, I have written at least weekly about the candidates, the campaign, and the pressing issues raised by this turbulent political season. I'm very grateful to The Huffington Post for this privilege, and to all those who read and often commented on what I had to say. So this letter is my way of saying thanks.

First, however, I want to reflect on what this election means and—especially—the defining choices we now face about what kind of country we want to be.

Donald Trump is now our president-elect. Our institutions and founding ideals will be tested as never in our lifetime. The election of an unstable and unqualified demagogue signals the beginning of a sustained national ordeal that will require the best from our leaders and ourselves. But unlike the times in our history when we were tested by foreign wars or economic crises, we have no common understanding of the challenges ahead—which, though unknown in their particulars, are suggested by the fissures that brought us to this moment.

The rancorous and divisive campaign that gave us Donald Trump has driven home some dire lessons. The Trump campaign was not a program—it was a desperate, last-ditch cry for something different. All too many Americans are alienated from their fellow citizens and from the government that exists to serve them. All too many face the future with a sense of anger and betrayal or, as enervating, a helpless, hopeless impotence. All too many doubt that we can escape political paralysis or partisan blame—shifting where a cacophony of voices shout past each other.

Those voices include our media. In better times, the established print or broadcast outlets served as a kind of informational glue, the principal means through which most Americans sorted out their political choices. But the destructive path of this campaign caught traditional journalism in its vortex. So it is well to consider its role in Trump's rise; the way his candidacy challenged its practices and traditions; the degree of damage he has already inflicted on its credibility; and whether and how it can still inform our national dialogue.

A September 2016 article by Frank Newport of Gallup describes how—at least until the campaign's latter stages—the media enabled Trump over Clinton, while slighting the issues at stake in our choice of the next president. Newport wrote:

> With a few exceptions . . . Americans have little recall of reading, hearing, or seeing information about the policies of the presidential candidates or their positions on issues. Our research shows instead that in the case of Mr. Trump, Americans monitor his statements, his accusations, his travel and his events . . . [I]n the case of Mrs. Clinton they report mainly hearing about her past behavior, her character and, most recently, her health.

In short, the media at large emphasized Trump's entertainment value over his character or positions. By doing so, it normalized him, particularly during the primary season, obscuring his ignorance, demagoguery, mendacity, and total lack of qualifications to be president. This was Joseph McCarthy's ideal, the media as megaphone.

But like McCarthy, Trump presented unique and troubling challenges to journalistic integrity. Over time it became ever more inescapable that this potential president was a shameless, incessant, and blatant liar and, in all likelihood, emotionally disturbed.

Thus our most principled media faced two excruciating ethical questions: At what point does a candidate's falsehoods become so constant and pervasive that it is insufficient to report them without comment? And when do his repeated behaviors suggest an emotional dislocation so potentially dangerous that it does not suffice simply to record each behavior in isolation?

As Edward R. Murrow demonstrated during the McCarthy era, there are times when strict journalistic neutrality serves neither truth nor decency. One year into Trump's candidacy, a handful of commentators began remarking on the mounting evidence of his psychological instability. And in September 2016, his mendacious press conference blaming Hillary Clinton for initiating the birther slur at last provoked the *New York Times* to catalog and label his stunning sequence of untruths for precisely what they were.

This corrective was imperative—Trump brought this rigor upon himself. But like so much about him, it has come at a cost to us all. With his usual projection, he used the "dishonest media" as a foil to stir his followers' outrage. As president, his own outrage and intolerance of criticism may pose real dangers to journalistic independence. And so, in a country that, more than ever, needs honest journalism to provoke thought and conversation, honest journalism has become ever more discredited, and truth ever more subjective.

All this raises a profound question for a country as roiled as ours: On what basis will Americans relate to each other, and how will we resolve the challenges that, whether we like it or not, all of us face in common? Our answer—for better or worse—will define our common future.

America is now a multiracial and multicultural society. We see it in our streets, in our electorate, on the Internet, and on our screens. We see it in our current president.

But the election of Donald Trump arose, in good measure, from the tensions, fears, and tragedies spawned by racial and social difference. These not only affect the justice system, but how different Americans view it. As but one example, the rates of incarceration for whites and nonwhites vary widely. Do we see this simply as reflecting criminal activity among particular groups? Or do we ask ourselves whether our laws, and our legal system, help drive this disparity?

Officer-involved shootings of African-Americans raise similar questions. Will we recognize that the facts of such shootings are often painfully particular? Will we acknowledge that, nonetheless, all too often blacks die the hands of police when whites would not? Will we render judgment based on pre-existing prisms—that we must protect our police, or prosecute racism—without caring, in any given case, which imperative most applies? What role will a President Trump play in how we respond to the ongoing trials of race?

These questions are seminal and raise other pervasive concerns about the role of race in our society—including, critically, with respect to voting rights, racial and religious diversity, and economic and educational opportunity. We cannot ignore them, for they will not ignore us.

For the passions that drove the Trump campaign are not simply—or even primarily—about economics. They also stemmed from deeply rooted white discomfort with, and fear of, the racial or religious "other"—blacks, Latinos, and Muslims—whether seen as criminals, terrorists, or symbols of societal change and social displacement.

This helped define the campaign of 2016. Racial animus against Barack Obama fueled Trump's entrée into presidential politics, the birther movement—were it otherwise, the Canadian-born Ted Cruz would have no place in the Republican Party. The principal engine of Trump's campaign was anti-immigrant sentiment, whether aimed at undocumented Mexicans—the scapegoats of his calls for massive deportation and the Wall—or Syrian refugees and other Muslims from abroad. And Trump and his party waged a multifaceted war against minority voting, both through bogus charges of voter fraud and cynical laws designed to deny the franchise to African-Americans and the poor.

The truth is inescapable—fear of the other was Trump's political petri dish. Though millions of diverse Americans opposed him, he has now become—at great cost to us here and abroad—America's human symbol to the world. Around the globe we have shaken allies, tarnished our self-professed ideals, and, quite possibly, forfeited our pre-eminent place—it is hard to gauge the full damage to our standing in the world. And at home, the racial and religious discord he exploited is now ours to deal with, far more toxic for his efforts.

Add to this the rocket fuel of paranoia and distrust. In Trump's world, every one of our institutions is incompetent, dishonest, or corrupt, if not part of a sinister conspiracy: government, the media, our electoral machinery, and our political parties. In his telling, there is nothing left for anyone to believe in save Trump himself.

In the process, he waged a scorched earth campaign against civil society itself. He trafficked in insults and lies, vilifying his opponents and degrading the standards of political dialogue in a way not easily repaired. By his vile words and actions, he lowered our sense of collective and personal decency, whether in our leaders, our society, or ourselves. Again and again, he asked Americans to believe that the electoral process was rigged against him, that minorities were engaged in massive voter fraud, that the media was conspiring to take him down, and that all those who opposed him were enemies of all they held dear. The damage to our societal mosaic is not easily repaired.

Many will be tempted by the siren song of complacency, the belief that Trump is sui generis. Others will dismiss his voters as worthy of our anger and contempt, but not our interest or concern. Both errors are dangerous to our future.

For Trump is not a bizarre aberration, a celebrity who inhabited a political party by sweeping a weak and divided field. He rose because millions of angry or terrified blue-collar workers believe that America has betrayed them. That feeling is neither transient or incomprehensible. So we must look through their anger to see, and address, the reasons for it.

A changing economy has left them adrift in a country that, in their view, no longer respects or even hears them. Their dislocation is real—and, to many of us, invisible. Instinctively grasping their desperation for change, Trump presented himself as the one leader who saw them. So when he conjured an economic revival from a compound of protectionism and racism, they listened.

Here, the GOP must search its soul. Both parties have their share of bigots; all of us harbor bias in some form or another. But Trump did not import racial animus to the Republican Party. Its antecedents include the massive migration of southern whites in reaction to the civil rights bills of the 1960s; the GOP's adamant opposition to any form of racial preferences; the hostility toward Latinos that began twenty years ago in California; the party's efforts to weaken the Voting Rights Act; its bogus voter fraud bills aimed at suppressing minority voting.

This history cannot be dismissed. And it merges with efforts by some within a fractured and incoherent party to distract blue-collar Americans with race-flavored tropes that blame their travails on the government, instead of honestly addressing their real problems—the very stratagem that gave us Trump.

As to those problems, both parties need to do better. Trafficking in the false promises of Trumpism—trade wars to repeal the global economy, or magically restoring jobs lost to automation and globalization—will only deepen the sense of betrayal and alienation among blue-collar workers. The path to hope must be grounded in reality: infrastructure programs, job retraining and education for the new economy, and help in moving to where the work is.

Too many Americans—white and non-white—are hurting. Too many kids lack the educational opportunity enjoyed by the children of affluence. Too many young people must choose between crushing debt and forgoing college. Trump's witchcraft must be replaced by a real commitment to create much more opportunity for many more Americans, enriching our societal talent pool while lessening social and racial friction.

The question is this: Do we as a society, including those we choose to lead us, have the will—and the goodwill—to act?

The answer, I suggest, depends on how Americans resolve our relationship to our government and to each other.

The rise of Donald Trump illustrates the degree to which our political parties are deepening the divide of class, race, religion, and locality. The Democratic Party includes minorities, the better educated, and the secular, often concentrated in metropolitan areas and on the coasts. The Republican Party is dominated by whites, including fundamentalists, and its base lives in rural and exurban areas, including in the Midwest, South, and Rocky Mountain states.

In our polarized politics, both parties depend on turning out their loyalists, not meeting in the middle. Both are divided within themselves, making it harder to search for common ground. Our gerrymandered Congress further elevates trench warfare over compromise. The result is a spiral of dysfunction, empowering other forces that erode our sense of common citizenship.

All too often, Americans of opposing backgrounds or beliefs no longer trust or even know each other. More and more, they sort themselves into separate camps living in different places. Worse, they live in gated communities of the mind, walled off by partisan media who profit by persuading them that many of their fellow Americans are their enemy, their suspicions further inflamed by the feverish effusions of social media unmoored from fact or reason.

So more Americans than ever think that our politicians are self-serving hacks, bent on buying off their favored interest groups with pernicious policies. They divine, correctly, that our system of campaign finance enhances the power of a privileged few. Thus, Americans of all political stripes and ages believe that our political institutions are incompetent or inimical, instruments of harm that no longer represent them. Sadly, the highly damaging intrusion of James Comey and the FBI in the election itself further eroded the trust of many in our organs of government. The certainty that government cannot address our real problems—indeed, that it aggravates them—becomes a self-fulfilling prophecy.

In this hotbed of gridlock and estrangement, those problems are compounded. Rising income inequality does not simply limit the prospects of those now left behind. Our failure to address it—sensibly and responsibly—strangles the optimism that has always made us, as a country, believe in ourselves. And it cheats our society of coming generations whose potential will be stunted by our failure to reach out.

Equally insidious, it deepens yet another social fissure, the divide between winners and losers who no longer know each other. As a nation we have no common bond—like national service—that brings diverse Americans together. We are losing the ability to see, or even to imagine, the lives of others.

This has never been our history. However indelible our sins—the horror of slavery, the mistreatment of native Americans, the internment of Japanese—since our beginnings we have always been a nation of others. We ended slavery; opened the country to immigrants; passed civil rights bills; put together a social safety net. Our sins toward the other have shamed us; new waves of others have enriched us. Seeing the other as each other allowed our consciences to grow.

This was the essence of American exceptionalism. Many countries in history have enjoyed great power and wealth. But America has combined democracy with an inclusiveness that made so many diverse peoples into fellow citizens with a shared sense of pride and purpose.

This common idea of what we are and could be enabled us to endure depressions, recessions, wars, assassinations, impeachment proceedings, electoral malfunctions, and racial and social upheavals. It empowered us to weave women, minorities, and the foreign-born into the fabric of a stronger, better country. More than anything else, it has been the means of our survival and the engine of our progress.

It could be still. But only if we can surmount the election of Donald Trump and rescue that vision of America from the forces that would tear it down by tearing us apart.

Many issues will illuminate the answer. But let me pose four problems that, in varying ways, pose existential tests of American exceptionalism.

First, can we continue to thrive as a multi-racial society in a time of changing demographics? The election of 2016 gives us disturbing evidence of discord, and the promise of more to come. And yet a principal component of resistance to Donald Trump was just that—that he sowed and exploited racial and religious antagonism. The question is whether, Trump notwithstanding, our government and our society will honor the common humanity that makes all Americans worthy of opportunity, compassion, and respect.

Second, can we defeat the scourge of terrorism while retaining our essential character? Trump stands for scapegoating American Muslims, barring refugees from abroad, curbing civil liberties at home, and employing torture abroad. But many Americans perceive that this will further disfigure the face we present to the world, and to each other, creating a breeding ground for terrorism both at home and abroad. The question is which vision of American resolve will prevail.

Third, can we reopen the paths of opportunity enjoyed by prior generations? Trump promises fake solutions to real problems not yet addressed by either party. As jobs vanished, economic security diminished, and special interest money burgeoned, too many Americans—including the young—felt their optimism curdle into hopelessness and mistrust. The question is whether we can work to make our free market economy more inclusive and secure, or whether our political entropy will make still more American strangers to hope.

Finally, will we passively allow climate change to choke the world we have received as an unearned yet priceless gift? Trump has added to our well of criminal ignorance by labeling climate science a "hoax." Such irresponsibility is the price we pay for the cynical politics and mass disinformation that promotes our most selfish and short-sighted delusions. The question is whether Americans, at large, still possess the vision to imagine and shape the future.

The past decades in our politics give us ample ground for skepticism; our fractious present gives us more. The GOP is splintered, and the Democrats are divided between progressive pragmatists and a newly empowered left. But the Republican Party now controls all three branches of government and must find, if it dares, a way forward more responsible than the shoddy demagoguery of our president-elect. In particular, leading Republicans in Congress must rise above their parochial political interests and recognize the weight of responsibility they must bear for keeping the country whole.

Their performance over the last two decades—not to mention in this election—does not augur well for rational governance. Thus much depends on whether we as citizens can see each other, our country and ourselves, as worthy of much better—and demand that our elected officials do the same. For if we slink back into our corners, closing our eyes and our minds, our leaders will be no better.

Despite all this, I continue to hope. I know too many Americans, of all origins and backgrounds, not to hope— which is why I chose to spend these last fourteen months as I have.

I did this, of course, because I knew you were there. There is no better gift for a writer who cares about these things than readers who care just as much. As I set writing aside, at least for now, please know how grateful I am.

With many thanks, and all good wishes in all things,

Ric

Epilogue

What else to say?

As the hours passed on Tuesday night, for many millions of Americans anticipation morphed into astonishment, foreboding into numbing disbelief. The oracles of cosmopolitan America had promised our first female president—an 84% favorite, the *New York Times* assured its readers early that evening. Four hours later, her prospects had shriveled to 7%.

Donald Trump had blazed his trail through white America to the Rust Belt.

Not even the Republican National Committee had imagined this—its internal projections, like those of the Clinton campaign, had Hillary Clinton becoming our 45th president. But the demographic foundation for the über-conventional wisdom had collapsed.

The outcome was defined by race and class—but not in the way pollsters, prognosticators, and professionals had envisioned. The Obama coalition turned out to be just that—personal to Barack Obama. That black people and the young would taper off at the polls was expected. But the much-vaunted Latino surge never materialized in full force nor, among those who voted, was the split between parties much different than in 2012. And white college-educated women turned out for the louche Donald Trump in the same proportion as for the genteel Mitt Romney. In the end, party loyalty trumped feminism.

So, too, did the raw emotion of Trump voters transcend the technological bells and whistles of Clinton's turnout machine. To an unprecedented degree, rural and working-class whites flooded the polls to support the avatar of their frustrations. The engine of race was powerful indeed— answering Trump's nativist call, white America had put a white man in the White House.

For many whites, the right-wing parody of Clinton was indubitable fact. She was dishonest, corrupt, and, as damaging, symbolic of the elite who condescended to ordinary Americans from distant redoubts of privilege. The facts prized by cosmopolites meant nothing in Trumpworld; instead, the elite media were bent on destroying a man in whom his followers reposed their hopes. Trump would rebuild the country or, at least, take a wrecking ball to Washington— the smug and privileged would at last hear the outcry of those they flew over. Nothing else mattered.

For Democrats, those final hours on Tuesday were wrenching—amidst their dismay, they clung to hope before resorting to blame. What Nancy Pelosi said that night is surely true: that in the campaign's final days James Comey "became the leading Republican political operative in the country, wittingly or unwittingly." It is indisputable that he changed the dynamic of the race; quite possible that he changed its outcome; intolerable to consider that the self-regard of a single man had made the singular Donald Trump president of the United States. But there Comey was, a boulder in history's stream.

Within the Clinton campaign, a bitter certainty prevailed that Comey had cost her the presidency. In a post-election call with donors, Clinton said that the FBI director had "stopped our momentum" and prevented her from ending the campaign with an optimistic closing argument. Prior to the Comey letter, internal polling showed Clinton ahead in all but two battleground states; in its wake came a fatal slippage. The break toward Trump was particularly marked among white suburban women, to whom Democratic pollsters attributed Clinton's narrow losses in Pennsylvania, Michigan, and Wisconsin—Trump's margin of victory in the electoral college.

Still, there were multiple tributaries to Clinton's defeat—not least an absence of passion among the voters she needed, including those traditionally affiliated with her party. Soon enough the dialogue among sharply divided Democrats will turn to fractious arguments about message and direction. Blame will be cast; conflicting lessons posed; a multiplicity of answers proposed—a process made more rancorous by the identity of the victor. But that was for later—Donald Trump had won, and there were rituals to observe.

There was irony in this. For all of his inveighing against foreigners, it is Donald Trump who is alien to our traditions, indifferent to all but self. There is little doubt that, in defeat, he would have been graceless and divisive, inflicting further damage on our polity. He spared us this much by winning.

So it fell to Hillary Clinton to begin the transfer of power. Though it was hard to watch—and surely wrenching to perform—she played her role well. "This is painful," she acknowledged, "and it will be for a long time. But I still believe in America, and I always will. If you do, then you must accept this result, and then look to the future. Donald Trump is going to be our president. We owe him an open mind and the chance to lead."

She was more emotional than usual, and had more to say. For young women, she offered encouragement: "Never doubt that you are valuable, and powerful, and deserving of every chance in the world." As for this passage, whatever its difficulties, "[t]he presidency . . . is bigger than any of us."

But she was big enough for the moment and, one knew, for the job she had hoped to win. So a hint of tragedy hung over the occasion.

She was a flawed nominee, to be sure, and her mistakes fed the attack line that she was untrustworthy and ethically challenged. Many who saw only the public person thought that she was calculating and synthetic. But those who knew her knew better. And anyone who cared to look could see that she was smart, conscientious, resilient, and highly capable—tough enough to hold the office, and compassionate enough to use it to make lives better. In every job she ever had—even this last painful task—she did her utmost.

But now she was done, and had passed the moment to Donald Trump.

The speech written for him was sufficiently gracious in tone to fulfill the requirements of impending power. In one passage, Trump sounded a bit more like himself. "America," he assured us, "will no longer settle for anything less than the best." And there he was, standing before us.

One could not help but think of the woman we had wasted and the man we had "settled for," Barack Obama. For it had fallen to this president of peerless integrity and grace to welcome as his successor a man who trafficked in xenophobia and racism.

Americans are "all rooting for his success," Obama said of Trump before welcoming him to the White House. There he told Trump "I want to emphasize to you, Mr. President-elect, that we now are going to . . . do everything we can to help you succeed, because if you succeed, then the country succeeds." Afterwards, Obama termed the meeting "excellent."

The president surely was. Together, he and Clinton had honored the rituals that are part of our healing, giving a veneer of normality to a wrenching transition. But they reminded us of who, and what, we are leaving behind, and who will take Obama's place as president of the United States.

Over the next few days and weeks, commentators will swath Trump in pieties about the grandeur of democracy, the majesty of peaceful transitions, and the power of the presidency to enlarge a man's spirit. Paul Ryan and Mitch

McConnell will be full of plans, somehow certain that they can bend Trump to their purposes. New Republican vistas will open, plucked from the old conservative wish list—repealing Obamacare, reversing our commitment to combat climate change, abandoning the Iran nuclear deal, passing tax cuts for the wealthy, and appointing a Scalia clone to the Supreme Court.

Unmentioned, one suspects, will be tariffs, starting trade wars and tearing up NAFTA, anathema to the GOP's donor classes. Nor are Republicans in Congress enthused about term limits or infrastructure spending, a Trump proposal that would actually help create jobs for the struggling Americans who supported him. Ryan and his friends will hope, as many hope, that Trump is far less serious about his ideas than he is about himself. The risk they are running is that Trump will get his ideas and himself confused.

But the presidency is fraught with risk—much of which involves the personal capacity of a president to respond to precipitous and unanticipated dangers. Think of John F. Kennedy and the Cuban missile crisis, then think of Donald Trump. By supporting his candidacy, with whatever ambivalence, the Republican Party has given us a combustible and erratic leader who is dangerous to them and, far more consequential, to us.

His roster of cabinet hopefuls is ominous, for Donald Trump repels people of genuine talent and integrity. The cast of suspects is like watching a TV retrospective from the '80s, peopled by the often eccentric human oddities who clung to his campaign—aging white retreads, mediocrities, apparatchiks and loons: Rudy Giuliani, Newt Gingrich, Jeff Sessions, Reince Priebus, and the man who will be one heartbeat away, the oleaginous and spineless Mike Pence.

For foreign policy advice in these perilous times, Trump will look to the frenzied hardliner, John Bolton—a man capable of frightening Dick Cheney—and the intemperate former general Mike Flynn, a close associate of the Russians who have been rooting Trump on. Alt-right racism will be represented in the White House by chief strategist Steve Bannon. The only man of color, the unfathomable Ben Carson, will likely never notice.

When a president in desperate need of the best advice has recourse only to the worst, it will accentuate the worst in him. The man himself is dangerous enough.

Though we are joined in common peril, one is tempted to think that, day-to-day, women will suffer most, and not simply because America chose a misogynist over a female. No doubt the repeal of Obamacare will mean a decline in women's health, and Trump's appointments to the Supreme Court will endanger women's rights, whether with respect to workplace equity or reproductive choice. One can also think of minorities deprived of the right to vote, or immigrant families ripped apart by deportation, or refugees from tyranny denied admission to our once compassionate country, or American Muslims scapegoated as incipient terrorists.

At least Trump has warned them of what to expect. What happens to the white Americans who placed their hope in his divisive bluster, only to discover that their lives, and the lives of their children, are even worse? And, should they care to notice, that their hero is surrounded by the very elite he warned them against—such as his presumptive candidates for Secretary of the Treasury, Wall Street figures like Steven Mnuchin, late of Goldman Sachs, or Jamie Dimon of J.P. Morgan. To whom do his embittered followers look then?

But that is the price of electing a demagogue who sees other people only as pawns, and whose campaign was marked by a conscienceless cruelty. In the end, Trump coarsens his surroundings wherever he goes. And now a scared and angry minority of Americans have sent him to the White House.

This is not a time for empty sentiment, or false hopes. Our president-elect is an ignorant and unstable seventy-year-old man with an unremediated personality disorder. That won't change; nor will he. For the lesson Trump learned from us is that he alone, once again, is sufficient to all moments. He won, after all—in his mind, he always does.

What else to say?

We cannot let him win anymore. No matter what we do, his presidency will mark us. But what we can do—must do— is to stand up for the values Trump contravenes: the civic institutions he disdains, the civility he abjures, the inclusiveness he shuns, the rule of law he resents, the compassion he diminishes. We must do all we can to reach across the divides he widened to address the ills that he exploited. We must always remember that what makes America great is that which makes it good. And we must never forget who this man is, and what our country yet can be if we strive to make it so.

RNP
November 12, 2016

Acknowledgments

This book would not be one without the help and support of others.

Arianna Huffington gave me the opportunity to write what I wanted about politics, every week for fourteen months on the front page of The Huffington Post. Without this as inspiration, nothing else would have happened. I can't thank her enough.

Many thanks, as well, to the people at HuffPost who shepherded every piece: Stuart Whatley, Bryan Maygers, Hayley Miller, and Alexandra Rosario Kelly. Week upon week they connected me with readers, which was all a writer could ever ask.

My terrific publisher, Nathaniel Marunas, inspired this project and was tireless and creative in brainstorming how to turn weekly articles into a narrative of the campaign. This, and his interest in what I was doing, helped keep me pushing forward.

My editor, Amelia Ayrelan Iuvino, helped to shape the narrative with a sharp and discerning eye, culling pieces that were less essential and pruning repetitious phrases and passages. It was with her considerable help that this became a book.

Numerous people—some mentioned herein, some who wished to go unmentioned—helped sharpen my analysis. All made my pieces better.

Finally, I'm very grateful to my wife, Nancy Clair, for all her understanding and encouragement of what was, at times, an around-the-clock undertaking. In so many ways, it is terrific to have a partner who is so caring and so smart.

About the Type

Typeset in Adobe Garamond at 10.5/14.25 pt.

Garamond is named for the famed sixteenth-century French printer Claude Garamond. The font is based on his designs. It is regarded as a classic.

Typeset and design by Scribe Inc., Philadelphia, Pennsylvania.